Christmas
CLASSICS

CREATIVE
PUBLISHING
international

MINNETONKA, MINNESOTA

CONTENTS

Copyright © 2000
Creative Publishing international
5900 Green Oak Drive
Minnetonka, Minnesota 55343
1-800-328-3895
All right Reserved
Printed in the U.S.A.

Please advise:
Christmas Classics draws pages from the
individual titles of The Home Decorating
Institute®, The Hunting & Fishing Library®,
and The Microwave Cooking Library®.
Individual titles are also available from
the publisher and in bookstores and
fabric stores.

Library of Congress
Cataloging-in-Publication Data
Christmas Classics.
      p.cm.   Includes index.
ISBN 0-86573-544-1
1. Christmas decorations. 2. Christmas cookery.
I. Creative Publishing International
TT900.C4 C438 2000
745.594'12—dc21   00-043152

CREATIVE PUBLISHING international

President/CEO: David Murphy
Vice President/Editorial:
Patricia K. Jacobson
Vice President/Retail Sales:
Richard M. Miller

Created by: The Editors of Creative
Publishing international, Inc.

Printed on American Paper by: R.R.
Donnelley & Sons
10 9 8 7 6 5 4 3 2 1

Creative Publishing international, Inc.,
offers a variety of how-to books.
For information write or call:

1-800-328-3895
Creative Publishing internationl, Inc.
Customer Service
5900 Green Oak Drive
Minnetonka, MN 55343

Visit us at:
www.howtobookstore.com

Christmas Traditions

Traditions enrich our lives, bond us with family and friends, and fill us with warm memories of times spent together. This is especially true at Christmas, when traditions are the heart of every gathering and celebration. Whether your traditions include making ornaments or baking cookies, stringing garlands or entertaining holiday guests, you will be delighted and inspired by the many projects and recipes in *Traditional Christmas Two*. Bursting with fresh ideas for Christmas crafting, decorating, and cooking, this book is sure to give you all kinds of ways to enhance your tried-and-true traditions, and even introduce you to a few new ones.

Traditional Christmas Two shows you how to spread Christmas cheer throughout your home with glorious mantel displays, original Christmas stockings, and even a holiday elf. Decorate wreaths with flair; make eye-catching wall trees and topiaries, or uniquely crafted tabletop trees. Create stunning floral arrangements to decorate the holiday table or buffet. Sew placemats, table runners, and toppers for elegant entertaining or everyday dining.

Trim your tree to suit your fancy, using ornaments, garlands, and tree toppers you make yourself. Select lace doily ornaments, trimmed fabric balls, and ribbon roses for a romantic Victorian tree. Or go for glitz, starting at the top with a bold wire-mesh bow and studding the tree with metallic folded stars, gold-leafed balls, and marbleized ornaments. For down-home country appeal, make ornaments from hand-cast paper or tea-dyed fabric and top the tree with a raffia-tied cinnamon-stick star. Sew a tree skirt that will be cherished for years, or try one of our quick and easy alternative skirt ideas.

The tastes and aromas from the Christmas kitchen build lasting memories. *Traditional Christmas Two* abounds with delicious recipes for entertaining your guests or simply treating the family. From appetizers and snacks to cookies and desserts, mouth-watering photographs entice you to try them all. Many of the recipes are microwavable, including specialty foods and crafts for inventive gift giving. Tantalize your tastebuds with savory Shrimp Wrap-ups or Antipasto Kabobs. Cater to your Christmas cravings with traditional favorites like Rosettes and Plum Pudding, or discover the exotic flavors of Poppy-Raspberry Kolachkes and Brandied Apricot Torte.

Christmas traditions, treasured and comfortably timeless, rekindle the holiday spirit every year. With vibrant photography and concise instructions, the ideas and recipes throughout these pages are sure to enliven the Christmas traditions in your home.

Decorating
The Tree

TREE TOPPERS

A tree topper adds the finishing touch to a Christmas tree. Select one that coordinates with the style or theme of the ornaments, such as a paper-twist angel to complement a tree with a homespun look. Make a wire-mesh bow to top a tree that is decorated with glittery or metallic objects, or make a cinnamon-stick star for a tree decorated with natural ornaments.

The angel shown opposite is crafted from paper twist, a tightly wrapped paper cording that, when untwisted, produces a crinkled paper strip. The angel is given dimension with the help of wire. The outline of the wings is shaped from paper twist with a wire inner core, and the garment and shawl have craft wire encased in the fold of the hems, allowing them to be shaped into drapes and folds. Embellish the angel as desired with a miniature artificial garland or tiny musical instrument.

For an elegant-looking tree topper, create a large wire-mesh bow from aluminum window screening. The window screening, available in shiny silver and dull charcoal gray, may be left unfinished or painted gold, brass, or copper. The bow may also be sprayed with aerosol glitter for added sparkle.

For a natural look, make a star from cinnamon sticks held together with hot glue and raffia. The star can be embellished with a raffia bow, miniature cones, and a few sprigs of greenery.

Angel *(opposite) is created from paper twist, sinamay ribbon, jute, and raffia, for a country look.*

Wire-mesh bow, *created from window screening, is sprayed with gold metallic paint for an elegant look.*

Cinnamon-stick star *is embellished with sprigs of greenery, red raffia, and miniature cones.*

HOW TO MAKE A PAPER-TWIST ANGEL TREE TOPPER

MATERIALS

- Poster board.
- Packing tape.
- Three 1½" (3.8 cm) Styrofoam® balls.
- ½ yd. (0.5 m) paper twist, 4" to 4½" (10 to 11.5 cm) wide, in skintone or natural color, for head, neck, and hands.
- 1 yd. (0.95 m) paper twist, 4" to 4½" (10 to 11.5 cm) wide, for shawl.
- 2 yd. (1.85 m) paper twist, 7" to 7½" (18 to 19.3 cm) wide, for dress.
- 1 yd. (0.95 m) paper twist with wire inner core, for wings.
- Sinamay ribbon, at least 2" (5 cm) wide, for wings.
- Raffia.
- 3-ply jute.
- Dowel, ⅛" (3 mm) in diameter.
- 24-gauge craft wire.
- Thick craft glue.
- Hot glue gun and glue sticks.
- Wire cutter or utility scissors.
- Miniature garland or other desired embellishments.

CUTTING DIRECTIONS

From skintone or natural paper twist, cut one 4" (10 cm) piece for the head, one 10" (25 cm) piece for the underbodice, and three ¾" (2 cm) pieces for the neck and hands.

From the paper twist for the dress, cut two 4½" (11.5 cm) pieces for the sleeves, six 8½" (21.8 cm) pieces for the skirt, and one 7" (18 cm) piece for the dress bodice.

From the paper twist with a wire inner core, cut one 12" (30.5 cm) length for the arms and one 24" (61 cm) length for the wings.

1 Cut a semicircle with 8" (20.5 cm) radius from poster board. Trim 6" (15 cm) pie-shaped wedge from one end; discard. Form cone with base 15" (38 cm) in diameter; secure with packing tape. Press the Styrofoam balls between fingers to compress to 1¼" (3.2 cm) in diameter.

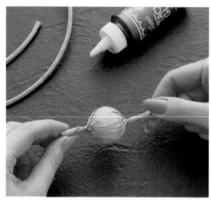

2 Untwist paper twist for head; glue width of paper around Styrofoam ball, using craft glue. Apply craft glue to ball at top and bottom, and tightly retwist paper; apply additional glue as necessary so paper stays twisted. Allow glue to dry.

3 Trim one end of the twisted paper close to foam ball; this will be top of head. Poke remaining twisted end into top of cone; trim top of cone, if necessary. Remove head, and set aside.

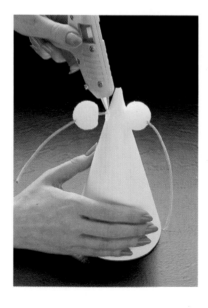

4 Poke a hole through each side of the cone, 1" (2.5 cm) from top; for the arms, insert the paper twist with the wire inner core through the holes. Push each wire arm through the center of Styrofoam ball; for shoulders, slide balls up to the cone. Shape balls to fit snugly against cone by pressing with fingers; secure to cone with hot glue, applying the glue to the cone.

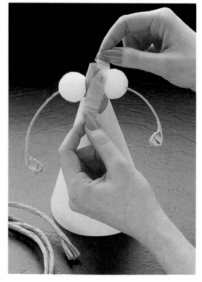

5 Bend each wire arm 1" (2.5 cm) from end; bend to form triangle shape for hands. Untwist a paper strip for hand; mist it with water. Wrap paper around the hand; secure with craft glue. Repeat for the other hand. Untwist and mist the paper strip for neck. Wrap paper around top of cone; secure with craft glue.

6 Untwist underbodice piece; cut a small slit in center. Position slit in paper over top of cone; smooth paper around shoulders and cone. Secure with craft glue. Glue head in place.

7 Untwist skirt pieces. Join the skirt pieces together by overlapping long edges ¼" (6 mm); secure with glue to form tube. Fold ½" (1.3 cm) hem on one edge; insert wire into fold, overlapping ends of wire about 1" (2.5 cm). Secure hem with craft glue, encasing wire.

8 Place cone on a soup or vegetable can. Slide skirt over cone, with the hem about 2" (5 cm) below the lower edge of the cone. Hand-gather upper edge to fit smoothly around the waist; secure with wire. Shape wired hem into graceful folds.

9 Untwist sleeve piece. Overlap the edges ¼" (6 mm) to form a tube; secure with craft glue. Fold the hem, encasing the wire as in step 7. Slide sleeve over arm, placing hem at wrist. Glue sleeve at shoulder, sides, and underarm, concealing underbodice at underarm. Shape wired hem. Repeat for other sleeve.

10 Untwist dress bodice piece; cut in half lengthwise. Fold strips in half lengthwise. Drape one strip over each shoulder, placing folded edges at neck; cross the ends at front and back; glue in place. Wrap wire around waist; trim excess.

11 Cut several lengths of raffia, about 25" (63.5 cm) long; mist with water. Tie raffia around waist, concealing the wire; trim ends. Cut thicker raffia lengths, and separate into two or three strands.

12 Bend the paper twist with wire inner core for wings as shown; allow the ends to extend 1" (2.5 cm) beyond center. Wrap ends around center; secure with glue.

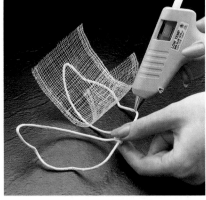

13 Bend edges and curve of wings as shown. Glue sinamay ribbon to back of wings, using hot glue. Allow glue to dry; trim away excess ribbon.

14 Position wings on back of angel at center, so wings curve away from back; secure, using hot glue.

(Continued)

15 Cut jute, and separate to make three single-ply 30" (76 cm) lengths. Wrap each ply tightly and evenly around dowel, securing the ends. Saturate jute with water. Place the dowel in 200°F (95°C) oven for 2 hours or until dry.

16 Remove jute from the dowel. Cut and glue individual lengths of coiled jute to head for hair, working in sections; for the bangs, glue short pieces across the front of the head.

17 Untwist the shawl piece. Fold ½" (1.3 cm) hem on one long edge. Insert wire into fold; glue hem in place, encasing wire. Repeat on opposite side.

18 Drape shawl around the shoulders. Shape the wired hems to make a graceful drape; adjust the shawl in back to conceal the lower portion of the wings. Fold ends of shawl to underside of the skirt. Glue shawl in place in several areas, using hot glue.

19 Shape the wire arms to hold desired accessories. Secure any other embellishments to angel as desired, using hot glue.

HOW TO MAKE A WIRE-MESH BOW TREE TOPPER

MATERIALS

- Aluminum window screening.
- 24-gauge or 26-gauge craft wire.
- Utility scissors.
- Aerosol acrylic paint in metallic finish, optional.
- Aerosol glitter, optional.

CUTTING DIRECTIONS

Cut the following rectangles from window screening, cutting along the mesh weave: one 8" × 38" (20.5 × 96.5 cm) piece for the loops, one 8" × 28" (20.5 × 71 cm) piece for the streamers, and one 2½" × 7" (6.5 × 18 cm) rectangle for the center strip.

1 Paint both sides of each rectangle, if desired; allow to dry. Fold up ½" (1.3 cm) on long edges, using a straightedge as a guide. Fold up ½" (1.3 cm) along short edges of streamers and one short edge of center strip.

2 Cut 16" (40.5 cm) length of wire. Form a loop from rectangle for loops, overlapping the short ends about ¾" (2 cm) at center. Insert wire at one overlapped edge; twist wire to secure, leaving 2" (5 cm) tail.

3 Stitch through the center of overlapped mesh with long end of wire, taking 1" to 1½" (2.5 to 3.8 cm) stitches. Pull up wire firmly to gather mesh; wrap wire around center, and twist the ends together; trim the excess.

4 Hand-pleat width of streamer at the center; place below the gathered loop. Wrap length of wire around the center of loop and streamers; twist ends together. Paint wire to match bow, if necessary.

5 Wrap center strip around the bow, concealing the wire. Stitch ends together with length of wire. Apply aerosol glitter, if desired. Secure a length of wire to the back of center strip for securing bow to tree.

HOW TO MAKE A CINNAMON-STICK STAR TREE TOPPER

MATERIALS

- Five 12" (30.5 cm) cinnamon sticks.
- Hot glue gun and glue sticks.
- Raffia.
- Embellishments, such as cones and sprigs of greenery.

1 Arrange two cinnamon sticks in an "X"; position a third stick across the top, placing one end below upper stick of "X" as shown.

2 Place remaining two sticks on top in an inverted "V." Adjust spacing of cinnamon sticks as necessary, to form star. Secure sticks at ends, using hot glue.

3 Tie raffia securely around ends at intersection of cinnamon sticks. Tie several lengths of raffia into bow; glue to top of star. Secure embellishments with glue.

TEA-DYED ORNAMENTS

Add an old-fashioned, homespun look to a Christmas tree with a variety of stitch-and-turn ornaments, such as stockings, stars, trees, and snowmen. Embellish the ornaments to make each one unique.

For an aged appearance, make the ornaments from cotton quilting fabrics, and tea dye the fabrics before cutting the ornaments. Tea dying works well on light-colored fabrics. The color change will vary with the type of tea used. Orange tea, for example, gives a yellowed look to fabrics, while cranberry tea produces a reddish appearance. The amount of color change will depend on the concentration of tea used and the length of time the fabric is soaked.

MATERIALS

- Scraps of cotton quilting fabrics, such as muslin, calico, and ticking.
- Polyester fiberfill.
- Embellishments, such as buttons, cinnamon sticks, artificial or preserved greenery, and artificial berries.
- 9" (23 cm) length of cording for hanger of each snowman, star, and tree ornament.
- Large-eyed needle.
- Small twigs and round toothpick, for snowman ornament.
- Orange acrylic paint and black acrylic paint or fine-point permanent-ink marker, for details of snowman ornament.
- Drapery weight or marble, for stocking ornament.
- Hot glue gun and glue sticks.

CUTTING DIRECTIONS

Transfer the ornament pattern pieces (page 314) onto paper. For a star or stocking ornament, cut two pieces from fabric, right sides together. For a snowman or tree ornament, cut two pieces from fabric, placing the dotted line of the pattern on the fold of the fabric. For the snowman, also cut one hat piece, placing the dotted line of the pattern on the fold of the fabric.

HOW TO TEA DYE FABRIC

1 Prewash the fabric to remove any finishes. Brew strong tea, about four tea bags per 1 qt. (1 L) of water; leave tea bags in water. Soak fabric in tea until desired color is achieved; areas with air pockets will not dye as dark, and areas of fabric touching tea bags will be darker.

2 Remove fabric from the tea, and squeeze out excess; do not rinse fabric. Place the fabric on paper towel; allow to dry. Press fabric to heat-set color; use scrap of fabric to protect ironing surface from any excess tea.

HOW TO MAKE A STOCKING ORNAMENT

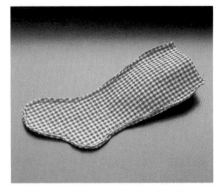  

1 Place stocking pieces right sides together. Stitch ⅛" (3 mm) seam around stocking, using short stitch length: leave top open.

2 Turn stocking right side out; press. Fold fabric to inside along dotted line; press. Placing drapery weight or marble into toe of stocking, loosely stuff stocking with polyester fiberfill.

3 Tear ½" × 6" (1.3 × 15 cm) strip of fabric for hanger; fold strip in half. Place folded strip at top of stocking; secure by stitching a button to strip, ⅜" (1 cm) from the ends, through all layers. Secure embellishments inside stocking, using hot glue.

HOW TO MAKE A STAR ORNAMENT

1 Cut a ¾" (2 cm) slit through center of one star piece. Place the pieces right sides together; stitch ⅛" (3 mm) seam around star, using a short stitch length. Trim off the points, and clip the inner corners.

2 Turn star right side out through the slit; stuff star firmly with polyester fiberfill. Hand-stitch opening closed, and take two or three stitches through center of star; pull stitches to indent center. Secure thread.

3 Glue embellishments to star over stitched opening in center. Thread cord for hanger through the needle; take a stitch through star at desired location. Knot ends of cord together.

HOW TO MAKE A TREE ORNAMENT

1 Place pieces for the tree right sides together. Stitch ⅛" (3 mm) seam around the tree, using a short stitch length; leave opening on lower edge of trunk. Clip corners and curves.

2 Turn tree right side out. Stuff tree with polyester fiberfill, stuffing branches first.

3 Turn raw edges to inside on lower edge of trunk; slipstitch closed. Stitch or glue buttons to the ends of the branches. Secure the hanger as in step 3, above.

HOW TO MAKE A SNOWMAN ORNAMENT

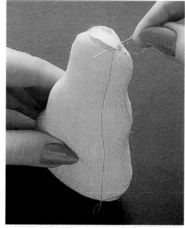

1 Place snowman pieces right sides together. Stitch ⅛" (3 mm) seam around the snowman, using short stitch length; leave a 1" (2.5 cm) opening at top. Clip seam allowances as necessary. Fold hat in half, right sides together, matching raw edges; stitch ⅛" (3 mm) seam on the edge opposite fold.

2 Turn snowman right side out; stuff firmly with polyester fiberfill. Turn raw edges to inside on upper edge; slipstitch opening closed.

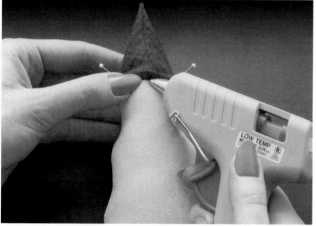

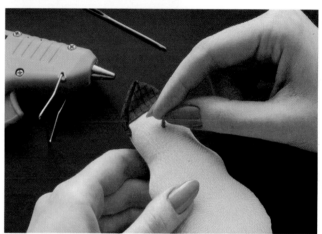

3 Turn hat right side out; fold fabric to inside along dotted line. Position hat on snowman with seam at center back; secure with hot glue. Fold the peak of the hat over to one side; secure with a dot of hot glue.

4 Break off ½" (1.3 cm) from round toothpick for nose; paint nose orange. Using a large-eyed needle, poke hole in fabric at desired location for nose. Apply a dot of hot glue to blunt end of nose; insert in hole.

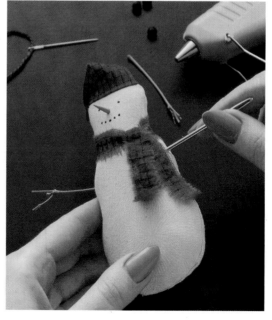

5 Make dots for eyes and mouth, using acrylic paint or a fine-point permanent-ink marker. Tear ½" × 8" (1.3 × 20.5 cm) fabric strip for scarf; tie scarf around neck of snowman.

6 Poke holes in fabric on each side of snowman at the desired location for twig arms; apply glue to end of each twig and insert into the holes. Secure any embellishments with hot glue. Secure cord for hanger as in step 3 for star, opposite.

COOKIE-CUTTER ORNAMENTS

Cookie cutters provide a variety of shapes to be used as patterns for tree ornaments. To make patterns, simply trace around the cookie cutters and add ¼" (6 mm) seam allowances. Stitch the ornaments wrong sides together and leave the seams exposed for a homespun look.

Make the ornaments from cotton or cotton-blend fabrics. Add decorative details to the ornaments with fabric paints in fine-tip tubes. Hand-paint your own designs or follow the imprints of plastic or metal cookie cutters as a guide for painting the details.

For best results in painting, prewash the fabrics to remove sizing. Practice painting on a scrap of fabric before painting on the ornaments to perfect the painting techniques. To keep the paint flow even, tap the tip of the bottle gently on the table to eliminate air bubbles. Wipe the tip of the bottle often while painting, to prevent paint buildup. If the tip becomes clogged, squeeze the tube to force paint through the tip onto a sheet of paper or a paper towel. If necessary, remove the cap and unclog the tip with a toothpick or needle.

HOW TO MAKE A COOKIE-CUTTER ORNAMENT

CUTTING DIRECTIONS

Make the patterns as below, step 1. For each ornament, cut two pieces from fabric, wrong sides together.

MATERIALS

- Scraps of cotton fabric in desired colors.
- Polyester fiberfill.
- 9" (23 cm) length of ribbon or cording, for hanger.
- Fabric paints in fine-tip tubes, for decorating ornaments.

1 Transfer cookie-cutter design to paper by tracing around cookie cutter with a pencil; add ¼" (6 mm) seam allowances.

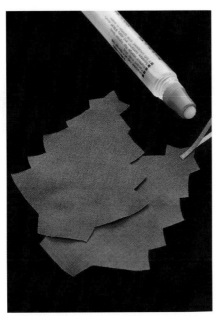

2 Cut fabric pieces for ornaments as in cutting directions. Fold ribbon in half to make hanger; glue-baste to top of ornament as shown.

3 Place the fabric pieces wrong sides together; pin. Stitch ¼" (6 mm) from raw edges, using short stitch length; leave 1" (2.5 cm) opening for stuffing.

4 Stuff the ornament with polyester fiberfill; use the eraser end of a pencil to push the stuffing into smaller areas.

5 Stitch the opening closed, using a zipper foot. Trim seam allowance to ⅛" (3 mm), taking care not to trim off hanger.

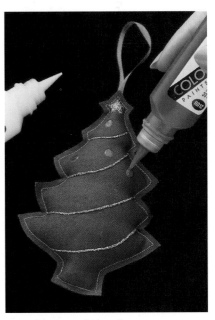

6 Add painted details to ornaments as desired, using fabric paints.

SPICE
ORNAMENTS

Spice ornaments are fragrant and colorful additions to the holiday tree. They are made by covering Styrofoam® balls with powdered or crushed dried spices. To create a variety of looks, the simple ornaments can be embellished with ribbons and preserved or artificial leaves or berries. For durability, the spice-covered ornaments are sprayed with an aerosol clear acrylic sealer.

MATERIALS

- Powdered or crushed dried spices, such as nutmeg, cinnamon, oregano, mace, paprika, parsley, poppy seed, crushed red pepper, allspice, mustard seed, chili powder, or dried orange peel.
- Aerosol acrylic paints in colors that blend with spices.
- Styrofoam balls.
- 20-gauge craft wire.
- 9" (23 cm) length of ribbon or cording, for hanger.
- Thick craft glue; hot glue gun and glue sticks.
- Aerosol clear acrylic sealer.
- Embellishments as desired.

Spice ornaments, *arranged in a bowl, are made with paprika, crushed red pepper, mace, allspice, mustard seed, cinnamon, and chili powder.*

HOW TO MAKE A SPICE ORNAMENT

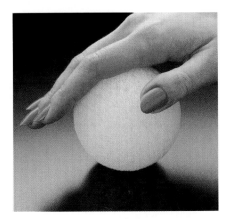

1 Roll Styrofoam ball lightly against table to compress the Styrofoam slightly.

2 Spray Styrofoam ball with aerosol acrylic paint; allow to dry.

3 Apply craft glue to the Styrofoam ball; roll in spice to cover. Allow to dry. Apply aerosol acrylic sealer.

4 Knot the ends of the ribbon or cording together. Bend 4" (10 cm) length of wire in half. Attach ribbon or cording to the ornament with wire as shown; secure with dot of hot glue.

5 Secure any additional embellishments to the ornament as desired, using hot glue.

METAL
ORNAMENTS

Metal ornaments made from either copper or tin add a whimsical look to a tree. The metals are available at craft stores in sheets of various sizes. Copper is the thinner of the two and cuts easily with household utility scissors; tin can be cut best with a jeweler's snips, available at jewelry-making supply stores. Both metals are suitable for flat ornaments; however, tin can also be used to make spiral ornaments. To create chained ornaments, two or more ornaments can be wired together.

Metal ornaments can be embellished, if desired, with craft wire or a punched design. Simple shapes for the ornaments and the punched designs can be found on gift-wrapping paper, greeting cards, and cookie cutters.

You may enlarge or reduce simple designs on a photocopy machine, if desired.

For a country or rustic look, copper can easily be given a weathered or aged appearance through a process called oxidizing. Heat oxidizing is done by placing the copper ornament over a flame until the color changes. The copper ornament is moved randomly over the flame to produce uneven coloring. A gas stove works well for oxidizing copper, because it produces a clean flame. Hold the copper with tongs while heating, because the metal becomes very hot. For additional texture, sand the surface of the copper before it is heated, using medium-grit sandpaper.

MATERIALS

- Copper or tin sheet.
- Awl and rubber mallet, or tin-punching tool.
- Utility scissors or jeweler's snips.
- Scrap of wood.
- Tracing paper and transfer paper.
- Masking tape.

- 22-gauge to 28-gauge brass or copper craft wire.
- Fine steel wool.
- 100-grit sandpaper.
- Tongs with handles that do not conduct heat, for oxidizing copper.
- Aerosol clear acrylic sealer.

HOW TO MAKE A COPPER OR TIN FLAT ORNAMENT

1 Cover the work surface with a newspaper. Transfer the desired design for the ornament onto tracing paper. Transfer design to metal sheet, using transfer paper.

2 Place ornament design over scrap of wood. Punch hole for hanger about ⅛" (3 mm) inside edge of design, using an awl and mallet. Embellish interior of ornament with a punched design, if desired (page 25).

HOW TO MAKE A COPPER OR TIN FLAT ORNAMENT (CONTINUED)

3 Cut out ornament, using scissors or jeweler's snips. Trim the tips off any sharp points.

4 Sand edges of ornament lightly, using sandpaper to smooth any sharp edges of metal; avoid sanding surface of ornament if smooth finish is desired.

5 Rub the ornament with fine steel wool to remove any fingerprints. Oxidize copper, if desired (opposite). Spray with aerosol clear acrylic sealer.

6 Embellish the ornament, if desired, by wrapping it with wire; for additional textural interest, layer two ornaments, then wrap with wire. Twist ends of wire together on back side; trim off excess.

7 Cut 7" (18 cm) length of wire, for hanger. Twist end of wire around awl, to make a coil, as in step 1, opposite. Insert opposite end of wire through the hole from the front of ornament; bend end to make hook for hanging.

HOW TO MAKE A TIN SPIRAL ORNAMENT

1 Cut ¼" × 6" (6 mm × 15 cm) strip of tin; trim ends at an angle. Trim off any sharp points, using jeweler's snips. Sand edges lightly with sandpaper. Punch a hole for hanger about ⅛" (3 mm) from one end of the strip, using an awl and mallet.

2 Wrap tin strip around pencil to make spiral; remove ornament from the pencil. Spray with aerosol clear acrylic sealer. Add hanger as in step 7, above.

HOW TO CONNECT METAL ORNAMENTS WITH WIRE

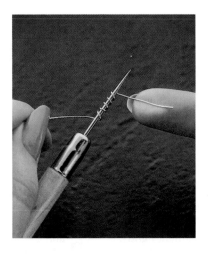

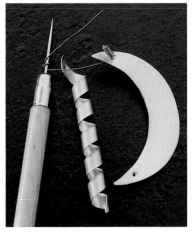

**1** Cut 6" (15 cm) length of wire. Twist end of wire around awl to make a coil, using about 2¼" (6 cm) of wire. Press coil together between fingers to compress slightly.

2 Insert opposite end of the wire through hole in one ornament from front. Insert wire through second ornament from back. Repeat coiling process to secure the wire to second ornament.

HOW TO PUNCH A DESIGN IN A METAL ORNAMENT

1 Transfer the design for punching to tissue paper as on page 23, step 1. Tape the design for punching to metal sheet inside lines for ornament.

2 Punch holes around the edges of design at ⅛" (3 mm) intervals, using awl and mallet. Remove tissue pattern.

HOW TO OXIDIZE COPPER

1 Texturize copper sheet, if desired, by sanding lightly with sandpaper.

2 Hold the copper ornament over flame with tongs; move it through flame randomly to produce color change. Remove the ornament from heat occasionally to check for desired color; holding the copper in flame too long can cause the copper to lose all its natural color.

FOLDED STAR ORNAMENTS

Using simple folding techniques, turn strips of paper or ribbon into delicate and dimensional folded star ornaments, sometimes called German stars. Each star ornament is made from only four strips of paper or ribbon. The width of the paper strips or ribbon determines the size of the ornament. Use the chart at right to help determine the width and length of the strips needed to make a folded star ornament of the desired size.

For folded star ornaments from paper, select papers of medium weight, such as parchment papers and gift-wrapping papers. Many art supply stores have large sheets of decorative papers with unique textures. To make gift-wrapping paper decorative on both sides, you can fuse two sheets together, using lightweight paper-backed fusible web. Test-fuse small pieces of paper to be sure the paper does not become too stiff to crease easily.

For folded star ornaments made from ribbon, select ribbons that are attractive on both sides and that hold a crease well, such as some craft and metallic ribbons; avoid satin or taffeta ribbons.

CUTTING DIRECTIONS

For each folded star ornament from paper, cut four strips of paper, using the chart below as a guide for determining the width and length of the strips.

For a folded star ornament from ribbon, cut four lengths of ribbon, using the chart below as a guide for determining the length of the strips; the length depends on the width of the ribbon used.

MATERIALS

• Paper or ribbon, amount depending on size of star desired.
• Lightweight paper-backed fusible web, for use with papers that are decorative on one side only.
• Thick craft glue; needle, decorative thread or cording, for hanger.

SIZE CHART FOR FOLDED STAR ORNAMENTS

APPROXIMATE SIZE	WIDTH OF STRIP	LENGTH OF STRIP	RIBBON YARDAGE REQUIRED
2" (5 cm)	½" (1.3 cm)	15" (38 cm)	1¾ yd. (1.6 m)
3" to 3½" (7.5 to 9 cm)	⅝" to ¾" (1.5 to 2 cm)	18" (46 cm)	2 yd. (1.85 m)
4½" (11.5 cm)	1" (2.5 cm)	27" (68.5 cm)	3 yd. (2.75 m)
6½" to 7" (16.3 to 18 cm)	1⅜" to 1½" (3.5 to 3.8 cm)	36" (91.5 cm)	4 yd. (3.7 m)
9" (23 cm)	2" (5 cm)	46" (117 cm)	5⅛ yd. (4.7 m)

HOW TO FUSE PAPER

1 Fuse adhesive side of paper-backed fusible web to the wrong side of decorative paper, using dry iron set at medium temperature; press for 1 to 3 seconds. Remove paper backing; set aside to use as press cloth.

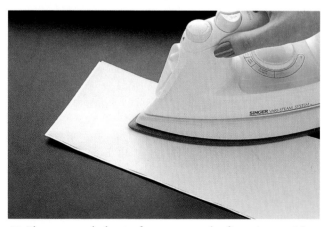

2 Place second sheet of paper over the first piece, with wrong sides together. Using paper backing as a press cloth, fuse layers together for 1 to 3 seconds.

HOW TO MAKE A FOLDED STAR ORNAMENT

1 Fold each of the four strips in half; trim ends to points. Place two folded strips vertically, with the tips of the left strip pointing up and tips of right strip pointing down.

2 Place the left vertical strip between layers of a third strip, positioning it near fold of third strip. Place ends of third strip between the layers of the right vertical strip.

3 Weave the fourth strip below third strip by placing ends of right vertical strip between layers of fourth strip. Place ends of fourth strip between layers of left vertical strip. Pull ends tightly.

4 Fold top layer of left vertical strip down; crease. Rotate woven square one-quarter turn clockwise.

5 Repeat step 4 to fold the next two top layers down; insert fourth strip between layers of the lower left square as shown. Crease and rotate one-quarter turn clockwise.

6 Fold upper right strip over itself at 45° angle as shown; crease.

7 Fold same strip over itself at 45° angle as shown; crease.

8 Fold same strip to left, aligning folded edges; insert end of strip between layers of upper right square to make one star point. Rotate woven square one-quarter turn clockwise.

9 Repeat steps 6 to 8 to make four star points.

10 Turn star over. Repeat steps 6 to 8 to make four more star points, for a total of eight star points.

11 Lift horizontal strip at upper right corner to the left, out of the way. Fold up vertical strip at lower right; crease.

12 Fold same strip over itself at 45° angle as shown; crease. Grasp end of strip; keep this side of the strip facing up as you complete step 13.

13 Turn the strip counterclockwise; insert end of strip between layers of upper left square. Strip will come out through star point; open point of star with finger or tip of scissors, if necessary. Pull tight to make star point that projects upward.

14 Rotate star one-quarter turn clockwise and repeat steps 11 to 13 to make four projecting star points.

16 Thread needle; insert needle through star between two outer points. Knot ends of thread for hanger.

15 Turn star over. Repeat steps 11 to 14 to make four additional projecting star points. Trim ends of strips even with edge of outer star points. Secure by applying dot of glue to both sides of ends, if necessary.

TRIMMED FABRIC ORNAMENTS

Create elegant ornaments by covering Styrofoam® balls with rich fabrics and trims. Four wedge-shaped fabric pieces are used to cover the Styrofoam ball. Use one fabric, or select up to four different coordinating fabrics, to cover the ball. The fabric pieces are glued to the ball, and the raw edges are concealed with flat trim, such as ribbon or braid. Cording, pearls, sequins, or beads can also be used to embellish the ornament. The hanger of the ornament is made from a decorative cord and an ornamental cap.

MATERIALS

- 3" (7.5 cm) Styrofoam ball.
- Fabric scraps.
- Cording and flat trims, such as ribbon or braid.
- Decorative beads, pearls, sequins, and bead pins, optional.
- 9" (23 cm) length of cording and ornamental cap, for hanger.
- Thick craft glue; hot glue gun and glue sticks.

HOW TO MAKE A TRIMMED FABRIC ORNAMENT

1 Transfer the pattern (page 314) to paper, and cut four pieces from fabric scraps.

2 Apply craft glue near the edges on the wrong side of one fabric piece. Position the fabric piece on Styrofoam ball; smooth edges around the ball, easing fullness along sides.

3 Apply remaining fabric pieces to ball; match points and align raw edges to cover ball completely.

4 Glue trim over the raw edges of the fabric pieces, butting raw edges of trim at top of ornament.

5 Poke hole in Styrofoam ball at top of ornament. Insert end of one or two pieces of cording into hole; secure with craft glue. Apply glue to fabric as shown; wrap the cording tightly around the ball in one continuous spiral, until desired effect is achieved. Poke end of cording into Styrofoam; secure with glue.

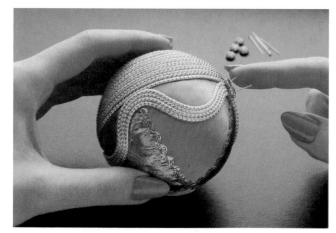

6 Embellish with additional cording, if desired. Attach decorative beads, pearls, and sequins, if desired, using bead pins; secure with dot of craft glue.

7 Insert cord in decorative cap; knot ends. Shape cap to fit top of ornament; secure with hot glue. Add bead or decorative cap to bottom, if desired.

GOLD-LEAF ORNAMENTS

Turn papier-mâché craft ornaments into elegant gold-leaf ornaments, using imitation gold leaf.

Imitation leaf, also available in silver and copper, can be found at craft and art supply stores. Several sheets are packaged together, with tissue paper between the layers. When working with the sheets of gold leaf, handle the tissue paper, not the gold leaf, whenever possible. The gold leaf is very fragile and may tarnish.

MATERIALS

- Papier-mâché ball.
- Aerosol acrylic paint, optional.
- Imitation gold, silver, or copper leaf.
- Gold-leaf adhesive; paintbrush.
- Soft-bristle brush.
- Ribbon, for bow.
- Thick craft glue; aerosol clear acrylic sealer.

HOW TO MAKE A GOLD-LEAF ORNAMENT

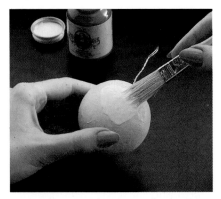

1 Apply aerosol paint to the papier-mâché ball, if desired; allow paint to dry. Apply gold-leaf adhesive to the ornament in small area, feathering out edges; allow the adhesive to dry until clear.

2 Cut the gold leaf and tissue paper slightly larger than adhesive area. Press the gold leaf over the adhesive, handling the tissue only. Remove the tissue paper.

3 Remove excess gold leaf with a soft-bristle brush. Apply gold leaf to additional areas of ball as desired. Apply aerosol clear acrylic sealer. Tie ribbon in bow around base of hanger; secure with dot of craft glue.

MARBLEIZED ORNAMENTS

Elegant marbleized ornaments are easy to make, using clear glass ornaments and craft acrylic paints. For best results, use paints that are of pouring consistency; paints may be thinned with water, if necessary. The marbleized effect is created by pouring two or three colors of paint into a glass ornament and swirling the paint colors together. Allow the paints to dry slightly after each color is applied, to avoid a muddy appearance.

MATERIALS

- Clear glass ornament, with removable top.
- Craft acrylic paints in desired colors.
- 9" (23 cm) length of cording or ribbon, for hanger.
- Ribbon, for bow.
- Disposable cups; hot glue gun and glue sticks.

HOW TO MAKE A MARBLEIZED ORNAMENT

1 Remove cap from ornament. Pour first color of paint into disposable cup; thin with water, if necessary. Pour small amount of paint into ornament; rotate to swirl paint. Place ornament, upside down, on the cup; allow any excess paint to flow out.

2 Repeat step 1 for each remaining color of paint. Place the ornament, upside down, on a cup, and allow the excess paint to flow out. Turn ornament right side up; allow to dry. Paint colors will continue to mix together during the drying process. Use additional coats of paint as necessary for opaque appearance.

3 Replace cap on ornament. Insert cording or ribbon through wire loop in cap; knot ends. Make a bow from ribbon; secure to top of ornament, using hot glue.

STRING BALL ORNAMENTS

Oversized string balls filled with nothing but air seem to magically keep their shape. An ornament is created by wrapping a balloon with string and decorative cords or narrow ribbons, then applying a liquid fabric stiffener and allowing it to dry. When the balloon is popped and removed, the stiffened string ball can be decorated with ribbons and other embellishments. Hang the ornaments on the Christmas tree, or arrange them around an evergreen garland on a buffet or mantel.

MATERIALS

- Round latex balloons, in desired sizes.
- Liquid fabric stiffener.
- Foam applicator.
- Wrapping materials, such as string, metallic cord, narrow braid, and narrow ribbon.
- Clothespins, dowel ⅜" (1 cm) or smaller in diameter, and deep cardboard box, for suspending wet balloon.
- Metallic cord, for hanger; large-eyed needle.
- Ribbon, for bows.
- Embellishments, such as glitter, sequins, and confetti, optional.

35

HOW TO MAKE A STRING BALL ORNAMENT

1 Inflate balloon to desired size; knot end. Grasp balloon by the knot; apply thin layer of liquid fabric stiffener to entire surface of balloon, using foam applicator.

2 Wrap end of string loosely around base of knot. Wrap string around balloon and back to knot.

3 Continue to wrap string around the balloon, changing directions gradually; sparsely cover entire surface of balloon. Wrap string loosely around knot; cut string. Apply another layer of fabric stiffener to string.

4 Repeat steps 2 and 3 for each additional layer of wrapping material. Continue to add layers of string until surface of balloon is evenly covered to desired density.

5 Apply generous coat of liquid fabric stiffener over the entire wrapped balloon. Sprinkle with glitter, if desired.

6 Suspend balloon from dowel, using clothespin; prop dowel across opening of deep cardboard box, allowing balloon to drip into box. Allow to dry completely.

7 Pop balloon; loosen any areas of balloon that may stick, using eraser end of pencil. Pull deflated balloon out of the ball through hole left by balloon knot at top. Remove any remaining residue between strings with eraser end of pencil or a pin.

9 Insert ribbons into same holes as cord; tie into bows. Embellish ornament as desired.

8 Attach cord at top of ball, using large-eyed needle; insert needle into hole left by balloon knot, and exit through any space, about 1/2" (1.3 cm) away. Knot ends of cord to form loop for hanging.

SCHERENSCHNITTE
ORNAMENTS & GARLANDS

Simple folding and cutting techniques turn ordinary paper into beautiful ornaments. The German craft of scherenschnitte (shear-en-shnit-tah), or scissors' cuttings, produces an intricate paper filigree that can be displayed as a single, flat ornament or a garland of repeated motifs. Single ornaments, glued to card stock, also make unique gift tags or Christmas cards. Two identical scherenschnitte pieces can be made and sewn together down the center for a three-dimensional ornament. Several patterns for each style are given on page 312. Ornaments can be antiqued, if desired, or painted with watercolor paints. For added sparkle, glitter may be applied to the ornament.

Choose art papers that have a sharp edge when cut. Parchment papers are particularly suitable for scherenschnitte, due to their strength and ability to accept stain or watercolors. Scissors with short, sharp, pointed blades are necessary for intricate work. Tiny detail cutting on the interior of the design is easier to do with a mat knife and cutting surface.

Three-dimensional ornament is created by stitching two identical symmetrical designs together through the center. You can also make single ornaments or a garland as shown opposite.

HOW TO MAKE A SINGLE SCHERENSCHNITTE ORNAMENT

MATERIALS

- Tracing paper.
- Art paper.
- Graphite paper, for transferring design; removable tape; scrap of corrugated cardboard.
- Scissors with short, sharp, pointed blades.
- Mat knife and cutting surface.
- Needle; thread, for hanger.
- Instant coffee and cotton-tipped swab, for antiquing, optional.
- Watercolor paints and glitter, optional.

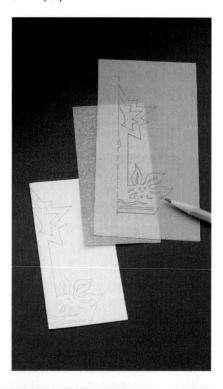

1 Cut a piece of art paper larger than the pattern dimensions (page 312); for a symmetrical design, fold paper in half, right sides together. Trace pattern onto tracing paper. Transfer the design from tracing paper to wrong side of folded art paper, using graphite paper; align the dotted line on design to fold of art paper.

2 Tape folded art paper to cutting surface, placing the tape in area outside design. Cut out interior shapes, using mat knife; begin with shapes nearest fold, and work toward cut edges of paper. Make any small holes by punching through paper with a needle.

3 Remove art paper from cutting surface, and cut outer edge of design with scissors. Open cut design.

4 Press flat with a warm iron. Antique or embellish as desired, using one of the three methods on page 17. Attach thread hanger at center of the ornament, ¼" (6 mm) from the upper edge, using a hand needle; knot the thread ends.

HOW TO MAKE A THREE-DIMENSIONAL
SCHERENSCHNITTE ORNAMENT

1 Follow steps 1 to 4, opposite, for two identical designs, omitting thread hanger. Place the cut designs on top of each other, aligning edges; secure to scrap of corrugated cardboard, using removable tape. Punch holes with pushpin every ¼" (6 mm) along the center fold, through both layers.

2 Thread a needle with 18" (46 cm) length of thread in same color as ornament. Sew in and out of holes from top to bottom of ornament.

3 Turn ornament over, and stitch back up to top hole. Tie the ends of thread together at desired length for hanger. Arrange the ornament sections at right angles to each other.

HOW TO MAKE A SCHERENSCHNITTE GARLAND

1 Cut strip of art paper 11" (28 cm) long and 2¾" (7 cm) wide. Fold in half, wrong sides together, to make 5½" × 4¼" (14 × 10.8 cm) strip. Fold short ends to center fold, right sides together, so the strip is accordion-folded, with wrong side facing out.

2 Trace design for garland (page 312) onto tracing paper. Transfer design from tracing paper to wrong side of folded art paper, using graphite paper; align dotted lines on design to double folded edges of paper.

3 Cut out the design, following steps 2 and 3 for single ornament on page 40. Open out garland. Embellish, if desired, using one of the three methods opposite.

4 Repeat steps 1 to 3 as necessary to make as many garland lengths as desired. Press the garland pieces flat with a warm iron. Join garland lengths with small pieces of tape on wrong side.

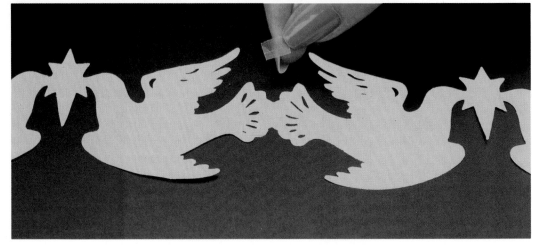

HOW TO EMBELLISH SCHERENSCHNITTE ORNAMENTS

Watercolored ornaments. Paint scherenschnitte ornament with watercolor paint and soft brush. Allow to dry; press with warm iron. Repeat on back side.

Glittered ornaments. Apply glue over areas to be glittered, using glue pen. Sprinkle with glitter; shake off the excess. Repeat on back side.

Antiqued ornaments. Mix 1½ teaspoons (7 mL) instant coffee with ½ cup (125 mL) hot water. Apply coffee to outer edge of ornament and around large openings with cotton swab. Allow to dry; press. Repeat on back side.

PAPIER-MÂCHÉ
ORNAMENTS

Create easy-to-make papier-mâché ornaments from ready-made forms, available at craft shops. Simply embellish the forms with a variety of paints, beads, or glitter for a shimmering holiday display.

TIPS FOR EMBELLISHING
PAPIER-MÂCHÉ ORNAMENTS

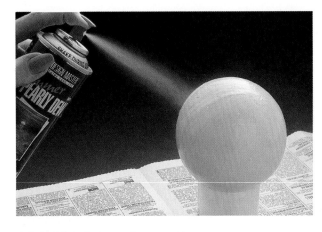

Paint the ornaments with aerosol acrylic paint; use pearlescent paint for a lustrous finish.

Apply glitter glue to painted ornaments to create a shimmering raised design.

Embellish the ornaments with beads; secure with craft glue.

HAND-CAST PAPER ORNAMENTS

Though they may appear to be very delicate, these hand-cast paper ornaments are durable enough to become lasting keepsakes. Cotton linter is soaked in water and processed to a pulp, using a household blender. Paper-casting powder is added to the pulp for strength. Water is then strained from the mixture, and the pulp is pressed into a ceramic mold and allowed to dry.

After the ornament is removed from the mold, it may be painted, using water-color paints, or shaded, using chalk pastels. Tiny sprigs of dried floral material and narrow ribbons may be added for a Victorian look. For sparkle, fine glitter may be applied.

Supplies for making hand-cast paper ornaments are available at craft or art supply stores. They may be purchased separately or in kit form. One sheet of cotton linter measuring 8" × 7" (20.5 × 18 cm) will produce enough pulp for three hand-cast paper ornaments. The decorative ceramic molds have many other uses, making them a worthwhile purchase. Preparation of the mold before casting may vary with each brand; read manufacturer's instructions before beginning the project.

Leftover pulp can be saved for later use. Squeeze out excess water, and spread the pulp out in small clumps to dry. It is not necessary to add more paper-casting powder when resoaking and processing leftover pulp.

MATERIALS

- Cotton linter.
- Paper-casting powder, such as paper clay or paper additive.
- Household blender.
- Strainer.
- Ceramic casting mold.
- Sponge.
- Kitchen towel.
- Narrow ribbon or cord, for hanger; darning needle, for inserting hanger.
- Watercolor paints or chalk pastels, optional.
- Embellishments, such as dried floral materials, narrow ribbons, and glitter, optional.
- Craft glue, or hot glue gun and glue sticks, optional.

HOW TO MAKE A HAND-CAST PAPER ORNAMENT

1 Tear 8" × 7" (20.5 × 18 cm) sheet of cotton linter into 1" (2.5 cm) pieces. Put in the blender with 1 quart (1 L) water; allow to soak for several minutes.

2 Blend the water and linter for 30 seconds on low speed. Add 1 teaspoon (5 mL) of paper-casting powder to mixture; blend on high speed for one minute.

3 Pour about one-third of mixture into strainer, draining off water. Put wet pulp into mold.

4 Spread pulp evenly around mold and out onto flat outer edges; pulp on flat edges will form deckled edge around border of ornament.

5 Press damp sponge over pulp, compressing it into the mold and drawing off excess water; wring out sponge. Repeat two or three times until excess water is removed.

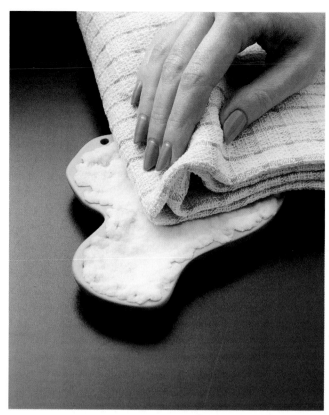

6 Press a folded kitchen towel over the compressed pulp, absorbing any remaining water and further compressing pulp.

7 Allow compressed pulp to dry completely in the mold. To speed drying, place the mold in an oven heated to 150°F (65°C) for about three hours.

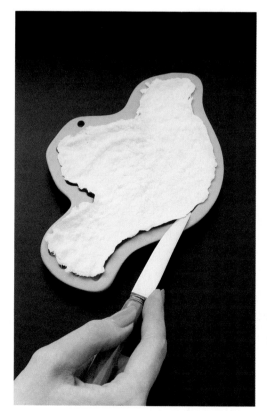

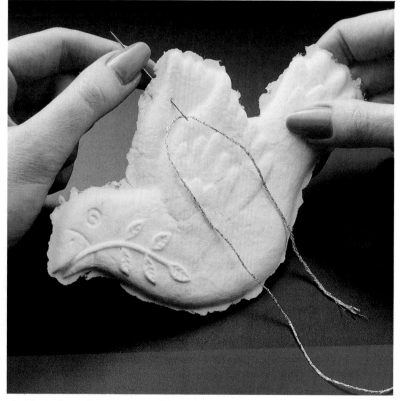

8 Loosen deckled edge of border around hand-cast paper ornament, using blade of knife; gently remove ornament from mold.

9 Thread cord or narrow ribbon into darning needle. Insert the needle through top of ornament at inner edge of border; knot ends of cord. Embellish ornament as desired (page 50).

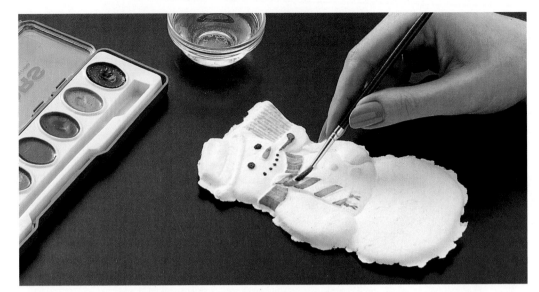

Painted ornaments.
Paint hand-cast paper ornaments, using diluted watercolors and small brush. Allow a painted area to dry before painting the adjacent area.

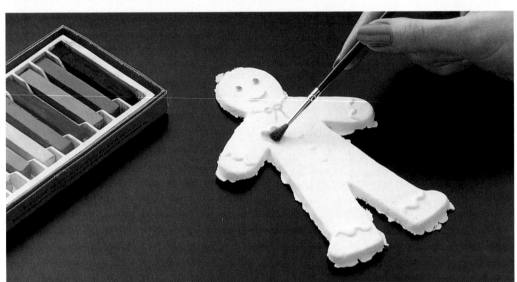

Color-shaded ornaments. Shade hand-cast paper ornaments, using chalk pastels or cosmetic powders. Apply with small brush or small foam applicator.

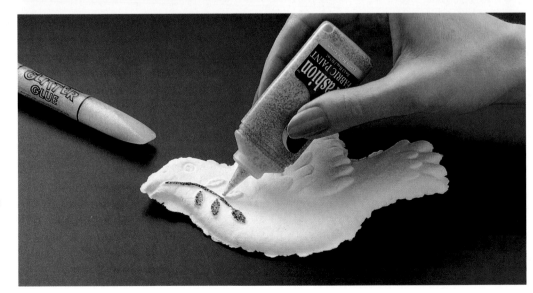

Glittered ornaments.
Outline or fill in small areas, using glitter glue in fine-tip tubes. Or, for large areas, apply glue over areas, using glue pen or glue stick. Sprinkle with glitter; shake off excess.

LACE DOILY ORNAMENTS

Lace doily ornaments, shaped as wreaths, semicircles, and baskets, give a Victorian look to a Christmas tree.

By using the ornaments, instead of bows, on packages, they become an extra keepsake gift.

Make the ornaments easily from Battenberg lace or cutwork doilies. Add ribbon hangers, and embellish the ornaments with trimmings such as dried or silk flowers or pearl strands.

MATERIALS (for lace doily wreath or semicircle ornament)

• Two 6" (15 cm) Battenberg or cutwork doilies, for lace wreath, or one for lace semicircle.

• Polyester fiberfill.

• 9" (23 cm) length of ribbon or braid trim, for hanger.

• Embellishments, such as dried or silk floral materials, pearl strands, and ribbon.

• Hot glue gun and glue sticks, optional.

MATERIALS (for lace doily basket ornament)

• One 8" (20.5 cm) Battenberg or cutwork doily: one doily makes two ornaments.

• 9" (23 cm) length of ribbon or braid trim, for hanger.

• Embellishments, such as dried or silk floral materials, optional.

• Hot glue gun and glue sticks, optional.

HOW TO SEW A LACE DOILY WREATH ORNAMENT

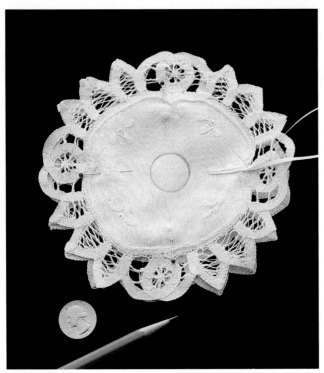

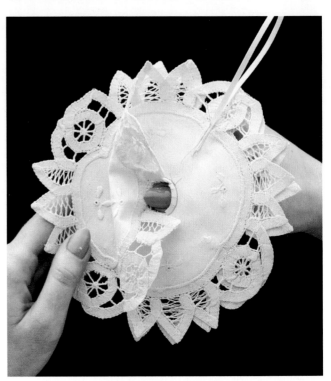

1 Baste ends of ribbon to wrong side of doily, about 1¼" (3.2 cm) from center. Mark 1" (2.5 cm) circle in center of one doily on wrong side. Pin the doilies right sides together.

2 Stitch around circle on marked line, using short stitch length. Trim away the fabric on the inside of circle ⅛" (3 mm) from stitching; turn right side out through center.

3 Stitch around the doilies, along the inner edge of lace trim, or 1" (2.5 cm) from the previous stitching; leave 2" (5 cm) opening.

4 Stuff the wreath with polyester fiberfill; stitch the opening closed by machine, using zipper foot. Secure embellishments with hot glue or by hand-stitching them in place.

HOW TO SEW A LACE DOILY SEMICIRCLE ORNAMENT

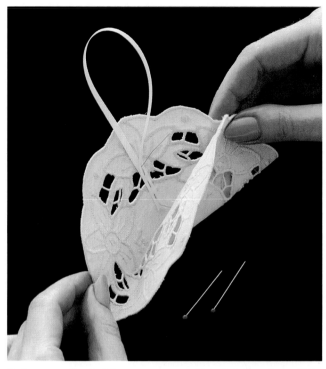

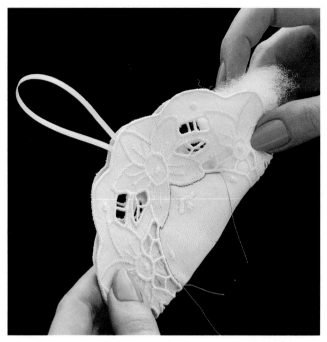

1 Baste ends of ribbon to wrong side of doily, about ¾" (2 cm) from center of doily. Fold doily in half.

2 Stitch around the semicircle, along inner edge of lace, or 1" (2.5 cm) from outer edge, using a short stitch length; leave 1" (2.5 cm) opening. Complete as in step 4, opposite.

HOW TO SEW A LACE DOILY BASKET ORNAMENT

1 Cut doily in half. Fold one doily piece in half again, right sides together; mark point on raw edge at fold. Mark point on outer curved edge ½" (1.3 cm) from cut edge; draw line connecting points.

2 Cut on the marked line. Stitch ¼" (6 mm) from the raw edge, using short stitch length. Turn right side out; press.

3 Stitch ribbon to each side of the basket; seam is at the center back. Secure any embellishments with hot glue or by hand-stitching in place.

FELT ORNAMENTS

These finely detailed ornaments are fun and easy to make, using craft felt or synthetic suede. Choose from a traditional dove or reindeer, or a whimsical cat and mouse. The body of each ornament is stitched before it is cut, making for quick assembly. Polyester stuffing gives added dimension.

HOW TO MAKE A MOUSE ORNAMENT

MATERIALS

- Felt.
- Polyester fiberfill.
- Thick craft glue.
- Black fine-point permanent-ink marker.
- Scrap of fabric for shawl.
- Gray embroidery floss.
- Scrap of yellow cellulose sponge, about ⅜" (1 cm) thick, for cheese.
- 9" (23 cm) length of ribbon, ⅛" (3 mm) wide, for bow on cheese.
- 8" (20.5 cm) length of fine brass wire, for glasses.

CUTTING DIRECTIONS

From felt, cut two ears and four arms, using patterns on page 310. Also cut one 5" (12.5 cm) strip of felt a scant ¼" (6 mm) wide, for tail. From fabric, cut one shawl, using pattern on page 310. Transfer mouse body pattern on page 310 onto heavy paper or cardboard; body is cut on page 56, step 3.

54

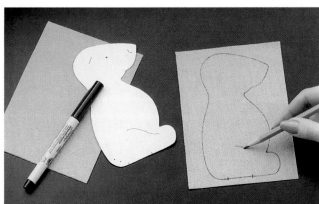

1 Place pattern for body on felt; using fine-point marker, trace around pattern. Lightly mark stitching line for leg definition, using pencil or chalk. Pin-mark tail placement. Place marked felt on second layer of felt.

2 Stitch around body ¼" (6 mm) inside marked line and on markings for leg definition, inserting tail as indicated on pattern; leave opening for stuffing at lower edge of body.

(Continued)

55

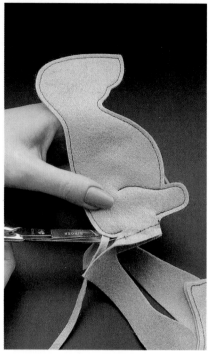

3 Trim felt ⅛" (3 mm) from the stitching, taking care not to trim off tail; do not trim at opening for stuffing.

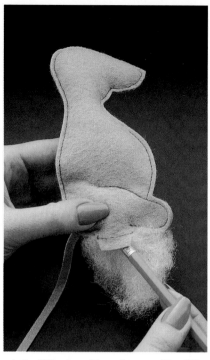

4 Stuff body with polyester fiberfill. Stitch the opening closed, using zipper foot; trim felt ⅛" (3 mm) from stitching.

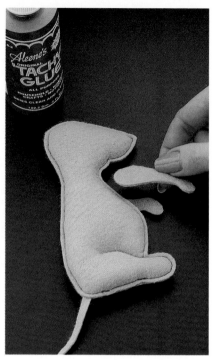

5 Glue two arm pieces together, matching edges; repeat for remaining arm. Allow glue to dry. Glue one arm to each side of body, as indicated on pattern. Allow glue to dry.

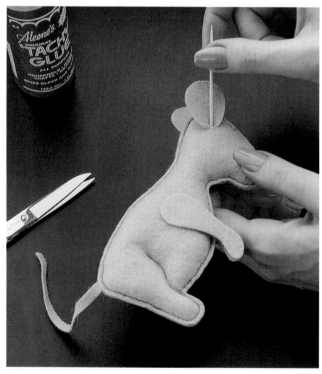

6 Cut slit for ear, about ¼" (6 mm) long, as indicated on pattern. Insert lower edge of ear into opening, using a toothpick. Secure the ear with small dot of glue. Repeat for remaining ear.

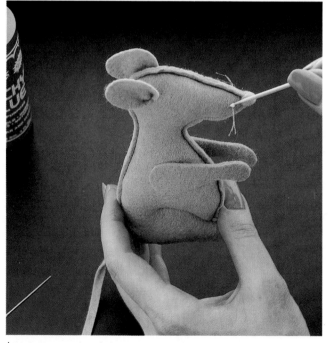

7 Cut two ¼" (6 mm) circles from pink felt; glue to each side of the snout as shown. Thread needle with three strands of gray embroidery floss, and insert through nose for whiskers; trim to ¾" (2 cm) on each side of nose. Using toothpick, place small dot of glue at the base of whiskers to secure.

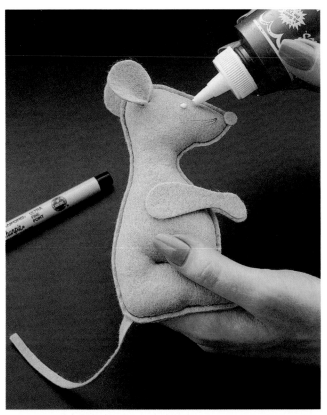

8 Apply small dot of fabric glue to felt at eye marks, as indicated on pattern. When glue is dry, mark each eye, using black permanent-ink marker.

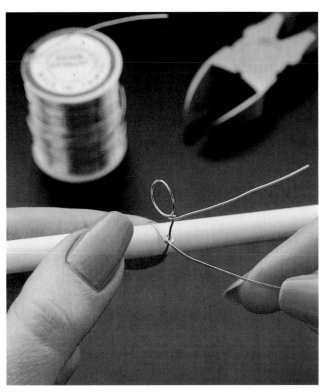

9 Form glasses by wrapping wire around a pen to make the first lens opening; twist wire to secure. Repeat to make the second lens, spacing circles about ½" (1.3 cm) apart. Place glasses on nose; secure by wrapping ends of wire around ears. Trim excess wire.

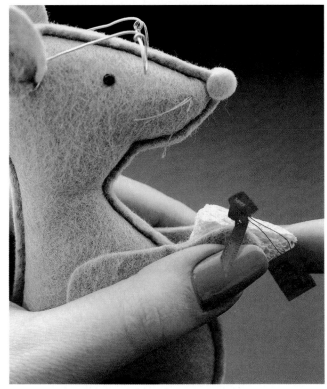

10 Cut wedge about 1" (2.5 cm) long from sponge, for cheese. Tie ribbon bow around cheese. Make gift tag from scrap of colored paper; secure to ribbon bow, using thread. Glue cheese to front paws.

11 Tie shawl around neck of the mouse. Secure loop of embroidery floss through top of the ornament, for hanger.

HOW TO MAKE A CAT ORNAMENT

MATERIALS

- Felt.
- Polyester fiberfill.
- Thick craft glue.
- Black fine-point permanent-ink marker.
- Miniature novelty mouse.
- 9" (23 cm) length of ribbon, ⅛" (3 mm) wide, for bow at neck.
- Brown embroidery floss, for whiskers.
- Pipe cleaner.

CUTTING DIRECTIONS

Cut two ears and one muzzle, using patterns on page 310. Cut two 1¼" × 5" (3.2 × 12.5 cm) rectangles, for tail. Transfer body and hindquarters patterns on page 310 onto heavy paper or cardboard; these pieces are cut below.

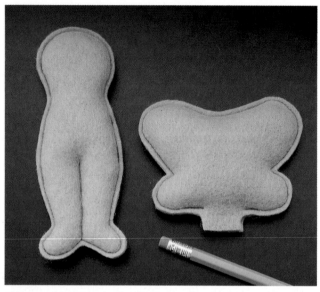

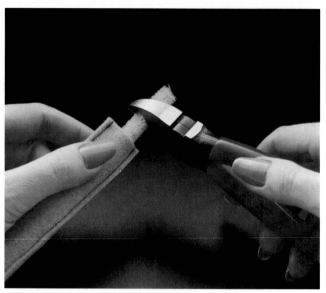

1 Assemble front body section as for mouse on pages 55 and 56, steps 1 to 4, omitting reference to tail; in step 2, leave opening just below neck, for stuffing. Repeat to make hindquarters section, leaving opening at lower edge, for stuffing and tail placement; do not stitch hindquarters section closed.

2 Layer tail pieces. Stitch around tail, using ¼" (6 mm) seam allowance and rounding corners at one end; leave opposite end open. Trim felt ⅛" (3 mm) from stitching. Insert pipe cleaner into tail; trim pipe cleaner ½" (1.3 cm) from edge of felt.

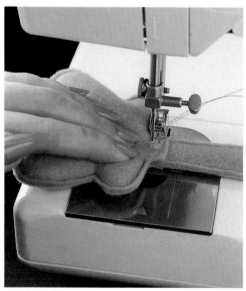

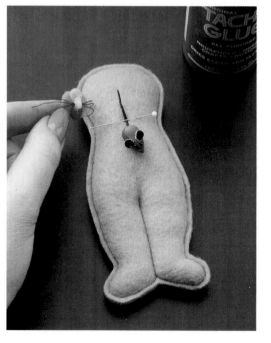

3 Insert the tail into hindquarters section; complete stitching. Trim the excess felt, taking care not to cut tail.

4 Cut one scant ¼" (6 mm) circle each from pink and red felt; glue to wrong side of muzzle piece as shown. Glue three 2" (5 cm) strands of brown embroidery floss to wrong side of muzzle, for whiskers. Glue muzzle unit to face, as indicated on pattern, tucking tail of novelty mouse under the muzzle.

5 Attach the ears as on page 56, step 6. Mark the eyes as on page 57, step 8. Hand-stitch or glue the body to the hindquarters.

6 Shape the tail into desired position. Tie ribbon around the neck. Secure loop of embroidery floss through top of ornament, for hanger.

HOW TO MAKE A REINDEER ORNAMENT

MATERIALS

- Felt.
- Polyester fiberfill; pipe cleaner.
- Thick craft glue; embroidery floss.
- Black fine-point permanent-ink marker.
- Golf tee, for horn; craft acrylic glitter paint.

CUTTING DIRECTIONS

From felt, cut two ears, two antlers, and one tail, using patterns on page 311. Cut one 1/2" × 8" (1.3 × 20.5 cm) rectangle for the scarf. Transfer body and leg patterns on page 311 onto heavy paper or cardboard; these pieces are cut below.

1 Glue antler pieces together, matching edges. Fold tail in half lengthwise; pin. Assemble reindeer leg section as for the mouse body on pages 55 and 56, steps 1 to 3, omitting reference to tail. Insert pipe cleaner into leg; trim pipe cleaner 1/4" (1.3 cm) from edge of felt.

2 Repeat step 1 on page 55 to prepare reindeer body section for stitching; pin-mark placement for antlers, tail, and extended leg. Stitch around body, inserting the antlers, tail, and leg at markings; leave opening at upper edge of back for stuffing.

(Continued)

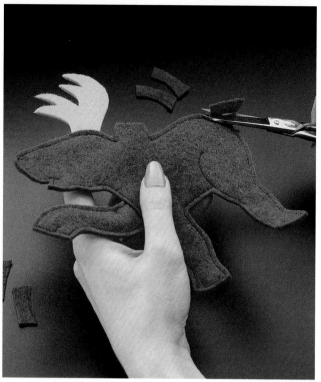

3 Trim felt ⅛" (3 mm) from stitching, taking care not to cut antlers, tail, or front leg. Stuff body with polyester fiberfill. Stitch opening closed, using zipper foot.

4 Attach ears as on page 56, step 6. Mark eyes as on page 57, step 8.

5 Apply glitter paint to golf tee; allow to dry. Glue golf tee to leg as shown, for horn.

6 Cut slits at ends of scarf piece to make fringe, using scissors. Tie scarf around neck of reindeer. Secure loop of embroidery floss through top of ornament, for hanger.

HOW TO MAKE A DOVE ORNAMENT

MATERIALS

- Felt.
- Polyester fiberfill.
- Thick craft glue; embroidery floss.
- Black fine-point permanent-ink marker.
- Small artificial leaves.

CUTTING DIRECTIONS

Transfer body and wing patterns on page 311 onto heavy paper or cardboard; these pieces are cut below.

1 Assemble body section as for mouse on pages 55 and 56, steps 1 to 4, omitting reference to tail. Repeat to make two wings, omitting stuffing.

2 Glue a wing to each side of the body, staggering the placement slightly so both the wings are visible from each side.

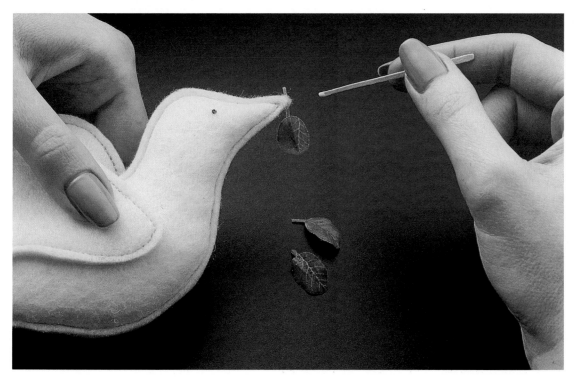

3 Mark eyes as on page 57, step 8. Glue artificial leaves to beak. Secure a loop of embroidery floss through the top of ornament, for the hanger.

RIBBON ROSES

Ribbon roses add an elegant touch to the Christmas tree. They are constructed using either standard ribbon for a traditional rose or wired ribbon for a cabbage-style rose, and are secured to wire stems. The stems are wrapped with floral tape, with artificial leaves inserted for a finishing touch.

Make roses of different sizes, using ribbon in different widths. The length of the ribbon needed for each rose varies with the width of the ribbon and the desired finished size. A rose made with ⅝" (1.5 cm) ribbon may require ½ yd. (0.5 m) of ribbon, while a rose made with 2¼" (6 cm) ribbon may require 1½ yd. (1.4 m) of ribbon. For impact, cluster several roses of different colors and sizes, forming a ribbon rose bouquet. Simply twist the wire stems of the roses around the tree branches to secure them to the tree.

MATERIALS

- Medium-gauge stem wire.
- Fine-gauge paddle floral wire, for traditional ribbon roses.
- Ribbon in desired width, for traditional rose, or wired ribbon in desired width, for cabbage-style rose; width of ribbon and desired finished size of rose determine length needed.
- Artificial rose leaves.
- Floral tape.

HOW TO MAKE A TRADITIONAL RIBBON ROSE

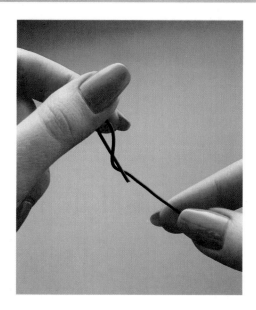

1 Bend a 1" (2.5 cm) loop in the end of stem wire; twist to secure.

2 Fold ribbon end over loop; wrap with paddle floral wire to secure.

(Continued)

63

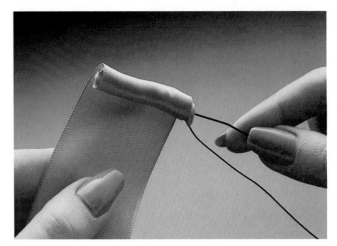

3 Hold ribbon taut in left hand and stem wire in right hand; roll stem wire toward left hand, wrapping ribbon tightly around the fold three times, forming rose center. Wrap paddle wire tightly around base to secure.

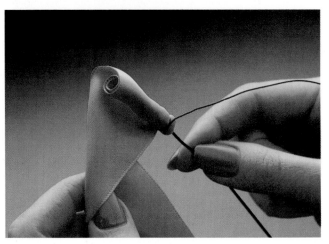

4 Fold ribbon back diagonally as shown, close to rose. Roll rose center over fold, keeping upper edge of rose center just below upper edge of fold; lower edges of ribbon will not be aligned.

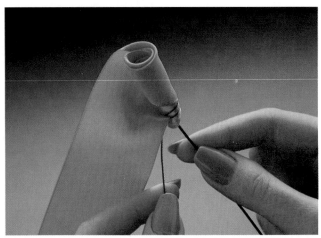

5 Roll to end of fold, forming petal. Wrap paddle wire tightly around base.

6 Repeat steps 4 and 5 for desired number of petals. Fold ribbon back diagonally, and secure with paddle wire at base; cut ribbon and paddle wire.

7 Wrap end of floral tape around base of rose, stretching tape slightly for best adhesion. Wrap entire base of rose, concealing wire. Continue wrapping floral tape onto stem wire. Place stem of artificial rose leaf next to stem wire; wrap stem wire and leaf stem together with floral tape. Continue wrapping until entire stem wire is covered with floral tape.

HOW TO MAKE A CABBAGE-STYLE ROSE

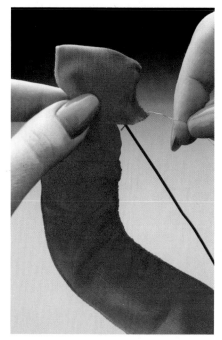

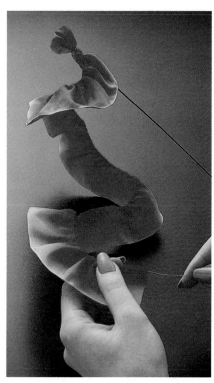

1 Follow step 1 on page 63. Cut a 1 to 1½-yd. (0.95 to 1.4 m) length of wired ribbon. Pull out about 2" (5 cm) of wire on one edge of one end of ribbon. Fold ribbon end over loop; secure with pulled wire, forming rose center.

2 Gather up one edge of remaining length of ribbon tightly by sliding ribbon along ribbon wire toward the rose center.

3 Wrap the gathered edge around the base of the rose, wrapping each layer slightly higher than the previous layer.

4 Fold the ribbon end down and catch under last layer. Wrap ribbon wire tightly around base several times to secure. Cut off excess ribbon wire.

5 Follow step 7, opposite, covering gathered edge of ribbon and wire.

MORE
IDEAS FOR
ORNAMENTS

Nature elements are used to embellish a miniature basket and wreath, creating clever ornaments. Miniature basket ornament is filled with sprigs of greenery and artificial berries. Miniature wreath is embellished with a small craft bird, sprigs of greenery, and artificial berries.

Ribbon, lace, and small cones (right) turn a plain ornament into an elegant tree decoration. Secure the embellishments using dots of clear-drying glue.

Torn fabric strips are tied around a cinnamon stick to make a Christmas tree ornament (below) Whole allspice and anise are used for embellishment. Secure raffia hanger with hot glue.

Large cones, painted like Santas, (below) make quick and inexpensive ornaments. Secure strings for the hangers, using a drop of hot glue. Form the face, beard, and hairline, using artificial snow paste; then paint the ornament, using acrylic paints. Trim the top of the completed ornament with snow paste.

QUICK & EASY ORNAMENTS

Wheat bundles (left), hung upside down, are attractive accents on trees with natural or country decorating styles. The wheat stems are secured in bundles with a rubber band, which is concealed with a fabric bow. Secure the ornaments to the tree using floral wire.

Wire garland, shaped into spirals, adds glitz to a Christmas tree. Wrap a 26" (66 cm) length of wire garland around a pen or pencil. Remove the wire, then gradually untwist the coil from one end to make the ornament. At the widest end, bend the wire to form a hanger.

Glitter adds sparkle to plain ornaments. Mark designs on the ornaments using a glue-stick pen, then sprinkle with extra-fine glitter.

Dried fruit slices *make aromatic ornaments. Orange slices, glued together, are decorated with sprigs of greenery, berries, and ribbon hangers. The apple slices have jute hangers and are embellished with anise and cinnamon sticks. Dried fruit slices are available at craft stores, or make your own as on pages 70 and 72.*

Torn fabric strips *are wrapped and glued around Styrofoam® balls to make country-style ornaments. Secure raffia bows and hangers with hot glue.*

Ribbons and berries *embellish the tops of purchased glass ornaments. Ribbons also replace the traditional wire hangers.*

Glitter glue *in fine-tip tubes is applied to a glass ball ornament, creating a unique dimensional design.*

GARLANDS

Tree garlands can be made in a variety of styles. Shown top to bottom, choose from a rope garland, wrapped ball-and-spool garland, a dried-fruit-slice garland, or a wired-ribbon garland.

For ease in assembling, make the garlands in lengths of about 72" (183 cm). The wired-ribbon garland can be made any length. Most garlands are constructed with loops at the ends for securing the garlands to the branches.

Decorate a tree with a country or natural look, using a rope garland embellished with berry or floral clusters. The clusters may be purchased ready-made, or you can make your own.

To make a wrapped ball-and-spool garland with a country look, wrap torn fabric strips around Styrofoam® balls and wooden spools, then string them together with a piece of jute or twine. Buttons can be added to the garland for more color. Adding buttons decreases the number of wrapped balls and spools needed.

For a dried-fruit-slice garland, combine dried apple and orange slices with cinnamon sticks and fresh cranberries. String the items together with a piece of raffia for a natural look. You can dry your own fruit slices by placing them in a low-temperature oven for several hours. The drying time will vary, depending on the moisture content of the fruit. Remove the fruit slices from the oven when they feel like leather. If the slices are dried too long, they will be brittle and break; if the drying time is too short, they will be soft and spoil. The fresh cranberries will dry naturally on the garland after it is made.

A wired-ribbon garland can be made inexpensively from fabric strips, beading wire, and paper-backed fusible web. Decorate a tree with one continuous garland or several shorter ones. Arrange the garland by weaving the ribbon between and into the branches to create depth.

HOW TO MAKE A ROPE GARLAND

MATERIALS

- 1⅓ yd. (1.27 m) two-ply or three-ply manila or sisal rope, ¼" or ⅜" (6 mm or 1 cm) in diameter.
- Sheet moss.
- Eight berry or floral clusters with wire stems, either purchased or made as on page 152.
- Wire cutter.
- Hot glue gun and glue sticks; thick craft glue.

1 Make 3" (7.5 cm) loops at ends of rope by inserting each end between plies; secure with hot glue.

2 Make eight berry or floral clusters, if necessary (page 152). Insert the wire stems of clusters between the plies of rope at 8" (20.5 cm) intervals, and secure them with hot glue; trim any excess wire, using wire cutter.

3 Conceal wire ends of clusters with pieces of sheet moss; secure with craft glue.

HOW TO MAKE A WRAPPED BALL-AND-SPOOL GARLAND

MATERIALS

- Scraps of cotton fabrics.
- Twenty-four ⅞" (2.2 cm) Styrofoam® balls.
- Twenty-four wooden craft spools.
- Assorted buttons, optional.
- Lightweight jute or twine.
- Large-eyed needle.
- Thick craft glue.

1 Tear twenty-four ¾" × 2¼" (2 × 6 cm) fabric strips on crosswise grain. Wrap around wooden spools; secure with glue. Tear twenty-four ½" × 13" (1.3 × 33 cm) fabric strips. Wrap randomly around Styrofoam balls; secure with glue.

2 Cut an 84" (213.5 cm) length of jute or twine. Form 3" (7.5 cm) loop at one end, and secure with knot; thread a large-eyed needle on opposite end.

3 String wrapped balls and spools onto jute or twine, alternating with buttons, if desired. Form loop at end; secure with knot.

HOW TO MAKE A DRIED-FRUIT-SLICE GARLAND

MATERIALS

- Firm apples and oranges.
- Fresh cranberries.
- Cinnamon sticks.

- 2 cups (500 mL) lemon juice.
- 1 tablespoon (15 mL) salt.

- Parchment paper.
- Raffia.
- 24-gauge floral wire.

- Wire cutter.
- Aerosol clear acrylic sealer.
- Paper towels.

1 Mix lemon and salt together; set aside. Cut fruit into scant ¼" (6 mm) slices, cutting crosswise as shown. Soak apple slices in lemon solution for 1 minute. Pat slices with paper towels to absorb excess moisture.

2 Place apple and orange slices on cookie sheet lined with parchment paper. Bake in 150°F (65°C) oven for 8 to 12 hours, until slices are dry, but still pliable; turn slices over and open oven door periodically while drying.

3 Apply aerosol clear acrylic sealer to cooled fruit slices. Break cinnamon sticks into 2" (5 cm) lengths. Select length of sturdy raffia; form loop at one end, and secure with knot.

4 Create needle for stringing fruit by folding a 6" (15 cm) length of floral wire in half around the unknotted end of raffia. Twist wire together at ends; trim excess, using wire cutter. Crimp the wire at fold, using pliers.

5 String the fruit slices, cranberries, and cinnamon sticks onto raffia; pierce fruit slices about ⅜" (1 cm) from the edges and gently ease along the raffia. Tie lengths of raffia together as necessary to make the garland about 72" (183 cm) long. Form a loop at end; secure with knot.

HOW TO MAKE A WIRED-RIBBON GARLAND

MATERIALS

- Fabric.
- One or more rolls of paper-backed fusible web, ⅜" (1 cm) wide.
- 26-gauge beading wire or craft wire.

1 Cut fabric strips to desired width of ribbon plus ¾" (2 cm). Piece strips as necessary, as on page 80, step 7. Apply strip of fusible web to wrong side of fabric along both long edges, following the manufacturer's directions. Remove paper backing.

2 Cut wire slightly longer than the length of fabric. Place the wire along inner edge of one fused strip. Fold and press fused edge to wrong side of fabric, encasing wire. Repeat for opposite side. Trim wire at ends.

MORE IDEAS FOR GARLANDS

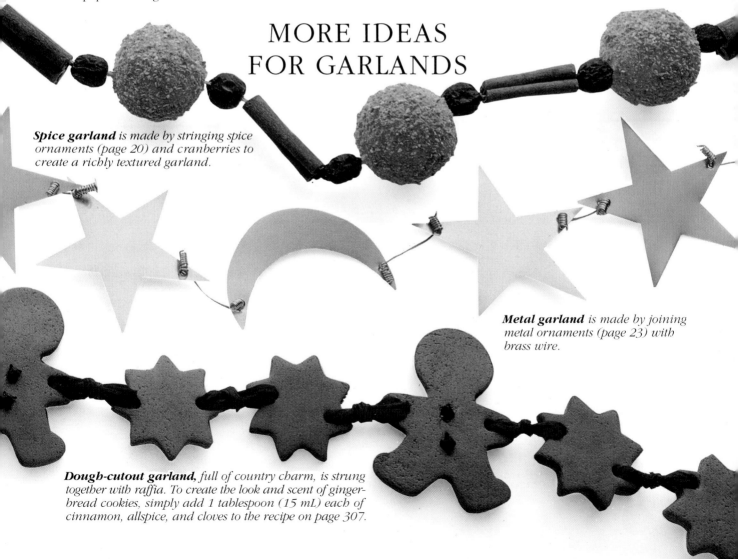

Spice garland is made by stringing spice ornaments (page 20) and cranberries to create a richly textured garland.

Metal garland is made by joining metal ornaments (page 23) with brass wire.

Dough-cutout garland, full of country charm, is strung together with raffia. To create the look and scent of gingerbread cookies, simply add 1 tablespoon (15 mL) each of cinnamon, allspice, and cloves to the recipe on page 307.

QUICK & EASY GARLANDS

Candy canes and mint candies *are tied together with red ribbon for a colorful garland.*

Large bells *embellished with cones and sprigs of greenery are tied together with raffia.*

Holiday garlands are traditionally used to decorate the Christmas tree. Make your own garlands by securing items such as candies, cookie cutters, or floral materials together with ribbon, raffia, or fabric strips.

Mini cookie cutters *in Christmas shapes are strung on lengths of jute. Beads are interspersed between the cookie cutters to add color to the garland.*

Pretzels, *tied to torn strips of fabric, make a country-style garland.*

TREE TRIMMING

Collectible metal toys and cookie cutters *are used as ornaments to create a country-style tree. Popcorn garland and fabric bows are used for contrast, and raffia streamers add to the country look.*

A variety of ornaments can be mixed successfully on a tree. Create a unified look by emphasizing a particular color or style, repeating it in several areas of the tree. For interest, add a few elements of surprise, such as an artificial bird's nest, oversize decorations, dried or silk flowers, or raffia streamers.

Wired-ribbon bow is used as a tree topper. Streamers of ribbon cascade down the tree and are tucked into the branches. Gold and bronze foliage and berry picks are tucked into the branches to complete the elegant look.

Dried floral materials, such as baby's breath, German statice, roses, and pepper berries, are tucked into the tree, creating a garland effect. Several craft bird's nests and birds add to the natural look. Dried flowers, tied with a bow, are used as a tree topper.

Artificial fruit garland gives a natural look to this tree. Aromatic dried-fruit-slice ornaments (pages 68 and 69) and honeysuckle vine are used to decorate the tree.

Oversize decorations, such as snowmen, can be used for impact on a tree. Place the oversize decorations on the tree first, securing them with floral wire, if necessary. Candy canes and frosted twigs are used to fill in bare areas.

TREE SKIRTS

A tree skirt offers the finishing touch to a Christmas tree. This simple lined tree skirt, finished with bias binding, has a layer of polyester fleece or batting for added body. It can be embellished in a variety of ways, using fused appliqués.

Make the patterns for appliqué designs by enlarging simple motifs found on Christmas cards or gift-wrapping paper. Use machine quilting or hand stitching around the outer edges of the appliqués to give them more definition.

MATERIALS

- 1¼ yd. (1.15 m) fabric, for tree skirt.
- 1¼ yd. (1.15 m) lining fabric.
- 45" (115 cm) square polyester fleece or low-loft quilt batting.
- ¾ yd. (0.7 m) fabric, for binding.
- Scraps of fabric, for fused appliqués.
- Paper-backed fusible web.

CUTTING DIRECTIONS

Cut the fabric, lining, and fleece or batting as in steps 1 to 3, below. Cut bias fabric strips, 2½" (6.5 cm) wide, for the binding.

HOW TO SEW A TREE SKIRT

1 Fold fabric for tree skirt in half lengthwise, then crosswise. Using a straightedge and a pencil, mark an arc on the fabric, measuring 21" to 22" (53.5 to 56 cm) from folded center of fabric. Cut on the marked line through all layers.

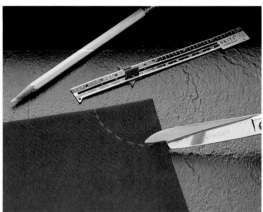

2 Mark a second arc, measuring 1¾" (4.5 cm) from the folded center of the fabric. Cut on the marked line.

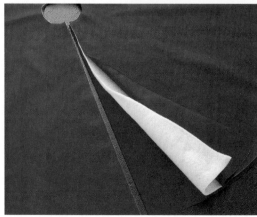

3 Cut along one folded edge; this will be the center back. Cut lining and fleece or batting, using fabric for tree skirt as a pattern.

4 Apply the paper-backed fusible web to the wrong side of fabric scraps, following the manufacturer's directions. Transfer design motifs onto paper side of the fusible web; turn pattern over if the design is asymmetrical.

(Continued)

5 Cut design motifs from paper-backed fabric; remove paper backing. Fuse motifs to the tree skirt as desired.

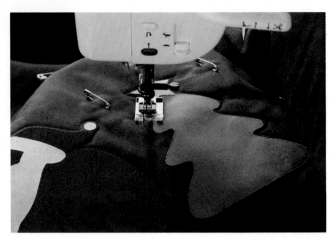

6 Layer the lining, fleece, and fabric for tree skirt, right sides out. Baste the layers together, using safety pins or hand stitching. Quilt design motifs by stitching around the outer edges of designs.

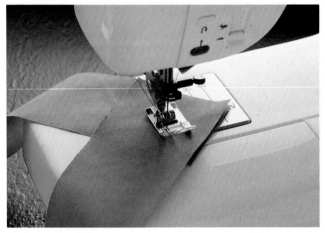

7 Piece binding strips to form 5½-yd. (5.05 m) length; join the strips together as shown; trim ¼" (6 mm) from stitching. Press seams open; trim off points.

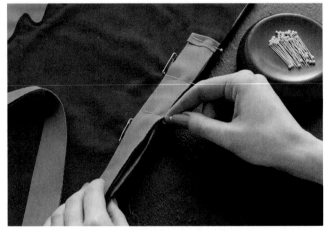

8 Press the binding strip in half lengthwise, wrong sides together; fold back ½" (1.3 cm) on one short end. Pin binding to tree skirt, matching raw edges and starting at center back.

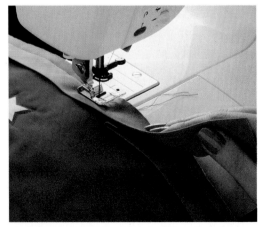

9 Stitch a scant ⅜" (1 cm) from raw edges, overlapping ends of binding ½" (1.3 cm); trim close to stitching.

10 Wrap binding strip snugly around edge of tree skirt, covering the stitching line on the wrong side; pin. Stitch in the ditch on right side of tree skirt, catching the binding on the wrong side.

MORE IDEAS
FOR TREE
SKIRTS

Gingerbread-men appliqués embellish this tree skirt. The outer edge is defined with contrasting bias binding and jumbo rickrack. The rickrack is applied to the underside of the tree skirt after the binding is applied. The gingerbread men are embellished with fabric paints in fine-tip tubes.

Star-and-moon theme is created using appliqués from lamé fabric. To prevent the delicate fabric from fraying, the raw edges of the appliqués were sealed, using fabric paints in fine-tip tubes.

Bullion fringe adds an elegant edging to a brocade tree skirt. Applied to the underside of the tree skirt, the fringe is secured in place by edgestitching along the inside edge of the binding from the right side.

Sheer organza overlay, placed over the fused angel appliqués, creates a shadow embroidery effect. The tree skirt is quilted around the outer edges of the appliqués, using two strands of embroidery thread and a hand running stitch.

LAYERED TREE SKIRTS

Decorate the base of a Christmas tree with a layered tree skirt embellished with ribbon bows. When arranged around the tree, it resembles an eight-pointed star. The skirt can be made for either an elegant or casual look, depending on the choice of fabrics and ribbon.

Easy to make, the tree skirt is simply two lined squares of fabric, stitched together around center openings. Back

openings in the layers allow for easy placement around the tree. Safety pins, used in place of permanent stitching, gather the fabric along each side, saving time and allowing the tree skirt to be stored flat.

Choose a lightweight lining fabric to prevent adding bulk to the skirt. For an inexpensive lining that is also a good choice for sheer fabrics, use nylon net.

**Layered
tree skirt is**
*made from printed
and plaid complementary
holiday fabrics. Solid-colored
fabrics are used for the lining. The
tree skirt is embellished with wired
ribbon bows.*

MATERIALS

- 1¼ yd. (1.15 m) each, of two coordinating fabrics.
- 1¼ yd. (1.15 m) each, of two lining fabrics.
- Eight large safety pins.
- Wired ribbon.

HOW TO MAKE A LAYERED TREE SKIRT

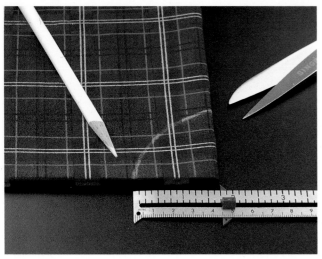

1 Cut outer fabric into a square, trimming selvages. Fold fabric in half lengthwise, then crosswise. Mark an arc, measuring 1¾" (4.5 cm) from folded center of fabric. Cut on marked line.

2 Pin-mark one folded edge at raw edges for the center back opening; open fabric and mark cutting line from raw edge to center opening, on wrong side of fabric.

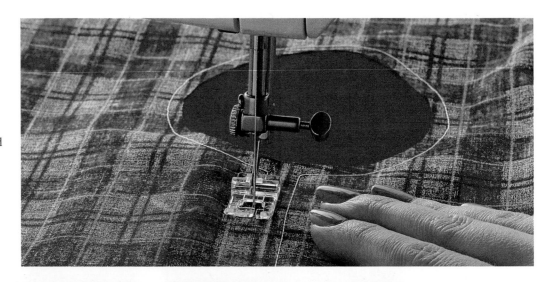

3 Place face fabric on lining, right sides together; pin the layers together. Stitch ¼" (6 mm) seam around tree skirt, stitching around all edges and on each side of center back line; leave 6" (15 cm) opening for turning. For sheer fabrics, stitch a second row scant ⅛" (3 mm) from first stitching.

4 Cut on marked line; trim lining even with edges of outer fabric. Clip seam allowances around center circle; trim corners diagonally. Turn right side out; press. Slipstitch opening closed.

5 Repeat steps 1 to 4 for the remaining tree skirt layer. Align skirts, right sides up, matching center back openings. Shift the upper skirt so corners of the lower skirt are centered at sides of upper skirt. Mark opening of lower skirt on upper skirt. Pin layers together around the center from marked point to opening in the upper skirt.

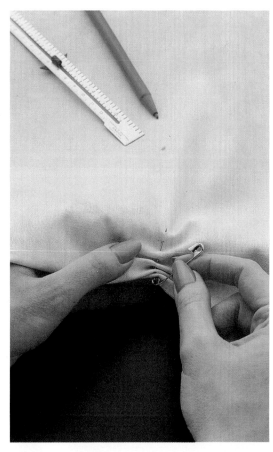

6 Topstitch ¼" (6 mm) from the raw edges around center, from opening to marked point, securing the two tree skirt layers together.

7 Gather and bunch fabric at the center of one long edge by inserting point of safety pin in and out of fabric for about 6" (15 cm) on lining side of the tree skirt as shown; close the pin. Repeat at center of each side for each tree skirt layer; do not pin back opening sides.

8 Place skirt around base of tree. Overlap back opening at outer edge; gather and bunch fabric for underlayer with safety pin. Repeat for remaining center back opening of upper layer of skirt.

9 Make four ribbon bows. Position a bow at each side of the upper layer, concealing safety pin; secure with pin.

MORE
IDEAS FOR
TREE
SKIRTS

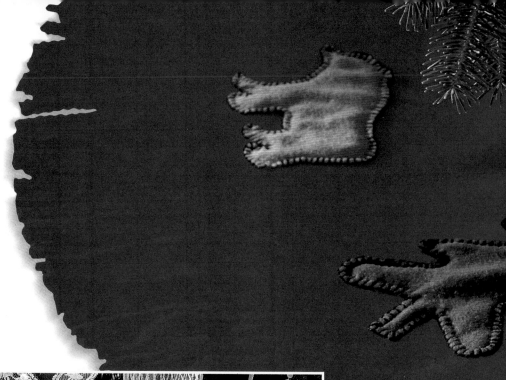

**Polar
fleece tree
skirt** (above)
is a quick and cozy
project. Simply cut a
polar fleece circle to
the desired size; cut
out a center circle for
the trunk, and cut an
opening slit, if desired.
Fringe the skirt, keeping
the blade of the scissors
perpendicular to the
fabric edge. Blanket-
stitch fleece appliqués
around the skirt for
rustic appeal.

Lace tablecloth,
draped around the
base of a tree,
complements a
Victorian-style tree.

Excelsior, highlighted with gold spray paint, is arranged around the base of a Christmas tree for a unique accent.

The Holiday Table

FRESH FLORAL
ARRANGEMENTS

Decorate for the holidays with fresh flowers by making a centerpiece or a buffet arrangement. A centerpiece used on a dining table is usually short in height so it does not interfere with conversation. A buffet arrangement is designed to be placed against a wall and can be taller, for more impact.

To make a holiday arrangement, use long-lasting flowers such as those on page 92 and add sprigs of greenery, such as Scotch pine, spruce, or juniper. For a more festive look, embellish the arrangement with canella berries, decorative pods, pepper berries, pinecones, feathers, or seeded eucalyptus.

A fresh holiday arrangement can be displayed in any container that holds water. For baskets, terra-cotta pots, or metal pots, use a plastic waterproof container as a liner.

Fresh flowers can be held in the arrangement by either of two methods, depending on the container selected. For glass containers, the flowers are held in place by making a grid over the mouth of the container with clear waterproof tape. For nonglass containers, the flowers are held in place by inserting them into floral foam designed for fresh flowers.

MATERIALS

- Flowers in three sizes.
- Sprigs of two or more varieties of greenery.
- Tall linear floral material, such as gilded devil's claw heliconia, curly willow, or branches, for the buffet arrangement.
- Gilded pods, berries, or twigs, for the centerpiece.
- Floral foam, designed for fresh flowers, for use with nonglass containers.
- Clear waterproof floral tape.
- Sharp knife.

TIPS FOR FRESH FLOWERS

Cut off 1" (2.5 cm) from stems, at an angle, before arranging; for roses, cut stems at an angle while submerging them in water.

Remove any leaves that will be covered by water in the finished arrangement; leaves left in the water will shorten the life of the flowers.

Add cut-flower food to the water.

Add fresh water to the floral arrangement as necessary.

Keep flowers out of direct sunlight and drafts.

Centerpiece *(above) combines chrysanthemums, roses, ornithogalum, leatherleaf, seeded eucalyptus, lotus pods, and cedar.* ***Buffet arrangement*** *(opposite) uses mums, lilies, leptosporum, roses, gilded devil's claw heliconia, leatherleaf, and seeded eucalyptus to create a dramatic display.*

Chrysanthemums

Ornithogalum

Lily

Carnations

Orchid

Yarrow

Heather

Roses

Alstroemeria

Stock

Leptosporum

Flowers shown above can be used to make long-lasting holiday arrangements.

HOW TO PREPARE THE CONTAINER

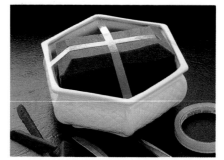

1 **Nonglass containers.** Soak the floral foam in water for at least 20 minutes.

2 Cut foam, using a knife, so it fits the container and extends about 1" (2.5 cm) above rim. Round off the upper edges of foam, if necessary, to prevent foam from showing in the finished arrangement. Secure with clear waterproof tape. Add water.

Glass containers. Make a grid over the mouth of container, using clear waterproof floral tape.

HOW TO MAKE A FRESH FLORAL BUFFET ARRANGEMENT

1 Prepare glass or nonglass container (above). Insert first variety of greenery into container, placing taller stems into center near back and shorter stems at sides and front.

2 Insert remaining varieties of greenery. Insert tall linear materials into container, spacing them evenly.

3 Insert largest flowers into the arrangement, one variety at a time, spacing them evenly throughout to keep arrangement balanced on three sides.

4 Insert second largest flowers into arrangement, spacing evenly. Insert the smaller flowers into the arrangement to fill any bare areas. Mist arrangement lightly with water.

HOW TO MAKE A FRESH FLORAL CENTERPIECE

1 Prepare the glass or nonglass container (opposite). Cut sprigs of greenery to lengths of 5" to 8" (12.5 to 20.5 cm); trim away any stems near the ends of sprigs.

2 Insert sprigs of greenery into the container, placing longer sprigs around the outside and shorter sprigs near the center.

3 Insert the largest flowers into the container, placing one stem in the center and several stems on each side to establish the height and width of the arrangement. Insert remaining large flowers, spacing evenly.

4 Insert the second largest flowers into the arrangement, one variety at a time, spacing evenly, so the arrangement appears balanced from all sides.

5 Insert additional sprigs of greenery as necessary to fill in any bare areas. Insert gilded pods, twigs, or berries, if desired, for further embellishment. Mist arrangement lightly with water.

Country arrangement *is created by filling small brown bags with popcorn, nuts, and dried fruits. The bags are tied with torn strips of fabric and placed in a rustic basket.*

Elegant decorating accent is created from a dried grapevine wreath, an artificial vine of grape leaves, dried artichokes, and gilded cones. Refer to pages 150 to 153 for information on embellishing wreaths.

Natural setting is created with a pine garland used as the base of the arrangement. Pillar candles placed in glasses and smaller votive candles are embellished with cinnamon sticks and raffia. Spice ornaments and dried flowers are scattered throughout, for additional interest.

HOLIDAY FLORAL ARRANGEMENTS

Use this unique floral arrangement to add color to your holiday table. Make the arrangement from the floral materials shown, or select floral materials to coordinate with your decorating scheme.

To help create the elegant natural look of the arrangement, the preserved leaves are highlighted with gold paint. Try this simple highlighting technique on other floral materials to achieve interesting effects. The gold highlights complement the gilded terra-cotta pots that are used for the base of the arrangement.

MATERIALS

- Two terra-cotta pots, about 5" (12.5 cm) in diameter.
- Gold aerosol paint, plus optional second color.
- Floral foam, for silk arranging.
- Artificial pine boughs.
- Latex grape clusters and apples; dried pomegranates.
- 3 yd. (2.75 m) stiff decorative cording.
- Artificial or preserved leaves on branches; twigs.
- Hot glue gun and glue sticks.

HOW TO MAKE A HOLIDAY FLORAL ARRANGEMENT

1 Place a sheet of plastic on a tabletop. Spray a generous pool of aerosol paint onto the plastic; drag the preserved leaves through the paint to gild them. Allow to dry. Repeat with additional paint colors, if desired.

2 Place one pot on its side, next to the other; secure pots together, using hot glue. When dry, apply gold aerosol paint to the containers.

(Continued)

3 Cut floral foam, using knife, so it fits container snugly and is even with edge of container; secure with hot glue. Repeat for remaining container.

4 Insert pine boughs and leaf branches into foam, so they rise from 5" to 8" (12.5 to 20.5 cm) above foam. Cut pine branches into small pieces to fill area around edges of containers. Insert a few twigs into vertical pot.

5 Insert apples and grape clusters, allowing some of the grapes to cascade slightly over sides of containers. Secure pomegranates into arrangement as desired with hot glue.

6 Apply tape to decorative braid at 8" to 12" (20.5 to 30.5 cm) intervals; cut braid through center of tape. Form loops from lengths of braid; wrap ends together with tape. Insert loops of decorative braid into arrangement, securing braid to foam with hot glue.

HOLIDAY COASTER SETS

As a gift for the hostess, make a set of holiday coasters and package them in a decorative box. Purchase a small cardboard box and lid in a holiday-motif shape, such as a star, heart, or tree. Make the padded coasters in the same shape as the box, using cotton quilting fabric and needlepunched cotton batting. Paint the box, and adorn the lid with an additional coaster, giving a clue to the contents of the box.

MATERIALS

- Cardboard box in holiday-motif shape, such as a star, heart, or tree, measuring about 2" (5 cm) high and 4" to 5" (10 to 12.5 cm) in diameter.
- ½ yd. (0.5 m) cotton quilting fabric in Christmas print.
- ½ yd. (0.5 m) needlepunched cotton batting.
- Pinking shears.
- Embellishments, such as tiny buttons or ribbons, optional.
- Acrylic paint and paintbrush.
- Craft glue.

HOW TO MAKE A HOLIDAY COASTER SET

1 Prewash fabric and batting, following the manufacturer's instructions. Fold fabric in half, wrong sides together, matching selvages. Trace the box bottom on right side of fabric eight times, for eight coasters; allow ½" (1.3 cm) between coasters. Trace the box lid once for larger coaster.

2 Insert batting between the layers of fabric. Secure fabric and batting layers together, using two or three pins in each traced coaster.

3 Cut coasters apart through all layers, leaving irregular margins around each coaster. Stitch layers together, using small stitches, and stitching ¼" (6 mm) inside traced lines.

4 Cut out coasters just inside traced lines, using pinking shears. Embellish the coasters with small buttons or other embellishments, if desired.

5 Paint all surfaces of cardboard box and lid, using acrylic paint and paintbrush. Allow to dry.

6 Insert the eight small coasters into box. Embellish large coaster for lid with bow or other embellishment, if desired. Secure large coaster to lid, using craft glue.

HOLIDAY PLACEMATS & TABLE RUNNERS

Create a variety of looks for the holiday table using simple stitched-and-turned placemats and table runners. Choose to make placemats and a matching rectangular table runner, or sew a table runner that has pointed ends. Embellish the placemats and table runner with coordinating braid, ribbon, or other flat trims.

The instructions that follow are for placemats with a finished size of 13" × 18" (33 × 46 cm). The length of the table runner is determined by the length of the table and the desired drop length, or overhang, at the ends of the table.

MATERIALS (for four placemats)

- 1⅝ yd. (1.5 m) fabric, for the placemat top and backing pieces.
- 1⅝ yd. (1.5 m) fusible interfacing.
- Braid or other flat trim.

MATERIALS (for table runner)

- Fabric, for table runner top and backing pieces; yardage varies, depending on length of runner.
- Fusible or sew-in interfacing; yardage varies, depending on length of runner.
- Braid or other flat trim.

CUTTING DIRECTIONS

For each placemat, cut two 13½" × 18½" (34.3 × 47.3 cm) rectangles from fabric, for the placemat top and backing. Cut one 13½" × 18½" (34.3 × 47.3 cm) rectangle from fusible interfacing.

For a table runner, cut two rectangles from fabric for the table runner top and backing, and cut one rectangle from fusible interfacing. The width of the rectangles is 18½" (47.3 cm); the length is equal to the length of the table plus two times the desired drop length, plus ½" (1.3 cm) for the seam allowances.

HOW TO SEW A BASIC PLACEMAT OR TABLE RUNNER

1 Apply interfacing to the wrong side of placemat or table runner top; if using fusible interfacing, follow manufacturer's directions.

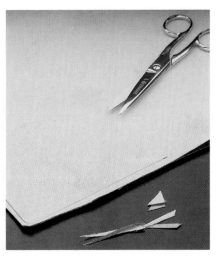

2 Pin top to backing, right sides together. Stitch around placemat or table runner, ¼" (6 mm) from raw edges; leave 4" (10 cm) opening for turning. Trim corners.

3 Turn the placemat or table runner right side out; press. Slipstitch the opening closed. If desired, embellish with braid trim (page 104).

HOW TO SEW A TABLE RUNNER WITH POINTED ENDS

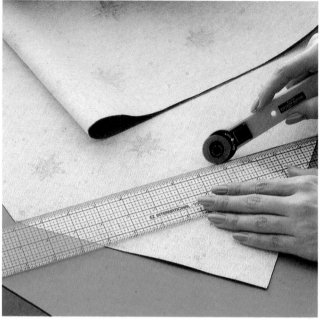

1 Mark the center of one short end on rectangle for table runner top. From same short end, measure distance on each long edge equal to the desired drop length plus ¼" (6 mm) for seam allowance; mark. Draw lines from marking on short end to markings on long edges.

2 Fold rectangle for table runner top in half crosswise; align the raw edges. Cut on marked lines through both layers. Cut backing and interfacing to match table runner top. Complete table runner as on page 103, steps 1 to 3.

HOW TO EMBELLISH A PLACEMAT OR TABLE RUNNER WITH BRAID TRIM

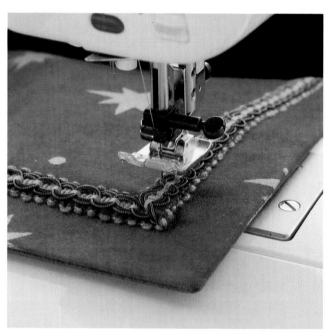

1 Pin braid trim to the placemat or table runner at desired distance from edge; miter the braid trim at corners by folding it at an angle. Fold end of braid diagonally at final corner; trim excess.

2 Edgestitch along inner and outer edges of braid trim; hand-stitch mitered corners in place.

MORE IDEAS FOR PLACEMATS
& TABLE RUNNERS

Braid trim (left) is used to make a mitered border around a placemat.

Purchased appliqués add a festive touch to a plain placemat. The appliqués are fused to the placemat tops before the backing is applied.

Assorted trims (above) are stitched to the placemat top before the backing is applied.

Layered trims are positioned 1" (2.5 cm) from the outer edges of a pointed table runner (right). A tassel is stitched to each point.

PACKAGE PLACEMATS

Dress up a holiday table with pieced placemats that have the three-dimensional look of wrapped packages. The dimensional illusion is achieved by using fabrics in light, medium, and dark colors. A simple bow, created from a pleated fabric square and a fabric loop, completes the package.

The placemat is made from either lightweight cotton or cotton blends, using quick cutting and piecing techniques for easy construction. The instructions that follow are for a set of four placemats that measure about 13" × 17" (33 × 43 cm). Stitch the placemats using ¼" (6 mm) seam allowances.

MATERIALS (for four placemats)

- ¼ yd. (0.25 m) light-colored fabric, for package top.
- ½ yd. (0.5 m) medium-colored fabric, for package front.
- ¼ yd. (0.25 m) dark-colored fabric, for package side.
- ⅝ yd. (0.6 m) fabric, for ribbon and bow.
- ⅞ yd. (0.8 m) fabric, for backing.
- Low-loft quilt batting.
- Quilter's ruler with an edge at 45° angle.

CUTTING DIRECTIONS

Cut the following strips on the crosswise grain, cutting across the full width of the fabric: two 6½" (16.3 cm) strips from the fabric for the package front; two 2" (5 cm) strips from the fabric for the package side; and four 2" (5 cm) strips from the fabric for the package top. From the fabric for the ribbon and bow, cut: four 1½" (3.8 cm) strips and one 1¼" (3.2 cm) strip, for the ribbon; eight 6½" (16.3 cm) squares, for the bows; and one 2½" × 15" (6.5 × 38 cm) strip, for the loop of the bow. Cut four 13½" × 17½" (34.3 × 44.3 cm) rectangles each from the backing fabric and batting.

HOW TO SEW A SET OF PACKAGE PLACEMATS

1 Stitch package front strips to each side of one 1½" (3.8 cm) ribbon strip, to make pieced strip for package fronts. Press the seam allowances toward ribbon strip. From pieced strip, cut four 9½" × 13½" (24.3 × 34.3 cm) rectangles.

2 Stitch package side strips to each side of one 1½" (3.8 cm) ribbon strip, to make pieced strip for package sides. Press the seam allowances toward ribbon strip. Cut off one end of pieced strip at 45° angle, as shown.

(Continued)

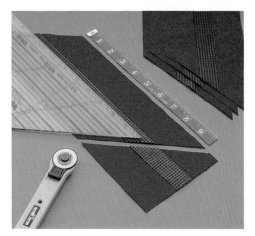

3 Measure and mark strip at 9¾" (25 cm) intervals. Cut four parallelograms for package sides, as shown.

4 Stitch package top strips to each side of one 1½" (3.8 cm) ribbon strip, to make the pieced strip for the package tops. Repeat to make two pieced strips. Press seam allowances toward ribbon strips. Cut off one end of each pieced strip at a 45° angle, as shown; the angle is cut in the opposite direction from the angle of package side strips.

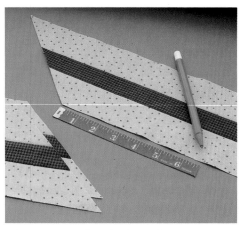

5 Measure and mark the package top strips at 6¾" (17 cm) intervals. Cut into eight parallelograms for package tops.

6 Stitch the 1¼" (3.2 cm) ribbon strip to one angled end of one of the parallelograms for package top; allow excess fabric from ribbon strip at each end. Press seam allowances toward ribbon strip; trim strip even with edges of the parallelogram. Stitch second parallelogram for package top to the opposite side of ribbon strip; press the seam allowances toward the ribbon strip. Repeat to make four package tops.

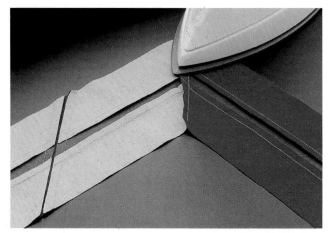

7 Align one package top to one package side along the angled edges, with right sides together and raw edges even. Stitch from sharply pointed end to ¼" (6 mm) from inside corner; backstitch to secure stitching. Press the seam allowances toward package top.

8 Align pieced strips for side and top to package front, matching ribbon strips of top and front. Stitch from outer edges exactly to the seam intersection. Press seam allowances toward top and side.

9 Place the backing and placemat top right sides together. Place fabrics on batting, with pieced design on top; pin or baste layers together.

10 Stitch around the placemat top, ¼" (6 mm) from raw edges; leave 4" (10 cm) opening for turning. Trim the excess backing and batting; trim corners.

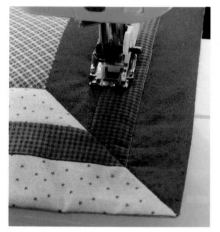

11 Turn the placemat right side out; press. Slipstitch opening closed. Quilt placemat by stitching on seamlines, using monofilament nylon thread in needle and thread that matches backing fabric in the bobbin. (Contrasting thread was used to show detail.)

12 Fold strip for loop of bow in half lengthwise, right sides together. Stitch ¼" (6 mm) seam; turn tube right side out. Press, with the seam centered on one side. Cut tube into four 3" (7.5 cm) strips.

13 Press raw edges ¼" (6 mm) to inside at one end of each tube; tuck opposite end inside the tube to make a loop. Stitch ends together. Pin loop, as shown, over intersecting ribbons on package top. Slipstitch in place.

14 Place two fabric pieces for bow right sides together, matching raw edges. Stitch ¼" (6 mm) from raw edges, leaving 2" (5 cm) opening for turning. Trim the corners; press the seams open.

15 Turn bow piece right side out; press. Slipstitch the opening closed. Hand-pleat fabric, and insert into loop for bow.

HOLIDAY PLACEMATS & NAPKINS

For a festive place setting at the table, make a set of quilted placemats that portray a winter landscape. A round napkin, folded to represent an evergreen tree, completes the setting.

The placements and napkins are made from 100 percent cotton fabric, using techniques for quick construction. Narrow piping or cording trims the edges of the lined napkin, making the napkins easy to turn and press. Simple stitch-and-turn construction eliminates binding on the placemats. The trees on the placemat are secured with machine-blindstitched appliqué.

The finished placemats measure about 12" × 18" (30.5 × 46 cm).

MATERIALS (for six placemats and napkins)

- ²⁄₃ yd. (0.63 m) fabric, for sky section.
- ³⁄₄ yd. (0.7 m) fabric, for lower ground section of placement.
- ¹⁄₂ yd. (0.5 m) fabric, for upper ground section.
- 1¹⁄₈ yd. (1.05 m) fabric, for backing.
- 1¹⁄₂ yd. (1.4 m) each of two coordinating fabrics, for napkins and appliquéd trees on placemat.
- 9¹⁄₂ yd. (8.7 m) cording or piping, for trim on napkin.
- Cardboard, spray starch, and monofilament nylon thread, for blindstitched appliqués.
- Low-loft quilt batting.

CUTTING DIRECTIONS

Cut the fabric for the napkins as on page 112, step l.

Make the pattern for the placemat and cut the fabric for the sky and ground pieces as on pages 113 and 114, steps 1 to 4. For each placemat, cut one 12¹⁄₂" × 18¹⁄₂" (31.8 × 47.3 cm) rectangle from backing fabric, and one 14" × 20" (35.5 × 51 cm) rectangle from batting.

Transfer tree templates for appliqués (pages 312 and 313) onto cardboard; cut. Using templates, cut one of each tree for each placemat, adding ¹⁄₄" (6 mm) seam allowances when cutting.

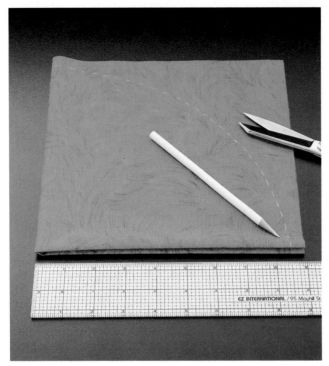

1 Cut one 18" (46 cm) square from fabric; fold in half lengthwise, then crosswise. Using a straightedge and pencil, mark an arc on the fabric, measuring 8½" (21.8 cm) from the folded center of fabric. Cut on the marked line through all layers. Using circle as pattern, cut six circles from each of the two napkin fabrics.

2 Pin trim to right side of one napkin piece, with raw edges even; curve ends of trim into seam allowance as shown, so ends overlap and trim tapers to raw edge. Machine-baste trim in place, using a zipper foot.

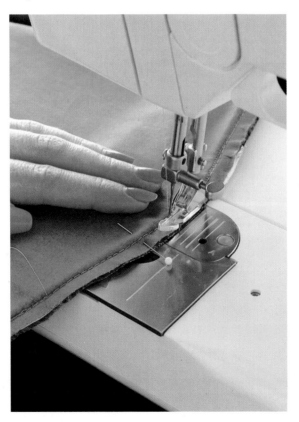

3 Place the napkin and lining right sides together, matching raw edges; pin. Stitch around the napkin, stitching just inside the previous stitches, crowding stitches against the trim; leave a 2" (5 cm) opening. Trim the seam allowance, using pinking shears.

4 Turn the napkin right side out; press. Edgestitch around napkin, using zipper foot and stitching opening closed.

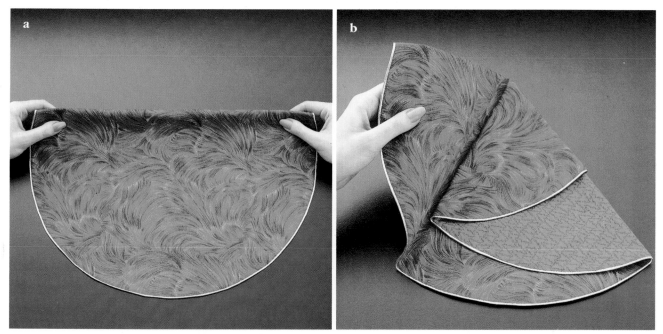

5 Fold under upper one-third of napkin **(a).** Fold right side over, then left side over, folding napkin into thirds **(b).**

HOW TO MAKE A LANDSCAPE PLACEMAT

1 Cut piece of paper 12" × 18" (30.5 × 46 cm). On left side of paper, make a mark 2½" and 9" (6.5 and 23 cm) from lower edge as shown. On right side of paper, mark 7½" (19.3 cm) from lower edge as shown.

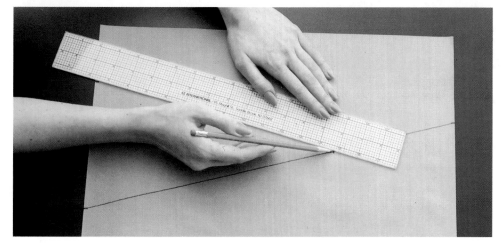

2 Draw a diagonal line connecting lower left mark to right mark as shown. Mark point on diagonal line 12" (30.5 cm) from left edge of the paper; draw a line connecting this point to the remaining mark on the left side.

(Continued)

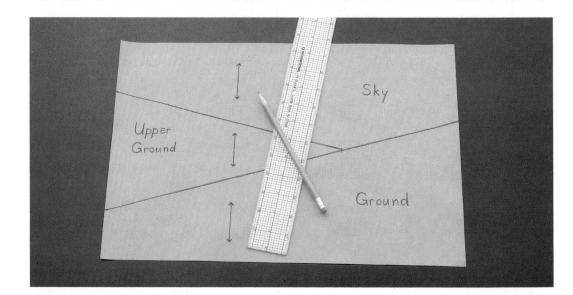

3 Label pattern sections for ground and sky, as shown; mark the grainline on each section.

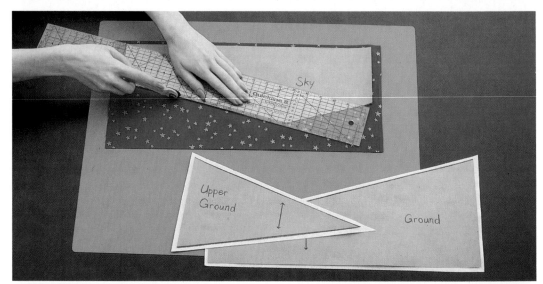

4 Cut pattern on marked lines. For each placemat, cut one of each piece from fabric, adding ¼" (6 mm) seam allowances to each side of pattern.

5 Mark each section on the wrong side of the fabric where ¼" (6 mm) seams will intersect. Align the upper ground piece and the sky piece, right sides together, matching markings for seam intersections. Stitch ¼" (6 mm) seam. Finger-press seam allowances toward upper edge of the placemat.

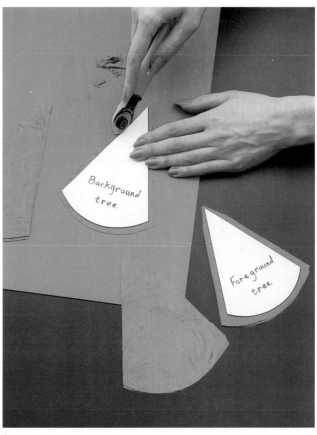

6 Align pieced unit and remaining ground piece, right sides together, matching markings for the seam intersections. Stitch ¼" (6 mm) seam. Press seam allowances toward upper edge of placemat.

7 Cut tree appliqués from fabric (page 111). Center tree templates on wrong side of fabric pieces. Trim points.

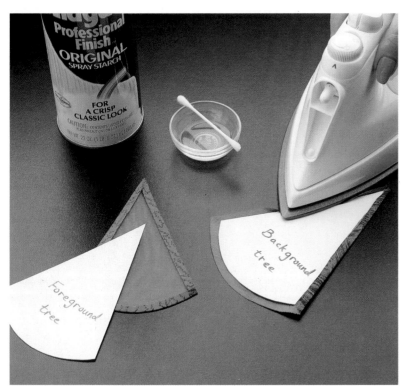

8 Spray starch into small bowl; dab starch on a section of the seam allowance. Using tip of dry iron, press seam allowance over edge of template. Continue around appliqués. Remove templates; press pieces, right side up.

9 Arrange trees on right side of pieced placemat top. Glue-baste background tree in place. Mark placement of foreground tree, using chalk; set aside.

(Continued)

10 Blindstitch around the outer edge of background tree, using monofilament nylon thread in the needle; stitch as close to the edge as possible, just catching the appliqué with the widest swing of blindstitch. Glue-baste the foreground tree in place; blindstitch. (Contrasting thread was used to show detail.)

11 Place backing and placemat top right sides together. Place fabrics on batting, with backing piece on top; pin or baste the layers together.

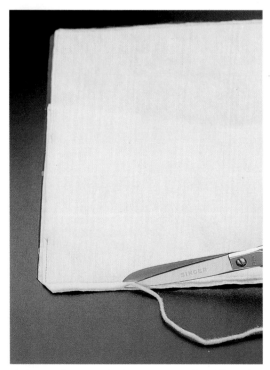

12 Stitch around placemat top, ¼" (6 mm) from the raw edges; leave 4" (10 cm) opening for turning. Trim batting to ⅛" (3 mm); trim corners.

13 Turn placemat right side out; press. Slipstitch opening closed. Quilt placemat by stitching around appliqués and on seamlines, using matching thread. Topstitch ¼" (6 mm) around outside edges. (Contrasting thread was used to show detail.)

MORE IDEAS FOR THE TABLE

Motifs cut from printed fabric are fused to a solid background to make an interesting table covering. Simply fuse motifs to background fabric, using fusible web; then conceal cut edges of fabric, using acrylic craft paints in fine-tip tubes.

Ribbon, wrapped package-style around a table, creates a holiday atmosphere. Secure the ribbon in place on the underside of the table, using masking tape.

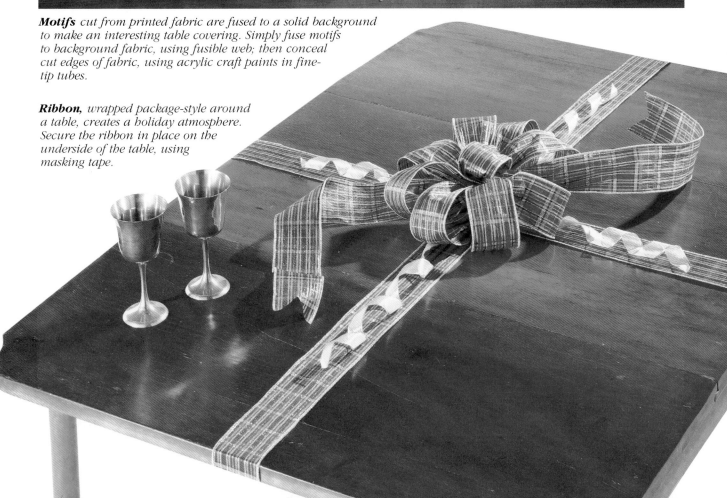

PIECED STAR TABLE TOPPERS

This eight-pointed reversible star adds a decorative touch to tables. Use it as a table topper over a skirted round table. Or drape it over a dining table, sofa table, or end table.

The star is made by stitching eight diamonds together. The outer half of each diamond is cut longer than the inner half, creating extended points that can be draped over the edges of a table. The finished star measures about 50" (127 cm) in diameter. Tassels can be added to the points of the stars for additional embellishment.

The star and the lining can be sewn from a single fabric. Or use two or more fabrics for variety. If more than one fabric is used, become familiar with the piecing technique in order to plan the placement of the pieces before you

begin to stitch. The lining is constructed using the same method as for the star, making the table topper reversible.

MATERIALS

- 3 yd. (2.75 m) fabric, for star and lining from one fabric, or ¾ yd. (0.7 m) each of four fabrics, for star and lining from four fabrics.
- Eight tassels, optional.

CUTTING DIRECTIONS

Make the pattern as on page 120. Cut eight diamonds from the fabric or fabrics for the star. Also cut eight diamonds from the fabric for the lining.

Pieced star table toppers *can be made in a variety of styles. Above, the star topper with a country look is made from four different cotton fabrics. Opposite, an elegant star topper is made from a single fabric and embellished with tassels at each of the points.*

HOW TO MAKE A PIECED STAR TABLE TOPPER PATTERN

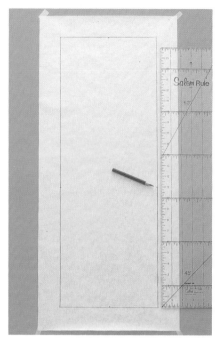 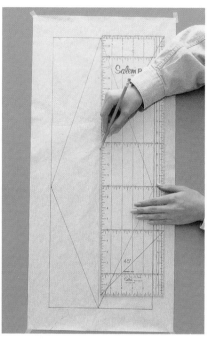 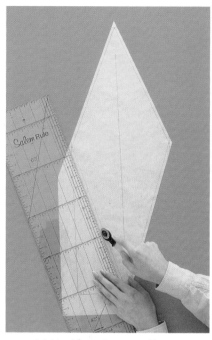

1 Draw 9¼" × 25" (23.6 × 63.5 cm) rectangle on paper. Mark a dot at the center of each short side. Mark a dot along each long side, 11" (28 cm) from one end.

2 Draw lines connecting the dots as shown. Mark grainline parallel to long sides of rectangle.

3 Add ¼" (6 mm) seam allowances to the diamond pattern, outside the marked lines. Cut out pattern.

HOW TO SEW A PIECED STAR TABLE TOPPER

1 Align two of the diamonds, right sides together and raw edges even. Stitch ¼" (6 mm) seam on one short side, stitching toward narrow point. Repeat for remaining pieces to make four 2-diamond units.

2 Stitch two of the 2-diamond units, right sides together, along one short side; finger-press seam allowances in opposite directions as shown. Repeat for the remaining two units.

3 Place the two 4-diamond units right sides together. Pin, matching inner points of diamonds at center. Fold seam allowances of each unit in opposite directions; stitch seam from outer edges toward center.

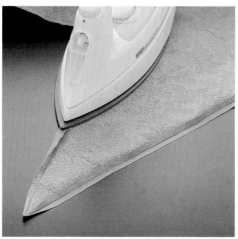

4 Release the stitching within the seam allowances at center of star, so seam allowances will lie flat. Press from wrong side, working from center out.

5 Repeat steps 1 to 4 for lining. Pin the star and the lining, right sides together, matching the raw edges and seams; the seam allowances will face in opposite directions. Stitch around star, stitching from inside corners to points; leave 6" (15 cm) opening on one side, for turning.

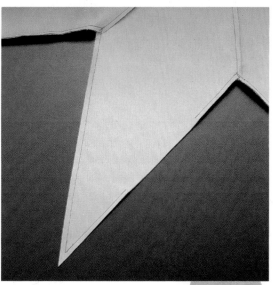

6 Clip inside corners, and trim points. Press the seam allowances open around the outer edges.

7 Turn star right side out; press. Slipstitch opening closed. Stitch a tassel to each point, if desired.

Around The
House

WOODEN BASKETS

Handcrafted wooden baskets are ideal for gift giving and can be used as decorative accents throughout the holiday season. Make the baskets using either a snowman or a Christmas tree design. An aged look, achieved by sanding the edges and applying stain, gives the baskets a rustic charm. They are inexpensive to make and require only basic woodworking skills and tools.

When cutting with a jigsaw, it is helpful to clamp the wood in place, protecting it with wood scraps or felt pads, if necessary. This also allows you to hold the saw firmly with both hands, to reduce vibration, and move the saw smoothly while cutting. Cut inside corners by sawing into the corner from both directions; cut curves slowly to avoid bending the blade.

MATERIALS

- 12 ft. (3.7 m) of ¼" × ¾" (6 mm × 2 cm) pine screen molding.
- 1 × 8 pine board.
- Wooden dowel, ½" (1.3 cm) diameter, 11¼" (28.7 cm) long.
- Jigsaw.
- Drill; ¹⁄₁₆" and ½" drill bits.
- Sanding block; medium-grit and fine-grit sandpaper.
- Acrylic paints; artist's brushes.
- Stain in medium color, such as medium walnut.
- 17 × ¾" (2 cm) brads.
- Wood glue; tracing paper; graphite paper.
- Scrap of wool fabric, for snowman scarf, optional.

HOW TO MAKE A WOODEN BASKET

1 Fold sheet of tracing paper in half lengthwise. Trace the partial pattern (page 313) for tree or snowman onto tracing paper, placing fold of tracing paper on dotted line of pattern. Cut out pattern. Open the full-size pattern. Transfer the pattern to 1 × 8 pine board twice, using graphite paper; align the arrow on pattern with grain of wood. Transfer mark for handle.

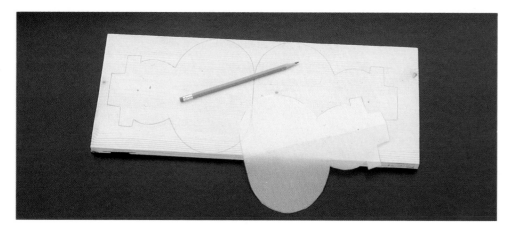

(Continued)

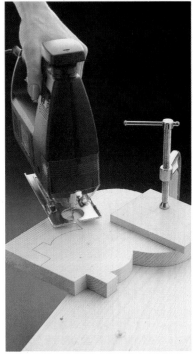

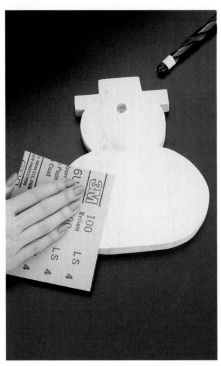

2 Cut along marked lines, using jigsaw.

3 Drill hole at mark for handle to 3/8" (1 cm) depth, using 1/2" drill bit; use masking tape on drill bit as guide for the depth. Sand basket ends smooth, using medium-grit sandpaper.

4 Mark and cut twelve slats from screen molding, in 12" (30.5 cm) lengths. Sand ends. Predrill nail holes 3/8" (1 cm) from each end of each slat, using 1/16" drill bit.

5 Paint outer surface of basket ends as desired, using acrylic paints and foam applicator. Allow to dry.

6 Sand edges of the basket ends lightly, using fine-grit sandpaper, to remove some paint and give an aged appearance.

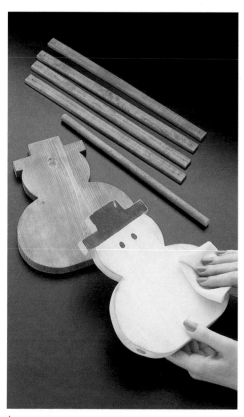

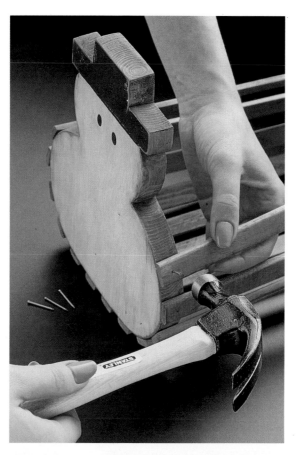

7 Apply stain to all pieces, using soft cloth; allow to dry.

8 Mark placement for slats on the basket ends, using pattern as guide. Secure slats to one basket end, using 17 × ¾" (2 cm) brads; align the end of slat to outer edge of basket end, with the rounded edges of the slat facing outward.

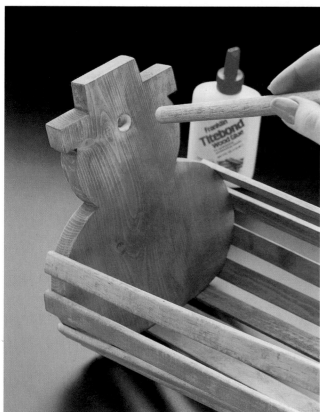

9 Apply small amount of wood glue in the holes for handle. Insert dowel ends into holes.

10 Secure slats to remaining basket end. For snowman basket, cut two 1½" × 22" (3.8 × 56 cm) fabric strips; clip ends to make fringe, and tie around necks, for scarves.

FRINGED
FABRIC TREE

Make a grouping of fabric trees in various sizes to display on a mantel. The trees are made from fringed strips of cotton fabric that are wrapped around a Styrofoam® cone. The fringe is given a frayed appearance by wetting it, then machine drying it with towels. Decorate the trees with purchased decorations or miniature dough cutout ornaments (page 307).

MATERIALS

- Styrofoam cone with height of 6" (15 cm), 9" (23 cm), or 12" (30.5 cm), depending on desired tree size.
- ½ yd. (0.5 m) fabric for small tree or ¾ yd. (0.7 m) for medium or large tree.

- Thick craft glue.
- 4" (10 cm) lengths of wire, for securing embellishments.
- Embellishments, such as miniature decorations and raffia, if desired.

HOW TO MAKE A FRINGED FABRIC TREE

1 Tear fabric strips, 4¼" (10.8 cm) wide, on crosswise grain; reserve sufficient fabric for covering cone. Fold fabric strip in half lengthwise, wrong sides together; edgestitch close to fold. Repeat for remaining strips.

2 Make the fringe by clipping the strips at ½" (1.3 cm) intervals, along the edges opposite the fold; clip to, but not through, stitching. Wet clipped strips, and squeeze out any excess water; machine dry with towels to create frayed edges.

3 Trim Styrofoam cone to a point. Roll trimmed end gently on table to make smooth.

4 Wrap fabric around the Styrofoam cone; trim off excess. Secure fabric to cone, using craft glue.

5 Apply glue to upper edge of the fringe, gluing about 4" (10 cm) at a time. Wrap fringe around the cone, starting 1" (2.5 cm) from lower edge of tree; continue to glue and wrap fringe to end of strip.

6 Continue to glue and wrap additional fringed fabric strips around cone until entire cone is covered; overlap ends of strips slightly. Trim off excess at top.

7 Embellish tree as desired, securing ornaments to tree with bent lengths of wire.

SANTA'S ELVES

Pose an elf or two on a table or mantel to add a whimsical touch to your holiday decorating. The body of the elf is stuffed with polyester fiberfill and is weighted down with a small bag of sand. Small quantities of sand are available, packaged as paint additives, at many paint stores.

MATERIALS

- Fabric scraps.
- 3" (7.5 cm) square of paper-backed fusible web.
- Assorted two-hole or four-hole buttons.
- Two small shank buttons, for eyes.
- Polyester fiberfill.
- Sand; plastic bag, such as a sandwich bag.
- Jute and ¼" (6 mm) dowel, for hair.
- Hot glue gun and glue sticks.
- Heavy-duty thread, such as carpet thread.
- Pink cosmetic blush.
- Embellishments as desired.

CUTTING DIRECTIONS

Make the full-size patterns for the upper body, lower body, and hat as in steps 1 to 3, opposite. Cut two lower body pieces and two upper body pieces from scraps of fabric for the body. Using the pattern for the upper body, also cut two hat pieces from scraps of fabric for the hat.

Trace the pattern pieces for the boot and ear (page 310) onto paper. Cut four boots and four ears from scraps of fabric.

For the pants legs, cut two 5½" × 6" (14 × 15 cm) rectangles from scraps of fabric that match the lower body. For the sleeves, cut two 4½" × 5½" (11.5 × 14 cm) rectangles from scraps of fabric that match the upper body.

1 Draw a 9½" (24.3 cm) vertical line on center of tracing paper. Draw a perpendicular line at lower end, 3¼" (8.2 cm) long. Mark a point 3½" (9 cm) above lower edge and 2½" (6.5 cm) from vertical line. Mark a second point 6½" (16.3 cm) above lower edge and 1¾" (4.5 cm) from vertical line.

2 Connect points to perpendicular lines, curving the line slightly. Fold on vertical line; cut on the marked lines. Unfold paper.

3 Draw line 3½" (9 cm) above lower edge, perpendicular to vertical line. Cut off lower portion on marked line; this section is pattern for lower body of elf. Remaining section is pattern for upper body and also for hat. Transfer the patterns to paper, adding ¼" (6 mm) seam allowances.

4 Cut body pieces from fabric (opposite). Apply paper-backed fusible web to scrap of fabric for face, following manufacturer's directions. Cut an oval for face, about 2" (5 cm) long and 2¼" (6 cm) wide, from paper-backed fabric.

5 Align upper and lower front body sections, right sides together; stitch ¼" (6 mm) seam. Repeat for the back body sections, leaving a 3" (7.5 cm) opening in center of seam.

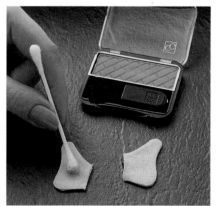

6 Stitch ⅛" (3 mm) seam around the ears, using short stitch length; leave straight edges open. Turn ears right side out, and press. Using cotton swab, rub pink blush in center of ears.

7 Remove paper backing from face. Make ⅛" (3 mm) tuck along the straight edge of each ear; baste to wrong side of face. Center face on upper body, with the face about 2¼" (6 cm) above the body seam. Fuse in place. Stitch around the face, using a narrow zigzag stitch.

(Continued)

8 Fold rectangle for sleeve in half, right sides together, matching short edges; stitch ¼" (6 mm) seam. Press seam open; turn tube right side out. Center the seam down front of tube. Make four ⅛" (3 mm) tucks, spaced evenly along upper edge of tube, so width is about 1½" (3.8 cm).

9 Pin tucked end of sleeve, seam side down, to right side of front upper body; match raw edges, and position sleeve about 1" (2.5 cm) above body seam. Baste. Repeat for other sleeve.

10 Fold rectangle for pants leg, right sides together, matching short edges; stitch ¼" (6 mm) seam. Press seam open; turn tube right side out. Center seam down back of tube. Repeat for other pants leg. Pin upper edge of pants legs to lower edge of front body section, centering them and matching raw edges; baste.

11 Pin front and back body sections right sides together. Stitch ¼" (6 mm) seam around body, taking care not to catch sleeves, pants legs, and ears in stitching.

12 Push in lower corners of elf, from right side, to shape the box corners. Slipstitch, or turn inside out and machine-stitch, across corners; turn right side out.

13 Roll up sleeves and pants legs. Thread needle with heavy-duty thread; secure thread to body, centered inside one pants leg. Thread a 2¾" (7 cm) strand of buttons, then thread back through the opposite holes of buttons; adjust the strand so top button of strand dangles about 3" (7.5 cm) below body. Secure thread. Repeat for other leg.

14 Stuff pants legs lightly with polyester fiberfill. On each pants leg, fold lower ¼" (6 mm) to the inside. Using hand running stitches, stitch close to the fold and tightly gather pants legs above buttons; secure thread.

15 Stitch ⅛" (3 mm) seam around the boot, using short stitch length; leave upper edge open. Clip inner curve. Turn right side out; stuff with polyester fiberfill. On each boot, fold upper ¼" (6 mm) to inside; slipstitch closed. Stitch the center of each boot to lower button of each button strand for legs.

16 Secure heavy-duty thread to body, centered inside one sleeve. Thread a 3" (7.5 cm) strand of buttons; secure thread inside other sleeve, allowing button strand to dangle from body about 2" (5 cm) at each side. Stuff sleeves and gather above buttons as in step 14.

17 Place about ⅔ cup (150 mL) sand in plastic bag. Tape bag closed, allowing space inside for sand to shift easily; this makes it easier for elf to sit. Insert the bag into the lower portion of body. Stuff remainder of body with polyester fiberfill; slipstitch opening closed.

18 Sew on buttons for the eyes; insert needle from back of body, and pull thread taut for a slight indentation. Rub pink blush on the face, for cheeks. Make jute hair, if desired, as on page 12, step 15; remove jute from dowel. Cut lengths of jute, and glue around face for the hair and beard.

19 Pin the hat pieces right sides together; stitch ¼" (6 mm) seam around curved sides. Turn right side out. Sew on buttons as desired at top of hat. Fold lower ¼" (6 mm) of hat to inside. Using hand running stitches, stitch close to fold; gather hat to fit head. Glue the hat to the elf. Secure any additional embellishments.

CAROLERS

Pose a pair of carolers, complete with a lamppost, on a table or mantel to spread holiday cheer. Crafted using wooden dowels and ball knobs, each piece is easy to assemble. The garments are assembled using simple rectangular fabric pieces, requiring no patterns and minimal sewing.

The carolers can be made in a variety of styles, depending on the fabrics chosen. For a country look, select fabrics such as corduroy or flannel. For a more elegant look, use fabrics such as velvet or taffeta. Floral wire in each arm allows the figures to be posed, holding a variety of embellishments.

MATERIALS (for pair of carolers and lamppost)

- Three wooden plaques, for base of each piece.
- Two 2" (5 cm) wooden balls, for heads.
- Four 1" (2.5 cm) wooden ball knobs, for feet.
- One 2¼" (6 cm) wooden ball knob, for lamppost.
- Four 18 mm wooden beads, for hands.
- Four 8" (20.5 cm) lengths of ⅝" (1.5 cm) dowel, for legs.
- One 11" (28 cm) length of ¾" (2 cm) dowel, for lamppost.
- Drill; ¹⁄₁₆" and ⅛" drill bits.
- Six 6 × 1⅝" (4 cm) drywall screws.
- One ³⁄₁₆ × 2" (5 cm) dowel screw; four 19 × ½" (1.3 cm) wire nails.
- 22-gauge paddle floral wire.
- Fabric scraps, for pants, shirt, and dress.

- Buttons, for shirt.
- Scrap of Ultrasuede® or felt, for cap.
- Scrap of ribbing, for leggings.
- ½ yd. (0.5 m) trim, such as gimp trim or ribbon, for pants.
- ⅝ yd. (0.6 m) eyelet or lace, at least 6" (15 cm) wide, for slip.
- ⅜ yd. (0.35 m) eyelet or lace, about 1" (2.5 cm) wide, for neck trim of dress.
- ¼" (6 mm) pom-pom, for cap.
- Doll hair; polyester fiberfill.
- Craft glue; adhesive felt.
- Acrylic gloss enamel paints; artist's brushes.
- Embellishments, such as miniature evergreen garland, ribbon, and small cones, for lamppost.

CUTTING DIRECTIONS

For the boy caroler, cut two 5½" (14 cm) squares from the fabric for the pants. For the shirt, cut one 4" × 12" (10 × 30.5 cm) rectangle for the body of the shirt and two 5" × 6" (12.5 × 15 cm) rectangles for the sleeves. For the scarf, cut one 1" × 14" (2.5 × 35.5 cm) rectangle. For the cap, cut one 1½" (3.8 cm) circle and one 4" (10 cm) circle from felt or Ultrasuede; cut the smaller circle in half for the brim.

For the girl caroler, cut one 6" × 20" (15 × 51 cm) rectangle for the slip. For the dress, cut one 12" × 20" (30.5 × 51 cm) rectangle. Cut two 5" × 6" (12.5 × 15 cm) rectangles for the sleeves of the dress. For the leggings, cut two 3" × 4" (7.5 × 10 cm) rectangles from ribbing, placing the rib of the fabric on the longest edge.

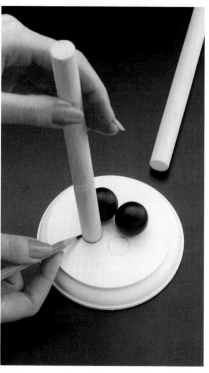

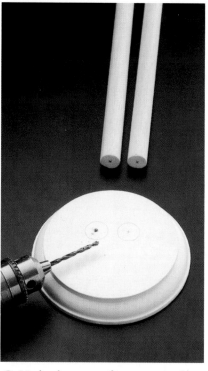

1 Paint 1" (2.5 cm) ball knobs for feet as desired. Paint 2" (5 cm) ball knob for head and 18 mm beads for hands flesh color. Paint or stain base plaque as desired.

2 Position dowels and ball knobs for feet on the plaque for desired placement, with dowels ¼" (6 mm) apart. Mark the position for dowels, using a pencil as shown.

3 Mark placement for screw in the center of each marking for dowel; mark center of each dowel at one end. Predrill holes at marks, using ⅛" drill bit.

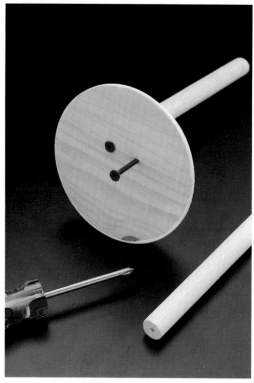

4 Secure dowels to base plaque, inserting screws from bottom of plaque.

5 Mark a 4" (10 cm) line, centered as shown, on wrong side of one pants piece, for pants inseam. Place pants pieces right sides together. Stitch ¼" (6 mm) side seams. Stitch inseam, stitching ⅛" (3 mm) from marked line and tapering stitches to line at top. With the needle down, rotate fabric and repeat stitching on remaining side of marked line.

6 Cut inseam on marked line; press seam allowances on sides open. Turn pants right side out. Using hand running stitches and double-threaded needle, stitch close to upper edge of pants, leaving thread tails. Repeat at lower edge of each pants leg.

7 Fold rectangle for body of shirt, wrong sides together, matching the short edges; stitch ½" (1.3 cm) from the folded edge to make center tuck.

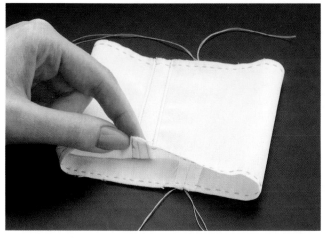

8 Press tuck, centering over seam; edgestitch on both sides through all layers. Fold the rectangle right sides together, matching short edges; stitch ¼" (6 mm) seam. Press seam allowances open, and turn tube right side out. Using hand running stitches and double-threaded needle, stitch close to upper edge of shirt, leaving thread tails. Repeat at lower edge.

9 Fold rectangle for sleeve, right sides together, matching long edges; stitch ¼" (6 mm) seam. Press seam allowances open; turn tube right side out. Stitch row of hand running stitches close to upper edge. Fold under 1" (2.5 cm) at lower edge; stitch row of running stitches ¾" (2 cm) from folded edge. Repeat for other sleeve.

10 Slip pants over the dowels, inserting one dowel in each leg of pants. Gather lower edge of each leg, and knot thread. Slip shirt over dowels; gather and knot lower edge of shirt, centering tuck and back seam. Glue lower edge of shirt to dowels; allow upper edge of shirt to extend slightly above top of the dowels.

11 Gather and knot upper edge of the pants; secure with glue. Secure gimp at waist and ankles. Glue feet to base. Lightly stuff body of the shirt with polyester fiberfill as necessary. Gather and knot the upper edge of the shirt; glue to dowels. Glue buttons to shirt.

(Continued)

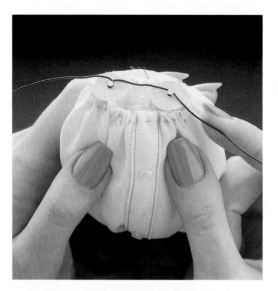

12 Cut wire about 16" (40.5 cm) in length. Secure the wire to the ends of dowels by wrapping wire around a wire nail inserted into each dowel; to prevent splitting the wood, predrill, using 1/16" drill bit.

13 Thread bead onto wire; wrap end of wire as shown so length of arm is about 3½" (9 cm). Repeat for opposite side.

14 Slip sleeve over wire arm. Gather and knot the upper edge of sleeve, centering seam down inside of arm; glue sleeve to upper edge of shirt. Lightly stuff the sleeve with polyester fiberfill. Tightly gather lower edge of sleeve; secure with knot. Repeat for second sleeve.

15 Glue head to top of dowels. Cut and glue individual lengths of doll hair to head for hair, working in sections; for the bangs, glue short pieces across front of head.

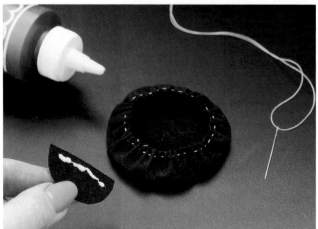

16 Stitch row of hand running stitches close to edge of 4" (10 cm) circle for beret. Gather circle to measure about 2¾" (7 cm) in diameter; knot the thread. Glue brim in place.

17 Stuff the cap lightly with polyester fiberfill. Glue the pom-pom to center of cap. Glue cap to caroler. Cut fringe on ends of scarf; tie scarf around neck.

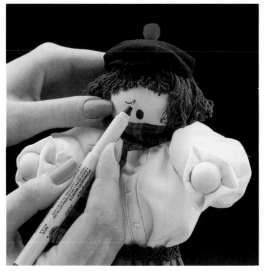

18 Draw eyes and mouth as shown, using fine-point permanent-ink marker.

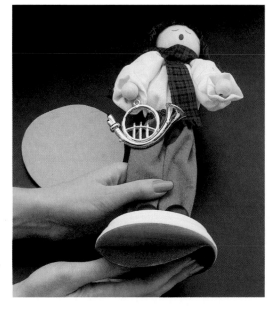

19 Place caroler on paper side of adhesive felt; trace around the base. Cut felt just inside the marked lines. Remove the paper backing, and secure felt to the bottom of the base. Secure any embellishments as desired.

HOW TO MAKE A GIRL CAROLER

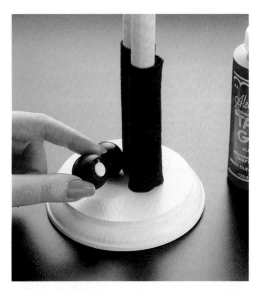

1 Follow page 136, steps 1 to 4. Fold rectangle for leggings right sides together, matching long edges; stitch ¼" (6 mm) seam. Turn tube right side out. Repeat for other legging. Slip one legging over each dowel leg, with seam centered down back of leg. Secure at lower edge with craft glue. Glue feet to base.

2 Fold the lace for slip right sides together, matching short ends; stitch ¼" (6 mm) seam. Press seam open. Repeat for dress.

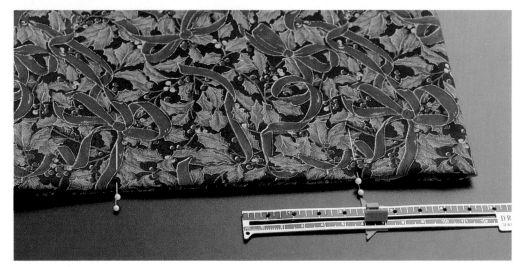

3 Fold the dress lengthwise, with wrong sides together and raw edges even; lightly press folded edge. Pin-mark lower edge of the dress 2⅜" (6.2 cm) to each side of dress center front and center back.

(Continued)

4 Stitch from pin mark at edge of dress to 1½" (3.8 cm) from the edge, using double-threaded needle. Stitch back to edge of skirt ⅛" (3 mm) from previous stitching as shown; leave thread tails. Repeat at remaining pin marks.

5 Place slip, right side out, inside dress, with raw edges even. Using hand running stitches, stitch close to the upper raw edges, stitching through all layers and leaving thread tails.

6 Gather the lower edge of dress at stitching, to create scalloped edge; knot threads to secure. Glue or stitch ribbon rose at peak of each scallop.

7 Assemble sleeves as on page 137, step 9. Slip the dress over dowels. Tightly gather upper edge, and knot the thread; glue dress to dowels at upper edge.

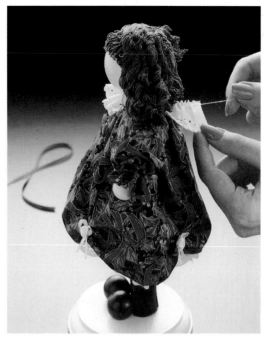

8 Attach wire arms and sleeves as on page 138, steps 12 to 14.

9 Glue on head and hair as on page 138, step 15. Stitch hand running stitches in heading of lace for neck trim. Gather and glue the lace around the neck, positioning raw edges at back of caroler. Complete caroler, following page 139, steps 18 and 19.

HOW TO MAKE A LAMPPOST

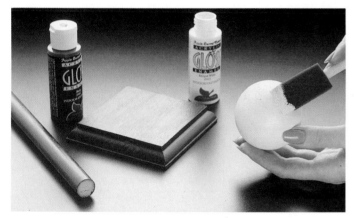

1 Paint or stain base plaque as desired. Paint ¾" (2 cm) dowel black for post. Paint 2¼" (6 cm) ball knob antique white for light globe.

2 Position the dowel as desired on base plaque; mark position, using pencil. Secure dowel to base as on page 136, steps 3 and 4. Predrill screw hole for dowel screw into upper end of dowel, using ⅛" drill bit; secure the dowel screw.

3 Secure the ball knob to dowel. Wrap the lampost with garland, securing with hot glue. Embellish the light globe as desired. Attach felt to base as on page 139, step 19.

BIAS-TRIMMED STOCKINGS

Large stockings, waiting to be filled with candy and trinkets, set the mood for the holiday season. A bias-trimmed stocking can be made in a variety of styles, depending on the choice of fabric and types of embellishments used. For a simple stocking, choose fabric that is distinctive and add embellishments such as purchased appliqués, ribbons, and buttons.

Make the binding from matching or contrasting fabric; a striped or plaid fabric can be used to create interesting effects. The stocking is lined and has a layer of fleece for added body.

MATERIALS

- ¾ yd. (0.7 m) outer fabric.
- ¾ yd. (0.7 m) lining fabric.
- ½ yd. (0.5 m) fabric, for bias binding.
- Polyester fleece.
- Embellishments, such as purchased appliqués, ribbon, or buttons.

CUTTING DIRECTIONS

Make the stocking pattern (below). With the right sides of the fabric together, cut two stocking pieces from the outer fabric and two from the lining. Also cut two stocking pieces from polyester fleece. Cut bias fabric strips, 2½" (6.5 cm) wide, for the binding, cutting two 10" (25.5 cm) strips for the upper edges of the stocking and one 60" (152.5 cm) strip for the sides. Piece the strips as necessary, as on page 80, step 7.

HOW TO MAKE A STOCKING PATTERN

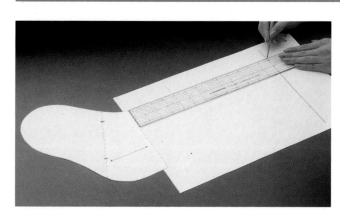

1 Transfer partial pattern pieces A and B (page 315) to paper. Tape pieces together, matching notches. Tape a large piece of paper to upper edge of partial stocking. Draw a line parallel to and 13" (33 cm) above dotted line, to mark upper edge of stocking. Align quilter's ruler to dotted line at side; mark point on line for upper edge. Repeat for the other side.

2 Measure out ⅞" (2.2 cm) from the marked points; mark. Connect the outer points at the upper edge to sides at ends of dotted line, to make full-size stocking pattern.

HOW TO SEW A BIAS-TRIMMED STOCKING

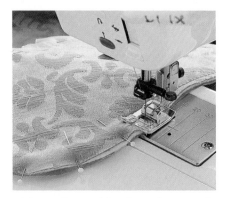

1 Layer the stocking front, fleece, and lining, right sides out. Baste layers together a scant ¼" (6 mm) from raw edges. Repeat for stocking back.

2 Position flat embellishments on the stocking as desired; pin or glue-baste in place. Stitch close to edges of trims.

3 Press the binding strips in half lengthwise, wrong sides together. Pin one 10" (25.5 cm) binding strip to upper edge of stocking front, right sides together, matching raw edges; stitch scant ⅜" (1 cm) seam.

4 Wrap binding around upper edge, covering stitching line on back of stocking; pin. Stitch in the ditch on the right side of stocking, catching binding on stocking back. Trim ends of binding even with stocking. Apply binding to upper edge of stocking back.

5 Align stocking front and back, with lining sides together; pin. Pin the binding to the stocking front, matching raw edges, with right sides together and ends extending ¾" (2 cm) on toe side of the stocking and 6" (15 cm) on the heel side; excess binding on the heel side becomes the hanger. Stitch scant ⅜" (1 cm) from raw edges; ease binding at heel and toe.

6 Fold the short end of the binding over upper edge of stocking. Wrap the binding around edge of stocking, covering stitching line on back; pin.

7 Fold up ½" (1.3 cm) on the end of the extended binding. Press up ¼" (6 mm) on raw edges of the extended binding. Fold the binding in half lengthwise, encasing the raw edges; pin. Edgestitch along pinned edges of the binding, for hanger. Stitch in the ditch around remainder of binding as in step 4.

8 Fold the extended binding strip to the back of stocking, forming a loop for hanger. Hand-stitch in place.

9 Hand-stitch ribbons, bows, or other embellishments to stocking front, if desired.

MORE IDEAS FOR BIAS-TRIMMED STOCKINGS

Written verses from "Jingle Bells" cover the front of this stocking. The verses are written using fine-point permanent-ink markers.

Buttons, stitched to the top of the stocking, give the appearance of a cuff.

Tea-dyed fabrics give a homespun look to this stocking. Fused appliqués are applied to the stocking front, using paper-backed fusible web as on pages 78 and 80. Fabric paint is used to personalize the stocking.

WOOLEN STOCKINGS

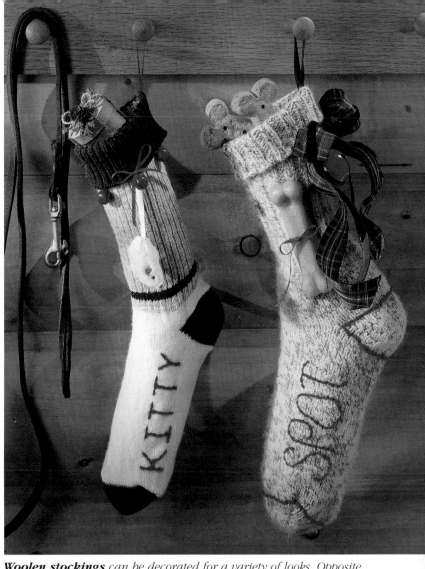

Turn woolen socks into personalized, one-of-a-kind Christmas stockings. Right at home hanging on a mantel, they also make a fun accent hung from an armoire.

Choose trims that complement the homespun look of the stockings. Add patches of flannel or wool fabric, and trims such as buttons, bells, or fringe. For a cuff, simply turn down the top of the sock. Or hand-stitch a fabric cuff to the top of the stocking. Most items can be stitched in place using a darning needle and narrow ribbon, yarn, or pearl cotton.

Wool socks are available at stores specializing in outdoor clothing. For extra-long stockings, purchase cross-country ski socks.

Woolen stockings *can be decorated for a variety of looks. Opposite, a stocking is embellished with sprigs of greenery and cones. Another features a snowman design, stitched in place using blanket stitches. Above, stockings are custom-designed for family pets.*

TIPS FOR MAKING WOOLEN STOCKINGS

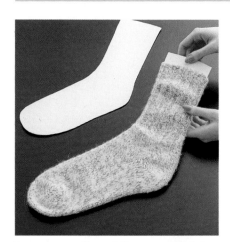

Insert a cardboard liner, cut slightly larger than the sock, into the sock before decorating with hand stitching; the liner will prevent catching stitches in the back of the sock.

Stitch letters, using yarn and back-stitches; secure stitches by taking one or two concealed small stitches.

Knot a loop of ribbon through top of sock for a hanger. Stuff finished stocking with tissue paper or with polyester fiberfill.

147

DECORATING MANTELS

Family photographs *from previous Christmases are grouped on a mantel for a nostalgic look. Honeysuckle vine and dried hydrangeas are used to embellish the artificial garland.*

Mantels are the perfect place to showcase Christmas decorations. Evergreen boughs or garlands displayed on a mantel can serve as a backdrop for a collection of family photos, Santas, unique ornaments, or hand-crafted Christmas items. For interest, mix a few dried or artificial floral elements with traditional Christmas accessories.

Safety note: Do not leave any open flame, including candles, unattended.

Gilded reindeer and candles in brass candlesticks (above) are arranged on an ornate mantel with greenery, cones, and berries. The papier-mâché reindeer were gilded with metallic paint.

Amaryllis (right) are set on each side of a picture, dominating this Christmas display.

Countdown calendar (below) is made by hanging twenty-four tea-dyed stocking ornaments (page 15), filled with holiday candies, along a fresh garland. A star ornament hangs at the end of the garland for Christmas Day.

EMBELLISHING
WREATHS

Honeysuckle vine *encircles an artificial wreath. A gilded reindeer and gold bow are elegant highlights. Artichokes, cones, hydrangea, and pomegranates add textural interest.*

Wreaths can be embellished for a variety of looks. For the base, select a fresh or artificial evergreen wreath, or a grapevine wreath. Embellish the base with items such as ribbons, ornaments, and floral materials to create a wreath that reflects your personal style.

Artificial evergreen wreaths are especially easy to decorate, because many items can be secured by simply twisting the branches around the embellishments. Items can also be secured to wreaths using floral wire or hot glue.

Embellish wreaths with one material at a time, spacing the items evenly to achieve a balanced look. Add large items first and fill in any bare areas with smaller ones. Secure embellishments to the surface as well as to the wreath base, to give a sense of depth.

Artificial evergreen garland is wrapped around a grapevine wreath. A natural look is created by adding birch bark and twig birdhouses, artificial birds, and stems of rose hips.

Santa's elf (page 130) is wired to the center area of this fresh wreath to create a focal point. Dried fruit slices, cinnamon sticks, and paper twist are added to give this wreath a country look.

Wire-mesh bow (page 9) and metal ornaments (page 23) are used to embellish a fresh evergreen wreath. The mesh strips for the bow measure about 4" (10 cm) wide and 24" (61 cm) long. Lights were added to the wreath before it was decorated.

Village house becomes the focal point of an artificial wreath. Additional sprigs of greenery, cones, and berries are added for texture and fullness. For a snowy effect, aerosol artificial snow is sprayed over polyester fiberfill.

TIPS FOR EMBELLISHING WREATHS

Attach wire to a cone by wrapping the wire around bottom layers of cone. Attach wire to a cinnamon stick by inserting it through length of stick; wrap wire around stick, and twist the ends at the middle.

Make floral or berry clusters by grouping items together. Attach wire to the items as necessary. Wrap stems and wires with floral tape.

Add texture to a wreath by inserting sprigs of other evergreen varieties. Secure sprigs to the wreath base, using wire.

Display Christmas collectibles, such as village houses and ornaments, on a wreath for visual impact. Wire items securely to the wreath base.

Gild embellishments, such as twigs, cones, artichokes, and sprigs of greenery, by applying gold aerosol acrylic paint.

Embellish wreath with ribbon by weaving it through the wreath; create twists and turns for depth. Secure the ribbon as necessary with hot glue.

Wrap honeysuckle vine loosely over a wreath, for added texture. Secure the vine with floral wire or hot glue.

Wrap artificial garland around a grapevine wreath to add color and dimension.

Add battery-operated lights to a wreath by weaving the cords into the wreath boughs.

Embellish bows with additional loops of contrasting ribbon. Fold length of ribbon in half to form loop the same size as loops on the existing bow; wrap ends tightly with wire. Secure to the center of bow, using hot glue.

CANDY WREATHS

A candy wreath is a festive holiday decoration full of little gifts. In one version, brightly wrapped Christmas candies nestle among coils of curled ribbon. For a fringed fabric wreath, candies are tied with raffia between knotted strips of cotton fabric. Small scissors hanging from the wreath invite each guest to snip out a piece of candy.

MATERIALS

- Metal ring, 8" (20.5 cm) in diameter.
- 50 to 70 yd. (46 to 64.4 m) curling ribbon in choice of colors, for ribbon wreath.
- ¼ yd. (0.25 m) each of three cotton print fabrics, for fringed fabric wreath.
- Raffia, for fringed fabric wreath.
- Wrapped Christmas candies.
- Small scissors.

HOW TO MAKE A CANDY & RIBBON WREATH

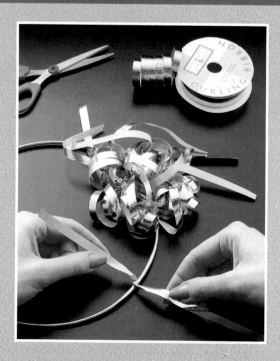

1 Cut a 12" (30.5 cm) length of curling ribbon. Wrap ribbon around metal ring; knot, leaving tails of equal length. Repeat, alternating ribbon colors as desired; cover about 4" (10 cm) of the metal ring.

2 Curl ribbon tails with blade of scissors. Tie pieces of wrapped candy to wreath; space evenly. Pack knotted ribbons tightly.

3 Repeat steps 1 and 2 until the entire wreath is covered. Fold 40" (102 cm) length of curling ribbon in half; wrap folded end around metal ring at top of wreath. Knot, allowing 2" (5 cm) loop for hanger.

4 Insert tails of ribbon through handle of small scissors; knot, allowing scissors to hang just below wreath. Curl ribbon tails.

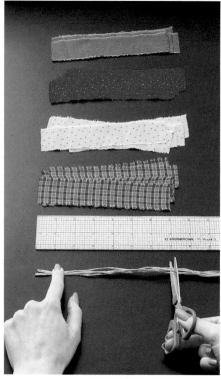

1 Cut selvages from fabrics. Tear fabric crosswise into strips, 1½" (3.8 cm) wide. Cut strips into 7" (18 cm) lengths. Cut raffia into 7" (18 cm) lengths.

2 Wrap length of fabric around metal ring; knot, leaving tails of equal length. Wrap length of raffia around metal ring next to knotted fabric; knot, leaving tails of equal length. Repeat until entire ring is covered, alternating fabrics and packing knots close together.

3 Tie wrapped candies to wreath where desired, using raffia tails.

4 Fold 36" (91.5 cm) length of raffia in half; wrap the folded end around the metal ring at top of wreath. Knot, allowing 2" (5 cm) loop for the hanger. Insert tails of raffia through the handle of a small pair of scissors; knot, allowing the scissors to hang just below wreath.

WALL TREES

Make a stunning wall accent from a miniature artificial pine tree. The branches of the tree are bent to the front, creating a flat surface in the back. This allows the tree to be displayed flat against a wall. The wall tree is embellished with a variety of fruit and is topped with a large bow.

MATERIALS

- Artificial pine tree with attached trunk, about 24" (61 cm) tall.
  - Four or five varieties of fruit, including apples, pears, grape clusters, and berries.
  - Preserved leaves on stems.
  - 3 yd. (2.75 m) wired ribbon, for bow.
  - Floral wire.

HOW TO MAKE A WALL TREE

1 Bend branches of artificial tree around to one side. Place flat on table, and arrange branches.

2 Secure pears to tree with hot glue, forming a curved diagonal line as shown.

3 Gild leaves as on page 97, step 1. Secure thin layer of gilded leaves along sides of pears, using hot glue. Lift pine boughs to surround the row of pears and leaves. Insert second variety of fruit and another row of gilded leaves, following the same line as the pears; secure with hot glue.

4 Continue to secure alternating rows of fruit and gilded leaves, until the entire tree is covered. Arrange pine boughs between rows of fruit and leaves.

5 Form large loops from wired ribbon as shown **(a).** Continue to make six loops. Make small loop at center. Bend wire around ribbon at center; twist wire tightly, gathering ribbon **(b).** Separate and shape the loops.

6 Secure bow to top of tree, using wire. Twist excess wire into loop at back, for hanging tree. Tuck ends of ribbon into sides of tree.

TOPIARY TREES

Make a classic topiary tree to accent your fireplace or display on a sideboard for the holidays. This finished tree measures about 24" (61 cm) tall. Embellish the top of this miniature tree with artificial fruit, floral materials, and decorative ribbon. The tree is set in a terra-cotta pot.

MATERIALS

- 4" (10 cm) Styrofoam® ball.
- Artificial pine boughs.
- Wired ribbon.
- Latex grape clusters and small pears.
- Dried yarrow.
- Small red-leaf preserved foliage; artificial green leaves.
- 7" (18 cm) terra-cotta pot.
- Floral foam, for silk arranging.
- Several dogwood stems.
- Hot glue gun and glue sticks.

1 Trim floral foam with a knife to fit pot snugly; secure with hot glue. Cut dogwood stems about 14" (35.5 cm) long. Insert several stems into center of the pot; secure with hot glue.

HOW TO MAKE A TOPIARY TREE

(Continued)

2 Secure the opposite ends of the stems to one side of the Styrofoam® ball, using hot glue.

3 Cut pine boughs into pieces about 3" (7.5 cm) long. Insert the pine stems into ball and foam in pot until the surfaces are covered.

4 Cut apart the grape stems and pears; insert as desired, securing with hot glue. Insert a large grape cluster into pot, allowing it to cascade over edge.

5 Cut red-leaf foliage into 4" (10 cm) stems. Secure leaf stems and yarrow pieces to ball with hot glue. Tuck the ribbon into ball; secure with hot glue, if necessary.

HANGING PINE BALLS

A holiday pine ball is created by decorating a Styrofoam® ball with pine stems, preserved leaves, and artificial berries. Display the pine ball indoors by hanging it from either a window or door frame, using a decorative ribbon and an upholstery tack. The pine ball can also be hung outdoors, offering a festive welcome to holiday guests.

MATERIALS

• 4" (10 cm) Styrofoam ball.

• Artificial pine boughs.

• Small-leaf preserved foliage.

• Artificial berries.

• Ribbon; floral wire.

HOW TO MAKE A HANGING PINE BALL

1 Cut several pieces of pine into 1½" (3.8 cm) lengths. Insert pine lengths into ball until surface is covered. Insert short pieces of small-leaf foliage into the ball, interspersing them among pine lengths. Cut sprigs of berries, and insert berries as desired.

2 Make six ribbon loops; secure with glue at center as shown. Cut ribbon to desired length for hanger. Cut 8" (20.5 cm) length of wire. Hold end of ribbon over wire; secure with glue. Bend wire ends down; insert wire ends into the foam ball over ribbon loops.

APPETIZERS

SHRIMP IN BEER ↓

- 2 pkgs. (12 oz./ 375 g each) frozen quick-cooking shrimp
- 1 can (12 oz./ 341 mL) beer
- 1 teaspoon (5 mL) garlic powder
- 1 teaspoon (5 mL) chopped chives

10 to 12 servings

Combine all ingredients in 2-qt. (2 L) casserole; cover. Microwave at High 8 to 13 minutes, or until shrimp are opaque, stirring 2 or 3 times. Drain all but ½ cup (125 mL) liquid before serving. Serve with cocktail picks.

↑ SPICED SHRIMP

- 2 lbs. (1 kg) raw shrimp, peeled and deveined
- ¼ cup (50 mL) butter or margarine
- 2 tablespoons (25 mL) all-purpose flour
- 2 teaspoons (10 mL) snipped fresh parsley or 1 teaspoon (5 mL) dried parsley flakes
- ½ teaspoon (2 mL) ground coriander
- ½ teaspoon (2 mL) ground cumin
- ¼ teaspoon (1 mL) salt
- ¼ teaspoon (1 mL) pepper
- ¼ teaspoon (1 mL) ground nutmeg
- Pinch ground cloves
- 1¼ cups (300 mL) milk

6 to 8 servings

1 Place shrimp in 1½-qt. (1.5 L) casserole. Microwave, covered, at High 5 to 8 minutes, or until shrimp are opaque, stirring 2 or 3 times. Do not overcook. Set aside.

2 Place butter in 4-cup (1 L) measure. Microwave at High 45 to 60 seconds, or until melted. Blend in flour, parsley, coriander, cumin, salt, pepper, nutmeg and cloves. Blend in milk. Microwave at High 3 to 6 minutes, or until thick and bubbly, stirring with wire whip 2 or 3 times. Drain shrimp; stir in sauce. Serve with cocktail picks.

← SHRIMP WRAP-UPS

- 8 slices bacon
- 8 large raw shrimp, peeled, deveined and cut in half
- 1 large green pepper, cut into 16 pieces
- 2 tablespoons (25 mL) soy sauce
- 2 tablespoons (25 mL) white wine or water
- 2 tablespoons (25 mL) chili sauce
- 2 tablespoons (25 mL) plum or grape jelly

6 servings

1 Place 3 layers of paper towel directly on microwave oven floor. Arrange 4 bacon slices on towel; cover with another towel. Arrange remaining 4 bacon slices on top; cover with towel. Microwave at High 4 to 5 minutes, or until bacon is slightly brown but not fully cooked.

2 Cut bacon slices in half. Wrap a piece of shrimp and green pepper in each bacon piece. Secure with a cocktail pick. Place in 9" x 9" (2.5 L) glass baking dish.

3 In 2-cup (500 mL) measure, mix remaining ingredients. Pour over wrap-ups. Cover. Refrigerate no longer than 8 hours or overnight, stirring once or twice. To serve, microwave at High 3 to 4 minutes, or until shrimp is cooked.

POLYNESIAN APPETIZERS →

- 1 tablespoon (15 mL) packed brown sugar
- 2 teaspoons (10 mL) cornstarch
- Pinch ground ginger
- Pinch garlic powder
- 1 tablespoon (15 mL) water
- 1 tablespoon (15 mL) soy sauce
- 1 can (8 oz./227 mL) pineapple chunks, drained and ⅓ cup (75 mL) juice reserved
- 8 oz. (250 g) frozen fully cooked brown and serve sausages

2 servings

In 1-qt. (1 L) casserole, blend brown sugar, cornstarch, ginger, garlic powder, water, soy sauce and pineapple juice. Cut each sausage into thirds. Stir into casserole with pineapple chunks. Microwave at High 3 to 7 minutes, or until sauce is thickened, stirring 2 or 3 times.

STUFFED CHERRY TOMATOES

- 1 pint (500 mL) cherry tomatoes
- ½ cup (125 mL) herbed cream cheese spread
- ⅓ cup (75 mL) shredded Cheddar cheese
- 4 slices bacon, cooked crisp, crumbled
- Snipped fresh parsley (optional)

6 to 8 servings

1 Cut thin slice from stem end of tomato. With small spoon or melon baller, scoop out pulp. Discard pulp and tops of tomatoes. Place tomatoes cut-sides-down on paper towel to drain.

2 Combine remaining ingredients in small mixing bowl. Mix well. Stuff tomatoes with cheese mixture. Arrange tomatoes on paper-towel-lined plate, with smaller tomatoes in center. Microwave at High 1½ to 2½ minutes, or until mixture is hot, rotating plate once. Sprinkle tomatoes lightly with snipped fresh parsley, if desired.

SAUSAGE-STUFFED MUSHROOMS

- 12 large fresh mushrooms (2" to 2½"/5 to 6 cm)
- ¼ lb. (125 g) bulk pork sausage
- 1 teaspoon (5 mL) instant minced onion
- 1 teaspoon (5 mL) dried parsley flakes
- 2 tablespoons (25 mL) seasoned dry bread crumbs
- 1 tablespoon (15 mL) grated Parmesan cheese

4 to 6 servings

1 Trim small portion of stem from each mushroom. Wipe caps clean with damp paper towel. Remove stems. Set caps aside. Finely chop enough stems to equal ¼ cup (50 mL). Place chopped stems in 1-quart (1 L) casserole. Discard remaining stems, or save for later use. Crumble sausage over chopped mushrooms. Sprinkle with onion and parsley. Cover. Microwave at High 1½ to 2½ minutes, or until sausage is no longer pink, stirring once to break apart. Mix in remaining ingredients.

2 Stuff sausage mixture evenly into mushroom caps. Arrange stuffed mushrooms on paper-towel-lined plate. Microwave at High 3 to 6 minutes, or until mushrooms are hot, rotating plate once.

SALMON-CUCUMBER CANAPÉS

- 2 cucumbers (8"/20 cm)
- 3 tablespoons (50 mL) chopped celery
- 2 tablespoons (25 mL) chopped onion
- 1 can (6¾ oz./192 g) skinless, boneless salmon, drained
- 2 tablespoons (25 mL) sour cream
- 1 teaspoon (5 mL) lemon juice
- ½ teaspoon (2 mL) grated lemon peel
- Pinch pepper
- Paprika

1 dozen canapés

1 Slice each cucumber crosswise into 6 equal pieces. With small spoon or melon baller, scoop out center of each piece, leaving ¼" (5 mm) shell. Flatten ends of rounded pieces by cutting thin slices from green ends. Place pieces hollowed-sides-down on paper towel to drain.

2 In small mixing bowl, combine celery and onion. Cover with plastic wrap. Microwave at High 1 to 2 minutes, or until vegetables are tender. Add remaining ingredients, except paprika. Mix well. Fill cucumber cups evenly with salmon mixture. Arrange canapés on plate. Microwave at High 3 to 6 minutes, or until canapés are warm, rotating plate once. Sprinkle with paprika to serve. (Canapés may also be refrigerated and served chilled.)

FLORENTINE CANAPÉS

- 2 pkgs. (9 oz./255 g each) frozen creamed spinach
- ¼ cup (50 mL) grated Parmesan cheese
- ¼ cup (50 mL) seasoned dry bread crumbs
- ¼ cup (50 mL) chopped tomato
- 2 teaspoons (10 mL) instant minced onion
- ¼ teaspoon (1 mL) ground nutmeg
- Melba cracker rounds

4 to 5 dozen

Place spinach in 2-qt. (2 L) casserole. Microwave at High 4 to 8 minutes, or until defrosted, breaking apart with fork once or twice. Drain. Stir in cheese, bread crumbs, tomato, minced onion and nutmeg. Spread on crackers. Place 12 crackers on paper-towel-lined plate. Microwave at High 1 to 1½ minutes, or until hot, rotating plate once. Repeat with remaining canapés.

Advance preparation: *Prepare spinach spread the day before. Cover and refrigerate. Canapés can be assembled 2 to 3 hours in advance and refrigerated. Add 15 to 20 seconds to microwaving time if spread is cold.*

CRAB CANAPÉS

- 1 can (6 oz./170 g) crab meat, rinsed, drained and cartilage removed
- ⅓ cup (75 mL) all-purpose flour
- 1 egg
- ¼ cup (50 mL) finely chopped green onion
- 1 jar (2 oz./57 g) chopped pimiento, drained
- 1 teaspoon (5 mL) lemon juice
- 1 teaspoon (5 mL) Worcestershire sauce
- ¼ teaspoon (1 mL) salt
- Pinch pepper
- 36 melba sesame rounds

3 dozen

1 Mix all ingredients, except melba rounds, in medium bowl. Drop by teaspoonfuls onto wax-paper-lined baking sheet. Cover and freeze overnight. Pack in freezer container; label. Freeze no longer than 2 weeks.

2 To serve, place 18 melba rounds around edge of paper-towel-lined 12" (30 cm) serving plate. Top each with frozen crab mixture. Microwave at 70% (Medium-High) 1¾ to 3 minutes, or until heated, rearranging after half the time. Repeat with remaining canapés as needed.

CHICKEN LIVER PÂTÉ

- 1½ lbs. (750 g) chicken livers
- 1 teaspoon (5 mL) instant chicken bouillon granules
- ½ cup (125 mL) water
- 1 hard-cooked egg
- ¼ cup (50 mL) butter or margarine, softened
- 2 tablespoons (25 mL) finely chopped onion
- 1 clove garlic, minced
- 1 teaspoon (5 mL) salt
- 1 teaspoon (5 mL) dry mustard

10 to 12 servings

In 1½-qt. (1.5 L) casserole, combine chicken livers, bouillon granules and water; cover. Microwave at High 8 to 12 minutes, or until livers are no longer pink, stirring after half the time. Drain. Purée livers and egg in meat grinder or food processor. In medium bowl, blend purée with remaining ingredients. Pour into well-oiled 2-cup (500 mL) mold. Chill at least 6 hours or overnight. Unmold onto serving plate. Garnish with chopped tomatoes and cucumbers, if desired.

← PICKLED SAUSAGES

- ¾ cup (175 mL) sugar
- 1 teaspoon (5 mL) pickling spice
- 1 teaspoon (5 mL) salt
- ¼ teaspoon (1 mL) peppercorns
- ½ cup (125 mL) water
- ½ cup (125 mL) cider vinegar
- 1 lb. (500 g) knockwurst or ring bologna
- 1½ cups (375 mL) pearl onions, or chunks of white onion

10 to 12 servings

In 2-qt. (2 L) casserole, mix sugar, pickling spice, salt, peppercorns, water and vinegar; cover. Microwave at High 1 to 3 minutes, or until boiling. Cut knockwurst lengthwise in half, then cut into ½" (1 cm) pieces. Add knockwurst and onions to sugar-vinegar mixture; cover. Refrigerate 4 to 7 days, stirring occasionally. Remove knockwurst and onions to serving dish with slotted spoon. Serve with cocktail picks.

CRAB-STUFFED ZUCCHINI ↑

- ¾ cup (175 mL) chopped fresh mushrooms
- 3 tablespoons (50 mL) butter or margarine
- 2 tablespoons (25 mL) all-purpose flour
- ¾ cup (175 mL) half-and-half
- ½ cup (125 mL) chopped green onion
- ¼ teaspoon (1 mL) paprika

- ¼ teaspoon (1 mL) salt
- Pinch pepper
- 2 tablespoons (25 mL) sherry
- 2 cans (6 oz./170 g each) crab meat, rinsed, drained and cartilage removed
- 1¼ to 1½-lb. (625 to 750 g) small zucchini, cut into ¾" (2 cm) pieces

4 to 4½ dozen

Advance preparation:
Prepare recipe as directed below, but do not sprinkle with paprika. Cover each plate with plastic wrap. Refrigerate no longer than 8 hours. Uncover. Sprinkle with paprika. Microwave one plate at a time at 70% (Medium-High) 2 to 5 minutes, or until heated, rotating once or twice.

1 Combine mushrooms and butter in 1-qt. (1 L) casserole. Microwave at High 1 to 2 minutes, or until butter is melted and mushrooms are tender. Stir in flour. Blend in half-and-half until smooth. Stir in onion, paprika, salt, pepper and sherry.

2 Microwave at High 2 to 4 minutes, or until very thick, blending with wire whip once or twice. Stir in crab meat. Set aside. With a spoon, hollow out each zucchini piece about halfway down leaving ⅛" to ¼" (3 to 5 mm) on sides. Spoon crab mixture into zucchini pieces.

3 Place on two paper-towel-lined plates. Sprinkle with additional paprika. Reduce power to 70% (Medium-High). Microwave one plate at a time 1 to 3 minutes, or until heated, rotating plate once or twice. Repeat with remaining plate.

SPINACH BALLS

- 1 pkg. (10 oz./300 g) frozen, chopped spinach
- ¾ cup (175 mL) shredded Swiss cheese
- ¼ cup (50 mL) dry bread crumbs
- 2 tablespoons (25 mL) grated Parmesan cheese
- 1 tablespoon (15 mL) grated onion
- ½ teaspoon (2 mL) salt
- 1 egg, beaten

2 dozen

1 Place package of spinach in microwave oven. Microwave at High 4 to 5 minutes, or until defrosted. Drain, pressing out excess liquid. Mix with remaining ingredients. Shape into 1" (2.5 cm) balls, about 1½ teaspoons (7 mL) each. Place on wax-paper-lined baking sheet; cover. Freeze overnight. Pack in freezer container; label. Freeze no longer than 2 weeks.

2 To serve, place all spinach balls on paper-towel-lined baking sheet. Microwave at High 2 minutes. Reduce power to 50% (Medium). Microwave 4½ to 6 minutes, or until hot and just set, rearranging once or twice.

SAUSAGE BALLS

- 1 pkg. (12 oz./375 g) bulk pork sausage
- ¾ cup (175 mL) seasoned bread crumbs
- ¼ cup (50 mL) grated Parmesan cheese
- Pinch ground red pepper
- 1 tablespoon (15 mL) dried parsley flakes
- 2 eggs

4 dozen

1 Crumble sausage into 2-qt. (2 L) casserole. Microwave at High 2 to 4 minutes, or until sausage is no longer pink, stirring to break apart; drain. Stir in remaining ingredients. Shape into balls, about 1 teaspoon (5 mL) each. Place on wax-paper-lined baking sheet; cover. Freeze overnight. Pack in freezer container; label. Freeze no longer than 2 weeks.

2 To serve, place 24 balls around edge of paper-towel-lined 12" (30 cm) serving plate. Microwave at High 1½ to 3½ minutes, or until heated and firm to the touch, rearranging once. Repeat with remaining sausage balls.

SPICED NUTS ↑

- ¼ cup (50 mL) butter or margarine
- 2 tablespoons (25 mL) Worcestershire sauce
- ¾ teaspoon (4 mL) seasoned salt

- ½ teaspoon (2 mL) garlic powder
- ¼ teaspoon (1 mL) cayenne
- 2 cans (12 oz./375 g each) mixed nuts

4 cups (1 L)

Place butter in 3-qt. (3 L) casserole. Microwave at High 45 to 60 seconds, or until melted. Mix in remaining ingredients except nuts. Add nuts, stirring to coat. Microwave at High 7 to 9 minutes, or until butter is absorbed, stirring 2 or 3 times during cooking. Spread on paper-towel-lined baking sheet to dry. Store nuts in tightly covered container.

HAM SALAD FINGER ROLLS

- 1 can (6½ oz./184 g) chunked ham
- ¼ cup (50 mL) mayonnaise or salad dressing
- 2 tablespoons (25 mL) sweet pickle relish
- 1 teaspoon (5 mL) grated onion

- 6 slices whole wheat bread
- ¼ cup (50 mL) butter or margarine
- 1 egg
- ¼ cup (50 mL) sesame seed

3 dozen

1 In small bowl, mix ham, mayonnaise, pickle relish and onion. Set aside. Trim crusts from bread. Roll to ¼" (5 mm) thickness with rolling pin. Spread each with ham mixture; roll up jelly roll style.

2 Place butter in shallow dish. Microwave at High 45 to 60 seconds, or until melted. Beat egg into butter. Roll sandwich rolls in butter-egg mixture, then in sesame seed to coat generously. Wrap, label and freeze. Freeze no longer than 2 weeks.

3 To serve, cut each roll into 6 pieces. Place around edges of two 12" (30 cm) plates. Microwave each plate at High 3 to 6 minutes, or until hot, rotating plate once or twice.

BAKED POTATO SKINS ↓

- 3 small russet potatoes (6 to 7 oz./175 to 200 g each)
- ½ teaspoon (2 mL) salt
- ¼ teaspoon (1 mL) ground cumin

- ⅓ cup (75 mL) finely chopped seeded tomato
- 3 tablespoons (50 mL) sliced green onions
- 1 jalapeño pepper, seeded and finely chopped

- 1 tablespoon (15 mL) snipped fresh cilantro (optional)
- ¼ cup (50 mL) nonfat or low-fat sour cream

6 servings

1 Heat oven to 425°F/220°C. Pierce potatoes several times with fork. Place potatoes on rack in oven. Bake for 45 to 50 minutes, or until tender. Cut each potato in half lengthwise. Scoop out pulp, leaving ½" (1 cm) shells. (Reserve pulp for other uses.)

2 Spray baking sheet with nonstick vegetable cooking spray. Arrange shells, skin-sides-up, on baking sheet. Spray shells with nonstick vegetable cooking spray. Bake for 10 to 13 minutes, or until skins are crisp. Turn shells over. Sprinkle inside of shells evenly with salt and cumin.

3 Combine tomato, onions, pepper and cilantro in small mixing bowl. Spoon tomato mixture evenly into shells. Top each shell with 2 teaspoons (10 mL) sour cream.

Arrangement is the secret of microwaving several foods with different cooking times. Place longer-cooking items around the edge of the platter. Make a second ring of vegetables with medium cooking times. Quick-cooking vegetables go in the center, where they receive less energy. The vegetables cook evenly and look beautiful.

← GARDEN BOUQUET VEGETABLE PLATTER

- 1 lb. (500 g) fresh asparagus, trimmed
- 4 oz. (125 g) fresh whole mushrooms, 1" (2.5 cm) diameter
- ½ lb. (250 g) yellow squash, cut into ½" (1 cm) slices
- 1 medium zucchini, cut into 2½" x ¼" (6 cm x 5 mm) strips
- 1 medium carrot, cut into 2½" x ¼" (6 cm x 5 mm) strips
- 2 tablespoons (25 mL) water
- 1 whole pimiento
- Browned butter

6 to 8 servings

1 Arrange asparagus spears in center of 12" to 14" (30 to 35 cm) round microwave-safe platter. Arrange mushrooms, squash, zucchini and carrots around spears, alternating colors and types of vegetables. Sprinkle with water. Cover with plastic wrap.

2 Microwave at High 8 to 9 minutes, or until tender-crisp, rotating platter 2 times during cooking. Feel through wrap to test doneness; vegetables should feel soft to the touch and pliable. Let stand 5 minutes. Cut pimiento into spiral strip and form a bow. Garnish asparagus spears with pimiento bow. Prepare browned butter. Serve with vegetables.

ELEGANT VEGETABLE PLATTER ↑

- 1 artichoke
- ½ lb. (250 g) fresh carrots, cut into 2½" x ¼" (6 cm x 5 mm) strips
- 4 cups (1 L) fresh cauliflowerets
- 8 oz. (250 g) fresh Brussels sprouts, trimmed and cut in half
- 2 tablespoons (25 mL) water
- Cheese Sauce (page 183)

6 to 8 servings

1 Trim artichoke 2" (5 cm) from top and close to base so it will stand upright. Snap off small lower leaves. Snip tips of outer leaves. Rinse; shake off excess water. Wrap in plastic wrap. Microwave at High 3 minutes. Remove plastic and place artichoke at one end of microwave-safe platter.

2 Place carrots in center of platter. Arrange cauliflowerets and Brussels sprouts around edge, alternating clusters of vegetables for color effect. Sprinkle water over vegetables. Cover platter with plastic wrap. Microwave at High 8 to 11 minutes, or until tender-crisp, rotating platter 2 times. Feel through wrap to test doneness; vegetables should feel soft to the touch and pliable. Let stand 5 minutes. Prepare Cheese Sauce as directed. Serve with vegetable platter.

WHOLE CAULIFLOWER

Wash a 1-lb. (500 g) head of cauliflower. Shake off water. Wrap in plastic wrap. Place on serving plate upside down. Microwave at High 3 minutes. Turn over. Microwave at High 2½ to 4½ minutes, or until base is fork tender. Let stand, covered, 3 minutes. Serve with Cheese Sauce, page 183.

TOMATO & FETA PITA PIZZAS

- 3 Roma tomatoes, finely chopped
- 1 tablespoon (15 mL) crumbled feta cheese
- 1 green onion, finely chopped
- 2 teaspoons (10 mL) balsamic vinegar
- 1 teaspoon (5 mL) olive oil
- ¼ teaspoon (1 mL) dried oregano leaves
- ¼ teaspoon (1 mL) pepper
- 4 whole soft pitas

8 servings

1 Combine all ingredients, except pitas, in small mixing bowl. Cover with plastic wrap. Let stand 20 minutes.

2 Heat oven to 350°F/180°C. Arrange pitas on baking sheet. Spread tomato mixture evenly over pitas. Bake for 10 to 12 minutes, or until hot. Cut each pita into 4 wedges to serve.

TIP: *These pizzas can also be served as a main dish.*

BBQ CHICKEN PITA PIZZAS

- 1 cup (250 mL) cubed cooked chicken breast (no skin; ½"/1 cm cubes)
- ¼ cup (50 mL) prepared barbecue sauce
- 4 whole soft pitas
- ¼ cup (50 mL) shredded reduced-fat Cheddar cheese

8 servings

1 Heat oven to 350°F/180°C. In small mixing bowl, combine chicken and barbecue sauce. Set aside.

2 Arrange pitas on baking sheet. Spread chicken mixture evenly over pitas. Sprinkle cheese evenly over top. Bake for 10 to 12 minutes, or until pitas are hot and cheese is melted.

- ½ cup (125 mL) ready-to-serve chicken broth, divided
- 1 large onion, sliced into ¼" (5 mm) rings
- 4 whole soft pitas
- 4 teaspoons (20 mL) shredded fresh Parmesan cheese
- 1 teaspoon (5 mL) snipped fresh rosemary leaves

8 servings

1 Heat ¼ cup (50 mL) broth in 10" (25 cm) nonstick skillet over medium-low heat until bubbly. Add onion. Cook for 35 to 40 minutes, or until onion is dark golden brown, stirring occasionally. Sprinkle only enough of remaining ¼ cup (50 mL) broth over onion as needed to prevent burning. (Adding too much broth at one time will make onions soggy and prevent browning.)

2 Heat oven to 350°F/180°C. Arrange pitas on baking sheet. Spread onion evenly over pitas. Sprinkle cheese and rosemary evenly over top. Bake for 10 to 12 minutes, or until pitas are hot and cheese is melted.

ANTIPASTO KABOBS

- 1 pkg. (9 oz./255 g) fresh cheese tortelloni or ravioli
- 1 can (14 oz./398 mL) quartered artichoke hearts in water, rinsed and drained
- 1 small red pepper, seeded and cut into 40 chunks
- 20 small fresh mushrooms, cut in half
- 10 jumbo pitted black olives, cut in half
- 10 large pimiento-stuffed green olives, cut in half
- 20 wooden skewers (10"/25 cm)
- 1 bottle (16 oz./500 mL) fat-free Italian dressing

20 kabobs

1 Prepare tortelloni as directed on package. Rinse with cold water. Drain.

2 Cut large artichoke heart quarters in half lengthwise in order to get 20 pieces. Thread ingredients on skewers as follows: pepper chunk, mushroom half, tortelloni, black olive half, artichoke heart, green olive half, tortelloni, mushroom half and pepper chunk.

3 Arrange kabobs in a shallow dish. Pour dressing evenly over kabobs, turning to coat. Cover. Chill at least 2 hours, turning kabobs occasionally. Drain dressing from kabobs before serving.

TIP: *Drained dressing may be reserved for other uses.*

EASY SNACK MIX

Seasoning Mix:

- 4 teaspoons (20 mL) dry buttermilk powder
- 1 teaspoon (5 mL) dry dill weed
- ½ teaspoon (2 mL) onion powder
- ¼ teaspoon (1 mL) garlic powder
- ¼ teaspoon (1 mL) paprika
- Pinch cayenne

- 4 cups (1 L) mixed cereals, pretzels and/or crackers (mini shredded wheat, nonfat low-sodium pretzels, corn squares, toasted oat cereal, oyster crackers)
- Butter-flavored nonstick vegetable cooking spray

4 servings

Combine seasoning mix ingredients in large plastic food-storage bag. Set aside. Spread cereal mixture on large baking sheet. Spray well with cooking spray (about 8 seconds). Stir mixture. Spray again (about 5 seconds). Pour mixture into bag. Seal bag. Shake to coat cereal mixture.

178

FRUITY POPCORN MIX

- 7 cups (1.75 L) unsalted air-popped popcorn
- 1½ cups (375 mL) miniature knot pretzels
- 2 tablespoons (25 mL) margarine
- ⅓ cup (75 mL) light corn syrup
- 1 pkg. (3 oz./85 g) fruit-flavored gelatin powder (any flavor)
- ¼ teaspoon (1 mL) baking soda

8 servings

1 Heat oven to 200°F/100°C. Spray 15½" x 10½" (40 x 25 cm) jelly roll pan with nonstick vegetable cooking spray. Combine popcorn and pretzels in prepared pan. Set aside.

2 Melt margarine over low heat in 2-quart (2 L) saucepan. Stir in corn syrup. Bring to full boil over medium heat. Remove from heat. Add gelatin. Stir until gelatin is dissolved. Add baking soda. Mix well. Immediately pour over popcorn mixture, stirring to coat.

3 Spread mixture evenly in pan. Bake for 1 hour, stirring after every 15 minutes. Remove from oven. Stir. Cool completely, stirring frequently to break popcorn mix apart. Store in airtight container in cool place.

ANIMAL CRACKERS

- 1½ cups (375 mL) whole wheat or graham flour
- ½ cup (125 mL) all-purpose flour
- ¼ cup (50 mL) sugar
- 2 tablespoons (25 mL) ground cinnamon
- ½ teaspoon (2 mL) baking powder
- ½ teaspoon (2 mL) baking soda
- ¼ teaspoon (1 mL) salt
- ⅓ cup (75 mL) light corn syrup
- ⅓ cup (75 mL) plain nonfat or low-fat yogurt
- 3 tablespoons (50 mL) vegetable oil
- ½ teaspoon (2 mL) vanilla

18 servings

1 Heat oven to 350°F/180°C. Spray baking sheets with nonstick vegetable cooking spray. Set aside. In large mixing bowl, combine flours, sugar, cinnamon, baking powder, baking soda and salt. In 1-cup (250 mL) measure, combine corn syrup, yogurt, oil and vanilla.

2 Add corn syrup mixture to flour mixture. Beat at low speed of electric mixer just until dry ingredients are moistened (dough will be crumbly). Form dough into ball. On lightly floured surface, knead dough for 3 to 5 minutes, or until smooth (adding additional flour as necessary to reduce stickiness). Divide dough in half. Wrap one half in plastic wrap. Set aside.

3 Roll remaining dough to ¼" (5 mm) thickness on lightly floured surface. Using 1½" (4 cm) assorted animal cookie cutters, cut shapes into dough. Place shapes 1" (2.5 cm) apart on prepared baking sheets. Repeat with remaining dough. Bake, one sheet at a time, for 7 to 9 minutes, or just until edges of crackers begin to brown.

Variation: *Prepare dough as directed. Roll all dough into 16" x 8" (40 x 20 cm) rectangle (¼"/5 mm thick). Using pastry wheel or sharp knife, cut dough into 1" (2.5 cm) squares. Place squares 1" (2.5 cm) apart on prepared baking sheets. Bake, one sheet at a time, for 7 to 9 minutes, or just until edges of crackers begin to brown.*

TIP: *Roll dough to ⅛" (3 mm) thickness for a crisper cracker.*

SAVORY SNACK MIX

- 3 cups (750 mL) thin pretzel sticks
- 1 cup (250 mL) Spanish peanuts
- 2 tablespoons (25 mL) butter or margarine
- 2 teaspoons (10 mL) Worcestershire sauce
- ½ teaspoon (2 mL) chili powder
- Pinch garlic salt
- ¼ teaspoon (1 mL) red pepper sauce

4 cups (1 L)

In large bowl, combine pretzels and peanuts. Set aside. In 1-cup (250 mL) measure, combine butter, Worcestershire sauce, chili powder, garlic salt and red pepper sauce. Microwave at High 45 to 60 seconds, or until butter melts. Stir. Pour over pretzels and peanuts, tossing to coat. Microwave at High 3 to 5 minutes, or until mixture is hot and butter is absorbed, stirring after each minute. Spread on paper towels to cool.

Variation: *Substitute ½ cup (125 mL) cashews for ½ cup (125 mL) of the Spanish peanuts.*

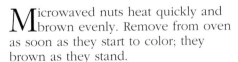

Microwaved nuts heat quickly and brown evenly. Remove from oven as soon as they start to color; they brown as they stand.

ROASTED PEANUTS

- 1 cup (250 mL) shelled raw peanuts
- 1 teaspoon (5 mL) vegetable oil

1 cup (250 mL)

Place peanuts in 9" (23 cm) pie plate. Add oil, tossing to coat nuts. Microwave at High 5 to 7 minutes, or until barely light brown, stirring every 2 minutes. Peanuts may be browner on inside and will continue to roast after they are removed from oven. Cool on double thickness of paper towels. Salt, if desired.

SUN-DRIED TOMATO & GARLIC SPREAD

- 1 whole bulb garlic
- 1 cup (250 mL) boiling water
- 2 oz. (60 g) dry-pack sun-dried tomatoes (about 1 cup/250 mL)
- 2 tablespoons (25 mL) pine nuts, toasted*
- 2 tablespoons (25 mL) shredded fresh Parmesan cheese
- 2 teaspoons (10 mL) snipped fresh basil leaves
- 1 fresh baguette (8 oz./250 g), cut into 24 slices, toasted

8 servings

To toast pine nuts, cook in a dry skillet over medium-low heat, stirring frequently to prevent burning.

1 Heat oven to 350°F/180°C. Remove outer peel of garlic bulb without separating cloves. Cut off and discard top ⅓ of each clove. Place garlic in center of 12" x 9" (30 x 23 cm) sheet of foil. Fold opposite edges of foil together, crimping edges to seal. Place foil packet on rack in oven. Bake for 1 hour. Let packet stand 10 to 15 minutes, or until garlic is cool enough to handle. Squeeze soft garlic from each clove peel. Set roasted garlic aside.

2 Meanwhile, in small mixing bowl, combine water and tomatoes. Let stand 30 minutes. Drain, reserving liquid. In food processor or blender, combine tomatoes, roasted garlic, pine nuts, Parmesan cheese and basil. Process until smooth, adding enough of reserved liquid to make smooth spread. Transfer spread to small mixing bowl. Cover with plastic wrap. Refrigerate overnight to blend flavors. To serve, spread tomato and garlic spread evenly on toast slices.

LAYERED CHEESE LOAF →

- ½ pkg. (8 oz./250 g) cream cheese
- 2 tablespoons (25 mL) butter or margarine
- ½ teaspoon (2 mL) dried basil leaves or dry mustard
- 3 slices Colby cheese, 3½" x 3½" (9 x 9 cm)
- 3 slices brick cheese, 3½" x 3½" (9 x 9 cm)
- 1 slice (¾ oz./21 g) salami
- 2 tablespoons (25 mL) snipped fresh parsley

One ¾-lb. (375 g) loaf

Place cream cheese and butter in small bowl. Microwave at 30% (Medium-Low) 15 to 60 seconds, or until softened, rotating every 15 seconds. Blend in basil. On serving plate, layer cheese slices and salami, spreading about 2 teaspoons (10 mL) of cream cheese mixture between each layer. Use remaining cream cheese mixture to spread on top and sides. Sprinkle with parsley, pressing gently to coat loaf. Refrigerate at least 3 hours before serving. Serve with crackers, if desired.

CHEESE SAUCE

- 2 tablespoons (25 mL) butter or margarine
- Pinch salt
- 2 tablespoons (25 mL) all-purpose flour
- 1 cup (250 mL) milk
- 1 cup (250 mL) shredded cheese (jalapeño, caraway, onion, garlic or dill)

1½ cups (375 mL)

Place butter and salt in 4-cup (1 L) measure. Microwave at High 30 to 45 seconds, or until butter melts. Blend in flour; stir in milk. Microwave at High 3 to 4 minutes, or until thickened, stirring with fork or wire whip after each minute. Add cheese, stirring until melted. Serve hot over cooked vegetables, or cover and chill to serve as a dip for raw vegetables.

HOT ARTICHOKE DIP

- 6 whole wheat pitas
- ½ to ¾ cup (125 to 175 mL) skim milk, divided
- 1 teaspoon (5 mL) olive oil
- ½ cup (125 mL) finely chopped leek
- 2 cloves garlic, minced
- 1 tablespoon (15 mL) all-purpose flour
- 1 can (14 oz./398 mL) artichoke hearts in water, rinsed, drained and coarsely chopped
- ½ cup (125 mL) plain nonfat or low-fat yogurt
- ½ cup (125 mL) low-fat cream cheese
- 2 tablespoons (25 mL) snipped fresh parsley
- ½ teaspoon (2 mL) Worcestershire sauce
- Pinch cayenne
- Pinch freshly ground pepper

1 Heat oven to 350°F/180°C. Cut each pita into 8 wedges. Arrange wedges on large baking sheet. Bake for 11 to 13 minutes, or until wedges are crisp. Set wedges aside.

2 Combine ½ cup (125 mL) milk and the oil in 2-quart (2 L) saucepan. Heat over medium heat until bubbly. Stir in leek and garlic. Cook for 2 to 3 minutes, or until leek is tender, stirring frequently. Stir in flour. Cook for 2 minutes, stirring constantly.

3 Reduce heat to low. Stir in remaining ingredients, except remaining milk. Cook for 4 to 5 minutes, or until dip is heated through, stirring frequently. Stir in just enough of remaining ¼ cup (50 mL) milk for desired consistency. Garnish with additional snipped fresh parsley, if desired. Serve dip with baked pita wedges.

12 servings

HUMMUS

- 2 cans (15 oz/426 mL each) garbanzo beans, rinsed and drained
- ¼ cup (50 mL) fresh lemon juice
- 2 tablespoons (25 mL) snipped fresh parsley
- 2 tablespoons (25 mL) water
- 1 tablespoon (15 mL) extra-virgin olive oil
- 2 cloves garlic, minced
- ¼ teaspoon (1 mL) cayenne
- 5 whole wheat pitas, each cut into 8 wedges

20 servings

1 Combine all ingredients, except pitas, in food processor or blender. Process until smooth. Transfer hummus to serving dish.

2 Place dish in center of serving plate. Arrange pita wedges around dish. Garnish hummus with parsley sprig, if desired.

TIP: *For a thinner hummus, add additional water, 1 tablespoon (15 mL) at a time, while processing, until desired consistency is reached.*

SEASONED CHIPS WITH LONE STAR CAVIAR

- 2 medium tomatoes, seeded and chopped (2 cups/500 mL)
- 1 can (15 oz./426 mL) black-eyed peas, rinsed and drained
- 1 medium green pepper, chopped (1⅓ cups/325 mL)
- ½ cup (125 mL) sliced green onions
- ½ cup (125 mL) snipped fresh cilantro leaves
- 2 tablespoons (25 mL) lemon juice
- 2 serrano peppers, seeded and finely chopped

- 1 to 2 jalapeño peppers, seeded and finely chopped
- 2 cloves garlic, minced
- 2¼ teaspoons (11 mL) ground cumin, divided
- ½ teaspoon (2 mL) salt
- 2 teaspoons (10 mL) chili powder
- 1 teaspoon (5 mL) garlic powder
- 16 whole wheat flour tortillas (6"/15 cm)

16 servings

1 Combine tomatoes, peas, green pepper, onions, cilantro, juice, serrano peppers, jalapeño peppers, garlic, ¼ teaspoon (1 mL) cumin and the salt in medium mixing bowl. Cover with plastic wrap. Chill Lone Star Caviar at least 4 hours to blend flavors, stirring occasionally.

2 Heat oven to 375°F/ 190°C. In large plastic food-storage bag, combine remaining 2 teaspoons (10 mL) cumin, the chili powder and garlic powder. Set aside. Spray both sides of each tortilla with non-stick vegetable cooking spray. Cut each tortilla into 8 wedges. Place wedges in bag. Secure bag. Shake to coat.

3 Arrange 32 wedges in single layer on baking sheet. Bake for 7 to 9 minutes, or until light golden brown. Repeat with remaining tortilla wedges. Cool completely. Serve chips with Lone Star Caviar.

MICROWAVE TIP: *Arrange 16 seasoned wedges in single layer on paper-towel-lined plate. Microwave at High 4 to 5 minutes, or until crisp, rotating plate once. Loosen chips from paper towel immediately. Repeat with remaining tortilla wedges. Continue as directed.*

LAYERED BEAN DIP

Garbanzo Bean Layer:

- 1 can (15 oz./426 mL) garbanzo beans, rinsed and drained
- 1 to 2 tablespoons (15 to 25 mL) fresh lemon juice
- 1 tablespoon (15 mL) olive oil
- 2 cloves garlic, minced
- ½ teaspoon (2 mL) ground cumin
- ¼ teaspoon (1 mL) salt

Black Bean Layer:

- 1 can (15 oz./426 mL) black beans, rinsed and drained
- ½ cup (125 mL) chopped freshly roasted red pepper or roasted red peppers in marinade, rinsed and drained
- 1 tablespoon (15 mL) snipped fresh cilantro
- 1 tablespoon (15 mL) finely chopped green onion

Yogurt Layer:

- 1 cup (250 mL) nonfat yogurt cheese
- 1 to 2 tablespoons (15 to 25 mL) snipped fresh cilantro
- 2 to 3 teaspoons (10 to 15 mL) snipped fresh mint leaves
- 1 to 2 teaspoons (5 to 10 mL) fresh lemon juice

- 1 cup (250 mL) finely shredded lettuce
- 1 Roma tomato, chopped
- 1 tablespoon (15 mL) chopped black or Kalamata olives (optional)

12 servings

1 Combine garbanzo bean layer ingredients in food processor or blender. Process until smooth. Spread the mixture evenly in bottom of 9" (23 cm) pie plate. Set aside.

2 Combine black bean layer ingredients in medium mixing bowl. Spread mixture evenly over garbanzo bean layer to within 1" (2.5 cm) of edge. In small mixing bowl, combine yogurt layer ingredients. Spoon yogurt mixture evenly over black bean layer. Cover with plastic wrap. Chill at least 1 hour.

3 Arrange lettuce and tomato around edges of dip. Garnish with olives. Serve dip with pita bread, chips or raw vegetable sticks, if desired.

TIP: To roast fresh peppers, first pierce the skin several times with a fork. If roasting over a gas burner, spear pepper with long-handled fork and hold over flame, turning until skin is blackened. If using a broiler, place peppers on broiler pan as close to heat as possible, turning until skin is blackened. Place peppers in closed paper bag for about 10 minutes; then peel and use.

SPINACH-FILLED BREAD

- 1 loaf (16 oz./500 g) round crusty bread
- 2 pkgs. (10 oz./300 g each) frozen chopped spinach
- 2 pkgs. (8 oz./250 g each) cream cheese
- 3 tablespoons (50 mL) milk
- 1 teaspoon (5 mL) lemon juice
- ½ teaspoon (2 mL) salt
- Pinch pepper (optional)
- Pinch ground nutmeg

8 servings

Advance preparation:
Prepare filling 1 day ahead; refrigerate. To serve, microwave filling at High 30 seconds to 1¼ minutes, or until warm. Fill bread. Microwave as directed.

4 Place cream cheese in medium bowl. Microwave at High 30 to 45 seconds, or until softened. Mix in remaining ingredients.

1 Cut 1½" to 2" (4 to 5 cm) slice from top of bread. Cut a circle 1½" (4 cm) from the outer edge of crust.

2 Remove the center, leaving at least 2" (5 cm) of bread on bottom. Cut center and top into pieces for dipping. Set aside.

3 Place packages of spinach in microwave oven. Microwave at High 4½ to 6½ minutes, or until heated, rearranging once. Drain, pressing out excess liquid.

5 Spoon into bread shell. Place on paper-towel-lined plate.

6 Microwave at High 45 seconds to 1¼ minutes, or until bread is warm. Serve with bread pieces for dipping.

FRESH ZUCCHINI DIP (a)

- 1½ cups (375 mL) shredded zucchini (1 medium)
- ¼ cup (50 mL) finely chopped onion
- ¼ cup (50 mL) finely chopped green pepper
- 1 tablespoon (15 mL) butter or margarine
- ¼ cup (50 mL) mayonnaise or salad dressing
- ¾ cup (175 mL) dairy sour cream
- 1 teaspoon (5 mL) garlic salt
- 1 teaspoon (5 mL) Worcestershire sauce
- Pinch cayenne

2 cups (500 mL)

Place shredded zucchini between layers of paper towel. Press to remove excess moisture. In 1-qt. (1 L) casserole, combine onion, green pepper and butter. Microwave at High 1 to 3 minutes, or until onion is tender. Stir in zucchini and remaining ingredients. Chill at least 2 hours.

CHIPPED BEEF DIP (b)

- ¼ cup (50 mL) chopped green onion
- 1 clove garlic, minced
- 1 tablespoon (15 mL) butter or margarine
- 1 pkg. (8 oz./250 g) cream cheese
- ½ cup (125 mL) dairy sour cream
- ¼ cup (50 mL) half-and-half or milk
- 1 pkg. (2½ oz./75 g) dried beef, chopped
- 2 tablespoons (25 mL) snipped fresh parsley
- 1 tablespoon (15 mL) prepared horseradish
- 1 tablespoon (15 mL) lemon juice

About 2 cups (500 mL)

In 1-qt. (1 L) casserole, combine green onion, garlic and butter. Microwave at High 30 to 60 seconds, or until butter melts. Add cream cheese. Microwave at High 45 seconds to 1½ minutes, or until cream cheese is softened. Mix in remaining ingredients. Chill at least 2 hours or overnight.

JALAPEÑO CHEESE DIP (c)

- 1 medium onion, chopped
- 1 tablespoon (15 mL) vegetable oil
- 2 cups (500 mL) shredded Monterey Jack cheese
- 2 cups (500 mL) shredded Cheddar cheese
- ½ cup (125 mL) half-and-half
- 2 tablespoons (25 mL) chopped jalapeño peppers

10 to 12 servings

Place onion and oil in 1½-qt. (1.5 L) casserole. Cover. Microwave at High 2 to 3 minutes, or until onion is tender. Stir in remaining ingredients. Reduce power to 50% (Medium). Microwave 3 to 6 minutes, or until heated and smooth, stirring every 2 minutes. Serve with taco chips, if desired.

CHEESE BALL

- ¼ cup (50 mL) chopped green pepper
- ¼ cup (50 mL) chopped green onion
- 1 teaspoon (5 mL) butter or margarine
- 1 pkg. (8 oz./250 g) cream cheese
- 2 cups (500 mL) shredded Cheddar cheese
- 1 pkg. (4 oz./125 g) blue cheese, crumbled
- 1 tablespoon (15 mL) chopped pimiento
- 2 teaspoons (10 mL) prepared horseradish
- 2 teaspoons (10 mL) Worcestershire sauce
- 1 clove garlic, minced
- ½ cup (125 mL) chopped pecans

10 to 12 servings

In small bowl, combine green pepper, onion and butter; cover. Microwave at High 30 to 45 seconds, or until vegetables are tender-crisp, stirring once. Place cream cheese in large bowl. Reduce power to 50% (Medium). Microwave 1 to 1½ minutes, or until softened. Stir in vegetables and remaining ingredients except pecans. Shape into ball. Wrap in plastic wrap. Chill 2 to 3 hours. Unwrap; roll in pecans. Serve with assorted crackers, if desired.

CURRY DIP (d)

- 1 pkg. (8 oz./250 g) cream cheese
- 3 tablespoons (50 mL) milk
- ½ teaspoon (2 mL) curry powder
- ½ teaspoon (2 mL) garlic salt
- 1 cup (250 mL) dairy sour cream
- 8 to 10 cups (2 to 2.5 L) raw vegetables (carrot and celery sticks, cauliflowerets, broccoli flowerets, zucchini strips)

6 to 8 servings

Place cream cheese in small bowl. Microwave at High 20 to 45 seconds, or until softened. Mix in milk, curry powder and garlic salt. Microwave at High 30 to 60 seconds, or until warm. Stir to blend. Mix in sour cream. Serve with raw vegetables.

Advance preparation: *Prepare the day before or the morning of the party. Cover and refrigerate. Before serving, microwave dip at High 45 seconds to 1½ minutes, or until softened, stirring once or twice. Add 1 to 2 teaspoons (5 to 10 mL) milk if needed for smoother consistency.*

CHEESY SEAFOOD SNACK DIP

- 2 pkgs. (8 oz./250 g each) cream cheese, cut into 1" (2.5 cm) cubes
- ¾ cup (175 mL) cocktail sauce
- 1 can (6 oz./170 g) crab meat, rinsed, drained and cartilage removed
- 1 can (4 oz./113 g) medium shrimp, rinsed and drained
- 2 tablespoons (25 mL) sliced green onion

6 to 8 servings

Arrange cream cheese cubes in single layer on 12" (30 cm) round platter. Microwave at 50% (Medium) 1½ to 3 minutes, or until cheese softens, rotating platter once or twice. Spread cream cheese into even layer on platter, to within 1" (2.5 cm) of edges. Top evenly with cocktail sauce. Sprinkle with remaining ingredients. Serve dip with assorted crackers.

MEXICAN SNACK DIP

- 2 pkgs. (8 oz./250 g each) cream cheese, cut into 1" (2.5 cm) cubes
- 1 cup (250 mL) refried beans
- ¾ cup (175 mL) taco sauce
- 1 cup (250 mL) shredded Cheddar cheese
- ½ cup (125 mL) seeded chopped tomato
- ¼ cup (50 mL) sliced black olives
- 2 tablespoons (25 mL) sliced green onion

6 to 8 servings

1 Arrange cream cheese cubes in single layer on 12" (30 cm) platter. Microwave at 50% (Medium) 1½ to 3 minutes, or until cheese softens, rotating platter once or twice.

2 Spread cream cheese into even layer on platter, to within 1" (2.5 cm) of edges. Spread refried beans in even layer over the cream cheese, to within ½" (1 cm) of edges. Top with taco sauce. Sprinkle with remaining ingredients. Serve snack platter with corn or tortilla chips.

CHEESE DIP ↑ IN PEPPER

SAVORY PEPPER WEDGES

1 In small mixing bowl, microwave 1 pkg. (3 oz./ 85 g) cream cheese at High 15 to 30 seconds, or until softened. Add ⅓ cup (75 mL) pasteurized process cheese spread and 2 tablespoons (25 mL) sliced green onion. Mix well and set aside.

2 Cut thin slice from top of large pepper (red, green or yellow). Set top aside. Remove and discard core and seeds. Spoon cheese mixture into pepper. Place pepper in a 6-oz. (175 mL) custard cup. Microwave at 70% (Medium High) 2½ to 4 minutes, or until pepper is warm and cheese mixture is melted, rotating 2 or 3 times. Stir cheese. If desired, place pepper in the center of the raw vegetable platter to serve. Replace top of pepper if desired.

- 4 teaspoons (20 mL) butter or margarine
- 1½ cups (375 mL) cooked rice
- ½ cup (125 mL) grated carrot
- ¼ cup (50 mL) finely chopped zucchini
- ¼ teaspoon (1 mL) dried thyme leaves
- ¼ teaspoon (1 mL) salt
- Pinch pepper
- 1 medium red pepper
- 1 medium yellow pepper

4 servings

1 In small mixing bowl, microwave butter at High 45 seconds to 1 minute, or until melted. Add remaining ingredients, except red and yellow peppers. Set aside.

2 Remove and discard core and seeds. Cut each pepper lengthwise into quarters and fill pepper quarters evenly with rice mixture.

3 Arrange pepper wedges on plate. Cover with wax paper. Microwave at High 5 to 7 minutes, or until rice mixture is hot and peppers are tender-crisp, rotating plate once. If desired, top peppers with snipped parsley to serve.

SEAFOOD & AVOCADO DIP ↑

- 1 large ripe avocado
- Lemon juice
- 1 pkg. (3 oz./85 g) cream cheese
- 1 tablespoon (15 mL) sliced green onion
- 1 small clove garlic, minced
- ½ cup (125 mL) shredded seafood sticks or rinsed and drained crab meat
- 1 teaspoon (5 mL) lime juice
- ¼ teaspoon (1 mL) Worcestershire sauce
- Pinch cayenne

6 to 8 servings

1 Cut avocado in half lengthwise and remove the pit. With small spoon, scoop out pulp, leaving ¼" (5 mm) shell. Chop avocado pulp and set aside. Brush surfaces of avocado shells with lemon juice. Set aside.

2 In small mixing bowl, place cream cheese, green onion and garlic. Microwave at High 15 to 30 seconds, or until cheese softens. Mix in chopped avocado pulp and remaining ingredients. Stuff seafood mixture evenly into avocado shells. Place one shell on plate. Microwave at High 30 seconds to 1 minute, or until dip is warm. Repeat with second avocado shell if needed. Serve dip with corn or tortilla chips, or assorted crackers.

TIP: *Dip is conveniently served in its own natural container. Microwave one avocado shell, and refrigerate second shell until more warm dip is needed.*

MIXED FRUIT WARMER →

- 4 cups (1 L) cranberry-raspberry drink
- 2 cups (500 mL) water
- 1 can (6 oz./170 mL)* frozen orange juice concentrate, defrosted
- ⅓ cup (75 mL) packed brown sugar
- 8 thin orange slices
- 1 stick cinnamon

8 servings

Combine all ingredients in 3-quart (3 L) saucepan. Stir until sugar is dissolved. Cook over Medium-High heat for 10 to 14 minutes, or until mixture is hot and flavors are blended, stirring occasionally. (Do not boil.) Remove and discard cinnamon stick before serving.

MICROWAVE TIP: *In 8-cup (2 L) measure, combine all ingredients. Stir until sugar is dissolved. Microwave at High 10 to 16 minutes, or until mixture is hot and flavors are blended, stirring once or twice.*

If 6-oz. (170 mL) can not available, use half of 12-oz. (341 mL) can.

MEXICAN HOT COCOA

- ²/₃ cup (150 mL) sugar
- ½ cup (125 mL) unsweetened cocoa
- ½ cup (125 mL) hot water
- 4 cups (1 L) skim milk
- 2 sticks cinnamon
- 1 teaspoon (5 mL) vanilla

5 servings

1 Combine sugar and cocoa in 2-quart (2 L) saucepan. Add water. Stir with whisk until smooth. Cook over medium heat for 3 to 5 minutes, or just until edges of mixture begin to bubble, stirring constantly.

2 Blend in milk. Add cinnamon sticks. Cook for additional 10 to 12 minutes, or until mixture is hot, stirring frequently. (Do not boil.) Remove from heat. Stir in vanilla.

TIP: *For stronger cinnamon flavor, let cocoa stand additional 10 minutes.*

Serving suggestion: *Place 1 stick cinnamon in each serving glass and garnish with a dollop of nonfat whipped topping.*

TEXAS MARY

- 1 can (46 oz./1.3 L) no-salt-added tomato juice
- 1 can (11½ oz./327 mL) vegetable juice
- ¼ to ½ cup (50 to 125 mL) fresh lime juice
- 2 tablespoons (25 mL) Worcestershire sauce
- 1½ teaspoons (7 mL) red pepper sauce

- 1 teaspoon (5 mL) prepared horseradish
- 1 teaspoon (5 mL) ground cumin
- ½ teaspoon (2 mL) freshly ground pepper
- Pinch celery seed, crushed
- 8 fresh asparagus spears, trimmed (optional)

8 servings

1 Combine all ingredients, except asparagus, in 8-cup (2 L) measure. Add asparagus spears to juice mixture. Cover with plastic wrap. Refrigerate overnight.

2 Pack serving glasses with ice. Pour mixture over ice. Add 1 asparagus spear to each glass.

RUSSIAN TEA

- 1 teaspoon (5 mL) ground cloves
- 1 teaspoon (5 mL) ground cinnamon
- 8 cups (2 L) water
- ½ cup (125 mL) sugar
- 2 single-serving black tea bags
- ¼ cup (50 mL) frozen orange juice concentrate, defrosted
- ¼ cup (50 mL) fresh lemon juice

8 servings

1 Cut 4-inch (10 cm) square cheesecloth. Place cloves and cinnamon in center of square. Bring corners of cheesecloth together to form bag. Secure spice bag with string.

2 Combine spice bag, water, sugar and tea bags in 3-quart (3 L) saucepan. Bring to boil over high heat, stirring to dissolve sugar. Remove from heat. Let stand for 5 minutes. Remove and discard spice bag and tea bags. Stir in concentrate and juice. Serve immediately. Serve with cinnamon sticks, if desired.

IRISH COFFEE

- ¼ cup (50 mL) packed light brown sugar
- 7 teaspoons (35 mL) instant coffee crystals
- 5½ cups (1.375 L) hot water
- 1¼ to 1½ cups (300 to 375 mL) Irish whiskey
- Sweetened whipped cream

6 to 8 servings

In 2-qt. (2 L) measure or bowl, combine brown sugar, coffee crystals and hot water; cover. Microwave at High 5 to 8 minutes, or until very hot. Stir to dissolve brown sugar. Stir in whiskey. Pour into individual cups. Top with sweetened whipped cream.

CAPPUCCINO FOR TWO

- 2 to 3 teaspoons (10 to 15 mL) packed light brown sugar
- 2 teaspoons (10 mL) instant coffee crystals
- 1⅓ cups (325 mL) hot water
- ¼ cup (50 mL) orange liqueur
- Sweetened whipped cream

2 servings

In 2-cup (500 mL) measure, combine brown sugar, coffee crystals, and hot water. Cover. Microwave at High 2 to 4 minutes, or until hot. Stir to dissolve sugar. Stir in liqueur. Pour into individual cups. Top with sweetened whipped cream.

CAPPUCCINO FOR EIGHT

- 2 to 3 tablespoons (25 to 50 mL) packed light brown sugar
- 2 tablespoons (25 mL) instant coffee crystals
- 4 cups (1 L) hot water
- ¾ cup (175 mL) orange liqueur
- Sweetened whipped cream

8 servings

In 1½- to 2-qt. (1.5 to 2 L) measure or bowl, combine brown sugar, coffee crystals and hot water. Cover. Microwave at High 4 to 6½ minutes, or until hot. Stir to dissolve sugar. Stir in liqueur. Pour into individual cups. Top with sweetened whipped cream.

ORANGE LIQUEUR

- 3 oranges
- 1 cup (250 mL) sugar
- 1 stick cinnamon
- 2 cups (500 mL) brandy

About 3 cups (750 mL)

1 Remove the peel from one orange with vegetable peeler or zester. Do not include white membrane. Cut oranges in half; squeeze juice. (Yields 1 cup/250 mL). In 4-cup (1 L) measure, combine orange peel, orange juice, sugar and cinnamon. Microwave at High 3 to 4 minutes, or until boiling, stirring after each minute. Boil 30 seconds. Watch closely; stir if necessary to prevent boilover. Cool to room temperature.

2 Remove cinnamon stick. Strain cooled juice mixture through cheesecloth. Add brandy to the strained liquid. Pour into bottle; cap. Let stand in a cool, dark place 1 month before serving. Shake bottle occasionally to mix.

CREME DE MENTHE

- 1½ cups (375 mL) sugar
- 1 cup (250 mL) water
- 1½ cups (375 mL) vodka or gin
- 1 teaspoon (5 mL) mint flavor
- ¼ teaspoon (1 mL) green food coloring

About 4 cups (1 L)

1 In 4-cup (1 L) measure or large bowl, combine sugar and water. Microwave at High 4 to 5 minutes, or until boiling. Boil 5 minutes. Watch closely; stir if necessary to prevent boilover.

2 Cool to room temperature. Skim any foam from top. Stir in remaining ingredients.

3 Pour into bottle; cap. Let stand in a cool, dark place 1 month before serving. Shake bottle occasionally to mix.

ANISE LIQUEUR

- 1½ cups (375 mL) light corn syrup
- ½ cup (125 mL) water
- ¼ teaspoon (1 mL) instant unflavored, unsweetened tea powder
- 1½ cups (375 mL) vodka
- ¾ teaspoon (4 mL) anise extract
- ½ teaspoon (2 mL) vanilla
- 2 drops yellow food coloring

3½ cups (875 mL)

1 In 4-cup (1 L) measure or large bowl, combine corn syrup, water and tea powder. Microwave at High 4 to 5½ minutes, or until boiling. Watch closely; stir if necessary to prevent boilover. Cool to room temperature.

2 Skim any foam from top. Stir in vodka, anise extract, vanilla and yellow food coloring. Pour into bottle; cap. Let stand in a cool, dark place 1 month before serving. Shake bottle occasionally to mix.

RASPBERRY LIQUEUR

- 2 pkgs. (10 oz./300 g each) frozen raspberries in syrup
- 1½ cups (375 mL) sugar
- 1½ cups (375 mL) vodka

3 cups (750 mL)

1 Remove raspberries from packages and place in large bowl. Microwave at 50% (Medium) 4 to 5 minutes, or until partially defrosted. Gently separate with fork. Let stand to complete defrosting. Drain juice into 8-cup (2 L) measure or large bowl. Set raspberries aside.

2 Add sugar to juice. Microwave at High 3 to 5 minutes, or until sugar dissolves and mixture boils, stirring every 2 minutes. Cool to room temperature. Skim any foam from top. Add reserved raspberries and vodka. Pour into bottle; cap. Let stand in a cool, dark place 1 month before serving. Shake bottle occasionally to mix. Strain through cheesecloth before serving. Serve raspberries over ice cream.

COFFEE LIQUEUR

- 1½ cups (375 mL) sugar
- 1 cup (250 mL) water
- ¼ cup (50 mL) instant coffee crystals
- 1½ cups (375 mL) vodka
- 1 vanilla bean or 1 teaspoon (5 mL) vanilla extract

2½ cups (625 mL)

1 In 4-cup (1 L) measure or large bowl, combine sugar and water. Microwave at High 4 to 5 minutes, or until boiling. Boil 5 minutes. Watch closely; stir if necessary to prevent boilover.

2 Stir in coffee crystals until dissolved. Cool to room temperature. Skim any foam from top. Add vodka and vanilla bean.

3 Pour into bottle; cap. Let stand in a cool, dark place 1 month before serving. Shake bottle occasionally to mix.

APRICOT BRANDY

- 1 pkg. (6 oz./175 g) dried apricots
- 1½ cups (375 mL) white wine
- 1 cup (250 mL) sugar
- 1 cup (250 mL) brandy

About 3 cups (750 mL)

1 If desired, chop apricots. In 4-cup (1 L) measure, combine apricots, wine and sugar. Cover with plastic wrap. Microwave at High 4 to 6 minutes, or until sugar dissolves and mixture boils, stirring every 2 minutes. Cool to room temperature. Skim any foam from top. Add brandy.

2 Pour into bottle; cap. Let stand in a cool, dark place 1 month before serving. Shake bottle occasionally to mix. Strain through cheesecloth before serving. Serve apricots over ice cream.

TIP: *Serve liqueurs in Chocolate Liqueur Cups, page 269; stir into softened ice cream, or give as gifts.*

201

Christmas
Cookies

CHRISTMAS COOKIE BASICS

This collection of Christmas cookies has recipes from a variety of countries. Austrian bakers get the credit for creating rich, buttery Florentines. These chocolate-glazed specialties are traditionally a mixture of honey, butter, sugar and candied fruit. Pfeffernüsse, or "peppernuts," are spicy cookies that are served at Christmastime in Germany. And Fattigmands are a crispy fried Scandinavian specialty, also a Christmas favorite. Italian Biscotti can be served any time. These intensely flavored cookies are twice-baked, making them crunchy and perfect for dipping in coffee or a sweet dessert wine.

Some of these recipes require specialized equipment, which is available at specialty cooking or kitchen stores.

Madeleine pans: These pans have special scallop-shell indentations for the cookies' signature look.

Cookie cutters: In a few recipes, we call for special cookie cutters. These can be found in many stores, or you can make your own.

Madeleine pan

Rosette iron

Special cookie cutters

204

Rosette irons: A heatproof handle is attached to one or two long metal rods. Various decorative forms can be attached to the rods. The forms are dipped in batter, then lowered into hot oil.

Krumkake and pizzelle irons: Krumkake and pizzelles are baked on the stovetop in hinged irons that leave designs on the thinly pressed cookies. Freshly made krumkake are shaped around a special cone. Pizzelles are served flat.

Krumkake iron

Krumkake cone

Pizzelle iron

← SOUR CREAM CUTOUTS

- 2 cups (500 mL) sugar
- 1 cup (250 mL) sour cream
- 3 eggs
- ½ cup (125 mL) butter or margarine, softened
- ½ cup (125 mL) vegetable shortening
- 5½ cups (1.375 L) all-purpose flour
- 2 teaspoons (10 mL) baking powder
- 2 teaspoons (10 mL) baking soda
- 1 teaspoon (5 mL) vanilla
- 1 teaspoon (5 mL) almond extract
- ¼ teaspoon (1 mL) salt
- Decorator Frosting (page 242)

About 10 dozen cookies

1 In large mixing bowl, combine sugar, sour cream, eggs, butter and shortening. Beat at medium speed of electric mixer until light and fluffy. Add flour, baking powder, baking soda, vanilla, almond extract and salt. Beat at low speed until soft dough forms. Cover with plastic wrap. Chill 1 to 2 hours, or until firm.

2 Heat oven to 350°F/180°C. On well-floured surface, roll dough to ¼" (5 mm) thickness. Using 3" (8 cm) cookie cutters, cut desired shapes into dough. Place shapes 2" (5 cm) apart on ungreased cookie sheets. Bake for 6 to 8 minutes, or until edges are light golden brown. Prepare frosting as directed. Decorate cookies as desired. Let dry completely before storing.

SPECIAL-OCCASION SUGAR COOKIES

- 1 cup (250 mL) sugar
- ¾ cup (175 mL) butter or margarine, softened
- 1 egg
- 3 tablespoons (50 mL) whipping cream
- 1 teaspoon (5 mL) vanilla
- 1 teaspoon (5 mL) almond extract
- 3 cups (750 mL) all-purpose flour
- 1½ teaspoons (7 mL) baking powder
- ½ teaspoon (2 mL) salt
- Granulated sugar
- Decorator Frosting (page 242)

5½ dozen cookies

1 In large mixing bowl, combine 1 cup (250 mL) sugar, the butter, egg, whipping cream, vanilla and almond extract. Beat at medium speed of electric mixer until light and fluffy. Add flour, baking powder and salt. Beat at low speed until soft dough forms. Cover with plastic wrap. Chill 1 to 2 hours, or until firm.

2 Heat oven to 400°F/200°C. On floured surface, roll dough to ¼" (5 mm) thickness. Using 3" (8 cm) cookie cutters, cut desired shapes into dough. Place shapes 2" (5 cm) apart on ungreased cookie sheets. Sprinkle shapes with sugar. Bake for 4 to 6 minutes, or until edges are light golden brown. Prepare frosting as directed. Decorate cookies as desired. Let dry completely before storing.

HOLIDAY MERINGUE COOKIES

- 3 egg whites
- ½ teaspoon (2 mL) white vinegar
- Pinch salt
- 1¼ cups (300 mL) sugar
- ½ teaspoon (2 mL) vanilla
- Any combination cinnamon candies, multicolored shot, chocolate-flavored candy sprinkles, etc.

About 1 dozen cookies

1 Heat oven to 300°F/150°C. Line cookie sheets with parchment paper. Set aside. In small mixing bowl, combine egg whites, vinegar and salt.

2 Beat at high speed of electric mixer until soft peaks form. Add sugar, 1 tablespoon (15 mL) at a time, beating at high speed. Beat until stiff peaks form. Beat in vanilla.

3 Fill pastry bag with meringue mixture. Using open star tip, pipe holiday designs 1" (2.5 cm) apart on prepared cookie sheets. Decorate as desired with candies, shot, sprinkles, etc.

4 Bake for 23 to 25 minutes, or until light golden brown. Cool completely before removing from parchment paper.

HOLIDAY HORNS

- ½ cup (125 mL) butter or margarine, softened
- 1 pkg. (3 oz./85 g) cream cheese, softened
- 1⅓ cups (325 mL) all-purpose flour
- 2 tablespoons (25 mL) sugar
- 1 tablespoon (15 mL) milk
- ½ teaspoon (2 mL) vanilla
- ½ cup (125 mL) favorite red jelly
- ½ cup (125 mL) finely chopped pistachios

4 dozen cookies

1 In small mixing bowl, combine butter and cream cheese. Beat at medium speed of electric mixer until light and fluffy. Add flour, sugar, milk and vanilla. Beat at low speed until soft dough forms. Cover with plastic wrap. Chill 4 to 5 hours, or until firm.

2 Heat oven to 325°F/160°C. Lightly grease cookie sheets. Set aside. Divide dough into quarters. On floured surface, roll one quarter dough to ⅛" (3 mm) thickness. Using 2" (5 cm) round cookie cutter, cut circles into dough. Place circles 2" (5 cm) apart on prepared cookie sheets.

3 Spoon ¼ teaspoon (1 mL) jelly onto center of each circle. Sprinkle ½ teaspoon (2 mL) pistachios over jelly on each circle. Lightly brush edges with water.

4 Fold opposite edges over filling and pinch together to form cone. Repeat with remaining dough, jelly and pistachios. Bake for 13 to 15 minutes, or until golden brown. Cool completely before storing.

TIP: *If dough becomes too sticky to roll, refrigerate until firm.*

209

COCOA PEPPERMINT PRETZELS →

- 1 cup (250 mL) powdered sugar
- 1 cup (250 mL) butter or margarine, softened
- 1 egg
- 1½ teaspoons (7 mL) vanilla
- 2½ cups (625 mL) all-purpose flour
- ½ cup (125 mL) unsweetened cocoa
- ½ teaspoon (2 mL) salt
- ½ cup (125 mL) vanilla baking chips
- 1 teaspoon (5 mL) vegetable shortening
- 12 hard peppermint candies, crushed

4 dozen cookies

1 In large mixing bowl, combine sugar, butter, egg and vanilla. Beat at medium speed of electric mixer until light and fluffy. Add flour, cocoa and salt. Beat at low speed until soft dough forms. Cover with plastic wrap. Chill 2 to 3 hours, or until firm.

2 Heat oven to 375°F/190°C. Shape level measuring tablespoons (15 mL) dough into 9"-long (23 cm) ropes. Twist ropes into pretzel shapes. Place pretzels 2" (5 cm) apart on ungreased cookie sheets. Bake for 8 to 9 minutes, or until set. Cool completely.

3 Line cookie sheets with wax paper. Set aside. In 1-quart (1 L) saucepan, combine chips and shortening. Melt over low heat, stirring constantly. Dip one end of each pretzel into melted chips, then roll dipped ends into crushed candies. Place pretzels on prepared cookie sheets. Let dry completely before storing.

MICROWAVE TIP: *In small mixing bowl, melt chips and shortening at 50% (Medium) for 2 to 4 minutes, stirring after every minute. Continue as directed.*

← MINT TRUFFLE COOKIES

- 1¼ cups (300 mL) sugar
- 1 cup (250 mL) butter or margarine, softened
- 2 eggs
- 1 teaspoon (5 mL) vanilla
- 2½ cups (625 mL) all-purpose flour
- ¼ cup (50 mL) unsweetened cocoa
- 1 teaspoon (5 mL) baking powder
- ¼ teaspoon (1 mL) salt

- 1 pkg. (4.67 oz./132 g) chocolate sandwich mints, coarsely chopped

Glaze

- 8 oz. (250 g) white candy coating
- 1 teaspoon (5 mL) vegetable shortening
- 1 or 2 drops green food coloring

4 dozen cookies

1 In large mixing bowl, combine sugar, butter, eggs and vanilla. Beat at medium speed of electric mixer until light and fluffy. Add flour, cocoa, baking powder and salt. Beat at low speed until soft dough forms. Stir in mints. Cover with plastic wrap. Chill 2 to 3 hours, or until firm.

2 Heat oven to 375°F/190°C. Lightly grease cookie sheets. Shape dough into 1" (2.5 cm) balls. Place balls 2" (5 cm) apart on prepared cookie sheets. Bake for 8 to 10 minutes, or until set. Cool completely.

3 In 1-quart (1 L) saucepan, combine candy coating and shortening. Melt over low heat, stirring constantly. Stir in food coloring. Pipe or drizzle glaze over cookies to form stripes. Let dry completely before storing.

MICROWAVE TIP: *In small mixing bowl, melt candy coating and shortening at 50% (Medium) for 2 to 4 minutes, stirring after every minute. Continue as directed.*

← POPPY SEED PINWHEELS

- ½ cup (125 mL) butter or margarine, softened
- ¼ cup (50 mL) granulated sugar
- 1 egg
- 1 teaspoon (5 mL) grated orange peel
- 1 teaspoon (5 mL) vanilla
- 1½ cups (375 mL) all-purpose flour
- ½ teaspoon (2 mL) baking soda
- 1 cup (250 mL) poppy seed filling, divided
- Powdered sugar (optional)

4 dozen cookies

1 In large mixing bowl, combine butter, granulated sugar, egg, peel and vanilla. Beat at medium speed of electric mixer until light and fluffy. Add flour and bak-ing soda. Beat at low speed until soft dough forms. Divide dough in half. Cover with plastic wrap. Chill 30 minutes to 1 hour, or until firm.

2 Roll half of dough between 2 sheets of wax paper into 12" x 10" (30 x 25 cm) rectangle. Repeat with remaining dough. Chill 30 minutes.

3 Heat oven to 350°F/180°C. Lightly grease cookie sheets. Set aside. Discard top sheet of wax paper from first half dough. Spread ½ cup (125 mL) fill-ing to within ¼" (5 mm) of edges. Roll dough jelly roll style, starting with long side. (Peel off wax paper when rolling.) Pinch edge to seal. Repeat with remaining dough and ½ cup (125 mL) filling.

4 Cut rolls into ½" (1 cm) slices. Place slices 2" (5 cm) apart on prepared cookie sheets. Bake for 10 to 12 minutes, or until edges are light golden brown. Cool completely. Sprinkle pinwheels with powdered sugar.

Optional Glaze:

- 1 cup (250 mL) powdered sugar
- 1 to 2 tablespoons (15 to 25 mL) orange juice

In small mixing bowl, combine sugar and juice. Stir until smooth. Drizzle over cooled pinwheels.

← HOLIDAY THUMBPRINT COOKIES

- 1 cup (250 mL) butter or margarine, softened
- ½ cup (125 mL) packed brown sugar
- 2 eggs, separated
- 2 cups (500 mL) all-purpose flour
- 1 teaspoon (5 mL) water
- 1½ cups (375 mL) finely chopped pecans
- 3 tablespoons (50 mL) currant jelly or other tart jelly

3 dozen cookies

1 Heat oven to 300°F/150°C. In large mixing bowl, combine butter, sugar and egg yolks. Beat at medium speed of electric mixer until light and fluffy. Add flour. Beat at low speed until soft dough forms. Set aside.

2 In small mixing bowl, beat egg whites and water at high speed until foamy. Set aside.

3 Shape dough into 1" (2.5 cm) balls. Dip balls into egg white mixture. Roll balls in pecans. Place balls 2" (5 cm) apart on ungreased cookie sheets. Indent top of each cookie with thumb. Bake for 18 to 20 minutes, or until set.

4 Immediately indent cookies again. Spoon ¼ teaspoon (1 mL) jelly into each thumbprint. Cool completely before storing. (Do not stack cookies.)

TIP: *Use end of spoon to make indentation in hot cookies.*

BRANDIED GINGER SNAPS

- ½ cup (125 mL) granulated sugar
- ½ cup (125 mL) butter or margarine
- ⅓ cup (75 mL) dark molasses
- 1 tablespoon (15 mL) apricot-flavored brandy
- 1¾ to 2 cups (425 to 500 mL) all-purpose flour, divided
- 1 teaspoon (5 mL) pumpkin pie spice
- Pinch salt

Frosting:

- 2 cups (500 mL) powdered sugar
- ¼ cup (50 mL) caramel ice cream topping
- 1 to 2 teaspoons (5 to 10 mL) milk
- ½ teaspoon (2 mL) vanilla

About 3½ dozen cookies

1 Heat oven to 350°F/ 180°C. Lightly grease cookie sheets. Set aside. In 1-quart (1 L) saucepan, combine gran-ulated sugar, butter and molasses. Bring to boil over medium heat, stirring constantly. Boil for 1 minute. Remove from heat. Stir in brandy. Set aside.

2 In large mixing bowl, combine 1¼ cups (300 mL) flour, the pumpkin pie spice and salt. Add butter mixture. Beat at medium speed of electric mixer until well blended. Stir or knead in enough of remaining ¾ cup (175 mL) flour to form stiff dough.

3 On prepared cookie sheet, roll out two-thirds dough to ⅛" to ¼" (3 to 5 mm) thickness. Using 3" (8 cm) star-shaped cookie cutter, cut shapes into dough at ½" (1 cm) intervals. Remove scraps and knead into remaining dough. Repeat with remain-ing dough on additional prepared cookie sheets. Bake for 7 to 8 minutes, or until set. Cool completely.

4 In small mixing bowl, combine frosting ingredients. Beat at high speed of electric mixer until smooth. Pipe star outline on cookies, or frost cookies with thin layer of frosting. Let dry completely before storing.

APPLIQUÉD ALMOND COOKIES

- ¾ cup (175 mL) butter or margarine, softened
- ⅓ cup (75 mL) almond paste
- 1 cup (250 mL) granulated sugar
- 1 egg
- 3 tablespoons (50 mL) milk
- 1 teaspoon (5 mL) almond extract

- 3 cups (750 mL) all-purpose flour
- 1½ teaspoons (7 mL) baking powder
- ½ teaspoon (2 mL) salt
- Food coloring
- Coarse sugar crystals

6 dozen cookies

1 In large mixing bowl, combine butter and almond paste. Beat at medium speed of electric mixer until smooth. Add granulated sugar, egg, milk and almond extract. Beat at medium speed until well blended. Add flour, baking powder and salt. Beat at low speed until soft dough forms. Divide dough into thirds. Cover ⅔ dough with plastic wrap. Add food coloring, one drop at a time, to remaining ⅓ dough, kneading dough until color is equally distributed and dough is desired shade. Cover with plastic wrap. Chill all dough 2 to 3 hours, or until firm.

2 Heat oven to 400°F/200°C. On floured surface, roll half of uncolored dough to ⅛" (3 mm) thickness. Using 2¼" (6 cm) round cookie cutter, cut circles into dough. Place circles 2" (5 cm) apart on ungreased cookie sheets. Set aside.

3 On floured surface, roll half of colored dough to ⅛" (3 mm) thickness. Using 2" (5 cm) cutter of desired shape (see Decorating Tip), cut shapes into dough. Place one colored shape on top of each uncolored circle. Repeat with remaining colored and uncolored dough. Sprinkle shapes with sugar crystals. Bake for 5 to 7 minutes, or until edges are golden brown. Cool completely before storing.

LEMON BLOSSOM SPRITZ ↑

- 1 cup (250 mL) butter or margarine, softened
- ½ cup (125 mL) granulated sugar
- ½ cup (125 mL) packed brown sugar
- 1 egg
- 1 teaspoon (5 mL) grated lemon peel
- 1 tablespoon (15 mL) fresh lemon juice
- 1 teaspoon (5 mL) vanilla
- 2½ cups (625 mL) all-purpose flour

- ¼ teaspoon (1 mL) baking soda
- ¼ teaspoon (1 mL) salt

Frosting:
- 1¼ cups (300 mL) powdered sugar
- ½ teaspoon (2 mL) grated lemon peel
- 2 to 4 teaspoons (10 to 20 mL) fresh lemon juice
- ½ teaspoon (2 mL) vanilla

About 5 dozen cookies

1 In large mixing bowl, combine butter, granulated sugar, brown sugar, egg, 1 teaspoon (5 mL) peel, 1 tablespoon (15 mL) juice and 1 teaspoon (5 mL) vanilla. Beat at medium speed of electric mixer until light and fluffy. Add flour, baking soda and salt. Beat at low speed until soft dough forms. Cover with plastic wrap. Chill 1 to 2 hours, or until firm.

2 Heat oven to 400°F/200°C. Place dough in cookie press. Using flower-patterned plate, press cookies 2" (5 cm) apart onto ungreased cookie sheets. Bake for 5 to 7 minutes, or until edges are light golden brown. Cool completely.

3 In small mixing bowl, combine frosting ingredients. Beat at low speed of electric mixer until smooth. Spread frosting evenly on cookies. Let dry completely before storing.

FATTIGMANDS

- Vegetable oil
- 3 tablespoons (50 mL) sour cream
- 3 tablespoons (50 mL) granulated sugar
- 3 egg yolks
- ½ teaspoon (2 mL) almond extract
- ¼ teaspoon (1 mL) ground cloves
- ¼ teaspoon (1 mL) salt
- 1¼ cups (300 mL) all-purpose flour, divided
- Powdered sugar

About 1½ dozen cookies

1 In deep-fat fryer, heat 3" (8 cm) vegetable oil to 375°F/190°C. In small mixing bowl, combine sour cream, granulated sugar, egg yolks, almond extract, cloves and salt. Beat at medium speed of electric mixer until smooth. Add 1 cup (250 mL) flour. Beat at low speed until soft dough forms. Knead in enough of remaining ¼ cup (50 mL) flour to form stiff dough.

2 On lightly floured surface, roll dough into ⅟₁₆" to ⅛"-thick (1.5 to 3 mm) rectangle. Using pastry wheel or sharp knife, cut dough into 2" (5 cm) strips. Cut strips diagonally at 4" (10 cm) intervals to form diamonds.

3 Cut 1" (2.5 cm) slit in center of each diamond. Pull one end of diamond completely through slit.

4 In hot oil, fry diamonds for 30 to 40 seconds, or until golden brown, turning over once. Drain on paper-towel-lined plate. Before serving, sprinkle fattigmands with powdered sugar.

MADELEINES

- 2 eggs
- Pinch salt
- ½ cup (125 mL) sugar
- 1 teaspoon (5 mL) grated lemon peel
- ½ teaspoon (2 mL) vanilla
- ½ cup (125 mL) plus 2 tablespoons (25 mL) all-purpose flour
- ½ cup (125 mL) butter or margarine, melted

2 dozen cookies

1 Heat oven to 400°F/200°C. Heavily grease 12-form madeleine pan. Set aside. In medium mixing bowl, combine eggs and salt. Beat at high speed of electric mixer until foamy. Add sugar, peel and vanilla. Beat at high speed for 10 to 12 minutes, or until light and airy, scraping sides of bowl frequently. Using whisk, gently fold in flour, 2 tablespoons (25 mL) at a time. Gently fold in butter, 1 tablespoon (15 mL) at a time.

2 Spoon 1 measuring tablespoon (15 mL) batter into each madeleine form. Bake for 5 to 7 minutes, or until edges are golden brown. Let cool for 3 minutes before removing from pan. Carefully remove madeleines from pan. Cool flat-sides-down on wire racks.

← CHOCOLATE ALMOND ROSETTES

- Vegetable oil
- 1 cup (250 mL) all-purpose flour
- ¼ cup (50 mL) unsweetened cocoa
- 3 tablespoons (50 mL) granulated sugar
- ½ teaspoon (2 mL) salt
- 1 cup (250 mL) milk
- 2 eggs
- 2 tablespoons (25 mL) vegetable oil
- ½ teaspoon (2 mL) almond extract
- Powdered sugar

4 dozen cookies

1 In deep-fat fryer, heat 3" (8 cm) vegetable oil to 375°F/190°C. In medium mixing bowl, combine flour, cocoa, granulated sugar and salt. Add milk, eggs, oil and almond extract. Beat at medium speed of electric mixer until smooth.

2 Heat rosette iron forms in hot oil for 30 seconds. Shake excess oil from forms. Dip hot forms into batter, making sure batter does not coat top side of forms. Immerse forms completely in hot oil. Fry for 30 to 40 seconds, or until edges begin to brown. (Rosettes may release from forms. If so, remove from oil with slotted spoon.)

3 Drain on paper-towel-lined plate. Repeat with remaining batter. Before serving, sprinkle rosettes with powdered sugar.

Optional Glaze:

3 cups (750 mL) powdered sugar

3 to 4 tablespoons (50 mL) milk

½ teaspoon (2 mL) almond extract

In small bowl, combine glaze ingredients. Stir until smooth. Dip tops of cooled rosettes into glaze.

← ROSETTES

- Vegetable oil
- 1 cup (250 mL) whipping cream
- 2 eggs
- 1 tablespoon (15 mL) granulated sugar
- 1 teaspoon (5 mL) vanilla
- ½ teaspoon (2 mL) ground cinnamon
- ½ teaspoon (2 mL) salt
- ¾ cup (175 mL) all-purpose flour
- Powdered sugar

About 4½ dozen cookies

1 In deep-fat fryer, heat 3" (8 cm) vegetable oil to 375°F/190°C. In medium mixing bowl, combine whipping cream, eggs, granulated sugar, vanilla, cinnamon and salt. Beat at low speed of electric mixer until smooth. Add flour. Beat at low speed until smooth.

2 Heat rosette iron forms in hot oil for 30 seconds. Shake excess oil from forms. Dip hot forms into batter, making sure batter does not coat top side of forms. Immerse forms completely in hot oil. Fry for 25 to 35 seconds, or until golden brown. (Rosettes may release from forms. If so, remove from oil with slotted spoon.)

3 Drain on paper-towel-lined plate. Repeat with remaining batter. Before serving, sprinkle rosettes with powdered sugar.

TIPS: *If batter does not adhere to forms, batter may be too thin (add additional flour, 1 tablespoon/15 mL at a time), or oil may be too hot or too cold. If rosettes adhere to forms after they are browned, rap top of forms gently with knife handle. If batter begins to thicken, thin with small amount of whipping cream.*

ORANGE-SPICED KRUMKAKE

- 1 cup (250 mL) sugar
- ½ cup (125 mL) butter or margarine, softened
- 2 eggs
- 1 teaspoon (5 mL) grated orange peel
- ¼ teaspoon (1 mL) ground cloves
- ¼ teaspoon (1 mL) ground cardamom
- 1½ cups (375 mL) all-purpose flour
- 1 cup (250 mL) milk

5 dozen cookies

1 In medium mixing bowl, combine sugar, butter, eggs, peel, cloves and cardamom. Beat at medium speed of electric mixer until smooth. Gradually add flour, alternating with milk, beating at low speed until smooth batter forms, scraping sides of bowl frequently.

2 Brush inside of krumkake iron with small amount of vegetable shortening. Heat iron over medium-low heat (if using gas stove) or medium heat (if using electric stove).

3 Place 1 measuring tablespoon (15 mL) batter in the center of open iron. Close the iron and firmly hold together. Cook for 5 to 20 seconds, or until light golden brown, turning iron over once. (Watch carefully to prevent burning.)

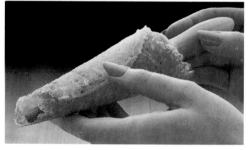

4 Remove the krumkake with spatula, and immediately roll into cone. Repeat with remaining batter. (The krumkake iron does not need to be rebrushed with shortening after the first krumkake is made.)

PIZZELLES

- 2 cups (500 mL) all-purpose flour
- 1 cup (250 mL) sugar
- 4 eggs
- ¾ cup (175 mL) butter or margarine, melted and slightly cooled
- ¼ cup (50 mL) finely ground hazelnuts
- 1 tablespoon (15 mL) anise extract

About 3½ dozen cookies

1 In medium mixing bowl, combine all ingredients. Beat at low speed of electric mixer until smooth batter forms, scraping sides of bowl frequently.

2 Brush inside of pizzelle iron with small amount of vegetable shortening. Heat iron over medium heat (if using gas stove) or medium-high heat (if using electric stove).

3 Place 1 measuring tablespoon (15 mL) batter in center of open iron. Close iron. (Do not squeeze shut.) Cook for 30 seconds to 1 minute 30 seconds, or until light golden brown, turning iron over once. (Watch carefully to prevent burning.)

4 With spatula, immediately remove pizzelle. Repeat with remaining batter. (The pizzelle iron does not need to be rebrushed with shortening after the first pizzelle is made.)

5 Cool pizzelles completely before storing. If desired, trim edges of cooled pizzelles with scissors.

TIP: *To recrisp pizzelles, bake at 250°F/120°C for 3 to 5 minutes.*

← ORANGE SNOWBALLS

- 2¾ cups (675 mL) finely crushed vanilla wafers
- 1 cup (250 mL) powdered sugar
- 1 cup (250 mL) finely chopped almonds
- ⅓ cup (75 mL) butter or margarine, melted
- ¼ cup (50 mL) frozen orange juice concentrate, defrosted
- Flaked coconut

3½ dozen cookies

1 Line airtight container with wax paper. Set aside. In large mixing bowl, combine wafers, sugar, almonds, butter and concentrate. Stir until well blended (mixture will be crumbly).

2 Shape mixture into ¾" (2 cm) balls. Roll balls in coconut. Place balls in prepared container. Store in refrigerator.

CHOCO-BRANDY → BALLS

- 2½ cups (625 mL) finely crushed chocolate wafers, divided
- 1¼ cups (300 mL) granulated sugar
- ½ cup (125 mL) butter or margarine, melted
- ½ cup (125 mL) finely chopped pecans
- ¼ cup (50 mL) brandy
- Powdered sugar

2½ dozen cookies

1 Line airtight container with wax paper. Set aside. In large mixing bowl, combine 2 cups (500 mL) wafers, the granulated sugar, butter, pecans, and brandy. Stir until well blended (mixture will be crumbly).

2 Shape mixture into 1" (2.5 cm) balls. Roll balls in remaining ½ cup (125 mL) wafers or powdered sugar. Place balls in prepared container. Store in refrigerator.

CHOCOLATE-GINGER →
ROCKING HORSE

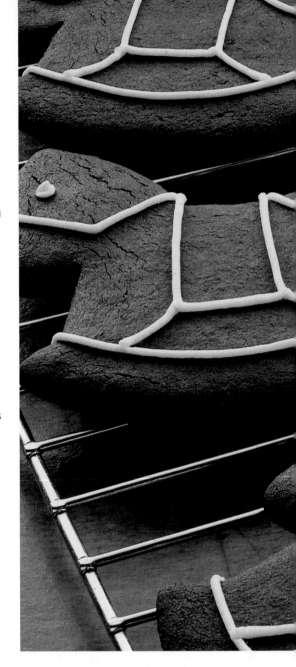

- 2¼ cups (550 mL) all-purpose flour
- ¾ cup (175 mL) unsweetened cocoa
- 1 teaspoon (5 mL) baking soda
- 1 teaspoon (5 mL) ground ginger
- ½ teaspoon (2 mL) baking powder
- ½ teaspoon (2 mL) ground allspice
- ¼ teaspoon (1 mL) ground cardamom
- ¼ teaspoon (1 mL) salt
- 1 cup (250 mL) sugar
- ½ cup (125 mL) butter or margarine, softened
- ½ cup (125 mL) light molasses
- 1 egg
- ½ teaspoon (2 mL) vanilla
- Decorator Frosting (page 242)

About 3 dozen cookies

1 In medium mixing bowl, combine flour, cocoa, baking soda, ginger, baking powder, allspice, cardamom and salt. Set aside.

2 In large mixing bowl, combine sugar, butter, molasses, egg and vanilla. Beat at medium speed of electric mixer until well blended. Add flour mixture. Beat at low speed until soft dough forms. Cover with plastic wrap. Chill 2 to 3 hours, or until firm.

3 Heat oven to 350°F/180°C. Lightly grease cookie sheets. Set aside. Divide dough in half. On lightly floured surface, roll half of dough to ⅛" to ¼" (3 to 5 mm) thickness. Using 3½" (9 cm) rocking horse cookie cutter, cut shapes into dough.

4 Place shapes 2" (5 cm) apart on prepared cookie sheets. Repeat with remaining dough. Bake for 8 to 10 minutes, or until set. Cool completely. Prepare frosting as directed. Decorate cookies as desired. Let dry completely before storing.

CANDY-FILLED CHOCOLATE WHEELS →

- 1½ cups (375 mL) powdered sugar
- 1 cup (250 mL) butter or margarine, softened
- 1 egg
- 1 teaspoon (5 mL) vanilla
- 2⅔ cups (650 mL) all-purpose flour
- ¼ teaspoon (1 mL) salt
- ¼ cup (50 mL) unsweetened cocoa
- 1 tablespoon (15 mL) milk
- ¼ cup (50 mL) finely crushed fruit-flavored hard candies

4 dozen cookies

1 In large mixing bowl, combine sugar, butter, egg and vanilla. Beat at medium speed of electric mixer until light and fluffy. Add flour and salt. Beat at low speed until soft dough forms.

2 Divide dough in half. Add cocoa and milk to half of dough. Beat at low speed until well blended. Roll chocolate dough between 2 sheets of wax paper into 12" x 8" (30 x 20 cm) rectangle. Discard top sheet of wax paper. Set dough aside.

3 Stir crushed candies into remaining half dough. Shape candied dough into 12"-long (30 cm) log. Place log lengthwise on long edge of rectangle. Roll chocolate dough jelly roll style around log. (Peel off wax paper when rolling.) Pinch edge to seal. Wrap in plastic wrap or wax paper. Chill 1 to 2 hours, or until firm.

4 Heat oven to 375°F/190°C. Cut roll into ¼" (5 mm) slices. Place slices 2" (5 cm) apart on ungreased cookie sheets. Bake for 8 to 10 minutes, or until set. Let cool 1 minute before removing from cookie sheets. Cool completely before storing.

← CHOCOLATE-DIPPED HAZELNUT BISCOTTI

- 1 cup (250 mL) slivered almonds
- 1½ cups (375 mL) sugar
- ½ cup (125 mL) unsalted butter, softened
- 2 tablespoons (25 mL) hazelnut liqueur
- 3 eggs
- 3¾ cups (925 mL) all-purpose flour
- 2 teaspoons (10 mL) baking powder
- Pinch salt
- 1 cup (250 mL) milk chocolate chips
- 2 teaspoons (10 mL) vegetable shortening
- 1½ cup (125 mL) finely chopped hazelnuts

3½ dozen cookies

1 Heat oven to 350°F/180°C. Lightly grease cookie sheets. Set aside. Place almonds in 8" (2 L) square baking pan. Bake for 10 to 12 minutes, or until light golden brown, stirring occasionally. Coarsely chop almonds. Set aside.

2 In large mixing bowl, combine sugar, butter and liqueur. Beat at medium speed of electric mixer until light and fluffy. Add eggs, one at a time, beating after each addition. Add flour, baking powder and salt. Beat at low speed until soft dough forms. Stir in almonds.

3 Divide dough into quarters. On lightly floured surface, shape each quarter into 2"-diameter (5 cm) log. Place logs 2" (5 cm) apart on prepared cookie sheet. Bake for 30 to 35 minutes, or until golden brown.

4 Immediately cut logs diagonally into ¾" (2 cm) slices. Place slices 1" (2.5 cm) apart on prepared cookie sheets. Bake for additional 10 to 15 minutes, or until dry and golden brown. Cool completely.

5 In 1-quart (1 L) saucepan, combine chips and shortening. Melt over low heat, stirring constantly. Remove from heat. Dip one end of each cookie diagonally into melted chocolate. Sprinkle hazelnuts evenly over dipped ends. Let dry completely before storing.

← STAINED GLASS COOKIES

- 1 cup (250 mL) sugar
- ½ cup (125 mL) butter or margarine, softened
- ⅓ cup (75 mL) vegetable shortening
- 2 eggs
- 1 teaspoon (5 mL) grated orange peel
- 1 teaspoon (5 mL) vanilla
- 2¾ cups (675 mL) all-purpose flour
- 1 teaspoon (5 mL) baking powder
- 1 teaspoon (5 mL) salt
- 5 rolls (.9 oz./22 g each) ring-shaped hard candies (assorted flavors)

4 dozen cookies

1 In large mixing bowl, combine sugar, butter and shortening. Beat at medium speed of electric mixer until light and fluffy. Add eggs, peel and vanilla. Beat at medium speed until well blended. Add flour, baking powder and salt. Beat at low speed until soft dough forms. Cover with plastic wrap. Chill 1 to 2 hours, or until firm.

2 Heat oven to 350°F/180°C. Line cookie sheets with foil. Set aside. Divide dough into thirds. On well-floured surface, roll one third dough to ¼" (5 mm) thickness. Using 3" (8 cm) cookie cutters, cut desired shapes into dough. Place shapes 2" (5 cm) apart on prepared cookie sheets.

3 Using smaller cookie cutters, straws or a sharp knife, cut desired shapes out of cookies on cookie sheets. (If cookies are to be hung as ornaments, make a small hole at the top of each cookie for string.) Repeat with remaining dough.

4 Place like-colored candies in small plastic bags. Coarsely crush candies by tapping each bag with back of large spoon. Fill cutout areas of cookies to the top with candies. Bake for 7 to 9 minutes, or until edges are light golden brown and candies are melted. Cool completely before removing from foil. Gently pull cookies off foil.

POPPY-RASPBERRY KOLACHKES →

- ½ cup (125 mL) butter or margarine, softened
- 1 pkg. (3 oz./85 g) cream cheese, softened
- ¼ cup (50 mL) granulated sugar
- ½ teaspoon (2 mL) vanilla
- 1½ cups (375 mL) all-purpose flour
- 1½ teaspoons (7 mL) poppy seed
- ⅓ cup (75 mL) raspberry jam

Glaze:
- ½ cup (125 mL) powdered sugar
- 4 to 5 teaspoons (20 to 25 mL) half-and-half
- ¼ teaspoon (1 mL) almond extract

About 3 dozen cookies

1 Heat oven to 375°F/190°C. In large mixing bowl, combine butter, cream cheese, granulated sugar and vanilla. Beat at medium speed of electric mixer until light and fluffy. Add flour and poppy seed. Beat at low speed until soft dough forms. Divide dough in half. On lightly floured board, roll half of dough to ⅛" to ¼" (3 to 5 mm) thickness. Using 2½" (6 cm) round cookie cutter, cut circles into dough. Place circles 2" (5 cm) apart on ungreased cookie sheets.

2 Spoon about ¼ teaspoon (1 mL) raspberry jam onto center of each circle. Fold top half of circle over bottom half. Press edges with fork dipped in flour to seal. Repeat with remaining dough and jam. Bake for 7 to 9 minutes, or until edges are light golden brown. Cool completely.

3 In small mixing bowl, combine glaze ingredients. Stir until smooth. Drizzle glaze over cookies. Let dry completely before storing.

← VIENNESE KISS COOKIES

- 1½ cups (375 mL) all-purpose flour
- ¾ cup (175 mL) butter or margarine, chilled and cut into 1" (2.5 cm) pieces
- ¼ cup (50 mL) sugar
- 3 tablespoons (50 mL) sour cream
- 1 teaspoon (5 mL) vanilla
- 24 chocolate kisses

2 dozen cookies

1 Heat oven to 350°F/180°C. Grease two 12-cup miniature muffin pans (1¾"/4.5 cm diameter). Set aside. In large mixing bowl, combine flour, butter and sugar. Beat at medium speed of electric mixer until mixture resembles coarse crumbs. Add sour cream and vanilla. Beat at low speed until soft dough forms.

2 Shape dough into 1" (2.5 cm) balls. Place 1 ball in each prepared muffin cup. Bake for 20 to 25 minutes, or until edges are golden brown. Immediately press kiss into center of each cookie. Let cool 1 minute before removing from pans. Cool completely before storing.

FRUITFUL FLORENTINES

- ½ cup (125 mL) butter or margarine, softened
- ⅓ cup (75 mL) honey
- ¼ cup (50 mL) sugar
- ½ teaspoon (2 mL) vanilla
- 1 cup (250 mL) uncooked quick-cooking oats
- ⅔ cup (150 mL) all-purpose flour
- 1 cup (250 mL) chopped candied fruit

Glaze:

- ¼ cup (50 mL) semisweet chocolate chips
- 2 tablespoons (25 mL) butter or margarine

2½ dozen cookies

1 Heat oven to 350°F/180°C. Lightly grease cookie sheets. Set aside. In large mixing bowl, combine ½ cup (125 mL) butter, the honey, sugar and vanilla. Beat at medium speed of electric mixer until well blended. Add oats and flour. Beat at low speed until soft dough forms. Stir in candied fruit.

2 Drop dough by heaping teaspoons 2" (5 cm) apart onto prepared cookie sheets. Flatten dough slightly with back of spoon. Bake for 10 to 12 minutes, or until edges are golden brown. Let cool 2 minutes before removing from cookie sheets. Cool completely.

3 In 1-quart (1 L) saucepan, combine glaze ingredients. Melt over low heat, stirring constantly. Drizzle glaze over cookies. Let dry completely before storing. Store in refrigerator.

MICROWAVE TIP: *In small mixing bowl, melt glaze ingredients at 50% (Medium) 2 to 4 minutes, stirring after every minute. Continue as directed.*

GREEK AMARETTO COOKIES

- 2 tablespoons (25 mL) honey
- 3½ teaspoons (17 mL) amaretto, divided
- 1 jar (6 oz./170 g) red maraschino cherries, drained (reserve juice)
- 1 jar (6 oz./170 g) green maraschino cherries, drained
- ¾ cup (175 mL) chopped pecans

- 2 tablespoons (25 mL) strawberry jelly
- 2 cups (500 mL) all-purpose flour
- ¼ teaspoon (1 mL) salt
- ¾ cup (175 mL) butter or margarine, chilled, cut into small pieces
- 5 to 6 tablespoons (75 to 90 mL) ice water

2 dozen cookies

1 Heat oven to 400°F/200°C. Lightly grease cookie sheets. Set aside. In 1-cup (250 mL) measure, combine honey and 2 teaspoons (10 mL) amaretto. Set glaze aside.

2 Cut 12 red and 12 green cherries in half. Set aside. Chop remaining cherries. In medium mixing bowl, combine remaining 1½ teaspoons (7 mL) amaretto, the chopped cherries, reserved red cherry juice, pecans and jelly. Set cherry mixture aside.

3 In large mixing bowl, combine flour and salt. Using pastry blender, cut in butter until mixture resembles coarse crumbs. Sprinkle with water, 1 tablespoon (15 mL) at a time, mixing with fork until particles are moistened and cling together. Form dough into ball. Divide dough in half. Wrap half of dough in plastic wrap. Chill.

4 On lightly floured surface, roll remaining dough to ⅛" (3 mm) thickness. Using 3" (8 cm) round cookie cutter, cut circles into dough.

5 Place heaping measuring teaspoon (5 mL) cherry mixture onto center of each circle. Overlap two opposite sides to form cylinders. Brush edges with water. Press edges to seal.

6 Place cylinders 2" (5 cm) apart on prepared cookie sheets. Repeat with remaining dough and cherry mixture. Insert 1 red and 1 green cherry half into opposite ends of each cylinder. Bake for 17 to 19 minutes, or until light golden brown. Immediately brush half of honey glaze over top and sides of cookies. Cool completely. Brush remaining glaze over cookies. Let dry completely before storing.

231

RUM BALLS

- 2 cups (500 mL) finely crushed vanilla wafers
- 1 cup (250 mL) granulated sugar
- ½ cup (125 mL) finely chopped walnuts
- ⅓ cup (75 mL) butter or margarine, melted
- ¼ cup (50 mL) light rum
- Powdered sugar

2½ dozen cookies

1 Line airtight container with wax paper. Set aside. In large mixing bowl, combine wafers, granulated sugar and walnuts. Add butter and rum. Stir until well blended (mixture will be crumbly).

2 Shape mixture into 1" (2.5 cm) balls. Roll balls in powdered sugar. Place on ungreased cookie sheets. Let stand 1 hour. Reroll balls in powdered sugar before placing in prepared container. Store in refrigerator.

TIP: *Flavor of rum balls improves after a few weeks' storage.*

CHOCOLATE SNOWBALLS

- 2½ cups (625 mL) all-purpose flour
- ½ cup (125 mL) unsweetened cocoa
- 2 teaspoons (10 mL) baking powder
- Pinch salt
- 3 cups (750 mL) sugar, divided
- 4 eggs
- ½ cup (125 mL) vegetable shortening
- 4 teaspoons (20 mL) vanilla, divided
- Granulated sugar
- 5 to 6 cups (1.25 to 1.5 L) flaked coconut
- 3 or 4 drops red food coloring
- 3 envelopes (.25 oz./7 g each) unflavored gelatin
- ⅔ cup (150 mL) ice water
- 1⅓ cups (325 mL) light corn syrup

8 dozen cookies

1 In medium mixing bowl, combine flour, cocoa, baking powder and salt. Set aside. In large mixing bowl, combine 2 cups (500 mL) sugar, the eggs, shortening and 2 teaspoons (10 mL) vanilla. Beat at medium speed of electric mixer until creamy. Add flour mixture. Beat at low speed until soft dough forms. Cover with plastic wrap. Chill 1 to 2 hours, or until firm.

2 Heat oven to 350°F/180°C. Lightly grease cookie sheets. Set aside. Shape dough into ½" (1 cm) balls. Place balls 2" (5 cm) apart on prepared cookie sheets. Flatten balls to 2"-diameter (5 cm) circles with bottom of drinking glass, dipping glass in granulated sugar to prevent sticking. Bake for 12 to 15 minutes, or until set. Cool completely.

3 Place coconut and food coloring in 1-gallon (4 L) sealable freezer bag. Shake to coat. Set aside. In top of double boiler, combine gelatin and ice water. Stir until gelatin is dissolved. Add remaining 1 cup (250 mL) sugar. In bottom of double boiler, bring additional water to boil. Place top of double boiler over boiling water. Cook gelatin mixture over medium heat until sugar is dissolved, stirring occasionally. Remove from heat.

4 In large mixing bowl, combine gelatin mixture, corn syrup and remaining 2 teaspoons (10 mL) vanilla. Beat at high speed of electric mixer for 15 minutes, or until topping is light and fluffy. Spoon about 1 tablespoon (15 mL) topping onto back of each cookie. Sprinkle topping with colored coconut. Let dry completely before storing.

TIP: *Chocolate cookie can be made in advance and frozen in airtight container.*

APRICOT-DATE BALLS (top)

- ¾ cup (175 mL) sugar
- ½ cup (125 mL) chopped dried apricots
- ½ cup (125 mL) chopped dates
- 2 eggs, beaten
- 1 cup (250 mL) finely chopped walnuts
- 1 teaspoon (5 mL) vanilla
- Granulated sugar

4 dozen cookies

1 Line airtight container with wax paper. Set aside. In 2-quart (2 L) saucepan, combine ¾ cup (175 mL) sugar, the apricots, dates and eggs. Cook over low heat for 6 to 8 minutes, or until mixture pulls away from side of pan, stirring constantly.

2 Remove from heat. Stir in walnuts and vanilla. Let stand for 45 to 50 minutes, or until mixture is cool enough to handle.

3 Shape mixture into 1" (2.5 cm) balls. Roll balls in sugar. Place balls in prepared container. Store in refrigerator.

SPICY GREEK JEWELS (bottom)

- 2 cups (500 mL) powdered sugar
- 1 cup (250 mL) butter or margarine, softened
- 1 egg
- 2½ cups (625 mL) all-purpose flour
- 1½ cups (375 mL) ground almonds
- 1½ teaspoons (7 mL) apple pie spice
- ¼ teaspoon (1 mL) salt
- Powdered sugar
- 24 red candied cherries, halved
- 12 green candied pineapple chunks, each cut into 8 pieces

4 dozen cookies

1 Heat oven to 350°F/180°C. In large mixing bowl, combine 2 cups (500 mL) powdered sugar, the butter and egg. Beat at medium speed of electric mixer until light and fluffy. Add flour, almonds, apple pie spice and salt. Beat at low speed until soft dough forms.

2 Shape dough into 1" (2.5 cm) balls. Place balls 2" (5 cm) apart on ungreased cookie sheets. Flatten to ¼" (5 mm) thickness with bottom of drinking glass, dipping glass in powdered sugar to prevent sticking.

3 Decorate each cookie with 1 cherry half and 2 pineapple pieces, pressing fruit lightly into dough. Bake for 12 to 14 minutes, or until edges are golden brown. Cool completely before storing.

MEXICAN BISCOCHITAS

- 3 cups (750 mL) all-purpose flour
- 1½ teaspoons (7 mL) baking powder
- ¼ teaspoon (1 mL) salt
- 1 cup (250 mL) sugar, divided
- 1 cup (250 mL) vegetable shortening
- 1 egg
- 1 tablespoon (15 mL) anise seed
- ¼ cup (50 mL) brandy
- 1 teaspoon (5 mL) ground cinnamon

About 4 dozen cookies

1 Heat oven to 350°F/180°C. In medium mixing bowl, combine flour, baking powder and salt. Set aside. In large mixing bowl, combine ¾ cup (175 mL) sugar, the shortening, egg and anise seed. Beat at medium speed of electric mixer until light and fluffy. Gradually add flour mixture, alternating with brandy, beating at low speed until soft dough forms.

2 On lightly floured surface, roll dough to ¼" to ½" (5 mm to 1 cm) thickness. Using 2½" (6 cm) flower-shaped or round cookie cutter, cut shapes into dough. Place shapes 2" (5 cm) apart on ungreased cookie sheets. Set aside.

3 In small bowl, combine remaining ¼ cup (50 mL) sugar and the cinnamon. Sprinkle shapes evenly with sugar mixture. Bake for 9 to 11 minutes, or until light golden brown. Cool completely before storing.

FRENCH LACE COOKIE CUPS

- 1 cup (250 mL) all-purpose flour
- 1 cup (250 mL) finely chopped almonds
- ½ cup (125 mL) packed brown sugar

- ½ cup (125 mL) butter or margarine
- ⅓ cup (75 mL) light corn syrup
- ½ teaspoon (2 mL) almond extract

4 dozen cookies

1 Heat oven to 350°F/180°C. Lightly grease cookie sheets and outsides of 4 inverted 6-oz. (175 mL) custard cups. Set aside. In medium mixing bowl, combine flour and almonds. Set aside.

2 In 1-quart (1 L) saucepan, combine sugar, butter and corn syrup. Bring to boil over medium heat, stirring constantly. Remove from heat. Gradually stir in flour mixture. Stir in extract.

3 Drop batter by measuring tablespoons (15 mL) onto prepared cookie sheets, spreading batter into 4" (10 cm) circles (4 circles per sheet). Bake for 5 to 6 minutes, or until edges are golden brown. Let cool 1 minute before removing from cookie sheets.

4 Place cookies over inverted custard cups, molding around cups and pinching edges to shape. Let cookie cups cool before removing from custard cups. To serve, fill cookie cups with cut-up fruit or ice cream.

GREEK HOLIDAY COOKIES

- 1 cup (250 mL) butter or margarine, softened
- ½ cup (125 mL) granulated sugar
- 1 egg
- ½ teaspoon (2 mL) vanilla
- ½ teaspoon (2 mL) brandy extract
- 2½ cups (625 mL) all-purpose flour
- 1 teaspoon (5 mL) baking powder
- ¼ teaspoon (1 mL) ground cloves
- ¼ teaspoon (1 mL) salt
- Whole cloves
- Powdered sugar

4½ dozen cookies

1 Heat oven to 350°F/180°C. In large mixing bowl, combine butter, granulated sugar, egg, vanilla and brandy extract. Beat at medium speed of electric mixer until light and fluffy. Add flour, baking powder, ground cloves and salt. Beat at low speed until soft dough forms.

2 Shape heaping teaspoons dough into crescent or S shapes. Place shapes 2" (5 cm) apart on ungreased cookie sheets. Press 2 whole cloves into each shape.

3 Bake for 9 to 11 minutes, or until set. Let cool 1 minute before removing from cookie sheets. Sprinkle cookies with powdered sugar. Cool completely before storing. Remove whole cloves before eating.

TIP: *Flavor of cookies improves after a few days' storage.*

CHOCOLATE-DIPPED PALMIERS

- 1 pkg. (1 lb./454 g) frozen puff pastry dough, defrosted, divided
- ½ cup (125 mL) sugar
- 2 cups (500 mL) semisweet chocolate chips
- 3 teaspoons (15 mL) vegetable shortening, divided
- 1½ cups (375 mL) vanilla baking chips

6 dozen cookies

1 Heat oven to 375°F/190°C. Lightly grease cookie sheets. Set aside. On lightly sugared surface, roll 1 sheet pastry into 12" x 10" (30 x 25 cm) rectangle.

2 Fold long sides of pastry toward center line, leaving ¼" (5 mm) gap in center.

3 Fold pastry in half lengthwise to form 12" x 2½" (30 x 6 cm) strip. Lightly press edges together to seal.

4 Cut dough crosswise into ¼" (5 mm) slices. Place slices 2" (5 cm) apart on prepared cookie sheets. Bake for 8 to 10 minutes, or until light golden brown, rotating cookie sheet after 5 minutes. Repeat with remaining pastry. Cool completely.

5 In 1-quart (1 L) saucepan, combine chocolate chips and 2 teaspoons (10 mL) shortening. Melt over low heat, stirring constantly. Repeat with vanilla chips and remaining 1 teaspoon (5 mL) shortening. Dip one end of each palmier in melted chocolate. Let dry on cooling rack. Dip again in melted vanilla chips. Let dry completely before storing.

THREE-CORNERED HATS

- 1½ cups (375 mL) butter or margarine, softened
- ½ cup (125 mL) sugar
- 1 egg
- ¼ cup (50 mL) evaporated milk
- ½ teaspoon (2 mL) vanilla
- 2¾ cups (675 mL) all-purpose flour, divided

Filling:

- 1 pkg. (12 oz./341 g) pitted dried prunes
- ½ cup (125 mL) finely chopped walnuts
- 2 tablespoons (25 mL) sugar
- 1 to 2 teaspoons (5 to 10 mL) grated orange peel
- 1 egg yolk beaten with 1 tablespoon (15 mL) water

About 3 dozen cookies

1 In large mixing bowl, combine butter, ½ cup (125 mL) sugar and the egg. Beat at medium speed of electric mixer until light and fluffy. Add milk and vanilla. Beat at medium speed until well blended. Add 1¾ cups (425 mL) flour. Beat at low speed until soft dough forms. Stir in remaining 1 cup (250 mL) flour to form stiff dough. Cover with plastic wrap. Chill 30 minutes to 1 hour, or until firm.

2 In food processor or blender, process prunes until smooth. In medium mixing bowl, combine processed prunes and remaining filling ingredients. Set aside.

3 Heat oven to 350°F/180°C. Lightly grease cookie sheets. Set aside. On lightly floured surface, roll dough to ⅛" to ¼" (3 to 5 mm) thickness. Using 3" (8 cm) round cookie cutter, cut circles into dough. Place circles 2" (5 cm) apart on prepared cookie sheets.

4 Place heaping measuring teaspoon (5 mL) filling onto center of each circle. Lightly brush edges with water. Bring sides of dough up and pinch together to form triangle, leaving top of triangle open to show filling. Lightly brush top and sides of dough with egg yolk mixture. Bake for 14 to 16 minutes, or until set. Cool completely before storing.

GERMAN PFEFFERNÜSSE

- 1 cup (250 mL) granulated sugar
- ¾ cup (175 mL) butter or margarine, softened
- 1 cup (250 mL) dark corn syrup
- 3 tablespoons (50 mL) hot water
- 2 teaspoons (10 mL) anise seed
- 1 teaspoon (5 mL) black pepper
- 1 teaspoon (5 mL) baking soda
- ¼ teaspoon (1 mL) ground allspice
- ¼ teaspoon (1 mL) ground cardamom
- ¼ teaspoon (1 mL) ground cloves
- ¼ teaspoon (1 mL) salt
- 4 to 5 cups (1 to 1.25 L) all-purpose flour, divided
- Powdered sugar

About 9 dozen cookies

1 In large mixing bowl, combine granulated sugar and butter. Beat at medium speed of electric mixer until light and fluffy. Add corn syrup, water, anise, pepper, baking soda, allspice, cardamom, cloves and salt. Beat at low speed until well blended.

2 Gradually add 4 cups (1 L) flour, beating at low speed. Stir or knead in enough of remaining 1 cup (250 mL) flour to form stiff dough. Cover with plastic wrap. Chill 3 to 4 hours, or until firm.

3 Heat oven to 350°F/180°C. Divide dough into 8 pieces. Roll each piece into ½" to ¾"-thick (1 to 2 cm) rope. Cut ropes diagonally into 1" to 1½" (2.5 to 4 cm) lengths. Place the lengths 2" (5 cm) apart on ungreased cookie sheets. Bake for 10 to 15 minutes, or until golden brown. Cool completely. Roll in powdered sugar before storing.

241

DECORATING WITH FROSTING

The quickest and easiest way to decorate cookies is with frosting. Here is a recipe for a basic decorator frosting that can be used for spreading or piping on cookies.

DECORATOR FROSTING

- ½ cup (125 mL) butter or margarine, softened
- ½ cup (125 mL) vegetable shortening
- 1 teaspoon (5 mL) vanilla
- 4 cups (1 L) powered sugar
- 3 to 4 tablespoons (50 mL) milk
- Food coloring (optional)

3 cups (750 mL)

In large mixing bowl, combine butter, shortening and vanilla. Beat at medium speed of electric mixer until creamy. Add sugar, 1 cup (250 mL) at a time, beating at low speed until well blended. Add milk. Beat at medium speed until light and fluffy. Beat in food coloring, 1 drop at a time, until frosting is desired color.

TIP: *One-half teaspoon (2 mL) almond extract, mint extract or other flavored extract can be substituted for vanilla.*

Dip corner or part of cookie in slightly thinned frosting. If desired, sprinkle with chopped nuts, coconut or other decorative topping (see page 246). Cookies can also be dipped in melted chocolate or vanilla chips, or in melted candy coating.

Place stencil over freshly frosted cookie, and lightly dust with sifted powdered sugar.

Pull fork tines through lines of frosting to create a marbled look.

242

Drizzle thinned frosting over the cookies with a spoon.

Use a small frosting spatula or table knife to spread frosting evenly on cookies. (Do not spread frosting too thick.) Frost cookies that are completely cooled, so the frosting does not melt. Also, warm cookies are more fragile and might break during the handling that is required.

Paint thinned frosting on cookies for a detailed look, or use a paintbrush to make designs and textures in frosting.

Thin frosting by beating in milk, 1 tablespoon (15 mL) at a time (for small amounts, ½ teaspoon/2 mL at a time), until desired consistency.

243

DECORATING WITH A PASTRY BAG

Use a pastry bag to pipe frosting on cookies. These bags are available at specialty kitchen stores and some supermarkets. Inexpensive metal or plastic decorating tips are also available at these stores. A coupler allows you to change decorating tips without emptying the pastry bag.

Pictured are six of the more common decorating tips.

#2 Writing tip

#5 Writing tip

#67 Leaf tip

#13 Open star tip

#27 Closed star tip

#18 Open star tip

HOW TO USE A PASTRY BAG

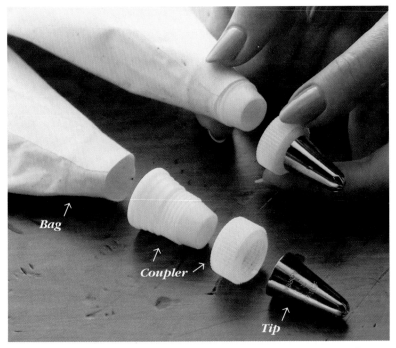

1 Place large part of coupler in bag, making sure bag fits snugly around coupler. Place tip through small part of coupler, then screw both halves of coupler together.

2 Scoop frosting into rolled-down pastry bag until bag is about two-thirds full. (Roll up bag while filling.)

HOW TO MAKE A PASTRY BAG

3 Twist or roll down the top of the bag to keep steady pressure on the frosting as you squeeze. Before decorating, hold the bag closed and squeeze out a small amount of frosting to eliminate air bubbles in the bag.

Fill a heavy, resealable food-storage bag half full of frosting; seal the bag. Snip off the tip (arrow) of one corner to create a writing tip that produces a line. Start with a small hole, and enlarge it, if necessary. A coupler and decorating tips can also be used with food-storage bags.

DECORATIVE TOPPINGS

Decorative toppings can be sprinkled over or pressed on frostings, as shown below. Add toppings to cookies before frosting dries, so toppings will stay in place. Or put toppings on cookies before baking, and leave the cookies unfrosted. Toppings like dried fruit, candies or nuts can sometimes be pressed into cookies fresh from the oven.

Colored sugar is tinted granulated sugar and is available in several colors and granule sizes.

Decorating or coarse sugar has granules about four times larger than those of regular granulated sugar. Dragées are tiny, round hard candies that come in sizes ranging from pinhead to ¼" (5 mm). Shot, confetti and sprinkles are commonly available decorative toppings.

Candies, dried fruit, nuts, miniature chocolate chips, licorice, coconut and grated citrus peel can also be used as cookie toppings.

Gumdrops

Cinnamon candies

Dragées

Whole nuts

Candied fruits

Shot

Chopped nuts

Miniature chips

Candy-coated chocolate pieces

Licorice

Confetti

Jelly beans

Colored sugar

Grated citrus peel

Sprinkles

Coarse sugar

Shredded coconut

MORE
DECORATING
IDEAS

Here are some additional ideas for decorating home-baked cookies or cookies you buy at the store:

Cut *dried fruit, gumdrops and licorice strings to make designs, eyes, hats, etc.*

Place *a small amount of fairly stiff frosting or a gumdrop in a garlic press. Carefully press out strands for "hair" or a textured look.*

Smooth *thin frosting base on cookies. Let it dry, then pipe outline or design on top. Decorative toppings can be added to complete the design.*

HOW TO TINT COCONUT

Color *coconut by placing it in a large, resealable food-storage bag. Add a few drops of food color to get the desired color.*

Seal *the bag and shake until coconut is uniform in color. Spread coconut on wax paper and let stand for a few minutes before using.*

Desserts
& Sweets

PLUM PUDDING

- 2 cups (500 mL) soft bread cubes (about 3 slices, trimmed)
- ½ cup (125 mL) all-purpose flour
- ½ cup (125 mL) currants
- ½ cup (125 mL) raisins
- 2 tablespoons (25 mL) packed dark brown sugar
- ½ teaspoon (2 mL) baking soda
- ½ teaspoon (2 mL) ground cinnamon
- ¼ teaspoon (1 mL) ground nutmeg
- ¼ teaspoon (1 mL) salt
- ¼ cup (50 mL) butter or margarine
- ½ cup (125 mL) half-and-half
- 2 tablespoons (25 mL) sherry
- 1½ tablespoons (20 mL) molasses
- 1 egg
- 2 tablespoons (25 mL) brandy

4 to 6 servings

1 Grease 2-cup (500 mL) measure. Cut two 1½"-wide (4 cm) strips of wax paper long enough to cover bottom and sides of measure, with 1" (2.5 cm) of overhang on each side. Overlap strips in base of measure. Set aside.

2 Combine all ingredients except brandy in medium bowl. Beat at medium speed of electric mixer, until well blended, scraping bowl frequently. Pour batter into prepared measure. Cover with plastic wrap. Place in oven on inverted saucer.

3 Microwave at 50% (Medium) 8 to 12 minutes, or until no uncooked batter appears through sides and cake feels springy to the touch, rotating every 2 minutes. Let stand, covered, 5 minutes. Remove plastic wrap. Loosen edges with small spatula. Invert measure, pulling wax-paper strips to remove pudding to serving plate. To serve, place brandy in small bowl. Microwave at High about 20 seconds, or until heated. Pour into large spoon or ladle; ignite and spoon flaming brandy over pudding.

HOLIDAY FRUITCAKE

Homemade fruitcake needn't take days or weeks to make. This recipe is uncomplicated and produces a fruitcake that's sure to become a family tradition.

- 1 cup (250 mL) chopped dried apricots
- 1 cup (250 mL) chopped dried figs or raisins
- ¾ cup (175 mL) brandy
- 1 cup (250 mL) unbleached white flour
- 1 cup (250 mL) granulated sugar
- 1 teaspoon (5 mL) salt
- ½ teaspoon (2 mL) baking powder
- 2 eggs plus 2 egg whites, slightly beaten (or ¾ cup/175 mL liquid egg substitute)

- ½ cup (125 mL) frozen orange juice concentrate, defrosted
- 1 10-oz. (284 mL) jar maraschino cherries, drained and patted dry
- 1 cup (250 mL) chopped pecans
- 1 cup (250 mL) chopped walnuts

Glaze:

- ½ cup (125 mL) powdered sugar
- 2 teaspoons (10 mL) frozen orange juice concentrate, defrosted
- 1 teaspoon (5 mL) water

TIPS:

If desired, omit brandy in step 1.

Use scissors to cut up dried fruit.

For easy cleanup, place wax paper under cooling rack before drizzling glaze over cake.

15 servings

1 Place apricots and figs or raisins in a small bowl. Cover with plastic wrap. Let stand overnight at room temperature. Drain. Set aside.

2 Preheat oven to 300°F/150°C. In a large mixing bowl, combine flour, granulated sugar, salt and baking powder. Stir in eggs or egg substitute and ½ cup (125 mL) orange juice concentrate. Stir in cherries, pecans, walnuts, apricots and figs or raisins. Mix well. Pour batter into a 9" x 5" (2 L) loaf pan that has been sprayed with vegetable cooking spray.

3 Bake fruitcake for 2 hours. Cover cake with foil. Bake for 15 minutes more, or until toothpick inserted in center comes out clean. Let cake cool 15 minutes before removing from pan. Remove cake from pan and place on wire rack to cool.

4 Meanwhile, combine glaze ingredients in a small bowl. Drizzle glaze over cake while cake is still hot. Cool completely. Wrap cooled cake in plastic wrap, then in foil. Store in refrigerator.

BRANDIED APRICOT TORTE

- 1 pkg. (10¾ oz./298 g) frozen loaf pound cake
- 1 cup (250 mL) apricot preserves
- 2 tablespoons (25 mL) brandy or homemade Apricot Brandy, page 201, divided
- 2 tablespoons (25 mL) butter or margarine
- 1 tablespoon (15 mL) light corn syrup
- 2 squares (1 oz./30 g each) semisweet baking chocolate

6 servings

1 Trim crust, top and sides from the pound cake. Cut lengthwise into thirds. Set aside. Place the preserves in 2-cup (500 mL) measure. Microwave at High 1½ to 2 minutes, or until hot and bubbly. Press through wire strainer into small bowl. Discard pulp. Add 1 tablespoon (15 mL) brandy to strained liquid. Set aside.

2 To assemble cake, place bottom layer on wire rack. Spread with 2 tablespoons (25 mL) strained preserves. Add second layer and spread with 2 tablespoons (25 mL) strained preserves. Add top layer. Spread top and sides with remaining preserves. Refrigerate about 1 hour.

3 To prepare chocolate frosting, place butter, remaining 1 tablespoon (15 mL) brandy and the corn syrup in 2-cup (500 mL) measure. Microwave at High 1½ to 2 minutes, or until butter melts and mixture just comes to a boil. Add chocolate, stirring to melt. Cool until warm. Spread top and sides of cake with frosting. Refrigerate about 30 minutes, or until frosting is firm. Transfer to serving plate.

EASY GERMAN CHOCOLATE CAKE

- ½ cup (125 mL) butter or margarine, divided
- ⅔ cup (150 mL) packed brown sugar, divided
- ⅔ cup (150 mL) flaked coconut, divided
- ⅔ cup (150 mL) finely chopped pecans, divided
- 1½ cups (375 mL) all-purpose flour
- 1⅓ cups (325 mL) granulated sugar
- ¼ cup (50 mL) cocoa
- 1½ teaspoons (7 mL) baking powder
- 1 teaspoon (5 mL) salt
- 1 cup (250 mL) milk
- ⅔ cup (150 mL) shortening
- 3 eggs
- 1 teaspoon (5 mL) vanilla

One 2-layer cake

1 Cut wax paper to fit bottoms of two 9" (2.5 L) round cake dishes. Place ¼ cup (50 mL) butter in each lined dish. Microwave, one dish at a time, at High 45 seconds to 1¼ minutes, or until butter is melted and bubbly. Mix ⅓ cup (75 mL) brown sugar, ⅓ cup (75 mL) coconut and ⅓ cup (75 mL) pecans into butter in each dish. Spread into an even layer. Set dishes aside.

2 Place remaining ingredients in large bowl. Blend at low speed of electric mixer, scraping the bowl constantly. Beat 2 minutes at medium speed, scraping bowl occasionally. Divide and spread the batter into cake dishes.

3 Place one dish on inverted saucer in microwave oven. Reduce power to 50% (Medium). Microwave 6 minutes, rotating ½ turn after half the time. Increase power to High. Microwave 2 to 4 minutes, or until cake is light and springy to the touch, rotating dish once. Sides will just begin to pull away from dish. Let stand directly on counter 5 minutes. Invert onto serving plate. Remove wax paper. Spread any topping from wax paper onto cake top. Repeat with remaining cake. Invert onto wire rack. Cool. Place second layer on top of first layer with frosting side up.

253

CARAMEL APPLE-TOPPED SPICE CAKE

- 3 tablespoons (50 mL) butter or margarine
- ¼ cup (50 mL) packed dark brown sugar
- 1 medium cooking apple
- 1 cup (250 mL) all-purpose flour
- ⅔ cup (150 mL) granulated sugar
- ¾ teaspoon (4 mL) ground cinnamon
- ½ teaspoon (2 mL) baking soda
- ½ teaspoon (2 mL) salt
- Pinch ground nutmeg
- ⅓ cup (75 mL) shortening
- ⅓ cup (75 mL) buttermilk
- 2 eggs
- ½ teaspoon (2 mL) vanilla

One 9" (23 cm) cake

1 Cut wax paper to fit bottom of 9" (2.5 L) round cake dish. Place butter in 2-cup (500 mL) measure. Microwave at High 30 to 45 seconds, or until melted. Stir in brown sugar. Microwave at High 30 seconds, or until boiling. Stir with fork until smooth. Spread evenly in wax-paper-lined dish.

2 Core and peel apple. Slice thinly. Arrange five slices in center of dish over caramel mixture. Arrange remaining slices around edge of dish, overlapping if necessary. Set aside.

3 Combine remaining ingredients in large bowl. Blend at low speed of electric mixer, scraping bowl constantly. Beat 2 minutes at medium speed, scraping bowl occasionally. Spread batter over apple slices. Place dish on inverted saucer in microwave oven.

4 Reduce power to 50% (Medium). Microwave 6 minutes, rotating ½ turn after half the time. Increase power to High. Microwave 2½ to 5½ minutes, or until cake is light and springy to the touch, rotating dish once. Let stand directly on counter 5 minutes. Invert onto serving plate.

BAKED APPLES

- 4 Rome or other firm red cooking apples
- ½ cup (125 mL) golden raisins
- ¼ cup (50 mL) chopped pecans or walnuts
- ¼ cup (50 mL) light brown sugar
- 2 tablespoons (25 mL) lemon juice
- 1 teaspoon (5 mL) ground cinnamon
- ¼ teaspoon (1 mL) ground ginger
- ¼ teaspoon (1 mL) ground nutmeg
- Plain or vanilla low-fat or nonfat yogurt (optional)

4 servings

1 Preheat oven to 350°F/180°C. With corer or paring knife, remove 1" (2.5 cm) diameter core from each apple without cutting through the bottom. Pare 1½" (4 cm) strip of peel around top of each apple.

2 In small bowl, combine raisins, pecans or walnuts, sugar, lemon juice, cinnamon, ginger and nutmeg. Spoon mixture evenly into apples.

3 Place apples in 8" (2 L) square baking pan. Fill pan halfway with water. Bake apples about 1 hour or until soft. Remove apples from pan with slotted spoon, and cool slightly. Serve with yogurt, if desired.

TIP: *If filling at top of apple begins to burn while baking, cover it loosely with a small piece of foil.*

CHERRY CHEESE ROLL

- 1 cup (250 mL) ricotta cheese
- 1 egg
- 2 tablespoons (25 mL) powdered sugar
- ¼ teaspoon (1 mL) almond extract
- ¼ cup (50 mL) sliced almonds
- 1 round sheet lefse or large crepe (about 12"/30 cm)
- 1 cup (250 mL) cherry pie filling
- Sliced almonds (optional)

4 servings

1 In small mixing bowl, blend ricotta cheese, egg, powdered sugar and almond extract. Stir in almonds. Spread mixture evenly down center of lefse.

2 Fold in opposite sides of lefse to enclose filling. Place roll on 12" (30 cm) platter.

3 Microwave at 50% (Medium) 7 to 11 minutes, or until center of roll is hot, rotating platter once or twice. Top with pie filling. Microwave at High 1 to 2½ minutes, or until pie filling is hot. Top cheese roll with sliced almonds.

GINGERBREAD

- 2¼ cups (550 mL) all-purpose flour
- ¼ cup (50 mL) unsweetened cocoa
- 1 teaspoon (5 mL) baking powder
- 1 teaspoon (5 mL) baking soda
- 1 teaspoon (5 mL) ground cinnamon

- ½ teaspoon (2 mL) ground ginger
- ¼ teaspoon (1 mL) ground nutmeg
- ¼ teaspoon (1 mL) ground cloves
- ¼ teaspoon (1 mL) salt
- 1 cup (250 mL) packed brown sugar
- ¼ cup (50 mL) margarine, softened

- ¼ cup (50 mL) unsweetened applesauce
- 1 cup (250 mL) skim milk
- ½ cup (125 mL) molasses
- ¼ cup (50 mL) frozen cholesterol-free egg product, defrosted, or 1 egg
- Powdered sugar

9 servings

1 Heat oven to 350°F/180°C. Spray 9" (2.5 L) square baking pan with non-stick vegetable cooking spray. Set aside. In medium mixing bowl, combine flour, cocoa, baking powder, baking soda, cinnamon, ginger, nutmeg, cloves and salt. Set aside.

2 Combine brown sugar, margarine and applesauce in large mixing bowl. Beat at medium speed of electric mixer until creamy. Add milk, molasses and egg product. Beat at medium speed until well blended. Gradually beat in flour mixture at low speed until well blended. Beat at medium speed for additional 4 minutes.

3 Pour mixture into prepared pan. Bake for 50 to 55 minutes, or until wooden pick inserted in center comes out clean. Before serving, lightly dust top of gingerbread with powdered sugar.

APPLE BRUNCH MUFFINS

- 6 tablespoons (75 mL) apricot preserves
- 3 plain or sourdough English muffins, split
- 1 medium red cooking apple, cored and thinly sliced (1 cup/250 mL)
- 1 tablespoon (15 mL) frozen orange juice concentrate, defrosted
- 1 tablespoon (15 mL) sugar
- ½ teaspoon (2 mL) apple pie spice

1 Heat oven to 350°F/180°C. Spray baking sheet with nonstick vegetable cooking spray. Set aside.

2 Spread preserves evenly on muffin halves. Top evenly with apple slices. Brush slices with concentrate.

3 Combine sugar and apple pie spice in small bowl. Sprinkle mixture evenly over apples. Arrange muffin halves on prepared baking sheet. Bake for 15 to 18 minutes, or until apples are tender.

6 servings

PUMPKIN PIE BREAD

- 1¼ cups (300 mL) all-purpose flour
- 2 teaspoons (10 mL) pumpkin pie spice
- 1 teaspoon (5 mL) baking powder
- ½ teaspoon (2 mL) baking soda
- ½ teaspoon (2 mL) salt

- 1⅓ cups (325 mL) sugar
- 1 cup (250 mL) canned pumpkin
- ⅓ cup (75 mL) fresh orange juice
- ⅓ cup (75 mL) processed prunes*
- ¼ cup (50 mL) frozen cholesterol-free egg product, defrosted, or 1 egg

- 2 tablespoons (25 mL) vegetable oil
- ½ teaspoon (2 mL) vanilla

16 servings

Process whole pitted prunes in food processor or blender until smooth. Approximately ½ cup (125 mL) whole prunes equals ⅓ cup (75 mL) processed prunes.

1 Heat oven to 350°F/ 180°C. Spray 9" x 5" (2 L) loaf pan with nonstick vegetable cooking spray. Set aside.

2 Combine flour, pumpkin pie spice, baking powder, baking soda and salt in large mixing bowl. Set aside. In medium mixing bowl, combine sugar, pumpkin, juice, prunes, egg product, oil and vanilla. Beat at medium speed of electric mixer until well blended. Add pumpkin mixture to flour mixture. Stir just until dry ingredients are moistened. Pour mixture into prepared pan.

3 Bake for 50 minutes to 1 hour, or until wooden pick inserted in center comes out clean. Let stand 10 minutes. Remove loaf from pan. Cool completely on wire rack before slicing.

↑ CHOCOLATE-COVERED CHERRIES

- ¼ cup (50 mL) butter or margarine
- 2 cups (500 mL) powdered sugar
- ¼ cup (50 mL) sweetened condensed milk
- 36 maraschino cherries
- 1 lb. (500 g) chocolate-flavored candy coating, broken into squares
- 1 tablespoon (15 mL) shortening

    3 dozen cherries

1 Place butter in medium mixing bowl. Microwave at 30% (Medium Low) 15 to 45 seconds, or until softened, checking after every 15 seconds. Add powdered sugar. Mix well. Blend in condensed milk. (Mixture will be stiff.)

2 Cover each cherry with about 1 teaspoon (5 mL) sugar mixture. (For easy handling, coat hands with powdered sugar.) Place cherries on wax-paper-lined baking sheet. Chill cherries 30 minutes.

3 Combine chocolate and shortening in 1-quart (1 L) casserole. Microwave at 50% (Medium) 5 to 8 minutes, or until the mixture can be stirred smooth, stirring once or twice.

4 Dip coated cherries in chocolate using two forks. Place on prepared baking sheet and chill until set. (If necessary, microwave chocolate at 50% [Medium] 1 to 3 minutes, or until remelted.)

5 Redip cherries in chocolate. Let cherries cool until chocolate sets. Cover loosely with wax paper. Set aside in cool place 2 to 3 days to allow centers to soften.

↑ CHOCOLATE APRICOT CHEWS

- 1 pkg. (3 oz./85 g) cream cheese
- 1 tablespoon (15 mL) powdered sugar
- ¼ teaspoon (1 mL) vanilla
- 1 pkg. (6 oz./175 g) dried apricot halves
- 1 pkg. (6 oz./175 g) semisweet chocolate chips
- 1 tablespoon (15 mL) shortening

About 15 candies

1 In small bowl, microwave cream cheese at High 15 to 30 seconds, or until softened. Add powdered sugar and vanilla. Mix well. Place small amount of cream cheese mixture between two apricot halves. Press halves together lightly. Repeat with remaining apricot halves and cream cheese mixture. Arrange stuffed apricots on plate. Chill 15 minutes, or until cream cheese filling is firm. Line a baking sheet with wax paper and set aside.

2 In small mixing bowl, combine chocolate chips and shortening. Microwave at 50% (Medium) 3½ to 4½ minutes, or until chocolate is glossy and mixture can be stirred smooth, stirring once or twice. Using two forks, dip stuffed apricots into chocolate mixture, turning to coat completely. Or dip one half only. Arrange apricots on prepared baking sheet. Chill 15 to 20 minutes, or until chocolate is set. Serve chilled.

↑ CARAMEL PECAN CLUSTERS

Remove wrappers from 12 caramels. Set aside. Line a baking sheet with wax paper and set aside. In small mixing bowl, combine ¼ lb. (125 g) chocolate-flavored candy coating and 1 teaspoon (5 mL) shortening. Microwave until mixture melts. Stir in 2 tablespoons (25 mL) finely chopped pecans. With spoon, dip each caramel into chocolate mixture to coat. Drop dipped caramels onto prepared baking sheet. Let clusters cool until set. Store in airtight container or plastic food-storage bag.

12 clusters

CHOCOLATE CHEWS

- 2 squares (1 oz./30 g each) unsweetened chocolate
- 2 tablespoons (25 mL) butter or margarine
- ⅓ cup (75 mL) light corn syrup
- ½ teaspoon (2 mL) vanilla
- 2 cups (500 mL) powdered sugar, divided
- ½ cup (125 mL) nonfat dry milk powder

1¼ lbs./625 g

1 In medium mixing bowl, combine chocolate and butter. Microwave at 50% (Medium) 3 to 4½ minutes, or until chocolate is glossy and mixture can be stirred smooth, stirring once or twice. Blend in corn syrup and vanilla. Microwave at High 1 minute.

2 Mix in 1¾ cups (425 mL) powdered sugar and the dry milk powder. Spread remaining ¼ cup (50 mL) powdered sugar on wooden board. Turn chocolate out onto sugared board and knead until extra sugar is absorbed. Divide dough into 8 equal portions. Roll each portion into ½" (1 cm) diameter rope. Cut each piece into 1½" (4 cm) lengths. Let chocolate chews cool. Wrap each in wax paper.

CANDY PIZZA

- 1 recipe pizza base (below)
- 2 cups (500 mL) stir-ins (opposite)
- ½ to ¾ cup (125 to 175 mL) toppings (opposite)
- 1 recipe frosting (opposite)

1½ lbs. (750 g)

1 Line baking sheet with wax or parchment paper. Set aside. Microwave candy pizza base. Add combined choice of stir-ins. Mix well to coat.

2 Spread the base mixture evenly on the prepared baking sheet to 10" (25 cm) diameter. Sprinkle with combined choice of toppings. Set aside.

Microwave frosting.
Drizzle frosting over candy pizza. Chill at least 1½ hours, or until set. Peel off wax paper. Break candy apart, or serve in wedges.

Candy Pizza Base

Light Chocolate:
In medium mixing bowl, combine 1½ cups (375 mL) milk chocolate chips and 3 squares (1 oz./30 g each) semisweet chocolate. Microwave at 50% (Medium) 4 to 6 minutes, or until chocolate can be stirred smooth, stirring twice.

White Chocolate:
In medium mixing bowl, combine ¾ lb. (375 g) white candy coating (broken into squares) and 1 tablespoon (15 mL) shortening. Microwave at 50% (Medium) 2½ to 5½ minutes, or until mixture can be stirred smooth, stirring twice.

Peanut Butter:
In medium mixing bowl, combine 1½ cups (375 mL) peanut butter chips and 3 oz. (90 g) white candy coating. Microwave at 50% (Medium) 4 to 6 minutes, or until mixture can be stirred smooth, stirring twice.

Dark Chocolate:
In medium mixing bowl, combine 1½ cups (375 mL) semisweet chocolate chips and 3 squares (1 oz./30 g each) unsweetened chocolate. Microwave at 50% (Medium) 4 to 6 minutes, or until chocolate can be stirred smooth, stirring twice.

Mint Chocolate:
In medium mixing bowl, combine 1½ cups (375 mL) mint-flavored semisweet chocolate chips and 3 squares (1 oz./30 g each) semisweet chocolate. Microwave at 50% (Medium) 4 to 6 minutes, or until chocolate can be stirred smooth, stirring once or twice.

Butterscotch:
In medium mixing bowl, combine 1½ cups (375 mL) butterscotch chips and 3 oz. (90 g) white candy coating. Microwave at 50% (Medium) 4 to 6 minutes, or until mixture can be stirred smooth, stirring twice.

Candy Pizza Stir-ins

Use one or more of the following, to equal 2 cups (500 mL):

- Crisp rice cereal
- Toasted round oat cereal
- Corn flakes cereal
- Crisp square rice, wheat or corn cereal
- Coarsely crushed pretzel sticks
- Coarsely crushed shoestring potatoes
- Salted mixed nuts
- Chopped nuts
- Salted dry-roasted peanuts
- Whole or slivered almonds
- Miniature marshmallows

Candy Pizza Toppings

Use one or more of the following toppings, to equal ½ to ¾ cup (125 to 175 mL):

- Miniature jelly beans
- Jellied orange slices, cut up
- Candied fruit
- Candied cherries, cut up
- Maraschino cherries, drained
- Red or black licorice pieces
- Shredded coconut
- Candy-coated plain or peanut chocolate pieces
- Candy-coated peanut butter pieces
- Chocolate-covered raisins
- Candy corn

Candy Pizza Frosting

- ¼ lb. (125 g) white or chocolate-flavored candy coating
- 1 teaspoon (5 mL) shortening

    Frosts one candy pizza

In 2-cup (500 mL) measure, combine candy coating and shortening. Microwave until melted. Drizzle frosting over candy pizza.

BASIC TRUFFLES

- 2 bars (4 oz./113 g each) sweet baking chocolate, cut up
- ⅓ cup (75 mL) whipping cream
- 3 tablespoons (50 mL) butter or margarine
- ½ teaspoon (2 mL) vanilla

Coatings:
- Powered sugar
- Cocoa
- Finely chopped nuts
- Shredded coconut

24 truffles

1 Line an 8 x 4" (1.5 L) loaf dish with plastic wrap. Set aside. In 1-quart (1 L) measure, combine chocolate, whipping cream and butter. Microwave at 50% (Medium) 4 to 6 minutes, or until chocolate melts and mixture can be stirred smooth, stirring once. Beat mixture until smooth and shiny. Blend in vanilla. Pour mixture into prepared loaf dish. Refrigerate 4 hours. Lift chocolate mixture from dish and cut into 24 equal portions. Let stand 10 minutes.

2 Coat hands lightly with powdered sugar and roll each portion into ¾" (2 cm) ball. Place desired coating in small bowl and roll each ball to coat. Place each truffle in paper candy cup and chill at least 1 hour before serving. Store truffles in refrigerator no longer than 2 weeks.

Variation: *Follow recipe above, except omit vanilla and substitute another complementary flavored extract (maple, almond, cherry, orange, peppermint, etc.).*

TIP: *Work quickly when rolling mixture into balls. Chocolate mixture is rich, and melts easily.*

264

← DELUXE TRUFFLES

- 2 bars (4 oz./113 g each) sweet baking chocolate, cut up
- ⅓ cup (75 mL) whipping cream
- 3 tablespoons (50 mL) butter or margarine
- 1 tablespoon (15 mL) liqueur (almond, cherry, orange, etc.)

Coating:

- ½ lb. (250 g) white or chocolate-flavored candy coating, divided
- ¼ cup (50 mL) shortening, divided

Decoration:

- 1 square (1 oz./30 g) semisweet chocolate
- 1 teaspoon (5 mL) shortening

10 truffles

TIP: For pastel-colored truffles, or decorative toppings, tint white candy coating with 1 or 2 drops food coloring.

1 Line an 8" x 4" (1.5 L) loaf dish with plastic wrap. Set aside. In 1-quart (1 L) measure, combine the chocolate, whipping cream and butter. Microwave at 50% (Medium) 4 to 6 minutes, or until chocolate melts and mixture can be stirred smooth, stirring once. Beat until smooth and shiny. Blend in liqueur. Pour into prepared loaf dish. Refrigerate 4 hours.

2 Lift chocolate mixture from dish and cut into 10 equal portions. Let stand 10 minutes. Line a baking sheet with wax paper and set aside. Coat hands slightly with powdered sugar and roll each portion into 1¼" (6 cm) ball. Place on prepared baking sheet. Chill 15 minutes.

3 Combine ¼ lb. (125 g) candy coating and 2 tablespoons (25 mL) shortening in 2-cup (500 mL) measure. Microwave until mixture melts. Using fork, dip each chocolate ball in candy coating. Place on prepared baking sheet. Chill until set.

4 Combine remaining candy coating and shortening in clean 2-cup (500 mL) measure. Microwave until melted. Redip truffles and chill until coating is set.

5 Place semisweet chocolate square and 1 teaspoon (5 mL) shortening in small bowl. Microwave at 50% (Medium) 2½ to 4½ minutes, or until chocolate is glossy and mixture can be stirred smooth, stirring once. Drizzle melted chocolate in decorative design over tops of coated truffles. Chill before serving. Store truffles in refrigerator no longer than 2 weeks.

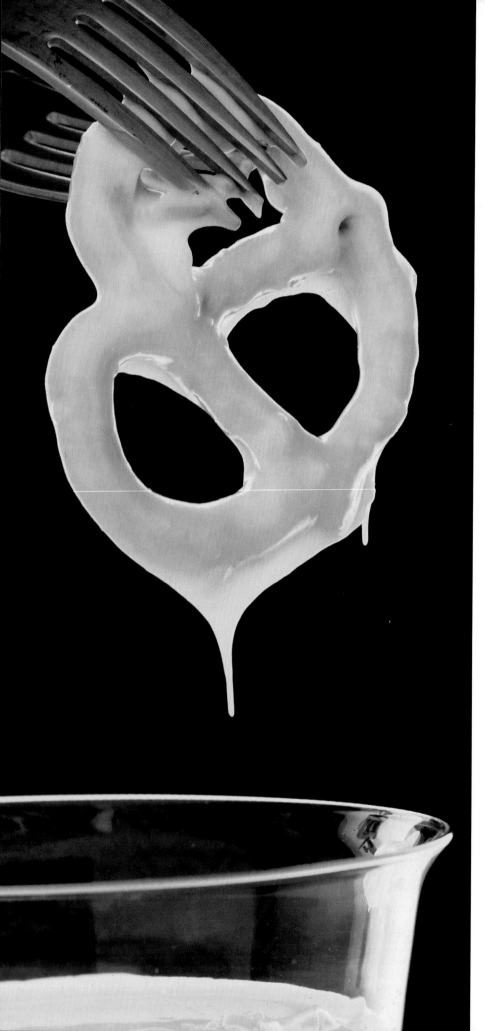

Use your microwave whenever a recipe calls for melted chocolate. No double boiler is needed because microwave energy penetrates from all sides rather than just the base as in range-top cooking. Microwaving also eliminates the need for constant stirring and reduces the possibility of scorching.

CHOCOLATE-DIPPED SNACKS & FRUIT

Coating:

- ½ lb. (250 g) chocolate-flavored candy coating or white candy coating

Or:

- ½ lb. (250 g) confectioners' candy coating plus 1 tablespoon (15 mL) shortening

Dippers:

- Potato chips, broken into 1" to 1½" (2.5 to 4 cm) pieces
- Pretzels
- Candied Peel (page 279)
- Candied Pineapple (page 278)
- Fresh strawberries

About 6 dozen pieces

1 Place candy coating in 2-cup (500 mL) measure or small deep bowl. Microwave at 50% (Medium) 3 to 4½ minutes, or until coating is glossy and can be stirred smooth, rotating after each minute. Stir to melt any small pieces. If coating begins to set, resoften at 50% (Medium) at 1-minute intervals, or until of proper dipping consistency.

2 Use two forks to dip pieces into coating. Let excess coating fall back into bowl. Cool on wire rack until set. Store pretzels or potato chips in wax-paper-lined container in cool, dry place. Refrigerate chocolate-coated fruit until serving time.

CHOCOLATE-COVERED MARSHMALLOWS

- 1 cup (250 mL) chocolate chips
- ¼ cup (50 mL) shortening
- 2 cups (500 mL) chopped nuts
- 1 pkg. (10 oz./300 g) large marshmallows
- 50 wooden picks

50 marshmallows

1 Place chocolate chips and shortening in 2-cup (500 mL) measure. Microwave at 50% (Medium) 1½ to 3½ minutes, or until chips are shiny and soft. Stir until smooth.

2 Place nuts in shallow dish. Insert pick in top of each marshmallow. Dip in chocolate to cover completely. Roll in nuts, coating about three-fourths of the way up. Set on wax paper. Repeat with remaining marshmallows. Let stand until firm. Stir together leftover nuts and chocolate. Drop by spoonfuls onto wax paper. Wrap marshmallows and candy drops individually in plastic wrap or store in covered container.

BUTTERMILK PRALINES

- 2 cups (500 mL) sugar
- 1 teaspoon (5 mL) baking soda
- 1 cup (250 mL) buttermilk
- ¾ cup (175 mL) butter or margarine
- 1 teaspoon (5 mL) vanilla
- 2 cups (500 mL) pecan halves

4 dozen pralines

1 Butter 3-qt. (3 L) mixing bowl. Stir in sugar, baking soda, buttermilk and butter. Microwave at 50% (Medium) 30 to 40 minutes, or until a soft ball forms in cold water, stirring 2 or 3 times during cooking. Add vanilla. Beat at high speed of electric mixer until soft peaks form. Stir in pecans.

2 Drop by teaspoons (5 mL) onto wax paper. Cool until firm. Store in tightly covered container in freezer no longer than 3 months or in refrigerator no longer than 1½ months.

CHOCOLATE BOURBON BALLS

- 1½ cups (375 mL) fine vanilla wafer crumbs
- ⅓ cup (75 mL) bourbon
- 1 cup (250 mL) semisweet chocolate chips
- 2 tablespoons (25 mL) butter or margarine
- ½ cup (125 mL) finely chopped pecans
- 1¼ to 1½ cups (300 to 375 mL) powdered sugar, divided

4 dozen balls

In small bowl, mix cookie crumbs and bourbon. Set aside. Place chips and butter in large bowl. Microwave at 50% (Medium) 2 to 5 minutes, or until chips are soft. Stir until smooth. Stir in pecans and crumb mixture. Gradually mix in enough sugar until mixture just holds together. Shape by teaspoons (5 mL) into balls; place on wax paper. Roll in remaining sugar to coat. Store in refrigerator, tightly covered, no longer than 2 weeks.

COCONUT DATE BALLS

- 2 cups (500 mL) chopped dates
- ¾ cup (175 mL) sugar
- ½ cup (125 mL) butter or margarine
- 1 egg
- 2 tablespoons (25 mL) milk
- 1 teaspoon (5 mL) vanilla
- ½ teaspoon (2 mL) salt
- 2 cups (500 mL) crushed corn flakes
- ½ cup (125 mL) chopped pecans
- 1 cup (250 mL) flaked coconut

5½ dozen balls

1 In medium bowl, combine dates, sugar and butter. Microwave at High 4 minutes, stirring 2 or 3 times. Stir until all butter is absorbed. In small bowl, mix egg, milk, vanilla and salt. Stir a small amount of hot dates into egg mixture, then return to dates, stirring constantly.

2 Reduce power to 50% (Medium). Microwave 5 to 8 minutes, or until thickened and mixture forms a ball when stirred. Mix in corn flakes and pecans. Shape into 1" (2.5 cm) balls; roll in coconut. Place on wax paper. Chill until set. Store in refrigerator or at room temperature, tightly covered, no longer than 2 weeks.

APRICOT CHEWS

- ½ cup (125 mL) butter or margarine
- 1 cup (250 mL) granulated sugar
- ⅓ cup (75 mL) all-purpose flour
- ½ teaspoon (2 mL) salt
- 2 eggs
- 1 cup (250 mL) chopped dried apricots
- 3 cups (750 mL) wheat flake cereal, coarsely crushed
- 1 cup (250 mL) chopped pecans
- 1 teaspoon (5 mL) vanilla
- ½ to ¾ cup (125 to 175 mL) powdered sugar

4½ dozen chews

1 Place butter in 2-qt. (2 L) bowl or casserole. Microwave at High 45 seconds to 1¼ minutes, or until melted. Blend in granulated sugar, flour, salt and eggs. Stir in apricots. Microwave at High 3½ to 6 minutes, or until very thick, stirring every 2 minutes. Cool 5 minutes.

2 In large bowl, combine cereal and pecans. Stir in apricot mixture and vanilla until all ingredients are well distributed. Shape into 1" (2.5 cm) balls. Place powdered sugar in plastic bag. Shake a few apricot balls at a time in bag until coated. Repeat. Refrigerate 2 to 3 hours, or until chilled.

THIN MINT LAYERS

- 1 pkg. (6 oz./175 g) semisweet chocolate chips
- 3 tablespoons (50 mL) butter or margarine, divided
- 1 cup (250 mL) powdered sugar
- ⅛ teaspoon (0.5 mL) peppermint extract
- 2 to 5 drops green food coloring
- 3 to 4 teaspoons (15 to 20 mL) milk

25 mints

1 In 2-cup (500 mL) measure, combine chocolate chips and 2 tablespoons (25 mL) butter. Microwave at High 45 seconds to 1½ minutes, or until chips are soft. Stir until smooth. Spread in 8" x 8" (2 L) baking dish. Chill about 1 hour, or until set.

2 In medium bowl, combine sugar, remaining butter, the peppermint extract and food coloring. Beat with electric mixer, adding milk as needed, until smooth and stiff frosting consistency. Spread on chilled chocolate layer. Chill 3 to 4 hours, or until firm. Cut into about 1½" (4 cm) squares. Store in refrigerator, tightly covered, no longer than 1 week.

CHOCOLATE DESSERT & LIQUEUR CUPS

Dessert Cups:

- 12 paper cupcake liners
- 4 squares (1 oz./30 g each) semisweet baking chocolate
- 2 teaspoons (10 mL) shortening

Liqueur Cups:

- 20 paper candy cups
- 2 squares (1 oz./30 g each) semisweet baking chocolate
- 1 teaspoon (5 mL) shortening

10 liqueur cups

1 Double paper liners to yield six dessert cup forms or ten liqueur cup forms. Arrange on a flat plate. Set aside. Place desired amount of chocolate and shortening in 2-cup (500 mL) measure.

2 Microwave at 50% (Medium) 3½ to 4 minutes (dessert cups) or 2½ to 3½ minutes (liqueur cups), or until the mixture is glossy and can be stirred smooth, stirring after each minute.

3 Spoon 1 tablespoon (15 mL) melted chocolate into each double thickness dessert cup liner or 1 teaspoon (5 mL) melted chocolate into each liqueur cup form. Tilt cups to coat sides to within ⅛" (3 mm) of top. Continue to tilt to form thick chocolate shell.

4 Return coated liners to flat plate. Refrigerate dessert cups 1 hour before removing paper, and liqueur cups 30 minutes. Return to refrigerator until serving time. Fill dessert cups with sherbet or ice cream; fill liqueur cups with liqueurs.

269

FRUIT-FLAVORED CRISPY BARS

- ⅓ cup (75 mL) butter or margarine
- ¼ cup (50 mL) fruit-flavored gelatin (half of 3-oz./85 g pkg.)
- 1 pkg. (10 oz./300 g) marshmallows
- 8 cups (2 L) crisp rice cereal

24 bars

1 Grease 12" x 8" (3 L) baking dish. Place butter in large bowl. Microwave at High 45 to 60 seconds, or until melted. Mix in gelatin. Stir in marshmallows, tossing to coat.

2 Microwave at High 1½ to 2 minutes, or until marshmallows melt, stirring after half the time. Immediately stir in cereal until well coated. Press into prepared dish with back of lightly buttered large spoon. Cool. Cut into 2" (5 cm) squares.

Remaining Gelatin*: Microwave ½ cup (125 mL) water at High 1 to 2 minutes, or until boiling. Stir in gelatin until dissolved. Stir in ½ cup (125 mL) cold water. Chill. 2 servings.*

CHOCOLATE-COVERED BANANAS

- 3 large firm bananas
- 6 wooden popsicle sticks
- 1 cup (250 mL) semisweet chocolate chips
- 2 tablespoons (25 mL) shortening
- ½ cup (125 mL) chopped peanuts

6 servings

1 Peel bananas; cut each in half crosswise. Insert wooden sticks. Place on wax-paper-lined plate or baking sheet. Place chocolate chips and shortening in 2-cup (500 mL) measure. Microwave at 50% (Medium) 2½ to 4 minutes, or until chips are glossy and can be stirred smooth.

2 Spoon melted chocolate over each banana to coat. Allow any excess to drip back into bowl. Sprinkle bananas with peanuts. Place on wax-paper-lined plate. Freeze until firm. Wrap in wax paper, label and freeze no longer than 2 weeks.

For Jo, who still believes

Contents

THE CYCLONES

1

A man-sized frog in a baseball jersey was sitting behind Alex on the bus.

"Gah!" Alex cried, and he dropped down below the back of his seat. A frog in a baseball jersey? A *gigantic* frog in a baseball jersey? Alex closed his eyes. He was dreaming. He had to be.

The springs in the seat behind him creaked, and he opened his eyes and came up again for another peek.

The giant frog was still there. This time it waved at him.

Alex slid down in his seat again and glanced around. This wasn't the bus he took to school, or the one his travel team took on trips, but in a way it was like every other bus he'd ever been on—the windows were grimy, the cracked green vinyl seat stuck to his skin, and the whole place smelled like exhaust and spilled soft drinks. It seemed real enough, but he couldn't remember getting on, or why he was here.

Or why there was a giant frog waving at him in the next seat.

Either he was dreaming, or else he'd gone completely crazy. There was only one way to know for sure.

Alex slid back up. "Um, are you a frog?" he asked.

The thing blinked. "A frog? Oh heavens no."

Alex slumped. He was going crazy then. Seeing things.

"I'm not a frog. I'm a toad," the thing told him. "Easy mistake. Happens all the time."

"I—you're—" Alex said, then he relaxed. A dream! That's what this had to be then. A really weird dream, but still.

"*The* Toad, actually," the creature told him. "As in Toad of Toad Hall. I'm sure you've heard of me." With a crisp, practiced snap he presented his card. On one side it had his address; on the other, it said: "VOTE TOAD."

Alex took the card, careful not to touch the thing's big webbed hands.

"Um, sure. Thanks."

The toad stood and tipped his green baseball cap. "Cheerio!"

"Right. Cheerio," Alex said. He hadn't had a dream this weird since he ate that bad burrito at Raging Taco.

A girl made out of cloth cartwheeled down the aisle to where Alex sat and stopped to examine him with black button eyes. Alex scrambled back in his seat, staring at her. She was a real-life rag doll, with a face patched together like Frankenstein's monster. Pieces of fabric were sewn together in a crazy, random pattern, and she wore a green and white baseball jersey just like the toad.

"*Definitely* a bad burrito," Alex decided.

"Dorothy!" the patchwork girl called. "We've got a live one!"

A girl and a boy—both normal-looking, Alex was relieved to see—came onto the bus. The boy was pale and had a mop of blond hair, while the girl was summer tan, with sandy brown hair pulled back in a ponytail through her green baseball cap. The cap said "OZ" on it. Up close, Alex thought they might be sixth graders, but he didn't recognize either of them from any of his classes.

"End of the line, pal," the girl told him. "No riders."

"The name's Alex," he told them, "and look, this is my dream. I can go wherever I—" He glanced out the window and stopped when he saw the baseball stadium across the street. "Is that—is that Ebbets Field?"

The boy with Dorothy smiled. "First time here. Must be."

"Okay," Dorothy told Alex. "I get it. We were all newbies once. But I don't have time to—"

"Ebbets Field," Alex said again, ignoring her. It had to be Ebbets Field! He'd know that rounded front and striped awning anywhere. Alex slid out of his seat and hurried down the aisle, leaving Dorothy and the others behind. He watched the stadium out the window the whole time, afraid that if he took his eyes off it, his dream would bounce somewhere else and Ebbets Field would disappear.

It didn't. To his delight, the stadium was still there when he got out onto the sidewalk. *Ebbets Field,* just like he'd seen in pictures! Only this time it wasn't a black-and-white photograph. It was color, and real: all brown bricks and white columns and red-white-and-blue bunting. He stood and stared at it in quiet wonder until the others joined him, barely even noticing that the bus he'd been on was painted pink on the outside.

"Awesome," Alex said. *"Awesome!* You know how much history happened in this stadium? Jackie Robinson's debut, the '55 World Series, the first TV game in major league history . . ."

"We know all that," Dorothy said, eyeing him. "What I want to know is how *you* know all that. Are you a Storybook?"

"He can't be from historical fiction. Not dressed like that," the boy said.

Alex looked down at himself. He was wearing his favorite jeans, his sneakers, and his Atlanta Braves T-shirt. He also noticed the girl's cleats for the first time—they were ruby red, with silver trim.

"What? No. I mean, I'm just dreaming all this."

The patchwork girl nodded like she understood. "He's a Lark."

"A what?" Alex asked.

"Then how does he know about Ebbets Field?" Dorothy said, now ignoring *him.* "They tore it down fifty years ago."

"I just did a research paper on it for English class," Alex told them.

The boy shrugged. "Well, somebody has to believe in it, or it wouldn't be here. Why not him?"

"One kid doing a book report on Ebbets Field is not keeping it around," said Dorothy.

"It only takes one to make a Lark," the patchwork girl argued, though Alex still didn't understand. Just past the turnstiles, he could see the famous rotunda with the baseball chandelier.

"Hey, will they let us in? I want to see inside."

"If you want to see it you can buy a ticket like everybody else. Meantime, I've got a game to win. Button Bright," Dorothy said to the blond boy, "see if you can find Toad. Jack? Tik-Tok? Get the equipment out of the luggage compartment."

Alex saw the other "people" standing near the pink bus for the first time. Besides Dorothy, the patchwork girl, and the boy, there was a rabbit, a brass robot, a flying monkey, and a scarecrow with a pumpkin for a head. They all wore the same emerald green uniforms with "OZ" written on the front.

"You're a team," Alex said, understanding. "You're a baseball team, and you're going to play a game at Ebbets Field! This is the best. Dream. Ever!" He ran up to Dorothy. "Come on. You gotta let me play!"

Dorothy looked like Alex's mother when she

was about to say "no" without thinking about it, but she stopped herself.

"You any good?" she asked instead.

"Am I good? Of course I'm good. I'm the cleanup hitter on my travel team."

"Dorothy," the patchwork girl said. "He's a Lark. You can't—"

She waved the rag doll quiet. "You said your name is Alex? Can you play first base, Alex?"

"It's my best position."

"Play a Lark? In the tournament?" the rabbit said. "It just ain't done."

Alex frowned. There was that word again. "What's a—?"

"Is it any worse than having the Steadfast Tin Soldier at first?" Dorothy said, talking over him. Everyone looked to the luggage bin under the bus, where the pumpkin-headed man and the robot were unloading a man-sized, one-legged metal soldier welded to a round base. They tipped him upright, and he teetered back and forth until they could steady him. In one hand he held a rifle, and on the other he wore a glove. He waved with the glove.

"He's your first baseman?" Alex asked. "How does he move? I mean, like, get around?"

"He doesn't," said Dorothy.

"We have to aim for his glove," Button Bright explained. "He has to use his rifle as a bat too. It's welded to his hand. Doesn't matter, really. If he manages to hit something, he can't run to first."

"The Tin Soldier's jersey should fit you just fine," Dorothy told Alex. "Get suited up."

"Dorothy," the patchwork girl said softly, as if trying not to hurt Alex's feelings, "he could disappear anytime. Maybe even in the middle of a game."

"I won't run off! I swear!" Alex promised.

It was hard for Alex to read the patchwork girl's face, but it didn't look like she was convinced.

"Alex is our new first baseman," Dorothy told them. "End of story."

But that, of course, was only the beginning of the story.

ALEX METCALF HAD A GREAT FALL

2

It was a day that would go down in baseball history, like Lou Gehrig replacing Wally Pipp, or Cal Ripken Jr. replacing Mark Belanger. Baseball fans all over the world would look back at the moment Alex Metcalf took over for the Tin Soldier as the beginning of his amazing career."

Alex spun around with his arms in the air, making a *"haaaaaaaaaaaaaaaaaaa"* sound, like the crowd giving him a standing ovation.

"What are you doing?" Dorothy asked. She stood next to him in foul territory with her arms crossed.

"I'm being the announcer. You know, building up the game. *'It had to have been a day like this, a hundred and fifty years ago, that someone first picked up a bat and a ball and drew lines in the dirt, like they had no other choice. Like the Earth said—'"*

"Shut up and get in the dugout," Dorothy told him.

"Aw, come on," Alex said. He followed her inside, where the rest of the team waited for them. "Where's the awe? The magic?"

"This isn't a game," Dorothy told him. "I need everybody to be serious and focus," she told her teammates. "We're going to win this one, right?"

"Right," Button Bright said, but he was the only one of them who looked particularly convinced. Not the patchwork girl, not the robot, not the flying monkey . . .

"Wait a minute," Alex said. "A flying monkey? The Oz Cyclones? And your name is Dorothy? Is this like *The Wizard of Oz* or something?"

"Well, at least I haven't been *totally* forgotten," Dorothy said.

Toad rolled his eyes and nodded sympathetically.

"Most of us are Oz characters, yeah," Dorothy explained, "but not all of us. There's me. I pitch. There's Scraps in right"—the patchwork girl, who was doing handstands—"Jack Pumpkinhead at second"—the pumpkin-headed scarecrow—"Tik-

Tok at catcher"—the robot man—"Button Bright in left"—the blond kid—"and Pinkerton in center." Pinkerton was the flying monkey. "We're all from Oz."

Alex frowned. "I know you and the flying monkey, but I don't remember the others."

Jack Pumpkinhead coughed uncomfortably. Scraps dropped back down to her feet. Even the machine man, Tik-Tok, managed to look unhappy.

"We ap-pear in a num-ber of se-quels," Tik-Tok said. His voice sounded like a music box, but his words came out like cubes from an ice dispenser.

"The rest of the roster is filled out with ringers," Dorothy explained.

"I get it," Alex said. "I play fantasy baseball."

"Not like this you don't," Dorothy told him. "So, Toad you met on the bus."

Toad tipped his cap. "I do hope I can count on your vote in the upcoming elections, old bean. If you're around then, of course."

"Sure. Yeah," Alex said, going with it. "And who are you supposed to be," he asked the rabbit. "The Easter Bunny? Peter Rabbit?"

The rabbit choked on the long piece of grass he was chewing.

"Peter Rabbit?"

"That's Br'er Rabbit," Dorothy said with a grin. "Br'er Rabbit plays third, and Toad's at short."

Br'er Rabbit crossed his arms and grumbled, glaring at Alex.

"Okay. So, who are we playing?" Alex asked. "Wizards on broomsticks?"

"The Mother Goose team."

Alex laughed. "Mother Goose! Excellent. My mom's been reading Mother Goose stuff to my little sister. So how good are they? Like, as a team?"

"Fair to middling," Button Bright told him. "We might actually have a shot."

"So . . . how good are we?"

"Oh. Well," Dorothy said. "We're . . ."

"Plumb awful," Br'er Rabbit said.

"Abominable," said Toad.

"We're the worst team in the whole tournament," said Scraps.

"I wouldn't say *that*," Dorothy argued.

"No, it's great that you're bad!" Alex told them.

Everyone stared at him like he was crazy.

"I'm serious. Don't you see? It's classic! '*A ragtag group of misfits comes together for the first time when a mysterious new player joins the team and leads them to victory!*'"

"This guy's a legend in his own mind," Br'er Rabbit said.

"I rather like him," said Toad.

"Think of the headlines," Alex told them. "'*Worst to first!*' '*Cyclones tear the roof off the tournament!*' We'll be like the '91 Twins. The '69 Miracle Mets. It's a Cinderella story!"

"Cinderella plays for the Royals," Dorothy told him.

"Aw, come on," said Alex. "Don't any of you guys ever read Matt Christopher books? You gotta believe! Who's with me?"

Only Toad looked enthusiastic. "I love it! Voters like a winner, you know."

The crowd in the stands cheered as the opposing team took the field. "Play ba-a-a-a-a-ll!" called a stuttering umpire.

"I don't care *what* the story is as long as we win," Dorothy told the team. "I want everybody focused out there. Got it? Pinkerton, grab a bat. You're up first."

"Go get 'em, Pinky!" Alex said.

The flying monkey stopped and stared at him.

"*Pinkerton,*" Alex quickly corrected himself. "I mean, go get 'em, *Pinkerton.*"

The flying monkey shook his head and stepped out onto the field.

"Wow," Alex said. "Tough crowd."

"Take heart, old man," Toad said, joining him at the dugout rail. "The rest of them just don't see the romance in the dark horse like you and me. We'll make them believers—just like I've done in my campaign for Prime Minister of Ever After. I used to be dead last in the polling, you know, but I've climbed to *ninth* place."

"Ever After?" Alex asked. Before Toad could explain, Pinkerton slapped a base hit to left, flapped his wings, and soared to first base.

"He can fly!" Alex cried. "I mean, *really* fly!"

"Well, he is a flying monkey, old man." Toad grabbed a bat. "Now it's time for me to do some damage!"

"To who? Us or them?" Br'er Rabbit asked.

"Just you wait," Toad told Alex with a wink. "Old Toady will drive him in. Marvelous Toad. Wonderful Toad! The greatest batsman any Storybook has ever seen!"

Toad strode to the plate, taking impressive-looking practice swings as he walked. Dorothy and Button Bright came up to the rail to watch with Alex.

"Looks like we're in business," Alex told them.

"You've never read *The Wind in the Willows,* have you?" Button Bright asked.

The pitcher went into her windup and pitched, and Toad flailed at it for strike one. If Alex didn't know better, he'd have sworn Toad had his eyes closed. The amphibian's second try was worse—Toad lost the handle on his bat mid-swing, and it ended up around first base.

"So, um, what can you tell me about the competition?" Alex asked the others, too embarrassed to watch Toad.

"Little Jack Horner at the hot corner is pretty good," Dorothy told him. "So's the pitcher, Mary Mary. She'll knock your head off with a fastball if you crowd the plate."

As it to prove her point, the pitcher made Toad hit the dirt with a ball at his head.

"Mary, Mary, quite contrary," Alex said. "Got it."

"Watch out for the catcher. She's the girl with the curl in the middle of her forehead. When she's good, she's very, very good. But when she's bad—you know the rest. Their four-six-three combination—the butcher, the baker, and the candlestick maker—they're tight. The outfield's weak, though. You can run on them if you hit a gapper.

Jack and Jill in right and left take a lot of falls, and Humpty Dumpty in center doesn't like to go near the wall."

"Humpty Dumpty! You gotta be kidding." Sure enough, a large round egg wearing the baby blue uniform of the Mother Goose squad patted his glove in center.

"I hope I remember half of this when I wake up," Alex said.

Toad struck out swinging and Dorothy grabbed a bat. "I hit next, then you, then Br'er Rabbit. *If* you're as good as you say."

"Just don't hit into a double play," Alex told her. "I want there to be base runners so my first at bat will be legendary!"

Dorothy shook her head again, and said nothing to Toad as he passed her on the way back to the dugout.

"I say, watch out for that bowler," Toad told the team. "She's awfully good."

"You make every pitcher look good," Br'er Rabbit told him.

Alex watched Dorothy dig in at home, then rap the first pitch she saw into the gap. When the dust cleared, Dorothy stood on second and the flying monkey was clutching third.

"Perfect! Two ducks on the pond," Alex said.

Jack Pumpkinhead leaned over to Tik-Tok. "Nobody said anything about ducks when they told me the rules."

"Now batting," the announcer boomed, "Cyclones first baseman, Alex Metcalf!"

Scattered applause greeted him as he stepped out onto the field. It wasn't exactly the *"haaaaaaaaaaaaa"* he had imagined, but he'd show them. Pretty soon, everybody would know the name Alex Metcalf.

"You gonna stand there all da-a-a-a-ay?" the umpire called.

"Sorry, sir, I just—"

Alex froze. The umpire was a *goat*. A goat wearing a black umpire's mask and chest pad. The other two umpires on the field were goats too. Alex shook his head and stepped in the batter's box. This wasn't bad burrito territory. It was a Halloween night, horror-movie-marathon, too-much-candy kind of crazy dream.

Mary Mary put a fastball over the plate while he was daydreaming.

"Stri-i-i-ike one!" called the goat.

"Hey, wait a minute! I wasn't ready!"

Alex blinked and tried to get ready for the next pitch, but it was on top of him before he could think. He took an excuse-me swing and missed.

"Stri-i-i-i-ike two!" the billy goat bleated. Over at first, Dorothy shook her head like he had already struck out. On the mound, Mary Mary was nodding at the catcher's next sign, ready to put him away.

"Time-out," Alex called. "Time-out!"

The home plate goat threw up his hooves and Mary Mary stopped mid-throw to glare at Alex. He took a few steps away from the batter's box and tried to get a grip. What kind of dream was this anyway? He hoped it wasn't one of those bad ones where he swung and swung and swung at pitches and never connected.

"Ba-a-a-a-tter up!" the goat called.

Alex took a deep breath and stepped back in. *I don't care what kind of dream this is supposed to be,* he decided. *I'll make it great.*

Mary Mary got her sign. She went into her windup. Alex hitched his bat—

—and hit the deck as the ball came screaming for his head and sent him falling to the dirt.

"Ba-a-a-a-all one," the umpire said.

"You think?" Alex asked. He got up and dusted himself off.

The catcher laughed. "Mary Mary doesn't like it when hitters step out on her."

"Oh yeah? Well, she's going to like what I do next even less."

Mary Mary came at him again with a fastball, but this time Alex was ready. He wiped the smile off her face with a towering drive that soared high and deep, over the left fielder, and into the bleachers for a home run.

Now the crowd did go *"haaaaaaaaaaaaaaaaaaaa!"* and Alex flipped his bat away and broke into the home run trot he'd practiced over and over again in his backyard. He put his hands up and spun like he'd just won the World Series, basking in the cheers of thirty thousand fans. He never would have hotdogged it in a real game, of course—showboating like that would have gotten him benched by his coach in a heartbeat—but this was just a dream. It didn't matter what he did here.

He was waving to the crowd with his back to third base when he heard a *zap!* and a *pow!* and a *boom!* and the *"haaaaaaaaaaaaaaaaaaaa!"* turned into screams. Were they shooting off fireworks? An enormous howl shook the stadium. It had to be something they were playing over the loudspeakers, but Alex couldn't figure out why.

The baker at second called out "No, no!" to Alex with a horrified look on his face, but Alex just laughed. *If the baker can't take the heat, he should stay out of the—*

Oof! Alex backed into someone, and they both went sprawling. The screaming crowd gasped, then fell silent. Dang. Had he hit Dorothy? If he'd run into her, they would both be out.

But it wasn't Dorothy. Standing around third base were three new people: a gray-bearded old wizard, a pudgy woman with tiny fairy wings on her back, and, weirdly, an ordinary-looking little boy in a blue hoodie. On the ground at their feet was the thing Alex had run into: an enormous wolf.

"Oh. Hey. Sorry," Alex said. "I didn't think anybody would be behind me."

The wolf stirred, and Alex offered a hand to help him up.

It was as though time stopped in the stadium for everyone but Alex. He could hear the blood pumping in his ears and feel his muscles twitch as he held out his arm, but everyone else was frozen in place, holding their breath, while the wolf stared at him. It felt like a lifetime went by.

And then someone laughed.

It was just a giggle from somewhere up in the stands, but it opened the floodgates. Soon everyone in the stadium was laughing, the way everyone always applauded when somebody dropped a tray in the cafeteria. The laughter shattered the ice that held Alex, the wolf, and the wizards in place, and the wolf roared and started to grow bigger. Really bigger, like nightmare bigger. Alex took a step back, and the laughing in the stands turned to screams as the fans started to flee. The wolf bared his big teeth and leaped at Alex, but the fairy flicked her wand, the wizard muttered an incantation, and the boy closed his eyes and squinted. A purple mist grabbed the wolf in mid-air and stopped him, inches away from Alex's face. The wolf yowled, fighting and clawing to break free of whatever the three were doing to him, but he was trapped.

"Back to the Black Forest with thee, Wolf," the wizard said.

"No! *No!*" the wolf howled. "I was finally free!" He huffed, and he puffed, and he tried to blow the three magicians down, but all he managed to do was spin around in the purple mist. "I'll get you for this! I'll get you!" he cried.

The audience had stopped running for the exits

when the wizards attacked, and now they cheered. The little boy came over and calmly shook Alex's hand.

"Thank you for your assistance," he said. He sounded older than he looked. "The Big Bad Wolf just escaped from his prison, and we've been pursuing him all over town. No doubt he came here to make it harder for us to fight him. All these innocent people around, you know."

"Um, sure. I didn't—I mean, I didn't know I was helping."

The wolf's eyes found Alex and stayed on him. He sniffed at the air.

"You—you did this to me," the wolf said. "What's your name?"

"Alex," he said without thinking. "Alex Metcalf."

"Let us away, Charles Wallace," the old wizard said, and he and the fairy woman dragged the wolf along, still trapped in their magic.

The little boy started to follow them, then turned back to Alex. "You probably shouldn't have told him your name," he said, "but thanks again."

The three left with their prisoner, and Alex stood on the base path between second and third, not exactly sure what had just happened. Everyone else seemed baffled too. The huge crowd, the Cyclones, the Mother Goose team—they all stared at him, waiting to see what he would do next.

Alex shrugged. "So, um, are we gonna finish this game, or what?"

LITTLE WOMEN

3

Ka-chung, ka-chung, ka-chung, ka-chung.
Hard plastic. Cold metal. A white tunnel.
Can't sit up. Can't turn over. Can't move.
Ka-chung, ka-chung, ka-chung, ka-chung.

Something shook Alex, and he woke. What a crazy dream he'd been having. The Big Bad Wolf, the Cyclones, Ebbets Field—he had played an entire baseball game in his dreams, going three for five and helping his team win. He'd gone back to the pink bus with them to celebrate, then fallen asleep on the way to their next game. That's when the dream had shifted. Bounced. The next part was hard to remember, but it was more scary. He'd been on his back, trying not to move for a long time, and it had been so cold . . .

Ka-chung, ka-chung. His world bounced again—
the real world this time, not his dream—and he
was almost tossed out of his bed.

Alex opened his eyes, and Jack Pumpkinhead
stared back at him.

He wasn't in his bed. He was back on the bus.

"I'm still dreaming?"

Ka-chung, ka-chung—the bus rattled over a pot-
hole and Alex bounced in his seat again.

"Sorry about the ride," Jack said. "Lester's a better Bible salesman than bus driver, and he's not
really all that good at selling Bibles."

Alex didn't have any idea what Jack was talking
about. He tried to sit up, but his legs and neck were
stiff from curling on the small bus seat to sleep.

"I thought I was done dreaming."

"You are. You were asleep for a little while, but
now you're awake again."

"No, I mean—" He was still too groggy to
explain. Jack, meanwhile, kept staring at him over
the back of the seat.

"Why are you looking at me like that?" Alex
asked.

"You made somebody laugh at the wolf."

"Yeah," Alex said. He shook his foot, trying to
wake it up.

"You made *lots* of people laugh at the Big Bad Wolf!"

"Yeah. Why is that such a big deal?"

The patchwork girl, Scraps, popped up from the seat behind Alex.

"Gaah!" Alex said, jumping back.

"Because you humiliated him," she said like she'd been in on the conversation the whole time. "In front of thirty thousand people. Nobody does that. Well, and not get eaten."

"Eaten?"

"That's what the Big Bad Wolf does. He eats Storybooks," Scraps told him.

"And Larks," Jack added.

Scraps made a "nom-nom-nom" sound like she was eating.

"But I'm not the one who laughed at him."

"No, but you made him look like a fool."

"I wasn't trying to. I was just trying to be nice!"

"Trying to be nice to the Big Bad Wolf," Jack said. He snickered, then quickly put his hands to his mouth. "Oh! I shouldn't laugh."

"Remember Anansi?" Scraps asked Jack. "That TV show he had? *Trick'd?*"

"Oh yes. He used to pull pranks on famous Storybooks. It was very funny!"

WHO'S AFRAID OF THE BIG BAD WOLF?

4

"By jingo. The Big Bad Wolf on ice. Who'd a thought it?" Tom Sawyer said. He sat on a metal bench inside an armored car, his bare feet stretched out onto the seat on the other side, where his companions, a pair of Arthurian knights, faced him. The older of the two, Sir Lancelot, had long, black hair and a dark, weathered face. His armor was dinted and dirty, and he sat with his legs sprawled, tapping Tom's seat with his long sword. The younger knight, the blond Sir Galahad, sat rigid on the bench, back straight, with his sword held upside down like a cross in front of him, as shiny as his polished armor.

Just beyond all three of them, toward the front of the car, lay the Big Bad Wolf—shackled,

"He made a fake house out of sticks, you know, like in that story? And when the Big Bad Wolf tried to blow it down, it popped right back up again. Over and over and over!"

"The wolf got so mad at being laughed at, Anansi had to go into hiding. Tracked him down for *six years,* the wolf did, until he finally caught him and ate him."

"Okay, whatever," Alex said. This was getting ridiculous. "What I want to know is, why am I still dreaming? My dreams don't usually last this long."

"I told you," Jack said. "You're not dreaming anymore. You woke up."

"No, I—" Alex said, but before he could finish, the bus driver slammed on the brakes and they were all thrown into the seats in front of them.

"Dadgummit, Lester!" Br'er Rabbit yelled. His head poked up from a seat in the back.

"S-sorry," the bus driver called. "There was a family of m-mice crossing the road." He stood and turned, wringing his hands. He was human, but so skinny he'd have to run around in a shower to get wet. He wore a stained pink tie with a matching carnation pinned to his faded blue overalls, and had a comb-over that wouldn't fool a blind man.

"C-couldn't see them until I was right on top of them," he said.

Toad's head appeared in a seat near the front. "I'm happy to offer my services as chauffeur, if—"

"*No,*" the team told him, almost as one.

Dorothy's head appeared over another seat. "Mice in the road means we're here. Everybody up and at it."

This new ballpark wasn't something Alex remembered from a research paper. Instead it reminded him of a world from one of his favorite fantasy series. The stadium looked like an ancient castle, with ivy climbing the gray stone walls. Out front stood a statue showing a heroic-looking mouse in white padded trousers and a collared jersey, holding a cricket bat aloft like a sword.

"Martin the Batsman," Toad said, coming up alongside him. "Test cricket batting average of 99.94."

Alex didn't have any idea what that meant, but he knew where he was.

"Redwall Abbey!"

"The Old Mossflower Cricket Grounds, actually," Toad told him. "But the abbey's not far from here."

Alex started to go for a closer look, but Toad

grabbed him by the arm. "Ah! Watch your step, old man." The road was crawling with little animals in medieval clothes. Some of them pulled carts, others carried children. A few even had swords.

The Cyclones stepped over the locals and went inside the stadium to begin their pregame warm-ups. Dorothy attached a bucket of baseballs to Tik-Tok's back, and he became a walking, talking pitching machine, firing fly balls to the outfielders and ground balls to the infielders.

"There we go, Kansas! Looking good, looking good," Alex called as Dorothy snapped up a grounder from Tik-Tok.

"'Kansas'?" she asked.

"It's a nickname."

"Nicknames?" said Jack. "Ooh! Ooh! I want one! I want one!"

"Here we go, Stretch, look alive now. Look alive—" Alex called.

"Stretch! He called me Stretch!" Jack said, more interested in his nickname than the ground ball Tik-Tok sent his way, which went bouncing past him into right. "I've never had a nickname before, you know!" Jack told the infielders.

"Not unless 'Lunkhead' counts," Br'er Rabbit said from third.

"Pick it up, Ears," Alex called to the rabbit. "Let's see some hustle."

Tik-Tok fired a ball to Pinkerton in center as the other team came on the field. Alex couldn't help but stare at them. They were all girls. Normal-looking, most of them, but all girls. The oddest one had red hair tied in pigtails that stuck out from the sides of her head like she had just licked an electrical socket. She had a little monkey on her shoulder too, dressed in a blue and yellow jersey that matched the rest of the team.

Across the field, Br'er Rabbit scooped up a grounder from Tik-Tok and threw the ball on a line to first. Alex didn't see it until the last second. He ducked just in time, and it missed his head and whacked against the dugout wall.

"Look alive now, Golden Boy," Br'er Rabbit jeered.

The Cyclones let the other team take the field for practice. Back in the dugout Alex sat next to Button Bright.

"So, I guess you don't need a nickname," Alex told him. "Unless Button Bright is your real—"

"Oh no," the boy said. "Don't call me Button Bright. I let Dorothy call me that, because we go

way, way back. But she's the only one. What kind
of name is 'Button Bright' anyway? No kid today
would take me seriously with a name like that."

"Yeah," said Alex. "I kinda wondered."

"The name's Saladin," the boy told him. "Saladin Paracelsus de Lambertine Evagne von Smith."
He offered his hand, and Alex shook it.

"Wow. You do need a nickname. A new one,
anyway."

Saladin clawed at his arm like he had the worst
case of poison ivy ever.

"You okay?" Alex asked.

"I've got The Itch."

No kidding, Alex thought. If Saladin wasn't careful he was going to hurt himself.

"All right everybody, grab your gloves. The
Avonlea Chicks hit first," Dorothy told them. "And
remember: Play like your lives depend on it."

"Will do, Kansas!" Toad said.

Dorothy gave Alex a look that said "Thanks a
lot," and he smiled.

She wasn't too put out, though. Dorothy looked
sharp, striking out the Chicks' first batter, a brown-
haired girl about eight years old who dragged her
bat all the way back to the dugout.

"The umpire hates me!" she said.

"Don't be so tragical, Baby," the next hitter told her.

"Don't call me Baby!"

The girl who replaced her at the plate was another one with red hair and pigtails, but hers didn't defy gravity. They sat next to her head like plain old ordinary pigtails should.

"Let's go, Cordelia!" her teammates called. "Get a hit!"

Alex didn't know any of these characters. He only ever read books about girls if his teacher made him. But whoever this girl was, she was a talker. He could hear her all the way from first. She talked to Tik-Tok. She talked to the umpire. She talked to herself. She even got a hit while she was talking, driving the sixth pitch she saw just over an incredible leap from Toad.

When Alex went over to hold her on first, the girl was already talking again.

"They call me Cordelia, but that isn't my real name, of course," she told him. "My real name is Anne with an *E*. A-N-N-E. We heard you Cyclones were using nicknames and thought it was a splendid idea. Most of us, anyway. The ones with imagination. Are you the new boy? The one who ran into the wolf? Everyone's talking about you. It's a wonder you weren't eaten. What storybook are you from? One of those Newbery things?"

"No, I—" Alex began, but she was already going again.

"A best seller then. Something contemporary, but with Greek gods and swords and great battles, I'm sure. Isn't this stadium lovely? I think it's one of the prettiest stadiums we've ever played in. The ivy, the flowers: Mossflower is the bloomiest place to play baseball there ever was. I just love how big and open it is too. More scope for the imagination, don't you think? You know what *I* imagined? I imagined getting a base hit to right, and that's just what I did. Not a double, or a triple, or a home run, mind you—there's no cause to be greedy, not at this point in the game, anyway. Just a single, a sensible little hit to get things going. You wouldn't think someone so homely and thin as me could hit a ball like that, would you?"

"Well, I—" Alex started to say, but before he knew what was happening, the girl at the plate smashed a ground ball between first and second— a ball he would have been able to get to if hadn't been distracted. He made a halfhearted dive for it and watched in dismay as it bounced into right field for a hit. The talking girl, meanwhile, broke for second as though she hadn't been in the middle of a conversation, and took third before Scraps could get the throw in.

Dorothy threw her hands up. "What was that?"

"She was—she kept talking to me!" Alex said.

Dorothy got the ball back with a snap of her glove. "Focus, Golden Boy!"

Alex grumbled all the way back to first. He was beginning to wish he hadn't started giving people nicknames.

"So what do they call you?" he asked the new girl standing at first.

"My name is Jo, but you may address me as Sir Roderigo."

"Great. Another head case."

Alex wasn't going to get caught talking this time, and he backed off a few steps. The cleanup hitter was at the plate, and he wasn't surprised to see it was the other redheaded girl. Her pigtails stuck out the sides of her batting helmet like wings on an airplane.

Dorothy turned and waved the outfielders deeper.

"Really?" Alex asked. "That deep for a girl?" Beside him, Sir Roderigo huffed and rolled her eyes.

Dorothy did everything she could to keep the

ball away from the girl with the pigtails—away, away, away, until she was on the verge of walking her. Whether it was stubbornness or an honest mistake, Alex didn't know, but Dorothy's next pitch was straight over the plate and Pigtails made her pay for it. With a swing that would make a major leaguer swoon, the redheaded girl belted the pitch to left. It just missed going over the wall for a home run, but it was just as well; if it had, it might have killed someone in the stands. The ball slammed into the outfield wall like a cannon shot, knocking mortar and rock loose in a shower of dust.

"Dang!" Alex said, ducking and covering his head with his hands. "Somebody could have warned me!"

The ball rolled around in left field until Button Bright chased it down, but for some reason he was having trouble picking it up. Wait—had Alex just seen the ivy-covered outfield wall through Button Bright? Was his character a ghost? But no, Alex had shaken hands with him, and he had been plenty solid then.

Chicks circled the bases. Button Bright still couldn't get a handle on the ball. Pinkerton flew over from center to help, but by then it was too late—Pigtails had an inside-the-park home run.

"It's all right, BB," Dorothy called to him. "Just hang in there."

Alex couldn't believe it. *She yells at me for missing a grounder, and all he gets is "It's all right, hang in there"?* Alex's coach would have benched him for playing like that.

Alex caught Dorothy as they were coming off the field at the bottom of the inning. "Dorothy, Button Bright—Saladin—"

"Will be fine," Dorothy said, ending the conversation.

Alex threw up his hands. It was her team. Besides, it didn't matter. He was going to wake up any minute now anyway.

Button Bright handled the rest of his chances in left field without any problems and the Cyclones hit well, but by the seventh inning the Chicks were ahead by three runs. Making up three runs in three innings was doable, but looking around at his teammates in the dugout, Alex wondered if this team could do it. They certainly had the talent—Br'er Rabbit, Scraps, Dorothy, Pinkerton, Button Bright, they could all handle a bat, and Toad was the best shortstop Alex had ever seen. But they didn't *believe*. Alex could see it in the way they slumped back on the bench. What they needed, Alex decided, was something to fire them up.

"Alex, you're up," Dorothy told him.

"All right, guys," Alex told the Cyclones, "pay attention now."

Alex studied the pitcher as he went to the plate. Her brown hair needed combing, she wore blue granny-glasses, and she was missing a tooth. She'd been cool on the mound all game, but he thought he could get to her.

"Hey pitcher," Alex called, "you're so ugly you make onions cry."

The catcher looked up at him and scowled.

"You're so ugly," Alex told the pitcher, "you give Dracula nightmares!"

"You're a big old meanie!" the pitcher yelled back, and she fired a pitch right down the heart of the plate for strike one.

Alex tried again. "You're so ugly that when you throw a boomerang, it doesn't come back!"

"Don't listen to him, Missy!" the catcher called. She looked up at Alex. "Lay off or you're going to get it."

"Oh yeah?" said Alex. He turned back to the pitcher. "You're so ugly, your parents had to tie a pork chop around your neck to get your dog to play with you!"

"That's not true! Tickle loves me!" the pitcher yelled back. She threw even harder, getting strike two.

"Alex, what are you doing?" Dorothy called. Every one of the Cyclones was at the railing now, watching. Alex smiled. Now, if the pitcher would just play along . . .

"Hey pitcher, you're so ugly—" he started to say, but before he could finish, the catcher popped up and punched him in the nose.

Alex stumbled back and fell on his butt. Ow! For a dream, that had really hurt!

The catcher threw her mask away and stood over him, fists clenched. "You think I can't handle a brat like you, boy? Let's go."

The catcher wasn't the girl he'd been trying to make angry, but she would do. He clenched his fists and smiled. A good fight would be just what the Cyclones needed to get fired up. Then—

Then, suddenly, Alex saw the major flaw in his plan. The catcher was a girl. All the Chicks were girls, and he wouldn't hit a girl. He couldn't.

Which meant he was going to get pummeled.

"Now hang on a minute," Alex said, holding up his hands. "I'm sure we can—"

The catcher dove at him and he threw his arms over his head to protect himself, but instead of fists there was an emerald flash, and an *oomph,* and when he looked up Dorothy was there, scrabbling in the dirt with the Chicks' catcher, punching and pulling and cursing.

"Yeah! Get her, Dorothy!" Alex cheered. "Hit her in the—*oof!*"

The pitcher landed on him with an elbow slam to his stomach that would have done a pro wrestler proud. Then Button Bright was there, pulling her off, and Br'er Rabbit was pouncing on a girl with a ferret on her shoulder, and the red-haired girl with the perpendicular pigtails was tossing Tik-Tok into the outfield like a superhero, and Sir Roderigo was pulling at the yarn on Scraps's head, and—and that was all Alex saw before he was at the bottom of a pile of Chicks and Cyclones. Over the grunts and the yells and the insults, he could hear the crowd roaring, cheering them on. It was an all-out, bench-clearing brawl.

When the umpires finally had everyone pulled off of each other and separated, Alex and the

Chicks' catcher were thrown out of the game and both teams were given official warnings that they would forfeit if they fought again.

"What were you doing?" Dorothy asked as she helped Alex back to the dugout.

"I was trying to get that pitcher to hit me, but the catcher did instead. Who is she, anyway?"

"Mary Lennox," Dorothy said. "She's always looking for a fight. But why were you looking for one?"

The Cyclones had regrouped in their dugout, and Alex directed his answer to all of them. "You have to get back at them. You gotta beat them, for me. All right?"

"Gladly," Br'er Rabbit said, nursing his bent whiskers.

Jack stuck his head back on. "You got it, Golden Boy!"

"We'll knock their socks off," Scraps told him.

"That's what I wanted to hear," Alex told them. "Now, I'll just—I'll just be in the locker room putting ice on every inch of my body."

behind home plate screamed and stampeded for the exits. Alex held his ground while the wolf grew twice as big as him.

"Still not afraid of me?" the Big Bad Wolf bellowed.

"You're not the worst nightmare I've ever had," Alex told him.

"Maybe not," the wolf said, grinning, "but I'll be your last one."

Alex raised his bat like a sword and charged, taking the wolf by surprise. "Yaaaaaaaaaaaaaaaaaah!" he cried, swinging.

Clang! His bat hit a lamppost. Alex stepped back, surprised, as the lamppost crumpled and bent in half.

"Hmph," said a woman pushing past with a baby carriage. "Vandals."

Alex blinked. He wasn't on the baseball field anymore. His dream had finally shifted! He was standing on a little footbridge outside a massive white-columned building decorated with banners and balloons. He still had his bat in his hand, though, and someone had her arms around him.

The person let him go and he turned.

Dorothy.

"What—? How—?"

chained, and bound for his prison in the Wild Woods. The wolf said something pleading, but the muzzle on his mouth made it come out like *"Mmm nnnd mm hmmm."*

The armored car bounced, and the Big Bad Wolf couldn't stop himself from rolling into the wall. The knights on the opposite bench grabbed the hand straps on the ceiling to brace themselves, their metal armor rattling, but Tom swayed easily with the car like a steamboat drawing nine feet of water, all the while playing with a piece of string stretched between his fingers.

"Heard tell of the Big Bad Wolf, of course," Tom said. "Hungry as a woodpecker with a sore beak, and single-minded as a hound dog when he gets latched on to something. And them videos he sends out, howling on about the Wizard's government. Shoot. Them's right scary. But all the rest of it . . ." He made double Xs out of the loop of twine stretched between his hands. "Ever After's greatest master of disguise, and all he can think to do is dress up like my aunt Polly and eat people? I could sure dream up better schemes if it were me." He held his hands out to the dark-haired knight. "Just pinch there, would you?"

Sir Lancelot looked down his nose at Tom and kept poking at the bench with his sword.

"Think you're all high and mighty, is that it?" Tom said. "I could lick you with one hand tied behind my back."

"Why doesn't thou, then?" Lancelot challenged him.

"Father! Remember thyself," Galahad said. "Thou art a knight of the round table. What matters this fool to you? We have in our charge the worst villain ever seen on these shores. Our attention cannot be led astray."

"Mmm nnnd mm hmmm!" the wolf tried to scream.

"What good is this runt of a boy in watching the wolf anyway?" Lancelot asked.

"The Ever After Department of Homeland Security claimeth he is as devious as the wolf, and can be counted upon to see through any subterfuge," Galahad told him. "On that score I have my doubts, but 'tis vital the Big Bad Wolf not escape 'ere he can be banished to the Waste Forest for good."

The wolf rattled his chains. *"Hnnn! Hnnn! Mmm nnnd mm hmmm!"*

"Don't forget, I was a detective once too. Here,"

Tom said. He offered his twine-tied hands again to Lancelot. "Just pull on that string."

Lancelot didn't bite. Tom turned to the shackled wolf. "What about you, hairy?"

"Mmm! Mmf! Mm hnn mm mmmm mm!" the wolf said.

Lancelot grinned. "Whatever that beast is telling you, it doth not sound very nice."

"Maybe we should take off his muzzle, let him say his piece."

"What? Art thou mad?" Galahad cried. "'Tis a poor joke indeed."

Tom shrugged and tried to reach the string with his bare toes. "Aw, the Big Bad Wolf ain't all that scary," he said. "Not anymore." He paused to hitch a piece of string over his thumbs with his teeth. "I mean, taken down by a day-old Lark in a baseball jersey? In front of all them people on TV?" Tom laughed. "I sure do wish I'd been there to see that. The Big Bad Wolf all laid out like a wolf-skin rug. *Whomp.*"

Lancelot slammed his sword into Tom's bench with a *clang*. "Thou dankish, base-court knave!"

"Father! Language!" Galahad scolded.

"There we go," Tom said. He leaned over to

Lancelot and held out a new pattern between his fingers. "Put your hand in there."

Lancelot met Tom's grin with a cold stare.

"Language aside, young Tom, my father dost have a point," Galahad said. "'Tis dangerous to bait the Big Bad Wolf, even though he be chained. He is as fierce as a dragon when laughed at, and thou appear to be *trying* to make him stir."

"Oh, I aim to," Tom said.

Galahad blinked. "What? Wherefore?"

Tom offered up the finger lacing again to Lancelot. "Go on, put your hand in," he said, but Lancelot still did nothing but glare.

"Fie upon this foolishness," Galahad said. He reached across his father and stuck his hand in Tom's string instead. "There. Art thou happy now?"

Tom let the twine go from two of his fingers and pulled, and it slipped into a harmless knot around Sir Galahad's wrist.

"There, see how easy that was?" Tom slid the string off the knight's wrist and strung it between his fingers again. "Here now, Lancelot. You give it a go."

"Stop these games," said Galahad. "Wherefore art thou trying to anger the Big Bad Wolf?"

"Because," Tom said, "I had to figure out which one of you was really the Big Bad Wolf in disguise."

Father and son stared at each other in stunned silence.

"Jmm! Jmm! Mmm hmm hmm hmmm mm jmm!" the muzzled wolf cried from inside the cage.

"Thou pig-faced git," Lancelot spat.

"Aw, come on," Tom told Lancelot. "These two may have just fallen off the turnip truck, but I've been at this a far sight longer. Like the man said, I know all the tricks. Heck, I invented half of them."

"But *I'm* not the wolf, and Lancelot—he cannot be the wolf!" Galahad said. "Art thou saying I do not know mine own father?" The perfect knight frowned. "But then, I did leave thee alone with the villain whilst I went to retrieve our neck pillows, Father. But the wolf couldn't have—"

Faster than Galahad could blink, Lancelot brought the back of his gauntleted fist up into his son's nose. *Whack. Thunk.* Galahad's head whipped back and hit the metal wall of the truck, and he was out cold. The armored car went over another bump, and Galahad's body slid to the floor.

"Hnnn! Hnnn!" the wolf in the cage tried to yell.

"You got me," Lancelot said. Only it wasn't

Lancelot's voice anymore. It was the wolf's. He stood and shed his disguise like a second skin.

"What big teeth you have," Tom told him.

"And you call me unoriginal," said the wolf, his voice low and gravelly. He took a step toward Tom.

"Catch, cradle! Catch!" Tom cried, and the little piece of twine sprang from his fingers, grew to a full-sized net, and swallowed up the Big Bad Wolf. The wolf struggled inside the net, but couldn't bite or claw his way out.

Tom leaned back and put his hands behind his head. "That there's a Catch Cradle, Wolf. Won that off a fat old king in a card game. Called himself a king, anyway. The ropes is strong as steel. And no matter how big or how small a thing gets, there's always just enough net to keep it caught."

To test that, the wolf grew big, then small, then normal-sized again. True to Tom's word, the Catch Cradle stayed tight the whole time.

"I knew you were up to something, Tom Sawyer. You're always up to something. Couldn't just let a sleeping dog lie, now could you?"

Tom nudged at Galahad's unconscious body on the floor. "Don't know what these boys was thinking. Putting you in chains? Locking you behind bars? When you can be any size you want? And you're a master of disguise? Dang. When I found out one of 'em had been alone with you, I knew you wouldn't have missed the chance to switch places. I sure wouldn't have. I just didn't know which of them it was. Both of 'em got their swords stuck so far up their—"

"Fall, cradle! Fall!" the wolf cried, using Tom's voice, but quick as an echo Tom said, "Catch, cradle! Catch!" right back, and the wolf was trapped all over again.

"I knew you'd try that," Tom told him. "But long as I'm awake, I can put that Catch Cradle back on you quick as a hiccup, and we'll be to McDougal's Cave or the Wild Woods or whatever everybody else calls it before I need to shut an eye." Tom stood and circled the wolf. "Ha! Caught twice in one day. That's downright embarrassing, I reckon."

The wolf's eyes narrowed. "And that's the second time you've had a laugh at my expense, Tom."

"Funny is as funny does, hairy," Tom said. The hair on the wolf's face stirred when Tom breathed the word "hairy," and in that moment they both realized the boy's mistake. The wolf didn't just use disguises and grow bigger and smaller; he could huff, and puff, and—

"Huck! Becky! Aunt Polly! Anybody!" Tom cried. He leaped for the back door, but the wolf was faster. He huffed, and he puffed, and he blew Tom into the wall with such force that he hit with a *clang* and slumped to the floor, unconscious.

"Fall, cradle. Fall," the wolf said in Tom's voice, and the net that imprisoned him turned into a simple loop of string and whispered to the floor.

"Mmm! Mm hnnn mm mmms!" the real Lancelot tried to yell. He was the only one left awake, but he was still muzzled and chained and disguised to look like the wolf.

"Oh, don't worry. I'm not going to let them send you away to the Wild Woods disguised as me," the wolf told him, taking off Tom's jacket and trying it on. "That's for my old friend Tom Sawyer here. He and I are going to switch places, and then I'm going eat what's inside this tin can here." He nudged the armored Galahad with his foot. "Unless, of course, you tell me where I can find a Lark named Alex Metcalf . . ."

BY THE HAIR OF HIS CHINNY-CHIN-CHIN

5

Alex Metcalf sat on the bench in the visitors' dugout at Dictionopolis's centrally located Center Field, talking with his teammates about the Cyclones' come-from-behind win against the Chicks. Only Dorothy and Button Bright were missing.

"After you were thrown out, Dorothy said we were shorthanded, so she put me at first," Jack Pumpkinhead said. "I suppose because I'm long-handed."

"It certainly ain't because you're long in the smarts department," said Br'er Rabbit.

"I never thought about you being down to eight players," said Alex. "How'd you manage?"

"Jack played a wide first, Br'er Rabbit played

a wide third, and I covered all the ground in between," Toad explained.

"That's quite a lot of real estate."

"It was nothing for old Toad. You should have seen me. I danced to my left. I leaped to my right. I corralled everything that came my way."

"Well, not everything," Scraps said.

Toad shrugged. "Seventy-five percent, perhaps."

Tik-Tok whirred and clicked like an adding machine. "Thirty-two—point six—per-cent, ac-tually."

"*The point is,*" Toad said quickly, "no one could have done better." He nudged Alex. "I came up two places in the overnight polls too."

"Ooh. *Seventh,*" Br'er Rabbit said. "You got about as much chance of getting elected as we do of winning this tournament."

Alex was more than a little tired of Br'er Rabbit's sniping. "Hey, Ears," he said. "Did you remember to bring the bucket with the curveballs in it?"

Br'er Rabbit sat up. "The what?"

"The bucket with the curveballs. Oh, don't tell me you forgot. How's Dorothy supposed to strike anybody out if she can't throw a curveball?"

"Nobody told me to bring no bucket," Br'er Rabbit said.

Tik-Tok frowned and put up a brass finger to interject, but Toad cut him off.

"Oh—oh yes. I distinctly remember Dorothy telling you to bring them."

"She'll be spitting needles if they're not here when she gets back," Scraps told him.

Br'er Rabbit looked around, worried.

"Well?" Alex asked. "You gonna sit there all day and wait for her to come back and notice there's no curveballs?"

Br'er Rabbit hopped off the bench and left at a gallop, running straight into Dorothy as she came into the dugout.

"Where are you going?" she asked him.

"I'm sorry. I'm sorry. I forgot to bring the curveballs. I was just going—"

Alex, Toad, and Scraps burst into laughter. Pinkerton, perched on top of the dugout, snickered with them. Br'er Rabbit's ears flattened as he realized the others had made a fool of him.

"Get back in the dugout," Dorothy told him.

"But what about the curveballs?" Jack asked.

"Don't worry about it, Stretch. I'll explain later," Alex told him. He turned to Dorothy to laugh about the joke and noticed she'd been crying.

"Kansas, you okay?" Alex asked.

Dorothy took a deep breath, and the team got quiet.

"Toad, I'm going to need you to play two positions again today," she said, "deep short and short left. Pinkerton, I need you to shift to left center. Scraps, you'll need to play right center."

Alex did the math. She was covering for an empty left field. "Wait, where's Button Bright? Did you kick him off the team?"

"No. He's gone."

It was like somebody unplugged the Cyclones. Dorothy stared at her ruby and silver cleats. Toad sat and clasped his webbed hands. Tik-Tok slumped. Even Br'er Rabbit's ears drooped.

Alex still didn't get it. "You mean he quit?"

Dorothy shook her head. "Not now, Alex, okay?" To the rest, she said, "Game's about to start. Pinkerton, you're up first."

Alex still didn't get what was going on with Button Bright. He stood in the middle of the dugout, waiting for someone to help him understand, but no one would meet his eyes.

"Okay. Fine. Whatever," Alex said. If this dream was supposed to mean something, he was totally lost. He was ready to wake up anyway.

Their opponents this time were a team of pigs,

all wearing red and white striped uniforms and red hats with the letter *P* on them. Pinkerton led off with a drive up the middle, but the pig in center came dashing in and caught the ball in his teeth on a dive.

Alex whistled to himself. "That's some pig."

Toad hit next. The pig on the mound practiced ballerina steps until her teammates told her to get on with it, and she struck Toad out looking. He came back to the dugout shaking his head.

"I do believe these porcine players are going to prove a handful today," he told his teammates. Nobody had anything to say to him, though—not even Br'er Rabbit. All the spirit of the last game's bench-clearing fight was gone.

Dorothy was still playing to win, though, and she stroked a single through the infield to keep the first inning alive for Alex. He didn't know where Button Bright was, or why nobody would talk to him about it, or when this dream was finally going to end, but all he could do was play along until he woke up.

The home plate umpire was a boy in a dirty white wolf costume, about half Alex's age. Alex recognized him from a picture book he'd loved as a kid.

"You're the one who made a fool out of the

Big Bad Wolf, aren't you?" the boy asked him.

"Yeah," Alex said. Talking about the wolf was something else he was tired of.

"Had a pretty good laugh at him afterward, I'll bet."

"No. Look. It was an accident. I bumped into him. It's no big deal."

"But then you tried to help him up. The scariest Storybook in Ever After, and you just offered him a hand. Now that was funny."

"Hey. This little piggy is ready to play ball," the catcher interrupted.

"Raaaaah!" the boy snarled. "Be quiet, or I'll eat you up!"

"I'm with the pig. Can I just hit?"

"I want to know why you weren't scared."

"Look, I didn't know he was some big monster, all right? I didn't know I was *supposed* to be afraid of him. Maybe next time I'll be scared."

"Maybe next time he'll eat you up," the boy said, his voice growing deeper and meaner. He started to swell and grow, his white wolf costume ripping away to reveal a brown wolf costume underneath.

Not a costume, Alex realized. *A real wolf. A wolf in wolf's clothing.*

The pig catcher squealed and ran, and the crowd

"I grabbed you and jumped out of there with the cleats," she told him. He looked down at her ruby and silver shoes. *She jumped out of the stadium?*

"I can click my heels and go anywhere, remember? 'No place like home' and all that?" She leaned back against the bridge railing to catch her breath. "Cripes. I hope people aren't forgetting."

"Where are we now?" Alex asked.

"The Ever After Exposition Hall. We passed it on the way into town. It was the first place I could think of."

Crowds poured through a door to the main building, and Dorothy grabbed Alex's hand and pulled him along to follow them.

"We have to keep moving. The wolf is the best tracker in all of Ever After. What were you thinking, going after him like that?"

"What was I supposed to do, let him eat me?"

"No, but you could have run like any sane person."

"Wait, what about everybody else? We have to go back for them!"

"The Wizard will have magicians there already. Besides, the wolf could have attacked everybody long before he did. He was waiting for you. Come on. We've got to hide."

A stuffed toy bear in a security guard uniform saluted them as they went inside. "Welcome to the Exposition!" he said.

"Why can't anything in this dream be normal?" Alex asked.

"This isn't a dream," Dorothy told him. "Come here. I'll show you."

She pulled him along into an exhibit hall with a huge scale model laid out on tables. It was a big island, with mountains and volcanoes and lakes and prairies. Cities with names like Dictionopolis, Busytown, Whoville, River Heights, and Emerald City dotted the interior. Surrounding everything was a barrier of forest labeled "Wild Woods," then a ring of beach marked "Shifting Sands," and beyond that a blue plastic ocean, called simply "The Sea." Writ large from one end to the other was the name "EVER AFTER."

"Cool model!" Alex said.

"This is where we are, Alex. This is Ever After. It's not a dream."

Alex bent low to look at a model pirate ship firing a cannon at a flying boy. "Well, it's sure not the real world."

"No. But it is *a* real world. And you're really a part of it. You're a Lark."

"Scraps called me that. A Lark. What is it?"

"Look, you know about the Storybooks, right? Me and the Cyclones, we're here because someone wrote us in a book, and children believe we're real. As long as children keep believing, we live on."

"'If you clap your hands very hard . . .'" Alex joked.

"Yeah. Something like that. Larks, though, they're not from any book. Each one is here because someone in the real world—just one person—dreamed him up and believes in him. It's like . . . a daydream. Say you're a kid in the real world, playing catch all by yourself in the backyard. You pretend you're the greatest baseball player in the world. The ball goes up. You go back. You go left. You go right. You're at the wall—you've got it! Alex Metcalf wins the World Series! The crowd goes wild! You don't just think it, you believe it—and in that moment, your belief makes that dream come to life here, in Ever After. That's what you are, Alex. A Lark. A daydream."

Alex laughed. "You're crazy." He stared across the diorama at her, waiting for her to say she was kidding, but she didn't. "You're crazy! I'm real, and this is just a dream."

"It's a dream, all right. But you're not the

one doing the dreaming. You're somebody else's dream."

"No," Alex said, coming around to her. "No, I know things. I know who won the World Series in 2004. I know who plays third base for the Atlanta Braves. I know who holds the record for the most hits in major league history!"

"All baseball stuff. Alex, face it: You're the daydream of a boy who wishes he was a baseball star. That's why you're so good."

"No. I remember other things too. My mom and dad. My little sister. Our house. My school in Decatur. I remember your book!"

"That's because you're him, Alex. You're just like the real you . . . only great at baseball. The real you is just some baseball-obsessed kid who dreams he's awesome."

"No way," Alex said. He took a step back. "No. You're wrong."

"Alex, it's the only reason I'd put you on the team. I needed your bat and your glove. We have to win the tournament this year. We just have to."

"Why?"

"Come on," Dorothy told him. "We've been here too long." She took his hand and clicked her heels together. "Hold tight—"

Alex's world shifted again, and he was standing in a grassy meadow.

"Where are we now?"

"The Ever After Theme Park."

It didn't look like any theme park Alex had ever been to. There were no roller coasters or gift shops. This was more like Piedmont Park, where they went to have picnics and fly kites back home. A paved path ran past a cluster of trees and a small pond, with wooden benches tucked away in shady places. The benches were weird, though—they had words painted on them in huge letters, things like "coming of age" and "sacrifice" and "identity."

Dorothy led Alex over to a bench with the word "death" written on it and sat with him.

"Alex, the tournament isn't just a game. Not to the Cyclones. The team that wins the tournament gets free wishes from the Wizard of Oz. One wish for each player."

"Okay. So?"

Dorothy took a deep breath. "Alex, Button Bright didn't quit. He's gone. He doesn't exist anymore."

"He—what?" Alex stood. "Are you saying Button Bright is dead?"

"He faded away this morning. Nobody in the real world believes in him anymore."

Alex paced around the grass in front of the bench. "This is crazy. It's nuts. You mean, that guy *died* this morning, and you still came to the ballpark like nothing happened?"

"Don't you dare tell me I don't care!" Dorothy shot back. "Who do you think sat up all night holding his hand while he faded in and out? Do you have any idea what that's like?" She closed her eyes. "I may look twelve, Alex, but I've been around for more than a hundred years. I've seen my fair share of friends be forgotten and fade away, and it never gets any easier. Button Bright was one of my oldest friends. He was just a little boy the first time he came here, and then—he changed."

"Changed?"

"He got his own spin-off novel where he was older, but it didn't sell. Then he was brought back in an Oz book and he changed again—got younger again. Then older. There was no rhyme or reason to it. No continuity. Sometimes he didn't even know who he was. I sort of looked out for him after that. He was like my little brother. And now—"

Alex sat beside her. "I'm sorry. Is that what was happening to him in the Chicks game? He was—disappearing?" Now Alex understood why Dorothy had gone easy on Button Bright for his error in the outfield.

"I thought he would make it. If we could just get to the end, see the Wizard, get our wishes— but Button Bright wasn't around long enough to get his. I failed him. But I'm not going to fail the others."

"You're going to use your wishes to stay alive. That's it, isn't it? That's why you have Jack, and Scraps, and Tik-Tok on the team, and why you had Button Bright. They're not the best baseball players you could get. You could have had a team full of ringers, but you chose them instead. Characters most people have never heard of. So they could get wishes if you won."

Dorothy nodded. "We weren't good enough. I knew that. But I kept adding more and more people I didn't want to see go. I couldn't help it. That's why I grabbed you up, even though you're a Lark. I needed somebody who could really play. You're some boy's dream of himself as a great baseball player, and I knew I could use that. With you, I think we have a real shot."

"But I'm not a Lark."

"Alex . . ."

"No, you said it yourself. Larks are like day-dreams, right? Well, daydreams don't last very long. So why haven't I disappeared already?"

"Maybe your dreamer really needs to hang on to that dream. Maybe you're all he's got left. I don't know."

Alex still didn't believe it. Until somebody proved otherwise, he was the only Alex Metcalf in this or any other world.

"You really think you can make kids believe in you?" he asked Dorothy.

"I don't know. But I have to try. We have to try. But Alex, you've got to accept that you're a Lark. You can't keep throwing yourself at the wolf like you're going to wake up soon. If he eats you, it won't matter how long you've got."

Alex knew it was pointless to argue with her, but he was sure she was wrong. He didn't know how, or why, but he was dreaming all this: the stadiums, the tournament, the Cyclones, the wolf, everything. And he wasn't afraid of the Big Bad Wolf.

All right, he admitted to himself, he was a little afraid of the Big Bad Wolf. But it was like when you dream that you're falling: You always wake up before you hit the ground, because if you don't, you die. At least that's what Ben Abbott had told him in fifth grade. So if this dream ever got really scary, he would just wake up. End of story.

Unless of course he didn't wake up in time, and he died in his dream. But it was dumb, really—the thought that something that happened in a dream could have any effect on you in real life. Dreams were dreams, and real life was real life.

Just in case, Alex slipped a hand down to his side where Dorothy couldn't see it and pinched himself.

He didn't wake up.

THE NANNY GOES TO WAR

6

Beep. Beep. Beep.

Up the baseball goes. He goes back. He goes left. He goes right. He's at the wall—

He's got it! Alex Metcalf wins the World Series!

The crowd goes wild!

Haaaaaaaaaaaaaaaaaaaaaaaaaaaaaa.

Beep. Beep. Beep.

Up the ball goes again. He goes back. He goes left. He goes right. He's at the wall—

The ball glances off his glove, into a beeping machine.

Crash! Bang!

His mother wakes with a start. A nurse comes running.

No more ball and glove in bed.

No! Please! The glove is all he has.

The glove can stay.

lex, you with us?" Scraps asked.

Alex blinked and looked around. He was sitting in the Center Field dugout again. They were back to finish the game they had started the day before against the Nine Little Pigs.

Called on account of Wolf.

"Sorry. Just daydreaming," Alex told his team-mates. Even now he couldn't remember what he'd been dreaming about.

"I was saying, Alex," Dorothy continued, "you're going to have to give Scraps some help down the line in right while she's shifted over. Same goes for you in left, Br'er Rabbit. Then maybe between now and our next game I can find us a replacement for Button Bright in left."

"*If* we have a next game," Br'er Rabbit said.

"We will have a next game." Dorothy glanced at Alex. "We're not going to lose. We can't."

He nodded. "We'll do it for Button Bright," Alex told the Cyclones, and at least upon that they all agreed.

"Does anyone hear a motorcar?" Toad asked.

"Toad, we're inside a baseball stadium," Scraps said.

"No, I distinctly hear a—"

And there it was, just as Toad had said. Alex heard it with the rest of them. A puttering *poop-poop-poop* sound like an antique car. But it wasn't a car; it was a motorcycle, an old military motor-cycle with a sidecar attached, driving toward them from the outfield.

"Is it the wolf again? In disguise?" Alex asked.

Dorothy stepped in front of him and put her arm across his chest, ready to whisk him away.

"No. Wait. I know that motorcycle! It's a Norton Big Four!" Toad leaped to the dugout rail, his amphibian eyes wider than ever. "Point-six-three-three-liter side valve air-cooled engine with a four-speed gear box. Maximum speed: sixty-eight miles per hour."

"And I know that driver," Dorothy said.

A trim young woman wearing a black dress, a brown trench coat, rubber boots, and a flat, round, World War I soldier's helmet, brought the motorcycle to a stop with a lurch in front of the dugout. A cat—a normal-sized one, black and white and brown like the woman—sat in the sidecar beside her, wearing little cat-goggles. Alex didn't recognize either of them from any storybook he'd ever read.

"Ooh. Nanny Mae!" Scraps whispered behind him.

"I have been dispatched by The Agency," the woman said in her slightly Scottish accent. "Which one of you is Alex Metcalf?"

Alex raised a hand, still not sure what was going on.

Nanny Mae dismounted and straightened her trench coat. "Front and center, Master Metcalf. Toot sweet."

Alex did as he was told, shooting a questioning glance over his shoulder. Toad urged him on. The nanny circled him, looking him up and down, then took in a deep breath.

"Not ideal, but we shall have to bear up. There's a war on, after all," she said.

"What war?" Alex asked.

"Mrs. P.," the nanny said, addressing the cat, "alert the Wizard that I am in position, and have The Agency contact me at once if they have further orders."

The cat nodded—*did cats nod?*—and bounded off into the stands.

"I'm sorry, I don't understand—" Alex began, but the woman ignored him and marched into the dugout. She sat down on the bench and pulled off her driving gloves.

"Ooh," whispered Toad. "The Agency sent a Nanny. They're an elite branch of the Wizard's Secret Service. Very hush-hush."

"I am assigned to the protection of Alex Metcalf until further notice," Nanny Mae told the team. "Wherever he goes, I go. Which includes the baseball field. I'll be needing a uniform."

"I decide who plays for the Cyclones and who doesn't," Dorothy told her.

"Dorothy, we do need a left fielder," Alex said.

Dorothy pulled him aside. "Alex, I wanted to give that spot to somebody who needs it."

"Maybe she needs it. I've certainly never heard of her. And maybe she's good. Maybe she can help us win."

"As a Nanny, I am trained for any contingency," the Nanny told them. She patted at her trench coat pockets. "I'm sure I have a mitt around here somewhere . . . ah, yes." From a pocket that was entirely too small to hold one she pulled a broken-in baseball glove.

"How did you—" Alex started, but he dropped it. He didn't know why he bothered asking about all the impossible things that happened in Ever After.

"Alex Metcalf does not play unless I play," the Nanny told them. "And I prefer right field, for I am always right."

"I'll bet you are," Dorothy grumbled. It made no difference to Scraps where she played, so the swap was made and the patchwork girl got busy sewing a jersey for the newest Cyclone.

The pigs took the field to warm up, and Alex went to the on-deck circle to take some practice swings. Nanny Mae stood with him and scanned the crowd.

"I don't need a babysitter," Alex said.

"You don't have a babysitter," she told him. "You have a Nanny."

Alex followed her gaze to the stands. Yesterday, the stadium had been packed. Today, minutes before the game was to resume, there was less than half the crowd. Was one of the people out there the wolf, waiting to shed his disguise and come for Alex? Maybe having a nanny watching over him wasn't such a bad idea.

"Where is everybody?" Alex asked.

"They're scared," the Nanny told him. "The stadium has tripled security and installed mental detectors at all the entrances to see through any disguise, but the Big Bad Wolf still has them hiding in their straw houses. You'd think it was the Blitz all over again."

A recorded message boomed over the PA system: "Your attention please. Due to the recent escape by the Big Bad Wolf, the Ever After Department of Homeland Security has raised the threat level from Tangerine, Florida, to Off-With-Her-Head

Red. The Wizard requests that you watch your neighbors, friends, and family, and report any suspicious behavior to the Ever After authorities at once. Thank you for your cooperation. Remember: The Big Bad Wolf could be anywhere!"

"Well, that should certainly should put everyone's fears to rest," said Alex.

The pigs taking infield looked at each other suspiciously, and the new umpire's call to play ball made everybody jump.

The pigs were nervous all game. They didn't hit well, they didn't pitch well, and they didn't field well. Runners in scoring position didn't score. Sure-fire double plays weren't turned. They had no patience at the plate. By the seventh inning, Dorothy had struck out eleven pigs and was approaching the Ever After Baseball Tournament single-game record.

Despite a 6–0 lead, the Cyclones were playing tight too. Alex could see it. Jack was jumpy. Toad was worried about how the low turnout would affect his polling numbers. Nanny Mae watched the stands. Even Scraps, who never seemed to be bothered by much of anything, missed a fly ball in warm-ups while she was staring at the rows of security guards who lined the foul lines.

"Let's hear some chatter in here," Alex told his teammates in the dugout.

Toad cleared his throat. "Well, I read an interesting article on motorcars this morning . . ."

"No. *Baseball* chatter."

"Oh. Of course! I say, Scraps," Toad said, "tell me again how earned run average is calculated."

"No, no, no. Not like that. Listen—" Alex climbed up to lean on the rail. "Let's go, Nanny Mae! Good eye now, good eye!"

"Good eye?" Tik-Tok asked.

"Yeah. It means, you know, judge the pitches well. Have a good eye."

"Good eyeball, Nanny!" Toad called.

"That's it. Kind of," said Alex. "We want a pitcher, not a belly itcher!" he called.

"What's a belly itcher?" Jack asked.

"It's a . . . It's like . . . You know, I have no idea. It's just something people say."

The Nanny stroked a double to the wall and slid in to second. Alex clapped. "That's the way now. That's the way. Keep it going, Scraps. Keep it going. You got 'em baby, you got 'em."

Soon most of the Cyclones were picking up on the chatter. Scraps bounced one through the hole at short, and they cheered.

"Wait, what's that smell?" Br'er Rabbit hollered. He made a show of sniffing the air. "I think it's bacon!"

The pig at first base glowered at him.

"All right, Br'er Rabbit," said Dorothy. "A little baseball chatter is fine, but can the pig jokes."

"Ooh. Canned ham," Br'er Rabbit said, loud enough for the infielders to hear him. "Now that does sound delicious!"

"That'll do, hare," said a British pig at short.

"Br'er Rabbit, that's not—" Alex began, but the rabbit was already shouting again.

"Can't put lipstick on this pig!" he joked.

Jack was at bat, and he managed to get his long arms around on a pitch and dribble it out into no-pig's-land between the pitcher, the shortstop, and the third baseman. The shortstop charged, scooped up the ball, and winged it to second—out! The pig at second pivoted and fired for first.

"Jack, be nimble!" Alex cried.

"Jack, be quick!" Dorothy called.

Bang went the ball. *Bang* went Jack's foot. "Out!" the umpire cried, and Jack stumbled and went sprawling.

The once chatty Cyclones dugout was silent.

"I say, they haven't looked that good all game," Toad observed.

"No," Dorothy said, staring straight at Br'er Rabbit. "They haven't."

The rabbit laughed meekly and shrank back onto the bench.

Over the next two innings, the Nine Little Pigs put on a rally rivaled only by the Cyclones' comeback against the Chicks, scoring five runs in two innings and drawing close enough to make the Cyclones sweat like pigs. In the top of the ninth the Cyclones were retired in neat order, and in the bottom of the inning the pigs' bats did their *oinking* for them. With two outs, a base hit by the pig who built his house out of straw was followed by a double by the pig who built his house out of sticks, and the tying run was at the plate.

"Little pig, little pig, drive me in!" called the pig on second. The Very Small Animal at bat did just that, and the pigs on base went "Wee-wee-wee" all the way home—making a particular point to show Br'er Rabbit each of their curly tails as they made their turns at third.

"Maybe next time you can keep your big mouth shut," Dorothy snapped at him. She sent Alex a nasty look as well to put part of the blame on him. He held up his hands in innocence, but Dorothy was already stalking back up the mound.

One more out; that's all they needed. But the radiant, humble center fielder was at the plate, and he had proven to be terrific. Dorothy got her signal from Tik-Tok and went into her windup. She pitched. The pig swung.

Dink! Up the ball went, a drifting foul ball toward the first base stands.

Alex went back. He went left. He went right. He was at the wall—

—and all at once he remembered his daydream. The beeping machines. His mother asleep beside him in the chair. The nurse running in—

Crash! Bang!

Alex fell into the stands, and the ball thwacked the concrete floor and bounced a few rows back, where the fans fought for the foul ball.

Dorothy and Jack came running over and helped Alex back to his feet.

"Nice try, Alex!" Jack told him. "Good hustle. Is that good chatter?"

"Hmm? Oh. Yeah. Good chatter."

Dorothy looked at him sideways. "You okay? You hit your head?"

"No. I'm okay."

"All right. Don't worry about it," Dorothy told him. "I'm gonna strike this swine out."

Alex went back to first, and hardly paid attention as Dorothy did just that and the Cyclones celebrated their victory.

He was too busy wondering why he had daydreamed he was in the hospital.

A WOLF IN SHEEP'S CLOTHING

7

Alex stared out the window of the Cyclones' bus, watching the streetlights go flashing by like UFOs. The way this dream was going, they might really be UFOs. The Cyclones had won their third game and were gathering steam in the tournament, but all Alex kept thinking about was being in the hospital. Why had he dreamed that? What was the dream trying to tell him?

"We might actually win this," Scraps was saying. "We *might. Actually. Win!*"

The Nanny was in the seat across from Alex, knitting, with Mrs. P. curled up in her lap. They'd strapped her motorcycle to the grille of the bus, and she was a full-fledged member of the team now. Dorothy sat two rows ahead of them, working on the lineups for the next day's game. Everyone else was sitting on their knees and leaning over their seats to talk about their victory.

"The odds—are now—539—to 1—that we—will win," Tik-Tok told them.

Jack pumped his fist. "Woo-hoo! Um, is that good?"

"No," said Br'er Rabbit. "But it's a whole lot better than what we started with," he allowed.

"You gotta believe," Scraps said. "Right, Alex?"

"Hunh?" He pulled himself away from the window. "Yeah. You gotta believe."

"What are you going to wish for, Toad?" Jack asked.

"If we win? Oh, dear. Well, let's see. There's a three-liter Lobster Quadrille I've had my eye on for some time—a splendid little two-seater automobile just perfect for getting out to see the world. But of course I will probably wish for victory in the coming election instead. What about you, Jack?"

"Oh! I know what I'm going to wish for. I'm going to wish I was good at baseball."

"But Jack, if you win the tournament with the Cyclones, won't that mean you've already gotten pretty good?" Alex asked.

"Not in Jack's case," said Br'er Rabbit.

Scraps did a handstand in her seat. "I think I'm going to ask for new stuffing." She sniffed her armpit and came away making a face. "My old cotton is getting pretty stank."

"I'm gonna wish for more wishes," said Br'er Rabbit.

Everyone groaned.

"You can't wish for more wishes!"

"Says who? In stories with wishes, they never wish for more wishes, even though nobody says they can't. Well, I don't aim to make the same mistake."

"What about you, Alex?" Scraps asked.

Alex sat up higher in his seat. "Who, me? I don't know. It doesn't really matter."

"There must be something you want, old man."

Alex already had everything he had ever wanted: He was the star of a travel team, riding from town to town on a team bus without his parents or his little sister or anybody else but his teammates, playing baseball every day and having a blast. But now, he was surprised to realize, he was homesick. He wanted to see his mom and dad again. His dog. His room. His school. Even his kid sister.

He wished he could go home.

He couldn't tell them that, of course. The Cyclones. They thought he was a daydream. A Lark. They didn't think he had a home to go back to, and they would just argue with him.

"I don't know," he told them. "I guess if I didn't have anything else to worry about, just riding around with you guys and playing baseball forever would be pretty great."

Scraps nodded sagely. "Good wish. How about you, Dorothy?"

Dorothy jumped. She'd been caught listening.

"You know what I'm going to wish for," she told them. "The same thing all of you should be wishing for." She turned back around in her seat and slapped her scorebook on her lap. "Right now I wish you guys would quit jabbering and let me finish figuring out the lineups so I can get to sleep."

Dorothy's scolding killed the conversation, and everyone sank back down into their seats. Alex stared out the window again, wondering when he would ever wake up from this dream, when he saw an orange glow up ahead.

"Fire!" Toad cried.

He was right. It was another bus. A bus like theirs—though not pink—turned over on its side and engulfed in flames.

"Lester, pull over!" Dorothy called. "Pull over!"

"Already on it," Lester called, and he slammed on the brakes. The pink bus skidded to a stop on the other side of the road, and he flipped on the lever that put out the old school bus stop sign even though there were no other cars on the lonely stretch of highway.

Toad pressed his face to the window. "Oh my, this is bad. A true test of my crisis response management skills. Has anyone got a megaphone?"

Alex stood with the rest of the Cyclones to go help, but Nanny Mae held up her hand.

"No. You'll stay here."

"But I have to help!" Alex told her.

"You'll do no such thing. It could be a trap. Besides, I was a Brigadier in Queen Alexandra's Royal Army Nursing Corps during the Great War. I'll be worth two of us."

"But—"

"Mrs. P. will remain here with you," Nanny Mae told him, and that was that.

Alex sat down in the front seat next to Mrs. P., who was wearing a little knitted scarf now. She sat and watched him like a guard dog. Out the window, Alex could see his teammates pulling people from the wreck against the bright yellow blaze.

"I wonder who was on that bus, Mrs. P.," Alex said.

"That there was the p-pig team you played today," Lester said.

"How do you know who it is?" Alex asked.

Lester's head turned around slowly, like a possessed man in a horror movie. "Because I'm the one who d-did it to them," he said, still stammering like Lester, but in a deeper voice like a growl.

Mrs. P. hissed and arched her back. It took Alex only a moment to understand what was going on as Lester grew thicker and hairier, busting out of his overalls like a werewolf. Alex lunged for the exit, but the Big Bad Wolf was there to cut him off, smiling. Mrs. P. was small enough to slip through though, and she darted between the wolf's legs and out the door.

"No, wait!" Alex called after the cat. Like a cat was going to be any help to him anyway.

"Looks like it's just you and me this time, Alex."

The wolf grew bigger and bigger, until he had to hunch over inside the bus. Alex scrambled over the back of his seat and fell face-first into the seat behind him.

"Help—help!" he screamed.

"Nobody's laughing now, are they?" the Big

Bad Wolf asked. He tore a seat from its bolts and tossed it behind him, blocking the door. Alex crawled over another seat, afraid that if he went for the aisle, the wolf would be on him in seconds. The wolf wrenched the next row of seats from the floor with a *krank* and threw them behind him.

"Help! Dorothy! Nanny Mae! Anybody!" Alex cried. It was no use. The dull roar of the burning bus was too loud. No one could hear him.

"Run, run, as fast as you can—" the Big Bad Wolf taunted. "Wait. Wrong fairy tale."

"Please wake up, please wake up, please wake up," Alex prayed. His leg got caught climbing over a seat, and he fell onto the floor. The wolf yanked up another vinyl seat, and the bus bounced.

The wolf was playing with him, Alex realized. He was not going to get away.

"Wakeupwakeupwakeupwakeup," he begged.

Chank! The wolf ripped away the seat where Alex was hiding, and he slithered along the dusty floor to hide under the next seat, and then the next.

"Do you know what you did to me, Alex Metcalf?" the wolf said. "You got me captured." *Krank!* "Made them laugh at me." *Shink!* "On national television." *Wronk.* "But the worst, the absolute worst, was that you acted like it was nothing. Like coming face-to-face with the Big Bad Wolf was an afternoon at the ballpark." *Ker-chank.* "So now I'm going to eat you up, Alex Metcalf. Devour you. Slowly. Until there's nothing left but your shredded jersey. Something they can show on the six o'clock news. Then everyone will remember that the Big Bad Wolf is no one to laugh at."

Alex hit the back wall of the bus. There was nowhere left to crawl.

"Wakeupwakeupwakeupwakeupwakeup," Alex whispered. He was supposed to be awake by now! That was how bad dreams worked!

Wrenck! The wolf pried the last of the seats away and leered at him. Saliva drooled from his huge, grinning teeth.

"This isn't supposed to happen!" Alex cried. "When the nightmare is too much, you're supposed to wake up! You can't die in a dream!"

"Want to bet?" said the wolf.

Alex was curling into a ball when he spied the words on the bottom of the wall behind him: EMERGENCY EXIT. The back door! Buses always had a back door!

Alex launched himself at the handle, but the wolf was on him like a beanball. Claws flashed. Alex's jersey ripped, and his stomach burned. He fell backward. His hands scrabbled for the handle. The wolf lunged, teeth gleaming. The door gave, swinging outward, and the wolf's jaws snapped right where he had been. Alex fell four feet down to the ground and landed on his back with an *oomph* that knocked the air out of him.

The wolf's head bent low and he lunged again, but his shoulders ground against the back wall of the bus. He was too big to fit through the door. For a few seconds at least.

"*Haaaaaa—haaaaaa—*" Alex rasped, trying to call for help, but it came out like a wheezy laugh instead. He tried to kick backward, but he was hyperventilating now, hysterical. He couldn't catch his breath.

The wolf shrank down to person size and leaped. Alex covered his head and turned, waiting for the bite that would finish him, but instead there was a *choom!* and an inhuman howl, and burning heat, and the smell of singed hair and burnt flesh.

Alex opened his eyes. The air was filled with smoke, and the Big Bad Wolf wasn't on top of him anymore. The wolf was struggling to his feet a few yards away, and on the other side of Alex was Nanny Mae, marching toward him with a long, black metal thing on her shoulder.

A bazooka.

"I have had just about enough of your naughtiness, Mr. Wolf!" she said.

Choom! She fired the rocket launcher as she advanced, cool as ice water at the end of baseball practice, Mrs. P. trotting along at her side. *Kathoom!* Alex flinched, feeling the searing heat from the explosion, and turned to see the Big Bad Wolf blown back into the darkness by the blast.

Nanny Mae pulled another missile out of her pocket and slid it into the smoking bazooka. Then Dorothy was there, grabbing Alex, ready to whisk him someplace else. But the Big Bad Wolf was gone. The Nanny had chased him away.

"I was right, of course. It was a trap," Nanny Mae said, sliding the bazooka into one of her trench coat pockets like it wasn't ten times too long to fit in there.

"Are you okay?" Dorothy asked Alex. She frowned at the cuts on his stomach. They stung like someone had slid into him cleats first.

"Great. Only I'd like to wake up now," Alex told her, and he promptly passed out.

THERE'S NO PLACE LIKE HOME

8

They are going to cut a hole in him. A hole to his heart.
"So we don't have to keep sticking you in the arm."
Alex puts a hand to his wrist. There is plastic there. A
tube in his arm. Taped to him.
The hole is for the poison. To kill the thing that's attack-
ing him.
To kill the thing that's killing him.
"The hole won't hurt," they tell him.
But the poison will. The poison feels worse than the
thing attacking him.
"Sometimes the only way to fight something terrible,"
they tell him, "is with something even more terrible."

Alex jerked awake. His stomach and arms
burned.

He was in the bus again. *That* bus. The one
the wolf had destroyed trying to get him. He was
lying on one of the ripped-out cushions. Beside
him sat Mrs. P. and Nanny Mae, who was reading

a book. The bus was stopped and the sun was up, but he didn't know if they had driven anywhere or not. He felt like he'd been asleep for days.

Alex sat up, and his stomach and arms screamed in pain. The bandages on his stomach he understood: That was where the wolf had clawed him. But what had happened to his arms?

"Minor burns," the Nanny told him. She checked a bag of clear fluid that ran down to his arm in a tube. "From the rocket launcher. I'm afraid you were caught in the crossfire. Had to be done, though. Sometimes the only way to fight something terrible is with something even more terrible."

Where had Alex heard that before? He shook his head. He'd been dreaming something, about tubes, and poison—

"Hold still while I take this out," Nanny Mae told him, and she removed the needle from his arm and wrapped it with a bandage.

"Thanks for going for help," Alex said to Mrs. P., and he could swear the cat nodded.

Dorothy joined them just as Nanny Mae was finishing up. "How is he?"

"We were right to bivvy up here. An overnight

rest is exactly what he needed. But no strenuous activity for at least twenty-four hours more—and that includes baseball."

"But we have a game today!" Alex said.

"Calm down. Calm down," Dorothy told him. "The game's been moved to tomorrow. The stadium's not ready yet."

Alex frowned. "How can the stadium not be ready?"

Dorothy led Alex and Nanny Mae off the bus, past the empty driver's seat.

"Poor Lester," Alex said. "Does anyone know what happened to him?"

"We're assuming the wolf ate him before taking his place," Nanny Mae told him.

Outside, the sidewalk was packed with men in top hats and women in bustles. Horse-drawn carriages passed by on the cobblestone streets.

"Victorian London," Dorothy explained. "A lot of classics take place here."

"Is this where your book is set?" Alex asked the Nanny.

"No, dear. I'm a thoroughly modern Twentieth-Century Nanny." She tapped her metal soldier's helmet as proof. "Still, it's good to be back home, no matter when it is."

Alex wished he could say the same thing.

Dorothy led them across the street and into Hyde Park, a big green place with trees and gravel paths and a curving river. Over the next rise, Alex could see what looked like a giant red Chinese pagoda, with golden roofs that curled up at the corners and carvings of long, snake-like dragons twisting around its pillars. The structure wasn't totally built, but it didn't have cranes and scaffolding and construction workers all over it. Instead it was like looking at an unfinished painting.

When they got closer, Alex saw that's exactly what it was. Toad and Scraps were standing at the entrance of the elaborate stadium, staring up at a small Chinese boy wearing what looked like red silk trousers, a brimless red hat, and a red jacket with a short yellow collar. He had a paintbrush in his hand, but no palette or paint can to dip it in. Still, wherever he moved the brush, new parts of the stadium appeared.

"*Ni hao,* old boy!" Toad called. "That means 'hello' in Chinese," he told his friends.

The boy in the silk outfit waved hello, then painted himself a winged dragon and hopped on its back to fly down and greet them. Alex stepped back as the dragon coiled and writhed, but the boy wiped it away with a damp rag as soon as his feet were on the ground.

"Ma Liang! Good to see you, good to see you," Toad said, pumping the boy's hand.

Ma Liang smiled. "I know what you want, Mr. Toad." He moved his brush like he was painting on the air, and something shiny and metal began to appear. A long, round body, four big wheels, a steering wheel . . . Before their eyes, Ma Liang painted an old-fashioned race car into existence.

Toad clapped happily. "What a clever lad! You remember!"

Ma Liang bowed. "Rivers and mountains may change; Toad, never."

Dorothy grabbed her shortstop by his jersey. "Toad, you promised. You swore off motorcars until we were finished with the tournament."

"But that was when I thought we were going to lose our first game! Please? He painted it especially for me!"

"It can't really work, can it?" Alex asked. "I mean, it's just a painting."

"Of course it can! It's a magic paintbrush," Toad told him. "Here, I'll show you."

Toad slipped free of Dorothy's grip, hopped into the car, and revved the engine.

"Toad, don't you dare!" Dorothy yelled, but she was too late. The car leaped away, its big wheels cutting tracks in the park grass as Toad swung the steering wheel this way and that.

"Ho-ho!" Toad cried as he swung back past them. "Make way for the amazing Toad, able batsman and daring motorcar racer! Skillful Toad, handsome Toad, glorious Toad! Say so long, fellows, for this is the last you'll see of old Toady. I'm off to see faraway places. Take the road less traveled. Grab life by the—"

Smash! Toad drove the painted car right into a tree and was thrown clear. He landed with a thud among some shrubberies.

"Toad!" Alex cried, rushing to his side. The daredevil lay unconscious among a scattering of "VOTE TOAD" cards that had come out of his pockets mid-tumble.

"Toad—Toad, speak to me," Alex said. Toad's eyes were closed, and Alex feared the worst.

Dorothy walked up and crossed her arms. "He'll be fine in a second."

She was right. Toad's eyes popped open and he came back to life. "Poop. Poop-poop," he said, imitating the car. "Did you see me, Alex? Did you? What a splendid ride! Hoo-hoo!"

Dorothy poked him with her foot. "I'm glad the team is so important to you that as soon as you hop into an automobile it's, 'So long, fellows! I'm off to see the world!'"

"Well, of course I didn't mean it," Toad said. "You know the team is the most important thing to me. Honestly. I think of nothing else, day and night. Hits and runs. Stolen bases. Double plays. Live for baseball: That's my motto in life."

A Victorian couple on a walk in the park stopped a few yards away to see what the fuss was about.

"Oh! Here." Toad handed Alex one of the strewn "VOTE TOAD" cards. "Run give this to those people, would you?"

Dorothy dragged Toad to his feet. "Let's go, Toad. You and me are going to put your automotive expertise to good use and see if we can't get Lester's bus fixed."

"But—I—" Toad tried to protest, but Dorothy dragged him away.

Scraps waved good-bye to Ma Liang as he painted a hot-air balloon for himself and floated back up to the top of the stadium to finish his work.

"Kind of seems out of place, doesn't it?" Alex said. "A Chinese pagoda in the middle of London?"

"We're all out of place here," Scraps told him. "Guess we have the day off then. Want to go into town with me? I need to buy a new bit of fabric." She pointed to her leg, and Alex saw the long gash there for the first time. Cotton batting stuck out through the hole.

"Scraps, you're hurt! Did the wolf do that?"

"I'm torn, not hurt," Scraps corrected him. She led him out of the park, with Nanny Mae and Mrs. P. a few watchful paces behind them. "And it wasn't the Big Bad Wolf. One of those pigs hoofed me when he slid into third yesterday. No big deal. Just another patch and I'm good as new."

"So that's really all you are? Fabric and stuffing? I mean, not 'all you are,' but you know."

Scraps smiled. "That's really all I am. Left-over scraps of somebody else's pretty fabric, sewn together all higgledy-piggledy."

"Please—no more pig jokes. Not after last night."

"Seconded," Nanny Mae said, listening in behind them.

Scraps tugged at one of her patches. "See this piece of red and white gingham? I like to think it came from an apron, or maybe a little girl's dress. Over here's my fanciest bit, a piece of silk with a crane pattern on it, from a kimono. And that scrap," she said, twisting around so he could see, "that's purple brocade, from a king's robe, maybe. Or maybe just somebody's drapes." She grinned. "Take me apart, and I'm just what my name says I am: a bunch of scraps."

"You don't know where all the pieces of you came from?"

"Do you?"

Alex watched another carriage rattle by on the street.

"Does that mean you can't die, Scraps?"

"None of us can. Not getting torn apart. The only way any Storybook ever dies is when people stop believing in us. Same for Larks. First you get The Itch, and then you're gone."

"The Itch? You mean like Button Bright? I saw him scratching in the dugout."

"The Itch comes when people start doubting you. Forgetting you," Nanny Mae explained from behind them. "Some people lose The Itch and make a full recovery, but for most, it means their time is up."

"Then Button Bright—"

Scraps shook her head. "Button Bright disappeared a couple of times before now, and he's been gone longer each time. I think this time it's for good. There are adults out there who remember him, but nobody believes in him anymore. You need kids for that."

They walked on quietly, and Alex saw a red and white Ever After Department of Homeland Security poster with a picture of the Big Bad Wolf's head and the words "Keep calm and carry on."

"If nobody in Ever After can die," he asked, "why is everybody so afraid of the Big Bad Wolf?"

"Oh. Well. The wolf doesn't kill you, see," Scraps said. "He just eats you up. Swallows you whole. You're inside the wolf, and inside the wolf is . . . well, nothing. It's just an empty void, no light, no sound, nothing—you're just there, waiting for someone to forget you. It's worse than dying."

"So the wolf, he can't die either?"

"No," the Nanny said. "You can knock him down. Hurt him. Isolate him. But he will always be there, waiting to come back again. And you never know when or if he will."

How long would Alex have to keep running from the wolf then? For as long as he kept dreaming?

But he wasn't dreaming. He knew that now. If he was really asleep and just dreaming all this, he would have woken up when the wolf was chasing him in the bus.

Alex stepped in a puddle on the sidewalk and felt the back of his pants leg get wet.

The wolf was real. The claw marks on Alex's chest were real, and they still hurt. This whole world was real. But he refused to believe what Dorothy and the others told him, that he was the daydream of some other Alex Metcalf somewhere else. It was crazy. There had to be some other explanation. If he wasn't dreaming this place, if it was a real place, and he was here, that meant—

Alex stopped in the middle of the sidewalk. "I'm real!"

"We all are," Scraps told him.

"No, I mean, I'm the only one here who isn't a fantasy. I'm not dreaming, and I'm not somebody else's dream. I'm the *one and only Alex Metcalf.* I don't remember falling down a rabbit hole or riding a tornado or anything, but somehow I ended up here, like Alice or Dorothy in their stories. That has to be it!"

"No, dear," Nanny Mae said. "You're a Lark."

"But I could be right, couldn't I?"

"Well . . ." Scraps began.

"No," the Nanny said again.

If the only other explanation was that he was a Lark, then Alex chose to believe he was a real live boy. That was the only answer. He had disappeared from the real world, gotten lost here in Ever After, and now the Big Bad Wolf was after him, and—

Alex put a hand to the bandages on his stomach.

—and he had to get out of here.

Scraps nodded to a shop window filled with bolts of cloth. "This is the fabric store I need. You coming?" she asked.

"Ah, no," Alex told her. He had spied an office across the street he wanted to visit. "No thanks, Scraps. I'll meet you back at the bus."

Scraps's eyes lingered on Alex for a moment, then she glanced at the Nanny.

"I'll watch him," Nanny Mae said. "I haven't lost one of my charges yet."

Alex wished they would believe him, but it didn't really matter. He would show them. He waited for a carriage to pass and hurried across the street to a shop marked "Ever After Holiday and Travel Services, Ltd." The Nanny gave him a disapproving look, but she didn't stop him from going in.

The walls of the tiny office were lined with posters advertising odd "vacation opportunities": a bank holiday spent inside a vault, a walk down Memory Lane, a trip down the stairs. Underneath each was listed the vacation's price, including airfare, taxes, and Ever After Department of Homeland Security fees.

"Hello and welcome!" said a perky woman behind the counter. "Where can we send you today? We have a number of specials right now, including our very popular Ego Trip. Or, if you're looking for something a little different, we have a number of day trips available. I understand Friday is beautiful this time of year."

"I—no. I already know where I want to go," Alex told her.

"Let's get right to it then!" The travel agent pulled her keyboard over. "Are you two together?"

Alex and Nanny Mae said *"No"* and *"Yes"* at the same time.

"Yes," the Nanny asserted. She pulled her knitting out of one of her impossible pockets and *click*ed away.

"All righty. Will this be a round trip, or a square trip?"

"Um, one way, if that's an option." Alex glanced at the Nanny. She raised an eyebrow but said nothing.

"Certainly! And how would you like to travel? Broomstick? Glass elevator? Magic wardrobe? I have some great rates on Giant Peach cruises—"

"It doesn't matter," Alex interrupted. "Um, magic wardrobe," he decided. At least that sounded safer than riding a piece of fruit somewhere.

"And where would you like to go?"

"Home, please."

The woman's fingers paused over her keyboard. Beside him, still knitting, Nanny Mae cleared her throat.

"Home?" the travel agent asked.

"Yes. My home. In Decatur, Georgia."

The woman tapped at her keyboard. Her computer beeped. Had she actually found it?

"I'm sorry, that destination again?"

Alex slumped. "Decatur, Georgia? Just outside Atlanta?"

"Atlantis?"

"No. Atlan*ta*."

"Is that near Camelot?"

"No. It's in the United States."

"Which is . . . ?"

"A country? You have to have heard of it."

"There's no place you can go we can't send you!" the woman said cheerfully. "Let me just look at my list of nations. Alienation, Divination, Elimination, Indignation, Pollination, Predestination . . . I'm sorry. I just don't see your home on here."

"But you said there was no place I could go you couldn't send me," Alex said.

"I do rather think that's the point, Alex," the Nanny said.

The woman behind the counter gave him a sympathetic smile. "I'm terribly sorry. Are you sure there isn't someplace else you'd like to go? The Emerald City? Sunnybrook Farm? Camp Green Lake? Free shovel with every purchase!"

"No. No thank you. I didn't have any money anyway."

"Oh, that's all right," the woman told him. "I'm not just a travel agent, I'm a free agent too. If you think of anywhere you'd like to go, you just let me know and I can send you there at no cost."

Alex thanked the woman and went back out onto the street. Nanny Mae pulled a bit of kibble from her pocket and fed Mrs. P. while they waited on Scraps to finish. *We're all out of place here,* Scraps had said. But Alex thought he was the most out of place of them all. He leaned back against the window of the travel agency, wondering how he could possibly get back to where he really belonged, and saw the gold pagoda roof of the new stadium poking up above the London skyline.

Ma Liang and his magic paintbrush! Alex nodded to himself. There might just be a way for him to get home after all.

ALEX AND THE MAGIC PAINTBRUSH

9

Whhat Alex needed was a distraction.

It was the next day, and the stadium was finished. Well-dressed London gentlemen and ladies, along with a fair number of odd-looking Storybooks and modern-looking Larks, were already streaming inside. The Cyclones' game was going to start soon. Toad was handing out "VOTE TOAD" cards. Scraps was doing cartwheels. Jack and Tik-Tok were unloading the baseball gear from the bus, and Dorothy was trying to collect the rest of the Cyclones for the game.

It was Nanny Mae Alex had to shake. He'd managed to sneak away from her and Mrs. P. for a few minutes the day before to talk to Ma Liang when they returned from the city, and she was not happy when she'd tracked him down. If it hadn't been her job to protect him, he thought, she might have killed him. Worse, now she was watching him like a pitcher eying a sixty-steals guy leading off first. If he disappeared behind the bus, Mrs. P. appeared at the other end. If he crossed the street to buy some boiled peanuts from a vendor, Nanny Mae was there fishing coins out of her pocket. He was beginning to think the only way he could get rid of her was to push her into one of those bottomless pockets on her trench coat.

Then the wind began to pick up. Gentlemen grabbed their top hats and ladies held on to their skirts. The trees in Hyde Park swayed and bent. Leaves thrashed. Newspapers swirled. Dark clouds blew in overhead.

The Big Bad Wolf again? Alex didn't stick around to find out. The Nanny's eyes finally left him as she whirled, one hand holding her metal hat, the other pulling a ray gun from one of her pockets. There was a crack, and a sound like shattering glass, and a booming voice said, "WEE ARRE HERRE!" but Alex was already gone. With Nanny Mae's attention elsewhere, he darted inside the red and gold stadium and sprinted to the upper deck, where the boy with the magic paint-brush was waiting for him.

"Did you figure out how to get me home?" Alex asked. If he hadn't, the Nanny was going to be more than cross with him when he got back. She would very likely turn that ray gun on him, orders or no orders.

"I have an idea," Ma Liang told him.

"Great! What is it? We have to hurry."

"A hasty man drinks his tea with a fork."

"Please!" Alex glanced over his shoulder. He thought he heard the soft padding of cat feet on the bleacher steps. "We don't have much time."

Ma Liang bowed and gestured toward a flight of stairs, and Alex took off at a run. After his failed attempt to leave Ever After with the help of the travel agency, he'd had the idea to ask Ma Liang to get him out. He could paint anything with his magic paintbrush—a car, a dragon, a doorway, even a flying carpet. If Ma Liang couldn't find a way to get him out of this place, Alex figured, no one could.

The stairs led to a platform high above the field, where an enormous red firework rocket with a fuse as thick as a rope and a bamboo trunk for a stabilizing stick lay propped up against one of the pagoda's sloped roofs.

"A . . . a bottle rocket?" Alex asked. He walked around the thing, not at all sure the boy had understood his request. "Um, how is this supposed to get me home?"

"We ride it, of course."

"I thought you were going to paint another dragon or a kite," Alex said. "Something Chinese."

"Are you kidding? The Chinese invented rockets. But are you sure you want to do this?"

"Of course! I mean, as long as the thing doesn't explode. Why not?"

"Because you can't find a fish by looking in a tree."

"Enough with the Chinese proverbs already! Come on. Mrs. P. is going to be here any second."

"All right. Climb on."

Alex shimmied up the outside of the rocket, where Ma Liang had painted two silk-cushioned palanquin chairs for them.

"So, wait. Is this really going to work?" Alex felt like Daffy Duck straddling a rocket ship in a cartoon.

"The longest journey begins with a single spark,"

Ma Liang said, grinning, and with a *shunk* he struck a match and touched it to the fuse. It flared to life and hissed as it burned toward the rocket.

Alex grabbed on for dear life. "You gotta believe, I guess."

Down below, Alex could see Hyde Park. He thought he could just pick out the Cyclones too. He didn't see the wolf, or any ray gun beams. But even if it hadn't been the wolf who caused that wind, it would only be a matter of time until he attacked again—and the next time, his nanny might not be able to save him.

The fuse struck the black powder inside the rocket, and it ignited with a *foosh!* The rocket kicked, skidded, then launched into the air, arcing up and away from the stadium.

Alex closed his eyes. He hated to bail on his friends, especially Dorothy, but he was getting out of here. He had to. He was going home, where the wolf would never get to him again.

The enormous firework steadied beneath him, and Alex felt Ma Liang poke him in the back. He had painted Alex a pair of goggles to help with the wind.

Alex put the goggles on and took one last look down at where his friends were. "So long, fellows," he said quietly, imitating Toad. "I'm off to see the world. The *real* world." He wished he could have said a proper good-bye, but he knew they never would have let him go otherwise.

The rocket flew higher and Ever After grew smaller. Alex saw baseball fields, and long stretches of river, and entire mountains, and octopus-like cities that swam in great oceans of green farmland. It was like flying over a real world, and he was more convinced than ever that this place was a real place. A real place he had to get away from. He spied London, and Dictionopolis, and Big Rock Candy Mountain, and a Thoughtful Spot, and a Yellow-Brick Road, and Neo-Tokyo, and more, and he knew what they were from so high up because he could read their names. There were letters and words—the names of cities and rivers and mountains—written right there on the ground, like a giant map. They rose even higher, and Alex saw the entire island was covered with the largest letters of all: EVER AFTER.

"It's like we're flying over that diorama," he said, the wind eating his words. "The one in the Ever After Exposition Hall."

For a strange moment, he wondered if he hadn't actually been *in* the diorama.

The little labeled dots on the map soon gave way to a large, dark wood, and the known became the unknown: the Wild Woods. The Briar Patch. The Shadowlands. The Forbidden Forest.

"We're doing it," Alex said. "We're leaving Ever After!"

The Wild Woods gave way to a desert, on one side called the Shifting Sands, on another the Deadly Desert. On and on they flew, the dunes below them rippling like a sea. And then they came to a real ocean, labeled only as "the Sea." A pirate ship fired a cannonball over the nose of their rocket.

"Can we go higher?" Alex yelled. "Faster?"

"Flying hurts least those who fly low."

"Come on, please?"

Ma Liang shrugged and painted two more rockets, each as big as the first, strapped to their rocket with rope.

Up they went, higher and faster. The water seemed to stretch on forever, and just when Alex thought he would never get there, he saw the thing he had most wanted to see all along.

"Land!" he cried. "I see land!"

He had no idea where it would be. America? Africa? Australia? Europe? There was no telling where Ever After was hidden, or if it was even real. But no matter where Alex ended up, he could always find a way to get in touch with his parents, find a way home. He leaned over the side and watched, eager for the first sign of where Ma Liang's rocket had taken them. The sea gave way to sand—a beach!—and Alex strained to see a city, a landmark, anything that would tell him where he was.

Then he saw the words "Great Sandy Waste" on the shore, as though written by some colossal cartographer.

"No," he said. "No, no, no, no, no—"

This was no beach; it was a desert. The one that surrounded Ever After. In the distance, beyond a wood labeled "Dark Forest," Alex could just make out enormous letters written on the earth: E-V-E-R—

EVER AFTER. They had flown all the way around the world and come back to where they started.

"No! We have to go higher!" Alex told the boy. "Higher!"

Ma Liang offered no Chinese proverbs this time, only a sad shake of the head. He added more rockets, and more rockets, and still they climbed.

The blue sky turned black, and they were in space, Alex's cartoon vision come true. He felt gravity leave them, and he held on now, not worried that he would fall off, but that he would fall up. Alex looked over the side again, hoping to see the Earth beneath them, but instead saw a world with only one continent, surrounded on all sides by water, desert, and woods.

Ever After.

Alex twisted away from the sight with his head in his hands. It was impossible. Inconceivable. He was trapped in this place, where not even a rocket could fly him to freedom.

Ma Liang was quiet behind him, waiting for Alex to tell him what more he wanted. But Alex didn't want to turn around. He didn't want to talk. What would he say, anyway? What he wanted wasn't possible. He would never get out of Ever After. Never.

Ma Liang waited a few moments more, then took out his magic paintbrush and painted a sickle-shaped moon in the black space beyond them. Then, using his wet rag, he wiped away all the other rockets but the one they rode, and they fell toward the moon he'd made as the firework petered out. Somehow, impossibly, the painted moon got bigger and bigger. They coasted down toward its cratered surface, and then with a jolt the nose of the rocket stuck like a fork in cheese and Alex and Ma Liang went tumbling, rolling to a gentle stop in the moon's low gravity.

Alex lay where he landed, staring down (*up?*) at the blue, green, and white world beneath them (*above them?*). They shouldn't have been able to breathe in space or on the moon, Alex knew, but it wasn't the real moon anyway. It was a painted moon, and the Earth that spun below them wasn't the real Earth either. It was Ever After. Nothing here was real. It was all a fantasy. A dream.

Alex rested his head on the rim of a crater and closed his eyes. "I just wanted to go home."

"Here. I will paint a home for you on the moon," Ma Liang said. "Who wouldn't like to live on the moon?" He took out his magic paintbrush and began to paint four walls, a roof, a rectangle for a door, a chimney with a trail of smoke trailing away—

"No," Alex told him. "No. Thank you. You've given me everything I've asked for, but all I really want is *my* home. Where I live. Where I'm supposed to be."

Ma Liang sat next to him. "Hmm. Where you are supposed to be . . ."

"I suppose you've got a Chinese proverb for that too."

"I do. Would you like to hear it?"

"No."

"I thought not. Here. I have something else for you instead." Ma Liang stood and painted a great kite shaped like a dragon.

"What is this Chinese proverb, 'Go fly a kite'?" Alex asked.

"In a way, yes," Ma Liang said. He handed the kite to Alex.

"Look, that's really nice of you, but I don't think flying a kite is going to—"

Ma Liang drew a gust of wind, and the kite pulled Alex to his feet. Ma Liang drew another gust, and another, and Alex lifted off the ground.

Alex kicked his feet, trying to come back down, but the wind kept coming. "Hey, wait! Ma Liang, what are you doing?" Soon Alex was already so high up off the ground that he was afraid to let go.

"There is an ancient Chinese proverb," Ma Liang called, already growing smaller as Alex drifted away. "One often finds his destiny where he most tries to avoid it. May you find yours where you are not looking, Alex Metcalf."

"Ma Liang!" Alex cried, but he was already dropping away from the moon toward Ever After. He grabbed on tighter to the kite and tried not to look down. High above him, he saw Ma Liang back at work, painting twinkling stars in the sky.

Alex closed his eyes, and a childhood rhyme came back to him. "Star light, star bright, first star I see tonight. Wish I may, wish I might, have the wish I wish tonight. I wish I could go home."

Nothing happened, of course. Nothing ever did when you made wishes. Wishes only came true in storybooks.

Storybooks, Alex realized, like *The Wizard of Oz*.

That was the answer. The wishes the Wizard promised the winners of the tournament! If the travel agency couldn't get him home, and the boy with the magic paintbrush couldn't do it, the Wizard could. All Alex had to do was find the Cyclones, rejoin the team, and do what he did best: play baseball.

The words on the land below grew larger, and Alex leaned toward London. The red and gold pagoda stadium stood out among the gray and brown buildings, but he could only do so much to steer himself. The stadium disappeared behind the city's rooftops, and the wind carried him around a tall clock tower and down to a busy sidewalk, where his arrival by kite was completely ignored by the citizens of Ever After. The giant clock struck twelve noon. He was just in time! Or he would be, if he could figure out where the stadium was.

"Big Bad Wolf on the loose!" cried a boy on the corner, holding up newspapers with the day's headlines. "Wizard declares War on Scariness! Read all about it!"

"Hey," Alex said. "Can you tell me how to get to Hyde Park?"

"What do I look like, Tourist Information?" The newsboy turned back to the passersby. "Read all about it! Big Bad Wolf on the loose! Pig team barbequed in late night weenie roast!"

"I was there," Alex told him. "That night. I mean, I was on the Cyclones' bus, when the Big Bad Wolf attacked. That's why I need to get to Hyde Park. I'm on the team. The Cyclones. I need to get there to play in today's game."

"The Cyclones?" the boy said. "The Cyclones ain't gonna play today. Nor tomorrow. Nor the

The Nanny was blow-drying everyone's wet jerseys with a hair dryer plugged in somewhere deep inside one of her pockets. Pinkerton shook himself dry like a dog, splattering them all over again.

Dorothy paced the dugout, clapping her hands and popping her bubble gum. "Let's see some spark out there today, all right Cyclones?" She slapped Alex on the shoulder. "You gotta believe, right Alex?"

"Right."

"I believe I have pneumonia," Br'er Rabbit grumbled.

"Hey, Br'er Rabbit, what's that?" Dorothy asked, pointing to the far end of the dugout.

"Huh? What?" he said. "I don't see anything." While his head was turned, Dorothy blew a bubble with her gum and stuck it to the top of Br'er Rabbit's hat.

"Hmm. Sorry. I guess it was nothing," she told him.

Alex and Toad snickered, and Dorothy gave them quiet high fives as she sat down between them on the bench.

"We can win this, guys. I feel it," she told them. "I mean, I always believed we could win, but I

day after that." The boy opened the paper to the sports page and stuck it in Alex's hands. The head-line across the top said: "OZ CYCLONES LOSE, CRASH OUT OF TOURNAMENT."

"Read all about it, pal," the newsboy told him. "You're a day too late."

A WIND IN THE PARK

10

The wind began to pick up. Gentlemen held their top hats and ladies held on to their skirts. The trees in Hyde Park swayed and bent. Leaves thrashed. Newspapers swirled. Dark clouds blew in overhead.

Nanny Mae's eyes left Alex and she whirled, one hand holding her metal hat, the other pulling a ray gun from one of her pockets. There was a *crack,* and a sound like shattering glass, and then a booming voice said, "WEE ARRE HERRE!"

Behind Nanny Mae, Alex Metcalf used the distraction to disappear inside the dragon stadium. Everyone else's eyes were on the three figures who had just appeared where the storm had formed: a blur that might have been a person and might have been a shimmer; a woman wearing a rough overcoat, a variety of colorful scarves, and a pink stole; and an oddly familiar twelve-year-old boy.

"Alex?" Dorothy asked.

Nanny Mae lowered her ray gun. "Mrs. Which? Mrs. Whatsit?" She looked suspiciously over her shoulder at where Alex had been, and whistled at her cat. "Mrs. P.! We have a runner," she said, and Mrs. P. bounded off into the stadium.

"No, I'm not—whoa." Alex lost his balance, and Dorothy was there to help hold him up. "That was weird. Traveling here. It was like, totally dark. And quiet. You couldn't hear anything—even your own heartbeat." He shook his arms and legs like they were asleep. "I feel all tingly!"

"Oh, that will wear off soon enough, dear," said Mrs. Whatsit, the kindly old woman with the multitude of scarves. "This is where and when you wanted to go?"

Something rumbled at the top of the stadium, and they all looked up to see a firework rocket lift off into the sky.

"Yes," Alex said with a smile. "Exactly. Thank you both."

Nanny Mae narrowed her eyes. "You're on that rocket, aren't you? That's what you were talking to that boy about yesterday. You used this distraction to slip away from me."

"What?" said Alex. "*Pfff.* That's crazy."

The Nanny's eyes bored holes in him. He glanced away, trying to look innocent.

"Thenn wee shhall bee ggoinnggg," said Mrs. Which. "Pplayy wwelll, Allexx. Thhe BBigg BBaadd Wwolff mmusst bee deffeatted."

The wind swirled again, and Alex put an arm up to shield himself. In the blink of an eye, his deliverers were gone.

The Cyclones gathered around Alex. "Well? Are you going to tell us what that was all about?" Dorothy asked.

Alex stepped a few paces away from Nanny Mae, where he hoped she wouldn't hear him. She could still see him, though, and she watched him with a frown.

"Okay. The Nanny's right. I'm on that rocket, trying to get home," Alex told them. "Back to the real world."

"Oh, Alex," said Scraps. "I should have known, after what you said."

"But this—is your home," Tik-Tok said.

"You're a Lark, Alex," Dorothy told him. "You need to stop fighting it."

"Yes," Toad said. "Some of my best friends are Larks."

"I just—I had to see for myself," Alex explained. "I snuck away when I heard the wind and the boom, and I tried to fly out of Ever After. But I can't. I get it now."

He didn't tell them he still believed he was a real boy lost in Ever After. He didn't want to argue about it now. He would show them when he helped them win the tournament and used his wish from the Wizard to go home.

"Wait," Jack said. His pumpkin head was scrunched up in thought. "How could you be your own distraction if you hadn't left yet?"

Alex waved the question away. "Look, all that matters is I'm back now, and I'm ready to play. After the rain delay."

"What rain delay?" Br'er Rabbit asked.

Thunder rumbled, and it began to sprinkle.

"That rain delay," Alex said. "I think maybe I brought the clouds when I transported here."

"Let's get on inside," Dorothy told everyone. "Maybe the umps won't call the game."

Alex held Dorothy back while the others scurried in out of the rain. "Dorothy, there's something else you should know. The Cyclones lose this game."

"What?"

"When I got back, I was going to come straight here to play—but it turns out I was gone overnight. The game was over. You'd lost. I thought we were finished until I remembered: the travel agent! I booked a trip to yesterday, which is today, and now we get a do-over."

"But how did we lose?"

Alex pulled out the paper the newsboy had given him and showed Dorothy the article. "The paper said you pitched awful," he told her. She snatched the paper from him and skimmed the article, and Alex hurried to soften the news. "Maybe you were mad that I bailed on you. I don't know. But I'm back now. We can beat them. I know it. We can beat anybody. We can win the whole thing."

The rain came harder now, and Dorothy pulled Alex along inside. Nanny Mae, watching a few paces away under a black umbrella produced from one of her pockets, came after them. By the time the three of them reached the dugout the rain was coming down in sheets, and the ground crew—a family of yellow ducks—was rolling a tarp over the infield.

"Rain delay," Br'er Rabbit confirmed.

"All right!" Alex said. "Who's got some socks?"

The Cyclones stared at him.

Alex took off his sneakers and pulled off his socks. "Come on, I need a few more pairs."

"Is this something that's supposed to help us play better?" Jack asked.

"Um, sure," Alex said.

Jack shrugged, and pulled off his socks. Scraps did too. They handed them to Alex, and everyone watched as he knotted them into a lopsided blob. He held it up proudly when he was finished.

"Er, what is it, old man?" asked Toad.

"It's a sockball."

Br'er Rabbit shook his head. "Genius."

Alex grabbed a bat and mounted the dugout steps.

"You're not going out there," Dorothy said.

"Sure! Come on. It's a rain delay. There's a tarp."

"So?"

"So we have to go play around! The rain's going to last for more than an hour anyway."

"You don't know that," Nanny Mae told him.

"Yeah I do. It was in the paper. Come on. Everybody take off your shoes and socks. They'll just get drenched anyway."

"I'm game!" Toad said. "It's been a good long time since I hit the water. I am an amphibian, you know."

"There we go," said Alex. "Me and Toad are captains. Toad, you choose first."

Scraps put her hand in the air and bounced on the bench.

"Scraps!" Toad said, and she jumped up and ran to his side.

Dorothy pulled Alex aside before he could pick. "Alex, we can't do this right now."

"Why not? What else are we going to do?"

"What about the tournament? The wolf? Everything you told me about the next game?"

"What are we supposed to do about any of that now? Dorothy, it's a *rain delay*. It's like—it's like the universe's way of hitting the pause button. We can't go back to the bus because it's got no seats, we can't practice because it's pouring, and there's nothing to do here in the dugout except tomorrow's crossword puzzle. Relax. Loosen up. Let's have some fun for a change." Alex pulled her back to the group. "I choose Kansas!" he announced.

"Br'er Rabbit!" Toad said.

"Pinky!" said Alex. The flying monkey didn't

move. *"Pinkerton,"* Alex said, and the flying monkey reluctantly joined Alex's side.

Scraps and Toad conferred. "Nanny Mae," he said finally.

"Absolutely not. Under no circumstances am I going out in that weather, and neither should any of you. It's raining pitchforks out there."

"But you're the only one of us actually dressed for it," Alex told her. "Besides, aren't you supposed to be watching me all the time?"

Nanny Mae tugged at the sleeves of her trench coat, clearly unhappy to be reminded that she had lost Alex, no matter how briefly. "I shall be umpire," she told them.

"Tik-Tok then," said Toad.

"That leaves you, Stretch," Alex said, and Jack popped up happily to join his team. "All right. Let's go! Everybody leave your gloves. You won't need them!"

Alex ran out onto the field, scattering the ducks who were waddling around on the tarp. "Make way, ducklings!" he cried.

Alex sprinted for where second would have been, tossed the sockball high in the air, and dove headfirst into a puddle on the canvas. Water shot everywhere.

"Woo-hoo!"

"You're soaked," Dorothy told him as she and the rest of the Cyclones caught up. She was hunched over to avoid the rain, but her ponytail was already drenched and lay flat against her back.

Alex got up, laughing. "So are you!"

"So how do we play?" Jack asked. The rain pounded on his hollow head, but he didn't seem to care.

"It's just like baseball, only different. Toad, you guys bat first. I'm pitcher. Dorothy, you're at first. Jack, Pinkerton, spread out on the infield. But play in."

Alex rolled the sockball around on the tarp to get it wet, then started to narrate using his announcer voice again. *"Yes, it's a beautiful day at the ballpark, sockball fans. Winds strong from the north-northeast, and a good steady rain that should keep up all game long. Just the right amount of standing water down there on the field. Absolutely perfect sockball conditions. Ace pitcher Alex Metcalf is on the mound. He's ten and oh as a sockball starter, with an earned run average of two point six. Just phenomenal what this boy can do with a sockball. Here he goes into his windup. He chucks it underhand at Toad, and—"*

Toad swung, his bat connecting with a solid *thunk* that sprayed him and Nanny Mae, who stood behind him holding an umbrella. The water-logged sockball spun through the air and died a few feet away.

"It's a hard line drive to short!" Alex narrated. Toad was off like a flash for first, his webbed feet gripping the tarp and sluicing away water as he ran. Alex fell on the ball, corralling it more than catching it. *"Alex dives for the ball. He's got it! An amazing play! He's up with it. Turns. Throws—"*

Alex slung the sockball as high and hard as he could at Dorothy. It left a trail of drops in the air as it twisted, a spinning spiral galaxy of water. Dorothy put up her hands to catch it, but the sock-ball was heavier than she expected and it slipped through her fingers and splatted her in the face, sending her sprawling.

"O-ho!" Alex said, laughing so hard he could barely do his announcer voice. *"She's—Dorothy's down! Oh, we haven't seen sloppy play like this in thirty years of sockball games."*

Dorothy pulled herself up, soaked through and through, and fired the ball not to Jack, who was frantically calling for it at second, but right at Alex. He was laughing too hard to catch it and it *splonk*ed him right in the side of the head. He fell on his butt on the tarp.

"Oh! And now the pitcher is down!" he cried, laughing. *"Oh, the humanity!"*

The few fans who had stayed behind in the stands in hopes the game would start sent up a cheer, and Dorothy charged in after the sockball. Alex splashed her with a puddle to slow her down, then heaved the leaden sockball at her. It drenched her as she caught it, but it was too heavy for her to hold and it slopped to the ground.

Pinkerton was hopping up and down and *"Eeep!"*ing, trying to get them to throw the ball to third, where Toad was making for home.

"They call him the Leaping Lizard!" said Toad, who needed no coaching on how to talk himself up like an announcer. *"The Amazin' Amphibian! The Toad Torpedo!"*

"Soak him! Soak him!" Alex yelled.

The sockball was so sodden it poured water like a hose when Dorothy picked it up. One of the socks had come half untied, and she used it to sling the sockball over her head like a ten-pound mace. Alex covered his head, expecting another sockball in the face from Dorothy, but she slung it at the sprinting Toad instead, nailing him in the side of the head and sending him flying. The scattered crowd cheered.

"You fiend!" Toad said. He pulled himself up and snatched the sockball. "You'll rue the day you soaked old Toad!"

Dorothy squealed and ran as Toad chased her down with the sockball, but his throw missed her and plunked Nanny Mae in the kisser instead. Pinkerton chirped with laughter, and Nanny Mae tossed her umbrella away (as she was now already thoroughly soaked anyway), plucked up the sockball, and came after the flying monkey. Soon every last one of them was dragged into the fight, hurling the sockball, kicking water at each other, screaming, and slipping around on the tarp. When the sockball came unknotted, they flung the wet socks at each other, laughing, forgetting all about teams and games and rules.

Nobody seemed to care, least of all Alex. A proper sockball game never did last very long anyway.

DRAGON BALL

11

Water. A white bowl. A toilet.
His head is in a toilet.
He heaves, but nothing comes.
His chest aches. His throat burns.
His mother rubs his back. Whispers.
He heaves again. And again. And again.
Nothing comes.
There's nothing left.

You'll catch your death, all of you. Mark my words," Nanny Mae scolded.

Alex woke from his reverie. He'd been daydreaming again. Sockball had ended with the rain, and the ducks were already rolling up the tarp. The game was due to start any time now. Tik-Tok and Jack were wringing Scraps out like a wet washcloth.

never *believed it* believed it. You know? For maybe the first time ever, I think we really can win the whole thing."

"Of course we can," Alex told her. "So who is this team we're playing today? The newspaper I read called them the Super Happy All-Star Manga Team Squad."

Dorothy frowned. "I thought we were playing some Japanese folklore team."

"No, manga are graphic novels from Japan," Scraps told them. She was properly wrung out now, and was fluffing herself back into shape. "They're very popular."

What was left of the rain delay crowd cheered as the manga team took the field, and Dorothy went to the rail to have a look at them. They all wore Day-Glo orange and neon green uniforms, even the towering robot mecha that made the ground shake as it strode out to left field. A boy with rockets in his legs flew out to center, followed at a run by a catgirl in right. A muscle-bound boy with huge spiky black hair ran out to third base, a girl in a short sailor skirt and super-long blond ponytails twirled out to second, and a thick black man with a golden Afro strutted over to first. The pitcher was the only one of them who didn't seem to be anything special—just a boy about Alex's age who was already sweating on the mound.

"I don't know any of these people," Dorothy said.

"They all have such big eyes and small mouths," said Toad.

Pinkerton was the first to bat, and he dropped a slick bunt down the third base line past the pitcher. It looked like he might beat it out, but the third baseman moved with superhuman speed, scooped the ball, then put his wrists together and fired the ball across the diamond in a blaze of blue energy. Pinkerton was out by six wing beats.

Toad came up next, and managed a little blooper over the scrawny boy at shortstop.

"Ho-ho! These newfangled manga fellows have nothing on the classics!" he cried, jogging down to first. "Nothing—" he began, then stopped and stared as the shortstop stretched like rubber to go up and catch a ball no one else could have gotten. "—beats . . . the original . . . model," Toad finished, sulking back to the dugout.

"This is why we lose," Dorothy whispered. "They're the future. We can't beat the future."

"No, come on," Alex said. "Sure, they can stretch,

and shoot energy balls, and fly, and who knows what else. But it's still baseball. And we know baseball. Right?"

Dorothy stared at the manga characters on the field like she hadn't even heard him.

"Dorothy, you gotta believe. Remember?"

She left the dugout without answering him. Standing in the batter's box brought her back to life a little, and she hitched her bat and stared down the pitcher. She took him to a full count, then slapped a hit over the head of the sailor girl at second.

"That's the way, Kansas!" Alex called. He grabbed his bat and jogged out onto the field. "All right. Time to show these guys who's boss."

Dorothy nodded and took a lead off first. If Alex could get a hit—even drive her in—he could make her believe again.

The pitcher wasn't ready, though. He picked the ball out of his glove with his thumb and forefinger and held it away from him. What he had wasn't a baseball. It was a tangle of hair that looked like a dead rat.

"What is this?" the pitcher asked.

"Is that what I threw back?" the big first baseman asked. "Wait. That's not a baseball—it's a hairball!" He put his hand into his huge Afro and rooted around like Nanny Mae searching for something in her oversized pockets. *"Here's* the baseball," he said. He pulled the game ball out and tagged Dorothy with it. A hidden ball trick for the third out!

The Super Happy All-Star Manga Team Squad came together at the mound for a team high five and froze for a few seconds like a cut scene in a video game. Alex shook his head and went back to the dugout for his glove. Dorothy just stood where she'd been tagged until Toad brought hers to her.

"Dorothy, you gotta shut them down," Alex told her. "They just got lucky that inning. We're good. We can beat these guys."

But Dorothy was gone, lost somewhere in her own head. Alex had seen players get like that on the field. Angry. Stubborn. You always wanted to get the other pitcher mad, because then he would stop pitching and start *throwing,* which is what Dorothy did from the start. Curveballs came in hard, straight, and fast. Changeups came in hard, straight, and fast. *Everything* came in hard, straight, and fast—and the Super Happy All-Star Manga Team Squad sat and waited on every pitch. The Cyclones did what they could behind her, but by the time they got three outs, the Japanese team already had a five-run lead.

Dorothy didn't slam her glove on the bench when she got back in the dugout, or kick the sun-flower bucket, or overturn the watercooler. She just sat down on the bench and stared at the wall.

"This is why we're disappearing," she said to no one in particular. "There are so many new char-acters. So many new stories. So much new stuff to read. They're just going to forget us. All those kids out there. Soon this is all that'll be left. These . . . *manga*, and all the new characters that're being written right now. There's just—there's just too many of them."

A pall fell over the Cyclones. Alex could see it in the way the others sat quietly on the bench, lost in their own thoughts. No one was chatting. No one was popping bubble gum bubbles. No one was having fun anymore. The Cyclones were packing it in, just like the first time they'd played this team.

Except Alex was here now. That one thing was different, and Alex was going to make sure that one thing changed history.

Alex walked to the plate again, this time with no one on base to drive in. Well, he'd just have to do what he could. He called time-out and studied the field. The left side of the infield was formidable, he knew—a supercharged third baseman, and an elastic boy at short. The girl at second hadn't been tested, but the first baseman was tricky—he'd proven that much. In the outfield, the mecha in left was like a big gray wall, taking that whole side out of play. Alex wasn't too excited about the boy with rocket boots in center, either. If the left-center part of the field was off limits, then he'd have to hit everything to the right—pretty tough for a right-handed pull hitter. But he was the Cyclones' only hope.

Alex tapped his cleats with his bat and stepped in to hit. *Right field,* he told himself. *Right field, right field, right field—*

A juicy fastball came in over the outside part of the plate and Alex took it high and deep to right. The girl with the cat tail and cat ears went back for it, but it didn't look like she could fly or jump any higher than a regular person. She was never going to get it. The rocket boy in center blasted off and zoomed over, but the ball sliced away from him, tucking just around the right field foul pole. *Home run!*

Chinese fireworks exploded over the stadium as Alex made his victory lap. The score was 5–1.

Now, he thought, *I just have to do this every time I come up to bat.*

But Dorothy kept throwing the ball up there, and the Super Happy All-Star Manga Team Squad kept hitting it. In the bottom of the fourth, the manga catcher, another boy with spiky black hair, got under one of Dorothy's pitches, shooting a towering pop fly up on the infield. Alex, Jack, Toad, Tik-Tok, Br'er Rabbit—they all came in after it, but Dorothy stood in the way. It was coming right for her, but she wasn't putting up her glove. An easy out, one of the few they were going to get, was going to fall.

"Tik-Tok!" Alex yelled as he dove, hoping the machine man would understand. Tik-Tok's defensive instincts kicked in, and he lifted Dorothy away just as Alex came flying in, catching the ball with an *oof* as he hit the hard dirt of the mound.

The infielders helped him up, patting the dirt off him and complimenting him on his catch, but Dorothy stood apart from them, staring down at the rosin bag like a zombie. She looked like she just didn't care anymore.

"Wait, time-out!" Alex said before the rest of the infield went back to their positions. "Listen up, guys. If we don't pull it together, we're going to lose this one."

"You mean if Dorothy don't pull it together," Br'er Rabbit said.

"Okay, look," Alex told them. "From the very beginning, Dorothy was the only one who ever really thought this team could win. Am I right?"

The Cyclones looked at each other guiltily.

"So now *she's* the one having a tough time believing, so we're just going to have to do the believing for her. Right?"

The Cyclones looked at each other again. Did they really believe? Could they?

"Right," Toad said. Good old faithful Toad.

"Right," said Tik-Tok. And Jack, and Br'er Rabbit.

"Right," Alex said again. "We play all out. Like we've never played before. And we win this one for Dorothy. In spite of herself."

And play all out they did. Dorothy kept throwing batting practice, but behind her, the Cyclones turned in some of the most sterling defensive plays the tournament had ever seen. Br'er Rabbit snared a blast down the line that dragged him halfway into left field with it, but hung on for the out.

Toad matched the rubber boy on the manga team catch for catch, snapping up the highest of them with his tongue like he was catching flies. Even the normally woeful Jack lifted his game, threading the ball right through the enormous legs of the charging mecha robot to finish off a spectacular double play.

Offensively, though, it was Alex who carried the Cyclones on his shoulders. Whenever anyone got on ahead of him, all they had to do was hug the bases and wait for him to drive them in. Hit after hit he sent to right—two doubles, a triple, and another home run. He might have hit for the cycle had he dropped in a simple base hit, but he was always swinging for the right field wall and beyond. When they put the rocket boy in right to foil him, he just hit the ball to deep center. He was unbelievable.

What Alex didn't stop to think about, of course—at least not until long after he and the Cyclones had won the ball game and rewritten history—was what it meant to be unbelievable.

THE GRIMM REAPERS

12

In 1908, following the introduction of the Model T Ford to the dreams of half the real world, Ever After caught automobile fever to rival Toad's own obsession. Automobile races were held in every city, village, and province in Ever After, but none was bigger or more anticipated than the Red Queen's Race, to be held at the newly built Wonderland Motor Speedway. Sixteen motorcars lined up and revved their engines, ready to race, while thousands of spectators crowded the grandstands to watch. The starting gun went off, the racers flattened their gas pedals, and sixty-four wheels spun—but nobody went anywhere. Every car sat at the starting line, wheels spinning uselessly, until each ran out of gas without moving an inch. It was a trick of Wonderland, the same thing that had happened to Alice when challenged to a foot race by the Red Queen, and on the spot the Queen of Hearts had decreed there would be no more silliness of the sort, and that the next person who brought an automobile into her realm would lose his head.

Thus, later that night after their win, the Cyclones boarded a train, not their pink bus, for their next game in Wonderland. Dorothy was still quiet and sullen even though they had won, and it rubbed off on the rest of the team, most of them choosing to just curl up and sleep for the evening-long train journey. Even Nanny Mae and Mrs. P. catnapped in the seat across the aisle from Alex, a bit more relaxed since they discovered the passenger car beyond theirs was full of wizards headed for a magic convention. Out of all the Cyclones, Alex thought he might be the only one awake.

"Got a lot on your mind?" Scraps said, popping up in the seat in front of him.

"Gaah! Scraps, you gotta stop doing that."

Scraps climbed over the back of her seat and plopped down beside him. "You're thinking so loud the whole train car can hear you."

"Oh yeah? What am I thinking?"

Scraps folded her legs underneath her. "You're asking yourself, 'How could I possibly be that good at baseball?' I mean, come on. Two doubles, a triple, and two home runs? To the opposite field? Against that team?"

"That? I just got lucky is all," Alex said. He didn't want to admit that was exactly what he'd been thinking.

"Oh. Well, it was a good thing you did for Dorothy, hitting like that, and rallying everybody together."

"I did it for the whole team."

"Maybe. But Dorothy needed it the most."

Alex watched the lights of a town slide by in the distance outside his window. "You know why she's playing, don't you? What she wants to wish for?"

"Yeah. She's going to wish that no one ever forgets her. And she wants the rest of us to wish that nobody ever forgets us either."

"So is that what you're really going to wish for?" Alex asked. "If we win?"

Scraps put her legs up on the back of the seat in front of them. "I've got something else in mind, I think," she told him. "And not just another piece of fabric."

"You're not worried about—you know, disappearing?"

"Let me ask you something. You ever know somebody so worried about staying alive she forgot to live? So focused on the end she didn't enjoy the getting there?"

"You mean Dorothy."

Scraps put a finger to where her nose would have been if she had one. "That's my wish. I wish Dorothy would loosen up a little. Stop and smell the popcorn."

Alex scratched his arm. "Maybe it's just in her nature. You know, how she was written. I don't know. It's been a while since I read her book."

"Well, we're all stuck with how our authors wrote us up," said Scraps. "I'm always going to be a patchwork girl, Toad's always going to be a toad, and Dorothy's always going to be a plain girl from the prairies. But beyond that, we can be whatever kind of patchwork girl or toad or prairie girl we want to be. Once we're here, we write our own stories."

A couple of seats down, Toad lay sprawled out, working the pedals of an imaginary car as he slept, muttering, "Poop! Poop-poop!"

"Well, for the most part," Scraps said with a

smile. "Dorothy didn't used to be like this, you know. Sixty, seventy years ago, we were playing in this very same tournament just for the fun of it. Then all these new characters started showing up. More and more of them. And a lot of the old guard, they started disappearing. Dorothy took it pretty hard. You're good for her that way. You get it. You have fun."

"I want to win just as much as she does," Alex told her.

"Got something more in mind for that wish after all?" Scraps said, like she could read his thoughts about that too.

The train's brakes squealed and the Cyclones stirred in their sleep. They weren't to their station yet—it would be daylight before they got there—and those who could turned back over to sleep through the stop. Alex looked out the window and blinked. Just beyond the tracks squatted a windowless log cabin on two-story-tall chicken legs.

"What in the world is that?"

"Ooh! It's Baba Yaga's witch house. The team bus of the—"

The door to their passenger car opened, and death itself walked in. Or so it seemed to Alex. A huge man with a long red cape and a horned skull for a mask ducked his way inside the cabin, and Alex gasped.

"—the *Grimm Reapers,*" Scraps finished. "One of the best teams in the tournament year in and year out. They must be playing in Wonderland tomorrow too."

Their uniforms were black with blood-red trim, and their red caps had black skulls and crossbones on them. Alex sighed in relief when the thing with the skull over its face passed them, then held his breath again when it turned around and came back to them. The thing leaned down, the antlers on its death mask scraping the ceiling and its empty eyes staring through them.

"Pardon me," the man in the horned helmet said. He gestured to where Scraps had been sitting. "Is this seat taken?"

"Oh, no. You can have it!" Scraps said happily.

Alex stared at her, dumbfounded, as the frightening thing took the seat in front of them.

"The King of Annwn, the Welsh King of the Dead," Scraps told him. "What? You don't mind if I sit with you the rest of the way, do you?"

Alex certainly didn't mind her sharing the seat, considering that the horrific thing in front of them came with equally horrific friends. First came a scraggly pirate on a crutch with a parrot on his shoulder, then a warty dwarf, a cruel-looking woman with a face like an ax, a raccoon-dog in a bathrobe and straw hat, and a shriveled old woman who flew along on a huge mortar—one of those bowl-like things pharmacists and alchemists used to crush up potions. She steered herself through the air with a baseball bat for a rudder.

"That's Baba Yaga," Scraps whispered. "She's a Russian Storybook."

The train car suddenly wobbled and groaned, sinking a foot down toward the tracks, and the talons of a huge dragon poked in through the open windows as it gripped the roof to ride on top.

The last Reaper through the door was a big yellow and orange cat with a great toothy grin on his face. He wore a black jersey and a red cap like the rest, and hopped up on the back of a seat near the front of the train car. The cat hadn't made so much as a sound, but Mrs. P. sat bolt upright in Nanny Mae's lap and gave a low, meowing growl that gave Alex goose bumps.

"Now, now, is that any kind of welcome for a fellow feline?" the orange cat asked. The unsettling grin never left his face.

Nanny Mae was awake in an instant. "There

now, Mrs. P. It's only the Cheshire Cat," she said. "No sense bothering with him. He's gone doolally. He was written that way."

A whistle blew, the train shuddered, and they were on their way again. Over the *chuff-chuff-chuff* of the steam engine, Alex could just hear the engine saying, "I think I can, I think I can, I think I can . . ." A wizard in colorful robes and a tall hat with half-moons all over it passed through their compartment on the way to the restaurant car as the train got under way, casting a wary eye on the assembled villains of the Grimm Reapers.

"So, here are the famous Oz Cyclones," the Cheshire Cat said. "I recognize all of you except . . ." The cat's big round eyes focused on Alex. ". . . that one. What storybook are you from?"

"He's a Lark," Scraps said.

"Mmmm," the Cheshire Cat purred. "I've eaten a lark or two. Very tasty."

A couple of the Reapers snickered.

"I don't think we're talking about the same kind of lark," Jack Pumpkinhead said.

"Aren't we?" the Cheshire Cat said, his smile growing even wider. "Speaking of eating Larks, is there a dinner service on this train?"

"Arr. The genie'll fetch us some snacks, matey,"

the pirate said. He pulled a brass lamp from his satchel and gave it a rub, and blue gas filtered out into the shape of a man.

"Say what thou wilt of me," the genie said. "Here am I, thy slave and the slave of whoso hath in his hand the lamp."

"Get the Cheshire Cat here a chicken sandwich from the dining car, Blue Man. And a soda?"

"Diet. I'm watching what I eat," the Cheshire Cat said, never taking his eyes off Alex.

"Arr. A diet soda. Anybody else be needing anything? Rumpelstiltskin? Tanuki? Wicked Step-sister?"

Everyone gave their orders.

"What about you, Baba Yaga, you want he should—"

The old woman shrieked and flicked her hand at him, and with a *pop* the pirate turned into a chicken. The raccoon thing the pirate had called Tanuki snickered.

"Baba Yaga loses a year off her life every time someone asks her a question," Scraps whispered.

"Turn Long John back into a pirate, you old witch," Rumpelstiltskin told Baba Yaga. "Genie, go get the snacks."

The genie did as he was bid, and the Cheshire

Cat turned his attention back to the Cyclones. "By the bye, how did you manage to defeat that Japanese comic book team? I'd nearly forgotten to ask. I heard you couldn't get a handle on your pitcher."

"Check the box score, cat," Alex said. "We won."

"Don't rise to that creature's bait," Nanny Mae told him. "He's just trying to make you mad."

"We're all mad here," the Cheshire Cat said. "Isn't that what I say?" He giggled, which Alex found even more disconcerting than his perpetual grin. "But the truth is, you wouldn't have won without your Lark. Your pitcher doesn't hold water."

"And you couldn't hit water if you fell out of a boat," Dorothy said, surprising Alex. He hadn't even known she was awake.

There were chuckles among the Reapers. The Cheshire Cat licked his lips. "Want to bet?"

"What, that I can't pitch, or you can't hit?"

"It seems to me there's a simple way to answer both questions at once."

"Like there's enough room to pitch on a train," Dorothy said, and she pulled her cap down low over her face and settled in to sleep again.

The Cheshire Cat reached over and pulled the emergency cord above the window. The train's brakes locked and shrieked, and everyone in the car was thrown to the floor. The genie was just coming back from the food car with an armload of sandwiches and soft drinks, and everything went flying.

The train ground to a halt, and everyone climbed back into their seats. Only the Cheshire Cat seemed unaffected, still sitting neatly on the back of his seat and still smiling that creepy smile.

"Oh, look," he said. "The train stopped. Now we can step outside for a moment. Unless, perhaps, you're as chicken as my sandwich?"

"Great. Fine," Dorothy said. She stood and screwed her cap down tightly on her head. "You and me, cat. Let's do this."

A GRIN WITHOUT A CAT

13

Word of the bet between Dorothy and the Cheshire Cat spread quickly through the train, and the wizards from the next car and the rest of the passengers spilled out to watch. It was dark outside, but a full moon—the real one or the one Ma Liang had painted, Alex didn't know—cast a silvery, dreamlike light over the broad meadow alongside the tracks.

Dorothy was already marking off sixty feet, six inches when Alex caught up to her.

"Dorothy, wait up. Dorothy, what are you doing?"

"I'm going to put a baseball so far down that smarmy cat's throat he chokes on it."

"Dorothy—Dorothy *stop*. You don't have to

prove anything to that jerk. Save it for the game tomorrow."

"No. I'm going to show him that I'm not going away. That *we're* not going away. I'm going to show them all. I'm going to strike out that loser in front of everybody here."

"No, you're not," Alex told her.

She swung around on him with a wild, angry look. "He hasn't even got opposable thumbs! You don't think I can—"

"Calm down. Of course you can strike him out. You're great. But you won't strike him out if you throw like you did today. You have to relax. You have to *pitch,* not throw. Do you understand?"

Dorothy seemed to hear what he was saying, and a little of the craziness went out of her eyes, even if the determination didn't. "Yeah. Okay. All right," she told him.

Alex still thought this was a bad idea, but there was no stopping her. Somebody tossed Dorothy a ball, and she started working it over in her hands. The crowd from the train made a big horseshoe around her and the Cheshire Cat.

"We never said what we were betting," the cat said. He stood on two legs now, and took what

Alex thought were good-looking practice swings with his bat.

"I'm betting I strike you out and make you look like my auntie Em," said Dorothy.

"That's what you're betting on. What are you betting? As in, what are you going to give me when I hit your pitch into tomorrow?"

"What do you want?"

The Cheshire Cat licked his lips again. "Your shoes are very sparkly."

He meant, of course, her ruby red baseball cleats with the silver trim.

"Dorothy, no!" Scraps said.

"Sure. Fine," said Dorothy. "It's not like I'm going to lose." She slapped the ball in her glove. "What about you? You haven't got anything I want."

"Are you so sure? You want to win the tournament, don't you?"

"Of course."

"Well, you'll certainly have to go through the Reapers to do it. So how about this? If you strike me out, the Reapers quit the tournament. Right here. Right now."

"Vait, now," said the old Russian witch. "I do not care who you are. Ve did not agree to—" she started to say, but Long John Silver cut her off with a hiss.

"Fair enough," Dorothy said. "Let's do this."

"Baba Yaga, seal the bet, if you please," the Cheshire Cat said. The old witch grumbled but flicked her hand, and—*zsssaaat!*—the air between them crackled like static electricity.

"Dorothy, you can walk away from this right now," Alex told her. "It doesn't matter."

Dorothy looked around at all the people watching. "It does matter," she told him. "Will you be my catcher?"

"Okay. Yeah. I guess. If you have to do this. Just remember: Pitch, don't throw."

Dorothy nodded and Alex got his glove and went to where the Cheshire Cat was standing.

"Who's going to be ump?" Alex asked.

"Long John will suffice," the Cheshire Cat said.

"No way!" Br'er Rabbit cried.

"The crowd," Dorothy said. "They'll decide what's a strike and what isn't. But I'm telling you right now: I'm only throwing strikes."

The Cheshire Cat grinned wider. "Shall we get on with it?"

The crowd grew quiet and waited for Dorothy's pitch. Alex didn't bother putting down a signal; whatever Dorothy threw, he would catch it.

Dorothy went into her windup. Her foot kicked.

Ruby and silver cleats glinted in the moonlight. The ball flashed. The Cheshire Cat swung—

—and missed. Bad. The ball smacked into Alex's glove before the cat was even halfway through his swing, and the crowd of wizards and other travelers oohed. Dorothy was *pitching*.

"Oh dear. She really is very good," the Cheshire Cat said. "Perhaps I was dreaming to think I could hit her."

"Yeah. You were," Alex told him.

Alex threw the ball back to Dorothy and waited. She stared in again, but she wasn't really looking at him, he could tell. She was looking past him, past the Cheshire Cat, past that meadow and that night. She was staring down the future. Daring it to leave her behind.

Dorothy's shoes sparkled again. Her glove went high over her head, and she fired. The ball twisted, spun, dropped—

"Speaking of dreams," the Cheshire Cat said, turning to Alex in the middle of the pitch, "I've been meaning to ask: Have you had any luck waking up yet?"

"W-what?" Alex said, watching the cat and the ball at the same time. He barely snagged the ball before it skirted past him.

"Strike two!" Jack called out triumphantly, and a murmur spread through the crowd. The Cheshire Cat hadn't looked at the pitch, much less taken a swing.

"Oh, dear. I forgot to swing, didn't I?" the cat said. "I suppose I was thinking of something else."

Alex frowned at the Cheshire Cat. What in the Sam Hill was that grinning idiot up to?

"Dorothy, watch out," Alex called as he threw the ball back. "He's playing with you."

"I don't care what he's doing," Dorothy told him. "He's going down." She tucked her glove under her arm, worked the ball over in her hands, and came set again, decades—*centuries*—of fight in her eyes.

The cat turned his lark-eating grin toward Dorothy one last time.

"This is going to hurt, Alex Metcalf," the Cheshire Cat whispered in a gravelly voice that wasn't his own. "Not as bad as a *rocket launcher* in the face, but it's going to hurt."

Alex gasped. "No, wait. Dorothy, don't! It's—"

But Dorothy was already pitching. Every ground ball, every swing of the bat, every run she had scored and out she had made and pep talk she had given—they all came down to this. The fastest ball she had ever thrown leaped from her hand like lightning, igniting the dark and sucking the air from the night. It crackled toward Alex like he was a lightning rod, but it never struck.

The Cheshire Cat swung his bat like a hammer of the gods and connected with a *BOOM* that shook the ground and made Alex twist away. The cat drove the ball like a rocket into the night sky, and it was still going up, up, up when it disappeared from sight.

"It's the Big Bad Wolf," Alex finished, staggering backward. But it was too late. Far too late. With a crackle and a *zsssaaat!* Dorothy's ruby and silver cleats blinked off her feet and onto the Cheshire Cat's.

"Now," the wolf said, stripping off his cat skin and starting to grow. "Time for that snack from the dining car." His great big eyes flashed, and his great big teeth glittered in the moonlight, and the watching crowd screamed. Alex fell back, terrified, but suddenly the wizards who had been watching the face-off were rushing forward, wands out and sparking. The wolf glanced at Alex, then at the wizards, then at Nanny Mae, who was pulling the long bazooka out of her pocket, and he smiled a Cheshire Cat smile.

"I have what I came for. Another time then, Alex Metcalf," the wolf snarled. "Be seeing you . . ."

And with a click of his new magic cleats, the wolf was gone.

A crush of robed magicians and Cyclones hurried to help Alex to his feet, but he didn't need it. It was Dorothy who needed the help, but nobody ran to her, and Alex couldn't get to her through the crowd. Nobody but him even saw her as she fell to her knees sixty feet and six inches away, alone, defeated, and forgotten.

ALEX'S ADVENTURES IN WONDERLAND

14

The way into Wonderland was usually just a trip and a fall down a rabbit hole, followed by a gentle landing on a heap of sticks and dry leaves—assuming your luggage did not land on your head, which it often did. But instead of the more traditional entrance, the next morning the Cyclones found a security checkpoint guarded by playing card soldiers with automatic rifles.

Alex scratched at his toes through his socks. "I still don't understand why I have to take off my shoes."

"Ever After Department of Homeland Security regulations, sir," a seven of clubs told him. "Word is the Big Bad Wolf got himself some magic slippers last night. Just put your shoes in the bin and slide them through the machine, please."

"Just be glad you're not Jack," Toad told him. "He has to put his whole head through the machine."

"Look Ma, no hands!" Jack's head cried, bumping down the ramp in a plastic tub.

Nanny Mae's trench coat, amazingly, went through the X-ray machine without any trouble, but Tik-Tok kept setting off the metal detector and had to have a full body search. While they were waiting, a teenage boy with a lick of blond hair and a trench coat of his own ran up, a white terrier trotting behind him.

"Ms. Gale! Ms. Gale! Ever After News Service. Any comment on why you gave your cleats to the Big Bad Wolf?"

Dorothy, who hadn't said two words all night and all morning, crossed her arms and stared at her feet.

"Overnight reports from all over Ever After put the total number of Storybooks eaten at twenty-six, with the world's wizarding community unable to anticipate where and when the wolf will strike next. Do you feel any personal responsibility for the Big Bad Wolf's current rampage?"

Alex jumped in between them. "She's not the one eating people! And she didn't know it was the wolf she was betting with anyway, or she never would have done it."

The reporter scribbled in his notebook. "You're the Lark, right? The one the Big Bad Wolf is after? What's your reaction to the wolf's announcement that he will stop devouring people if the Wizard hands you over to him?"

"I . . . wait, what?"

"Sixty-three percent of Storybooks polled by EANS are in favor of giving you up. Will you turn yourself in?"

Alex stammered, and it was Nanny Mae's turn to come to the rescue.

"Preposterous. Cowards all, that's what I say," she said, whisking Alex and Dorothy away. "Toad? I could use reinforcements here."

Toad popped up in their place and straightened his jersey like he was on television.

"Toad of Toad Hall, candidate for prime minister," he said, launching into politician mode. "The current crime rate is appalling, I tell you. Appalling! If elected, I shall crack down with the sternest measures. Tough on crime, that's my motto. Except of course for automobile theft, where some degree of leniency is required . . ."

Dorothy jumped down the hole that led to Wonderland and away from the reporter. Nanny Mae took Mrs. P. in her arms, and after assuring Alex that this was a magical fall, not a real one that would hurt, she and Alex followed. They fell slowly, as Nanny Mae promised, and along the way Alex had time to look around. Plastered all over the tall, round walls were advertisements for Wonderland businesses and posters announcing the next game in the Ever After Baseball Tournament.

"Nanny Mae, will they do it?" Alex asked as they fell. "Will the authorities turn me over?"

"Don't be silly," she said. "The Agency doesn't negotiate with terrorists."

That might have given Alex comfort if they hadn't been greeted when they landed by a horde of angry Storybooks holding signs that said "If you're not dinner, you're against us!" and chanting "Feed him the Lark!"

Nanny Mae hurried him along to the ballpark. "This game I suggest you keep your head down, soldier," she said.

The Flamingo Grounds, Wonderland's baseball stadium, was odd, to say the least. The stands were pink and red, and in dead center, just beyond the wall, was a small cluster of topiary Tumtum trees cut in the shape of hearts, diamonds, clubs, and spades. Flamingos roamed on the outfield grass, which was cut in a chessboard pattern, while three playing-card groundskeepers, under the direction of an officious lizard, were painting the white foul lines red. In left stood the stadium's answer to the Green Monster—an immense purple wall that would stop all but the most towering of home runs.

"Beware the Jabberwock, old man!" Toad said, joining him.

"The Jabberwock?"

"That's what they call the big wall in left. Jaws that bite and claws that catch, and all that."

Alex sighed. It wasn't the Jabberwock he was worried about—it was Dorothy. Playing the manga team had rattled her, but losing her cleats to the wolf was worse. It had sucked the life out of her. There was nothing left when Alex looked in her eyes, and he wondered how she could even bear to be here with the rest of them, let alone take the field.

Then he realized: She *wasn't* there. All the other Cyclones had joined them in the stadium, but Dorothy was nowhere to be seen.

Scraps and Toad shared a knowing look. "Everybody spread out," Scraps said. "Check all the exits."

They found her slinking out through the bullpen

in right. She struggled at first to get away, but soon enough they had her hauled back to the dugout, where she sat slumped on the bench. Br'er Rabbit kept an eye on her while the others huddled a few feet away.

"She was headed for the Forest of Fighting Trees," Scraps said.

"The what?" Alex asked.

"The Wild Woods," Toad explained. "The dark place at the edge of Ever After. Everyone has a different name for it: the Briar Patch, the Black Forest, the Shadowlands, the Doldrums."

Alex remembered flying over it in the rocket. "Isn't that where they were taking the Wolf? I thought it was a bad place. Why would Dorothy want to go there?"

"It's where you go when you've given up and want to wallow in your own misery," Nanny Mae told him.

"The people there become shadows of themselves, old man, tearing themselves apart. They become monsters."

Jack shivered. "Awful place."

"And Dorothy's not going to end up there," Scraps told everyone. "We'll have to watch her."

A black cat jumped down into the dugout from above, startling everyone, and crossed over to Nanny Mae and Mrs. P.

"Well, that can't be a good sign," Jack said.

"Hello, Winkie. What's the rumpus?" Nanny Mae asked.

Winkie and Mrs. P. sat face-to-face, about a cat's length apart, and stared at each other for a few moments. Mrs. P. glanced at Nanny Mae, who frowned, and then Winkie was off, leaping up onto the field and then into the stands.

Nanny Mae buried her hands in her trench coat pockets, but not, apparently, to pull anything amazing from them. "Gadzooks," she muttered.

"What is it? What did the cat say?" Alex asked.

"What? Don't be daft," Nanny Mae said. "Did you hear her say anything?"

"Well, no, but can't you—?"

"Are we going to play baseball today," the Nanny interrupted, "or are we just here for the tea and cakes?"

The Cyclones looked to Dorothy to rally them, but she still sat staring at her feet.

"Dorothy has apparently become useless," Nanny Mae announced. "Toad, Jack, see that the equipment is ready. Alex and I will deliver the lineup card." She was halfway out of the dug-out already, and Alex hurried to catch up. He didn't know why Nanny Mae was so angry, but he didn't want to do anything to make it worse. As they crossed to home plate, Alex noticed the Nanny was more vigilant than usual. She was scanning the stands like always, but she glanced at the skies as well. What had that cat told her?

The home plate umpire—a white rabbit with a gold pocket watch—stood with a large, mopey turtle with a hangdog face, and a plump, unhappy woman wearing a crown over her black umpire hat. The Nanny introduced them as the March Hare, the Mock Turtle, and the Queen of Hearts.

"You're late," the March Hare told them.

"We, uh, we had to track down our pitcher. She'd gone missing."

"Off to the showers!" the queen cried.

"What? You can't throw somebody out before the game even starts," Alex told her.

"Can't I?" she asked. She squinted at Alex. "Say, you're not that Lark, are you? The one the wolf is after?"

Nanny Mae cleared her throat, and Alex remembered her advice to lay low.

"Um, no," Alex told her. "I'm nobody you know."

"Did you say your name is Nobody?" the queen asked.

"Yes," said the Mock Turtle. "That's what he said. 'I'm Nobody, you know.'"

"No, I meant—"

"You mean they don't have a first baseman?" the hare asked, studying the Cyclones' lineup card.

"Of course they do," the queen told him.

The March Hare took out his pencil. "Then who's on first?"

"Nobody."

"Nobody's on first?"

"That's right."

The March Hare looked terribly confused. "Now look here. When the third baseman picks up the ball and throws it to first, who catches it?"

"Nobody," the queen told him.

"Nobody catches it?"

"That's right."

The March Hare frowned. "And if the Cyclones' first baseman wins the MVP award for the tournament, will nobody's name be inscribed on the award?"

"Proudly," said the queen.

"No—it'll be my name," Alex told the Hare.

"And you are?"

"He's Nobody," the queen said.

"No, I'm *somebody*. I'm just not—"

"You're Somebody now?" the Mock Turtle lamented. "Oh, nobody tells me anything anymore."

"He does? When did you last speak to him?" the March Hare asked.

"That is *quite* enough of this silliness," Nanny Mae cut in. "Say 'Play ball' toot sweet," she told the hare. "Say it."

"Um, play ball?" the March Hare said.

"Play ball!" the queen repeated, and the game was under way.

"You have to be stern with Wonderlanders," the Nanny told Alex on the way back to the dugout. "They can go on like that all day. Everyone is going to have to be particularly careful about what they say and what they do here," she told the rest of the team. "That means no talking to strangers, no opening strange doors, and no eating the concession stand food."

Br'er Rabbit froze with a small "EAT ME" cake halfway to his mouth. "Aw, Nanny! I'm starving!"

"You'll just have to tough it out then," she told him. "Those cakes are liable to turn you ten stories tall."

Br'er Rabbit tried to pop the cake into his

mouth when Nanny Mae wasn't looking, but Alex snatched it away.

"Pinky, you're up first," Alex said.

The flying monkey just stared at him.

"Pinkerton," Alex said, and the leadoff hitter grabbed his bat and fluttered to the plate.

They were playing a team called the Misfits, which sounded promising to Alex. Maybe this one would be a cakewalk. They could certainly use one: Dorothy might play, but her heart wasn't going to be in it until they figured out a way to get her fired up again. At that very moment she sat on the bench staring at her shoes. Her plain, black shoes, which Nanny Mae had magically dug out of her pockets to replace Dorothy's ruby and silver cleats.

But perhaps the worst result of Dorothy's lost wager—at least for the Cyclones' chances at winning the tournament—revealed itself later that inning. Dorothy stood on third and Alex was on second, with Br'er Rabbit at the plate. Br'er Rabbit hit a screaming line drive base hit to right center, and Dorothy walked home from third. Alex, seeing the big-eared mouse in center and the vampire rabbit in right misplay the ball, rounded third and followed Dorothy home at full speed. What he expected to see standing in between him and home plate was the Misfits' catcher—an over-weight bald man in diapers and a red cape. Instead he saw Dorothy, still standing a foot from home. She hadn't scored.

"Dorothy, keep going! Go go go!"

"I can't," Dorothy said.

Alex pulled up behind her, glancing nervously over his shoulder. The floppy-eared mouse had lobbed the ball back to the infield, and the first baseman, who was as thin as home plate, was trying to pick up the ball in his flat, smooth hands.

"Dorothy, look—you can mope around all you want in the dugout. Just step on home so we can score!"

She turned on him, angry. "Look at what I'm telling you! *I can't touch the plate.*" She aimed her cleat at the house-shaped plate, but every time she tried to step on it her foot bounced off like there was a force field around it.

Alex looked back at the first baseman. He'd given up picking up the ball and was kicking it along, using his flat foot like a hockey stick.

"Dorothy, we have to do something!"

"Well, you try it!" she said.

Alex stepped around her and put his foot on home plate without any problem.

"Why can't I touch home?" Dorothy asked, dismayed. She was being replaced by new characters, she couldn't touch home, she'd lost her cleats—

Alex suddenly understood. "Dorothy, your ruby and silver shoes. In your book, they let you go home, right? Now that you don't have them—"

"I can never go home," she finished quietly.

The first baseman rolled the ball over, and the catcher picked it up and touched it to Dorothy.

"Tra-la-laaaaaaaaaaaa!" he cried.

"Out," the March Hare said. "And I really hate to mention this, but rules are rules. Any runner who passes another runner on the base paths is out, which means you're out too—whoever you are."

"He's Nobody!" the queen cried from her place near the first base bag.

The March Hare looked bewildered. "Then . . . nobody's out?"

"Dang!" the catcher said. "I thought we had him! Oh well, tra-la-laaaaaaaaaaaa!"

Dorothy's inability to score was disastrous, but Alex being "nobody" quickly offset it. Every time he was called out, the Queen of Hearts announced, "Nobody's out!" and he got to stay on base. Soon the Cyclones had a commanding lead, but being nobody backfired on Alex in the bottom of the eighth inning when he hit a moon shot over the manxome Jabberwock in left field to put the game away for good.

"Nobody has hit a home run!" the queen announced.

"Er, nobody has hit a home run," the March Hare said, trembling. "Next batter."

Alex stopped his home run trot. "What? No way! I knocked that one out of the park! Everybody saw it!"

"*Everybody*'s not here," the Queen of Hearts told him. "Nobody is."

"No, look—*somebody* just hit a home run, right?" Alex argued.

The Queen of Hearts got in his face. "I know Somebody. Somebody's a friend of mine. You're not Somebody. *Off to the showers!*"

"Alex," Toad called, "just let it go! We're winning by eleven runs! It's in the bag, old man."

"No! No, you don't understand," Alex told the Queen of Hearts. "I am *a* somebody, lowercase. I'm Alex Metcalf."

"The Lark!" the queen cried. "I knew it! And playing under a false name! Guards, seize him! *Off to the wolf!*"

An army of life-sized playing card people

hopped out of the stands and came running, cutting him off from the dugout.

"No, wait—Nanny Mae! Toad! Somebody do something!"

"I thought you said *you* were Somebody," moaned the Mock Turtle.

"I am," Alex said, and with sudden inspiration he pulled the cake he'd snatched from Br'er Rabbit out of his pocket and took a bite. In moments he was growing big, bigger, bigger, until the soldiers were nothing more than a pack of cards. Alex shook off the guards and lumbered around the bases, finishing the home run trot he deserved.

"Come back here this instant!" the queen commanded. "Nobody disobeys me!"

"Somebody just did," Alex said, and he jumped on home plate so hard he shook the stadium's foundations.

BAD TUESDAY

15

His head burns.
His skin is wet.
He wakes. Kicks the covers off.
Stacks of baseball cards spill to the floor.
Thermometer. Phone. Suitcase.
The red lights bring out the neighbors.
A bed with straps, like he's a prisoner.
His mother squeezes his hand.
He rolls inside. The doors close.
A siren wails.
Emergency.

Somebody's hand on Alex's shoulder woke him as the train slowed to a stop at their station. Nanny Mae. "We're here," she said. She scanned the station platform outside through the windows. *The Big Bad Wolf having Dorothy's cleats must have her spooked,* Alex thought as he yawned and stretched. He didn't see how watching out the window would help when the wolf could be there beside them and gone with a click of his heels, but he supposed that was his nanny's job, and she was going to do it.

The Cyclones dragged their bags away from the station and onto a busy sidewalk where they were almost run over. Animals in human clothes walked, cycled, drove, and flew everywhere. A dog in a police uniform whistled at traffic. A pig chased after his hat. Farther down the road, a hippopotamus in a business suit paid more attention to his newspaper than to the freshly poured concrete he was about to walk into.

"Look out, Mr. Hippo!" Jack cried.

The startled hippopotamus jumped out of the way in time, but hit a board hanging on a rope at a construction site, which knocked over a pile of bricks, which fell on a bear welding a pipe, which made him drop his blowtorch. The flames touched the wooden building next door, and it lit up with a *whoosh*. Within seconds, a zoo's worth of crazed animals came running from the burning building.

"Fire!" Alex said. "We should do something!"

"Not our problem," Nanny Mae told him, scanning up and down the street. "Move along, everyone. Let's not muck about."

Alex couldn't believe a nanny would just walk away when someone needed help, but Toad put his arm around Alex and led him away.

"Don't worry, old chap. They live for this kind of thing here."

Before Toad had even finished, a fire engine came screaming down the street with firefighting pigs hanging off it. The fire engine was followed by a zooming ambulance with cat nurses and doctors inside, its red lights flashing, its siren wailing.

Suddenly Alex remembered his dream from that night. There had been an ambulance there too. And his mother and his family again. An emergency.

His dreams were so real, and this world, with its cat doctors and EAT ME cakes and wolves in human clothing, was so *un*real. What was real and what wasn't?

A tiger zoomed by in a truck, and a bear wearing a crossing-guard uniform escorted a line of cat children across the street to school.

"What a busy town," Alex said.

"I always get along famously here," Toad was saying as he tipped his baseball cap and handed out "VOTE TOAD" cards to passersby. "Animals in automobiles are my core demographic."

"I think we're booked into a hotel for dogs," Scraps said, checking a map. "We should go . . . that way."

"No. I changed our reservations," Nanny Mae told everyone. "Follow me."

The Nanny led them through a maze of back alleys and narrow streets, and Alex began to wonder if she really knew where they were going at all.

"Are we there yet?" Jack asked.

"We'll be there when we get there," Nanny Mae snapped. "In the meantime, I'll thank you to—"

The Nanny turned the next corner and stopped short. Standing in her way were three identical women, each carrying black umbrellas and wearing identical black hats, black dresses, and black sunglasses. There was a sheepdog with them, and it had black sunglasses on too.

"Hello, Agent Mae," said the woman standing in front.

"Agent Smith," Nanny Mae said.

They were all Nannies, Alex realized. Like his

nanny. Government agents. But if they worked together, why did Nanny Mae have her hands in those magic pockets of hers, and why was Mrs. P.'s tail bushy?

"You changed your itinerary without letting the Agency know," Nanny Smith said. "That's very naughty."

"Oh, I was sure I sent word back to the brass hats at HQ," Nanny Mae said. "Perhaps my carrier pigeon got pipped."

"There was no carrier pigeon, Nanny Mae," Nanny Smith said. "If we didn't know any better, we would think you were planning to disobey your new orders."

"New orders?" Alex asked. "What new orders? Is that what that black cat told you?"

"Is that him? The Lark?" Nanny Smith asked. She pulled on a pair of black leather gloves and tugged them tight while the Nannies behind her fanned out to close them in.

Nanny Mae stepped in between them and him.

"Wait a minute, have they come for me? Why?" Alex asked. "Where are they going to take me?" Dorothy and Toad stepped up beside him, and the others gathered in close behind.

Nanny Mae pulled a long samurai sword from her pocket and leveled it at the other Nannies. "They're not taking you anywhere."

With a *shink,* Nanny Smith drew a sword from her umbrella. "I'm disappointed in you, Agent Mae," she said. "You know the first rule of Nannying. Don't become attached to your *charges.*"

On the word "charges" Nanny Smith leaped at Nanny Mae and their swords *clinked. Ching ching ching ching*—the alley became a tornado of steel blades. The other Nannies—everyone but the dog—drew swords from their umbrellas, and soon Nanny Mae was keeping them all at bay.

"Jerry up!" Nanny Mae cried.

"What?" Alex asked.

"Run!" Nanny Mae said.

Alex broke from the Cyclones and sprinted back the way they had come, and Dorothy, Toad, and Mrs. P. took off with him.

"Nana! Golly! Maria!" Nanny Smith cried. "After him!"

The dog *woof*ed and dashed right through the Cyclones, but Jack got a long leg out to trip one of the women, and Tik-Tok's arms windmilled with a *whirr,* knocking the other woman into a clatter of trash cans. Pinkerton and Br'er Rabbit hopped on them to keep them down while Nanny Mae continued to hold off Nanny Smith with her sword.

In an alley a few blocks away, Alex slid to a stop, trying to decide which turn to take.

"This way, old man!" Toad cried.

"No, this way!" Dorothy said, and they were following her again. "I can't believe the Wizard wants to give you up!"

"It is an election year," Toad observed.

"I don't care if it's Backward Day," Dorothy said. "We're not giving you up. *We're a team.*"

"I didn't think you cared much about the team anymore," Alex said.

Dorothy shot him a look, but they were interrupted by a *woof.* Agent Nana had cut them off, and they threw on the brakes and ran back the way they had come.

"There! That ladder!" Dorothy cried, pointing to a fire escape.

Alex shot a look over his shoulder. The dog was gaining on them. "She's going to catch us!"

"Not to worry, fellows! Brave, loyal Toad shall save you!"

"Toad, no!" Dorothy cried, but the Cyclones' shortstop had already turned and thrown himself in the dog's path. Dog and toad tumbled into a heap of paws and webbed feet, buying Alex, Dorothy, and Mrs. P. enough time to climb the ladder to the fire escape.

Up and up they went. Alex didn't count the landings or turn back to look down, but by the time they reached the top of the building, he and Dorothy were winded.

Mrs. P. meowed.

"She's right," Dorothy said between panting. "We've got to keep moving. Those Nannies won't stop until—"

The door to the roof burst open, and Nanny Smith stepped out. Her hat was crooked, her sleeve was torn, and she didn't have her sword anymore, but she'd somehow gotten past Nanny Mae.

Alex and Dorothy turned back to the fire escape, but the other two Nannies were already climbing up behind them. They were trapped.

"Sorry, chaps!" Toad called up to them, pinned down by the dog in the alley. He was so far away he looked the size of a *real* toad.

Dorothy pulled Alex to the far corner of the rooftop, away from the Nannies on the fire escape and Nanny Smith on the other side. Together they glanced over the edge, hoping for some other way out, but there was nothing but a fifteen-story drop to the busy street below.

Mrs. P. darted away, sneaking through the legs of the other Nannies at the top of the fire escape.

"That darn cat!" Dorothy said.

"No, no—the last time she took off on me, she brought back help," Alex told her.

The Nannies drew closer.

"I can't believe you would do this!" Dorothy said. "There are rules! Things you just don't do!"

"Do you think the Big Bad Wolf plays by the rules?" said Nanny Smith. "This is a war, child. A war on terror. We can't *afford* rules."

Alex's heels hit the low wall of the rooftop as he backed away, and he grabbed on to Dorothy to keep his balance.

"You don't understand!" Alex told the Nannies. "I'm not a Lark! I'm a real boy!"

Nanny Smith rolled her eyes. "All Larks think they're real, boy. They just never stick around long enough to learn the truth. You're not going to be around much longer either, so what difference does it make if we give you to the wolf? It's worth it to save the lives of more Storybooks."

Dorothy got red in the face. "It doesn't matter if

he's a Storybook, a Lark, or a real boy—the good guys don't give the bad guy what he wants!"

"Nor do they weigh the worth of one life against another," Nanny Mae said, parachuting down to the rooftop. Nanny Mae kicked a leg out and caught Nanny Smith square in the chest, and Alex and Dorothy cheered.

Nanny Smith put a hand down to steady herself as she skidded to a stop, then jumped and flew at Nanny Mae. The two Nannies met in midair, kicking and punching each other like ninjas in a martial arts movie. *Whack! Thwack! Smack!*

The fight blocked Alex and Dorothy's route to the roof's exit, and the other two Nannies were almost on top of them.

"Now what?" Alex asked.

Dorothy clenched her fists. "Now we fight."

Alex watched Nanny Smith deliver a wicked roundhouse kick to Nanny Mae, slamming her up against an air-conditioning unit.

"You gotta be kidding! They'll tear us up!" he said, but they had no other choice. The other Nannies were already on top of them.

"Auf Wiedersehen," said one of the Nannies, and she grabbed at Alex. He pulled back to keep away from her, but lost his balance against the low wall

of the roof. His arms flailed as he tipped over the edge.

"Dorothy! Help! I'm—"

Dorothy caught his hand, but he was already too far out. His fingers slipped from hers, and Dorothy's horrified face was the last thing he saw before he pitched over the wall and fell.

Alex had always thought that falling from a great height would be like falling down the rabbit hole; that he would be able to look around on the way down and notice things like birds and billboards and people in windows, and have time to wonder things like how far he had fallen, and how much farther he had to go. But falling for real was much quicker and much crazier than that. All he saw were smears of white cloud and red brick, and all he could think was, *Wake up wake up wake up wake up,* and then the sidewalk was rushing up to meet him and he closed his eyes and then—

And then Alex died.

In Between

Machines beep and hum.

Tubes run from his arms.

He is in the hospital.

A nurse slips into the room. She puts a finger to her lips and winks.

His mother sleeps in a chair beside his bed. They won't wake her.

She takes his temperature. His blood pressure. Draws blood.

Does he need anything?

He needs to get out of this bed. Out of this hospital. He needs to go home.

He needs his video games, his books, his bike.

He needs to play baseball again.

No, he tells her. He doesn't need anything.

The nurse leaves, and Alex sees himself in the mirror. He's bald.

He touches the baseball glove on his table, then pushes it away.

He is in the hospital, and he's dying.

BE HE 'LIVE, OR BE HE DEAD

16

Alex wasn't dead.

He woke up on the pavement, blinking in the afternoon sun. Ambulance sirens blared, and a crowd of concerned animals gathered around him. High above, he saw Dorothy leaning out over the edge of the rooftop. One of the Nannies held her, and another disappeared, heading for the fire escape.

I'm not dead, but I should be, Alex thought. He propped himself up on his elbows and looked at his body. His legs, his arms, his head—everything worked fine. There wasn't a scratch on him.

It was impossible.

"Alex!" Scraps cried, and in moments she and the rest of the Cyclones were pushing back the crowd to get to him. "Toad! Jack! Drag him back here, into the alley. Alex, can you walk? Is anything broken, or did you just die?"

"I—I just died," he said, not so much to her but to himself. "I died, but now I'm not dead."

"Rather shocking the first time, isn't it, old sport?" said Toad. "You get used to it, though. Happens to me all the time."

Alex stared at him.

"Oh, sure," said Toad. "I died just the other day. You were there. When I drove that car into the tree in Hyde Park?"

"But—how?"

"I told you," said Scraps, "the only way a Storybook or a Lark can die is if whoever's dreaming about them forgets them. You can get hurt here, but if you ever do something that would kill you, you just . . . pop back into existence."

"It's really better to just die and come back whole again rather than get hurt," Toad told him. "Ever so much less painful."

But Alex *was* hurt. Not physically. Physically, he was fine. He had never felt better. But that's what hurt so badly. He knew now that he couldn't be a real boy trapped in Ever After.

Real boys died when they fell off buildings.

Br'er Rabbit peeked around the corner, into the street. "Those Nannies are gonna be on us in no time. Somebody better figure out what we're going to do, and fast!"

"I'm not somebody," Alex said quietly. "I'm nobody." He looked up at Scraps. "When I was— when I was dead, I dreamed I was in the hospital again. Is that me? I mean, is he the *real* me? Is he the one who's dreaming me?"

"We'll worry about that later," Scraps told him. "Right now, we've got to—"

She never got to finish. Nanny Smith landed in the entrance to the alley, followed closely by Nanny Mae. The other Nannies rounded the corner, holding Dorothy, and everyone was right back to the standoff where they had begun— except this time the alley was a dead end. There was nowhere to run.

"You're not leaving this alley with the Lark," Nanny Smith said.

Nanny Mae pulled a bazooka from her pocket. "Neither are you."

The Nannies crouched, ready to fight, and Alex's teammates formed a wall around him. The alley was moments from exploding into a storm of fists and feet and rockets when a gray cat jumped off a trash can and strutted out in the no-man's-land between them, making everyone pause. The Nannies waited as Mrs. P. and Nana the dog consulted silently with the new arrival. After a time, Mrs. P. turned and looked at Nanny Mae, and Nana let out a *woof*, and the Nanny holding Dorothy let her go.

"Well," Nanny Smith said. "That's that then. Sorry, Mae. Nothing personal, of course."

"No," Nanny Mae said coldly. "Of course not."

"Ladies?" Nanny Smith said, and the other Nannies filed out of the alley behind her. The chase was off.

"What—what just happened?" Dorothy asked.

Nanny Mae slid the bazooka back down into her pocket. "The Wizard has rescinded his order," she told them.

"He changed his mind?" Scraps asked.

"No. The wolf did. He struck a deal with the Wizard. The wolf will cease eating people if he is granted a pardon and allowed to play in the Ever After Baseball Tournament as a member of the Grimm Reapers."

"He *what?*" Dorothy asked. "He wants to play? Why?"

Nanny Mae beat dust from her trench coat. "I don't know."

"The Big Bad Wolf never gives up. *Never*," said Scraps.

"Indeed," the Nanny said. "I don't like it one bit. But the ceasefire gives us a moment's peace, and leaves us with only one front."

"But the wolf can't promise not to eat people!" Dorothy said. "It's what he *does!* It has to be a trick."

"Maybe he just wants a wish from the Wizard, like the rest of us," Jack said.

That made them pause for a moment, each picturing just what awful things Ever After's most notorious villain could do with a wish.

"Nanny Mae, you're going to stay with us, aren't you?" Dorothy asked.

"Yes. A good soldier never abandons her regiment. Now, I do believe we're going to have to give her the gun if we're to make it to our game on time. Shall we get moving?"

Alex wasn't thinking about their next game though, or what the wolf wanted with a wish, or how the Wizard could have agreed to give him up. All he could think was: *I'm not real.*

"Unreal," said Br'er Rabbit.

Toad threw up his hands. "To have come all this way for nothing!"

"We've lost," Jack wailed.

"I—I don't understand. What?" Alex said, coming out of his trance. He had followed the team to the hotel and then to the stadium, but he'd been too stunned by falling off a building and bouncing back up to pay much attention to anything else.

"We play the Giants," Dorothy said. "At home."

Alex still didn't get it.

"The Giants bat first," Scraps told him.

"Which means we ain't never gonna bat," Br'er Rabbit explained. "On account of the Mercy Rule."

"The tournament has a Mercy Rule?"

"They have to," Dorothy told him. "Otherwise some games would go on for weeks. One team's all trees."

"Another's all mice," said Toad. "Fine chaps, but they can't catch a ball without being squashed."

"Any team up by twenty runs at any point in the game automatically wins," Scraps explained.

"Twenty runs?" Alex said. "There's no way a team could score twenty runs on us."

"You ain't never played against giants," Br'er Rabbit told him.

Alex understood as the Giants stepped over the outfield wall into the stadium to the cheers of the fans. *Thoom, thoom, thoom.* The bats in the bat rack clattered with every step they took.

"Well, it was a good run while it lasted," Nanny Mae said.

"Eat me," Alex said.

The Nanny raised herself up. "I beg your pardon, young man?"

"EAT ME cake. I still have some in my pocket from Wonderland. The EAT ME cake—"

"Makes you grow taller!" said Toad. "Good show, old man!"

"You want me to eat two-day-old cake outta this boy's pocket?" Br'er Rabbit asked.

"Put a sock in it, hare," said Nanny Mae. She dug in her pockets. "Here. I believe I have some butter in here somewhere . . ."

"But I don't eat," Jack said. "Neither does Scraps. Or Tik-Tok."

Alex hadn't thought of that.

"We're just going to have to play shorthanded," Dorothy told them.

"So to speak," Toad said.

The Cyclones who could eat swallowed equal portions of the cake, and soon they began to grow to enormous size. It was dizzying being that tall, but fun too. The fans in the stands looked like action figures to Alex. Then he remembered how small Toad had looked from atop the roof, and how far he had fallen.

Of course I can grow to be a giant here, he thought. *I'm not—I'm not—*

He couldn't think what he was or wasn't.

"Can't think straight," he told the other Cyclones. "It's like there's a, a cloud-thing. Covering my brain."

"Guess your insides are starting to match your—you know," Br'er Rabbit said. "You're dumb-looking."

"It's being giant," Dorothy told them. "Giants in storybooks are stupid. Having big brains doesn't make them smarter. It makes the . . . the thinks they think . . . have farther to go. Don't know how long cakes will last. Need to win before we small again."

The players who couldn't become giant-sized were put on the bases, and Dorothy spread the rest of the team inside and outside of the stadium.

"Giants hit ball *long* way," she told them, already sounding more stupid.

Even though the Cyclones were now their size, the Giants were still a formidable team. A big, friendly giant proved to be a clever hitter, and Paul Bunyan was as good with a bat as he was supposed to be with an ax. The Cyclops at least was easy to strike out—no depth perception—but a massive Indian giant named Kumbhakarna tore the cover off the ball (literally) and stomped around the base paths, taking each base in two big strides.

Scraps kept a foot on second waiting for Pinkerton's throw from two miles away, and paid no attention to the giant trudging at her.

"Cloth girl!" Dorothy cried. "Big man coming! Get away!"

Scraps didn't move. She hung in for the throw, but the giant beat it to the bag and stomped her flat. Her body kicked up behind him and flopped lifelessly to the ground as the giant turned toward third.

Alex thundered over and plucked Scraps's trampled remains off the ground.

"Patchwork girl!" he wailed. His huge tears sent the ground crew running for a tarp to cover the infield.

"I'm all right!" Scraps told him. "Just give me a shake and knead my stuffing around a bit, will you?"

Dense as he was as a giant, Alex understood. "Pretend people no die," he said.

"That's right," Scraps told him. "I'm sorry, Alex."

The game resumed, and Alex took his place half a mile away, straddling a busy sidewalk. All those little people, all those Storybooks and Larks—he was just like them. He was somebody else's dream.

The next giant fought off Dorothy's first pitch with a towering foul ball that sliced out of the stadium, and Alex's instincts took over. He thundered through the busy streets and out into the suburbs like a dog chasing a firefly. Ten miles outside of town he tripped over an interstate overpass and went sprawling, but he caught the ball in his outstretched hands and slid to a stop against a tall line of trees. He stood, smiling down at the little pebble he held in his hand, but then a sad, lonely feeling tugged at him, and he saw where he was: the Wild Woods. The name was written right there on the tops of the trees.

The Wild Woods were unlike any other forest Alex had ever seen. There were no birds tweeting, no animals darting about, no empty spaces between the trees. There wasn't even a wind to rustle the leaves. There was something about the place that made Alex want to run away, but there was something in there that pulled at him too. Like it would be the perfect place to crawl inside and hide forever, where there would be no Big Bad Wolves and no falls from buildings and no bad dreams to deal with. They belonged together, the forest whispered: Alex and the Wild Woods. Like a ball needed a glove.

Alex put a foot inside the woods, knocking down a clump of trees. He was about to put his other foot in, to plow through to the middle of the forest and lie down and hide away from everyone and everything forever, when a giant hand grabbed his shoulder and held him back.

Dorothy.

"Forest am bad," she said. "No go forest."

"Me want go forest. Me no want to think anymore. Me confused."

"Me know. Must fight. Must be strong. Me help you," Dorothy told him. She reached out a hand and he took it, letting her pull him away from the dark place that whispered his name.

THE PITCHER AT THE GATES OF DAWN

17

Defeating a team of giants—even when temporarily the same size—is a difficult thing. The Giants were used to being big, dumb, and slow; the Cyclones were not. Besides, if there was one thing every Storybook in Ever After knew, it was that the smallest of heroes could take down the biggest of giants—if they were clever. And the Cyclones—when in their right, normal-sized minds—were clever.

Halfway through their turn at bat, the effects of the EAT ME crumbs wore off and the Cyclones shrank back down to regular size, turning the tables on the Giants. Where the Giants beat teams who could not pitch *up* to them, it was now equally impossible for them to pitch *down* to the Cyclones. Unable to throw anywhere near the strike zone, the Giants walked batter after batter, until finally—thirty-eight straight walks and thirty-five runs later—the Cyclones won by the Mercy Rule. (Dorothy, unable to score, had tactfully withdrawn by claiming injury, so as not to clog the base paths.) The game might not have been the most exciting one its twenty-five thousand booing spectators had ever seen, but the Cyclones were not in the business of entertaining people. They were in the business of winning, and with their victory they were three games away from winning the whole tournament.

Dorothy's fake injury, however, proved to be not so fake, which she revealed to the Cyclones before their next game. A tournament's worth of pitching complete games, plus the added stress of throwing three hundred miles an hour as a giant, had left her with a dead arm that would need at least a game's rest—perhaps more.

"Which means I can't pitch," she told them. "So who's going to do it?"

There were blank stares all around.

"Come on. Somebody here has to be able to pitch."

"I thought Somebody was on first," said Jack.

"Oh, let's not start *that* again," moaned Alex.

"Br'er Rabbit? Scraps? Pinkerton?"

They all shook their heads.

"Nanny Mae?"

"The only thing I know how to pitch is grenades, dear."

"Toad, what about you?"

"Does it mean I get to drive the bullpen car? The one they have here is shaped like a baseball, you know! Poop! Poop-poop!" he said, imitating the sound of a motorcar.

Dorothy threw up her hands. "Okay. Alex, you have to pitch."

"What? No. I've never pitched before. I'll get destroyed."

Dorothy leveled a "do we really have to have this conversation?" look at him. "Alex, you know you can. You're the best player on the team. You were born to be a baseball star. It's who you are."

"What about . . . what about Tik-Tok?" Alex asked. "You can be programmed to throw the ball any distance, right?"

"Of—course," the machine man said.

"There you go. Tik-Tok will be pitcher, I'll play catcher, and Dorothy, you can move to first, since there's less throwing to do there."

Dorothy didn't like it, but short of ordering Alex to pitch, there was nothing she could do. The necessary adjustments were easily made to Tik-Tok, but Alex had to borrow a set of catcher's gear from the other team, Pinocchio's Puppets, because Tik-Tok never wore any.

Alex was trying on a shin guard when he caught himself scratching an itch. Was it The Itch, or just *an* itch?

"You all right?" Scraps asked, sneaking up on him again.

"I—yeah," Alex said, trying to hide that he'd been scratching. "No," he confessed. "No, I'm not. Scraps, where did I go when I was out? After I, you know—after I hit the ground?"

Scraps shrugged. "You went . . . away."

"But where? I could still dream, Scraps. I dreamed I was in the hospital. That my mother was there. That I was sick. Dying. It felt—it felt real."

"Maybe it was," Scraps told him. "I don't know. I'm a Storybook. The only other me is on paper."

Alex scratched at his elbow when Scraps wasn't looking.

"Scraps, what happens when you die? I mean for good. Like Button Bright. Where do you go?"

"Oh, let's not talk about that. Let's talk about baseball."

"Scraps, please."

She sighed. "I don't think Storybooks or Larks go anywhere when people stop believing in them. I think we just . . . aren't. We were all just make-believe to begin with."

Alex stared at the shin guard in his hands.

Scraps nudged him. "Hey. I ever tell you about this boy I knew who was always so worried about when it was all going to be over he forgot to have fun while it lasted?"

"Hmm? Oh. Yeah . . . Yeah."

Scraps gave him a playful punch in the arm and cartwheeled away, and Alex went to stand with Dorothy at the dugout railing.

"You doing okay?" Dorothy asked.

Alex shrugged. "You?"

"I'm better. You were right, though. I kind of gave up for a little while there."

Alex nodded at the other team as they took the field. "They're all boys and girls," he said, doing everything he could not to scratch his arm. "I mean, with a name like Pinocchio's Puppets, I thought they'd all be, you know, wooden or something."

"No. You're right. I know who they are now—

they're characters from baseball books!" Dorothy smacked the dugout rail. "They're ringers! Pinocchio's stacked his team with aces this year!"

The rest of the Cyclones came to the rail to see.

"That one there, he's the boy who saved baseball," Scraps said. "And over there is the boy who only hits homers."

"And I know that shortstop," Br'er Rabbit said. "He's a samurai. And that boy there, he's got himself a bat carved from the World Tree."

"I'm afraid we've got our work cut out for us today, fellows," said Toad.

"We'll win though, right?" Jack asked. "You gotta believe. Right, Alex?"

Alex was scratching at his neck, and he dropped his hand and tried to look interested. "Yeah. Absolutely."

But no amount of believing helped the Cyclones score a run in the first, and no amount of believing turned Tik-Tok from a pitching machine into a Cy Young winner. Everything he threw was driven into the outfield for a hit. After the machine man gave up a three-run home run without getting any outs, Dorothy called a meeting on the mound.

"No offense, Tik-Tok," she told him, "but this isn't working."

"I—am not—pro-grammed—to take—of-fense."

"Alex, you have to pitch," Dorothy said.

"I told you. I can't. I've never pitched before in my life."

"Alex, you're a Lark who only knows baseball, and you know it. It doesn't matter that your dreamer's never pitched. In his dreams, he's the best baseball player ever. He can do anything on a baseball field."

"I'm not—" Alex started to say, but he knew he couldn't argue with her. "I'm not comfortable with this," he told her.

"Get comfortable," she said. She put the ball in his glove. "Alex, we need this."

Alex scratched his arm as the Cyclones went back to their positions, Tik-Tok taking up his usual place at catcher. How was he supposed to just know how to pitch? Pitching was an art. It was like painting. You didn't just pick up a paintbrush the first time and paint a masterpiece.

"Batter up!" the ump cried, and a new boy stood in. Alex got his sign, reared back, and aimed for Tik-Tok's glove. A swing and a miss—strike one! The Cyclones clapped and shouted encouragement behind him, but getting a strike just made Alex feel worse. *He shouldn't be able to pitch.*

His second pitch didn't make him feel any better. Another strike.

"Come on, Alex!" Dorothy called from first. "Strike him out!"

Alex wanted to be the hero and help his team, but he almost wished he couldn't strike the boy out. Maybe if the boy got a hit, it would mean Alex had been right all along.

Alex went into his windup. Pitched.

Crack! The batter hit the ball back, back, back—and over the wall for a home run! *Yes!* The home run put the Cyclones down by four runs, but Alex pumped his fist like he'd won the game. He wasn't some real boy's dream of a perfect baseball player after all!

"Shake it off," Dorothy told him. "That's the kid who only hits home runs. He's almost impossible to get out."

Alex's heart sank, and it kept sinking as he struck out the next three batters in a row without even trying.

Alex hit first the next inning, and as he stood in and waited for the first pitch, he considered all the evidence: his baseball skills, the dreams, his inability to wake up, his death and rebirth, The Itch. There was no denying it anymore. He was a Lark.

The pitcher, a girl who threw knuckleballs, floated strike one over the plate.

"Come on, Alex!" Dorothy called from the dugout. "Wake up out there!"

That's what Alex had been trying to do since he first appeared in Ever After—wake up. But now he knew for sure that he would never wake up. *He* was the dream.

To prove it, Alex closed his eyes as the girl went into her windup. He waited, waited, waited, his eyes still closed, then swung.

Crack!

Alex opened his eyes to see the ball leaping away from him, high up over the second baseman, over the center fielder, and out over the wall, where it disappeared into the seats.

"Run, dummy!" Br'er Rabbit called. "You hit a home run!"

Alex circled the bases in a daze, and when he finally came back to where he started he put his foot on home plate and wondered if that wasn't the only home he'd ever had.

With Alex's amazing hitting and pitching, the Cyclones clawed their way back into the game, despite Toad having easily the worst game Alex had ever seen him play. Always a poor batter but usually fleet of foot and sure-handed in the field, the amphibian missed balls he had once easily run down, and overthrew Dorothy at first five times in five innings.

"What is going on with you today?" Dorothy asked Toad as they went back to the dugout, down another run thanks to another of his throwing errors.

"Oh, there's nothing to be done. Nothing!" Toad said. "I'll—I'll be better presently. Don't be unduly anxious. I hate being such a burden to my friends, and I do not expect to be one much longer."

Though he apologized profusely all game long, Toad didn't appear to be sick or injured, smiling and bouncing happily on the bench and in the field as the innings rolled by. Alex, meanwhile, single-handedly kept the Cyclones in the game. He was the boy who only hit homers and the boy who only threw strikes, the boy who caught balls with his eyes closed and ran faster than any real boy could ever run. He was the Golden Boy. He was magic. He was the greatest baseball player anyone had ever seen, because that was the dream some sick boy in the real world was clinging to.

But Pinocchio's Puppets were impossibly good

too—all but Pinocchio himself, who was wooden and stiff at the plate and a tangle of strings in the outfield—and by the seventh inning the Cyclones were down by two runs.

Toad was due up first, but he was nowhere to be found.

"Where the devil could he have got to?" Dorothy asked. "Br'er Rabbit, check the stands. Maybe he's up there handing out those dang 'VOTE TOAD' cards."

Br'er Rabbit never got a chance. The audience went crazy, laughing and cheering about something on the field, and the Cyclones ran to the rail to see the stadium's bullpen car—a golf cart shaped like a giant baseball—careening out of a padded door in center field with Toad at the wheel.

"Make way! Make way!" Toad cried, scattering Pinocchio's team. The golf cart tipped as Toad swung it hard to the left, chewing up the outfield grass, then right as it barreled toward the field exit behind home plate.

"Toodle-oo, friends! I'm off to explore the farthest reaches of Ever After—and beyond! It's a classic tale: a humble toad, the open road, and a baseball-shaped golf cart! Don't come looking for me. I shall be cruising from town to town, finding odd jobs, fighting injustice, falling in love—"

"Toad! No!" Dorothy cried as the golf cart swerved for the exit.

Crash!

The molded plastic baseball was too tall for the exit. The golf cart smashed into the roof of the doorway and Toad went flying, tumbling to a stop on the cement ramp that led up and out of the stadium. Both teams ran over to see if Toad was all right, and Alex followed along slowly, lost in his own thoughts and scratching at his itchy arms.

Toad lay deathly still for a moment, then his eyes popped open and he sat up, grinning.

"What a thrill! I've never driven a baseball before, you know."

"That's the truth," said Br'er Rabbit.

"Toad, where did you get the key to the bull-pen car?" Dorothy demanded. "They know better than to leave it lying around when you come to town."

Toad looked sheepish. "Oh. Well, um—the key was *given* to me. As a gift. Yes. That's it. Mystery solved!"

Dorothy folded her arms and waited.

Toad went on his knees and wailed. "Oh, have pity on poor Toad! I am weak. I admit it. Foolish. Pathetic. A slave to my own desires. I need professional help. Motorcar rehab. Freudian analysis. Driver education—"

"Well, he certainly apologizes like a politician," one of the Puppets said.

"Toad," Dorothy warned.

The shortstop saw there was no way out but to tell the truth. "He told me if I played awfully he would give it to me!" Toad said quickly. "Just strike out once or twice, boot a ball here or there . . ."

"You took a bribe to throw the game!?" Dorothy cried.

"Oh, I am fate's plaything!" Toad cried. "The victim of a vast conspiracy! A minor pawn in some nefarious game. Well, not so minor, perhaps. A knight or a bishop maybe . . ."

"Toad," Dorothy said, "who bribed you?"

"He did!" Toad said. He pointed a webbed finger at Pinocchio, who had just started to slip away.

Pinocchio's wooden legs clattered as he broke into a run, but Pinkerton took to the air and pounced on him before he could escape. The players from both teams gathered around.

"You bribed him?" one of Pinocchio's own players asked.

"I just—I wanted to win so badly!" the puppet wailed.

"Well, that's it then," said the samurai shortstop. "Honor dictates we forfeit."

"What!?" Pinocchio cried, but his players were already taking off their yellow and red Puppets hats and tossing them on the ground. "No! No no no no! I put together the best baseball team this tournament has seen. The best team *anyone* has ever seen! Better than the 1937 Hobbiton Hobbits. Better than the 1894 Jungle Book Team. Better than the 1904 Lost Boys! Come back! We can go all the way! We can beat the Reapers!"

But Pinocchio's teammates did not come back, and the umpires were forced to call the game in the Cyclones' favor. Both teams wandered back to their dugouts as the crowd filed out of the stadium, leaving only Alex and Pinocchio together on the field.

"I was so close. So close!" Pinocchio sobbed. "Now I'll never be a real boy."

Alex scratched at his neck. "You were going to use your wish to become real?"

"Of course. That's all I've ever wanted since I first got here. But nobody ever imagines me as a real boy. I'm always a stupid wooden puppet."

"And the Wizard can do that? He can make you real?"

"The Wizard can do anything. But he's not going to do anything for me now."

Pinocchio kicked at the infield dirt as he clattered away, but Alex was feeling better already. If the Wizard could turn a wooden puppet into a real boy, maybe he could turn a daydream into one too.

THE GREAT ESCAPE

18

The afternoon sun is bright from the window.
He wakes, a baseball in his hand.
He closes his eyes and turns over.
Is it Saturday? Monday? Wednesday?
His room is a mess. There are crumbs in the bed. He
sleeps in his clothes.
It doesn't matter. None of it matters anymore.
Alex? Are you awake? Some of your friends are here.
Leave me alone, he says.
You wanna play a video game or something?
Go away, he says.
Maybe tomorrow, his mother says.
But not tomorrow. Not ever again. It doesn't matter.
None of it matters anymore.
The baseball rolls from his hand and thunks on the floor.

A baseball *thunked* to the floor of the Cyclones'
refurbished team bus and rolled past Alex's seat.
The team was taking a fairy—not a ferry, as Alex
had at first thought—to a stadium at the top of a
beanstalk, high up in the clouds. Rather than make

the long climb, most Ever Afters paid to have pixie dust sprinkled on them and fly up. There was a time when Alex would have been fascinated to watch out the window of a flying bus, or to chat excitedly about the big game tomorrow, the last one they had to win to get to the finals. But Alex didn't care about flying buses or big games. Yesterday, after hearing what Pinocchio wanted to wish for, he'd gotten the idea to use his wish to become real. If he were real, and not a daydream, it wouldn't matter if anyone believed in him. He'd be real—alive! He could go home to his parents and—

—and what? Share a bunk bed with the other Alex? The real Alex? That's where his fantasy about becoming real had come crashing down around him. There already *was* an Alex in the real world. There wasn't room for two. So what did it matter if he won the tournament and got a wish? There was nothing to wish for. He was a Lark. The daydream of a real boy. A baseball-obsessed boy.

A baseball-obsessed boy who was dying.

He understood everything now. When the boy had gotten sick, he had dreamed of being well. Better than well: He had dreamed of being super-human. Why? Had it made it easier, being trapped in bed when the sun was shining and the sky was blue and the kids in the neighborhood were playing a pickup game the next house over? Alex had gotten better and better every game in Ever After, while somewhere, in the real world, the boy dreaming him had gotten worse and worse, always clinging to the hope that he would get well and become the Alex of his dreams.

But now the real Alex was dying, and the dream Alex was dying with him. He didn't need his visions of the real Alex to tell him that. The Itch was so strong now he wanted to claw at his arms and legs and neck and chest. He wanted to tear himself apart.

Dorothy leaned over the back of her seat and called everyone to attention.

"Who'd have thought we'd make it this far, huh guys?"

Everyone but Alex applauded and cheered, but Dorothy hushed them.

"Just two more games, but we can't start looking ahead. We have a tough team standing in our way tomorrow: the Royals. For those of you who don't know, they're good. Really good."

"Is it because they are so beautiful?" Jack asked.

"They—no," Dorothy said. "It's because they

play hard and they play mean. They can't be bribed either. They're incorruptible."

At the mention of bribing, Toad sank miserably in his seat.

"Is that because they are so virtuous?" Jack asked.

"No. It's because they already have everything anyone could ever want," Dorothy told them. "Looks, brains, money, power . . . and Prince Charmings," she added for Jack's benefit. He blushed a shade of burnt orange. "They're in this to win it, to prove they're better than everyone else, and they'll be tough to beat. Alex, my arm's better, but you're ten times the pitcher I ever was. I want you to stay on the mound, and I'll play first again. Alex? You with us?"

"Huh? Yeah. Right. I'll play first again."

"No, *I'll* play first again."

"Right. Sorry."

Dorothy's look lingered on him, then she was back to business. "All right. We're landing. Breakfast first, then practice in thirty minutes," she told them, and the Cyclones started gathering their things to leave the bus.

Alex didn't join them. He curled up on his seat, arms wrapped around himself and scratching, wishing he didn't have to talk to anyone. Soon there were footsteps on the bus stairs, though, and he knew he wasn't going to get his wish.

"I told you," Scraps said. "He's got The Itch." She, Dorothy, Jack, and Toad stood over him.

"Go away," he told them.

"We're not going to let you do this, old man. You've got to fight it."

"Why? What's the point?"

"Most Larks don't have to deal with this, Alex," Scraps told him. "Let us help you."

"You didn't let me give up, and I'm not letting you give up," Dorothy told him. "If you don't get up and come practice with us, I'll have Tik-Tok drag you out of here."

Alex didn't think she'd really go through with it, but when he didn't move Dorothy sent the machine man in. More gently than Alex thought was possible, Tik-Tok picked him up and carried him out into the bright sunshine of the world above the clouds. The wind was stronger up here, much stronger, but Tik-Tok was too heavy to be swayed. Alex felt like a baby being toted around, and as soon as he could he wriggled free.

"All right. All right! I can walk."

"If you don't, Tik-Tok can always carry you to the field," Dorothy told him.

Alex kicked at the white, fluffy clouds that covered the ground while Tik-Tok cooked up eggs and bacon for everyone in an oven in his chest. Alex wasn't hungry. All he wanted to do was get away, go somewhere he could be alone. How could any of them understand? Storybooks lived for decades. Centuries. And Dorothy was worried people wouldn't believe in her anymore? Like she had anything to worry about! She would probably live forever. She could afford to relax and enjoy herself. Not Alex. And he certainly didn't feel all rah-rah about some stupid baseball tournament when he could disappear at any moment.

The Wild Woods. That's where he could go. They weren't far from here, he knew. Just down the beanstalk. They called to him. Told him how easy it would be to sneak onto one of the carts or trucks or buses lined up to take the fairy back down to Ever After. The Wild Woods. That's where he could hide from them. That's where he could finally be alone and die in peace.

Alex slinked around the back side of the bus to run away, but Dorothy, Scraps, and Nanny Mae were waiting for him.

"Going somewhere?" Dorothy asked.

Alex bolted, kicking up clouds as he ran. Let

them chase him! He was faster than any of them, even Br'er Rabbit! He was the fastest boy in the whole tournament. *Exactly the way the real Alex dreamed me,* he realized. *At least I owe him something for that—*

Foomp. Something hit his back and rode him to the ground. Pinkerton! Alex fought and kicked, but the flying monkey held on tight and flew him back to where Dorothy and the others waited.

"Witch!" Alex yelled at Dorothy over the wind. "You're wicked. All of you are! Why don't you let me go? You don't understand!"

"We understand well enough, old bean," Toad told him. "And we don't want to lose you."

"Let me go!" Alex raged. "You don't care about me! None of you do. You just want me for your stupid team because I'm a Lark who only knows baseball. You just want to use me until I fade away!"

"It looks as though someone will need to stand watch," Nanny Mae said. The wind came even stronger, and she put a hand to her metal hat to keep it from blowing away. "Mrs. P. and I—Mrs. P. and I will—"

The wind was so strong they all had trouble keeping their footing. Even up here, in the clouds, this must have been unusual. The wind roared in

Alex's ears and his hair whipped around his head, and he put an arm up to shield his eyes.

Dorothy, being a child of the great Kansas prairies, understood the sudden, dangerous change in the weather like no one else. Alex saw her perk up, like she was listening to what the wind was telling her, and then she was screaming at them.

"Twister! We have to find shelter!"

"The dugout inside the stadium," Nanny Mae told them. "Everybody make your way—" she began, but she never got to finish. Tumbling out of the clouds came a red farm tractor, half carried on the wind, half bouncing end over end on the ground, hurtling right for her. Nanny Mae held her hat and dove out of the way, but the tractor clipped her, knocking her back into the bus with a *thud*. Her body slumped lifelessly to the ground.

"Nanny Mae!" Dorothy cried.

Then, as suddenly as the wind had come, it died down again. It still lashed at their jerseys and swayed them in gusts, but it wasn't sending them for cover. Nanny Mae was unconscious, but breathing, with a large dent in her helmet where she'd struck the bus.

"That wind," Dorothy said. "If it was a tornado, it should have lasted longer . . ."

Alex tried to use the distraction to slip away

again, but Pinkerton and Br'er Rabbit were there to hold him.

"Let me go!" Alex told them. "I'll disappear by tomorrow anyway, and nobody will care. Nobody! Just like with Button Bright!"

Dorothy eyes flared. "Maybe we *should* let you go to the Forest!"

"Dorothy!" Scraps scolded.

Nanny Mae moaned as they took off her helmet, revealing a nasty bump on her noggin. Mrs. P. paced restlessly back and forth, mewling.

"Oh dear. I've been in my share of accidents," Toad told them, "and that one's going to put sugar in her tank for some time. I'll stay here and watch her, and Alex too."

"Toad, are you sure?" Scraps asked.

"Oh, I know all the tricks, for I've used them all myself. Don't worry. I won't let him get away." Toad saluted. "Ever vigilant: That's my motto."

They tied Alex to part of the beanstalk with some of Scraps's extra fabric, and Toad was left to watch him and tend to Nanny Mae with Mrs. P. while the Cyclones got in a short practice. Dorothy lingered for a moment, watching Alex, but he turned away. *She was only pretending to be my friend to get me to play,* he told himself.

When he looked back, she was gone.

Toad dabbed at Nanny Mae's bruised forehead with a damp cloth. "I say, you were rather hard on Dorothy, don't you think?"

Alex didn't say anything. He tried to scratch his Itch without his hands and think of a way he could escape to the Wild Woods.

"Oh. Ooh. Oh," he moaned.

"What is it, dear boy? Something wrong?" Toad asked.

"It's my stomach. I think I need a doctor . . ."

Toad leaned back against the bus and smiled. "Oh, good show. Playing sick is a dandy con."

"Seriously, Toad. I think I might be dying."

"You know what helps? Hold your breath until you're red in the face and all perspirey. Dashed effective! Particularly if your hands are bound and you can't fake a good swoon."

Alex dropped the act.

"You're right, Toad. I guess you can't con a con," he said, desperately trying to think of some other trick he could use. "Say, I'm glad they got the old bus fixed."

Toad's eyes lit up. "Oh yes! A 1939 Crosley, with a Waukesha air-cooled flat twin engine. A sterling piece of engineering."

"How's it handle?"

"Oh, like a dream! At least, that's what I imagine. I'm not allowed to drive it."

"You could, you know. While everybody else is gone. I won't tell a soul."

Toad rubbed his webbed hands together. "Oh. Oh, that's an intriguing notion. I have rather wanted to see what she can do in the hands of an expert driver."

"Just a little turn around the field," Alex told him. "No one will ever know."

"Yes. Yes, I—wait a moment. You're trying to trick me. Make me leave you alone! O-ho, a fine attempt. A fine attempt indeed. But old Toad's too smart for all that. You're not going to pull the ball cap down over this amphibian's eyes, I tell you."

"You win," Alex said. "I give up. You've got too much willpower for me. And Toad, I never said it, but thank you for throwing yourself at that dog when the Nannies were chasing us. That was incredibly brave."

Toad smiled. "Anything for a friend: That's my motto."

"Well, since we're here with time on our hands, why not have a little after-breakfast snack?"

"Oh, quite! I'll fetch the toast and jam."

Mrs. P. meowed at Toad.

"Oh, don't worry! I'm sure I can rustle up a bit of fish for you."

Mrs. P. kept meowing at Toad. When he didn't understand, she meowed at Nanny Mae, trying to wake her up.

"I'll get the picnic blanket and plates," Alex said. He turned his bound hands toward Toad. "If you would?"

"Of course, of course," Toad said. He untied Alex's hands, and Mrs. P. meowed louder and more insistently. "Now now, my dear cat, no need to be so pushy. I'll just pop round and get the fixings."

Toad disappeared around the other side of the pink bus, humming happily to himself.

Mrs. P. growled at Alex, low and angry, Nanny Mae still unconscious by her side.

"Yeah, well, just try and stop me," Alex said, and he took off for the fairy.

Toad trotted back a few minutes later with an armful of groceries, humming a little song about himself. His eyes fell on the empty ground where Alex should have been and he dropped the food, realizing his mistake.

"Oh poop."

THE WILD WOODS

19

"I wish Badger were here," Toad said.

Tik-Tok *whirr*ed and *kachunk*ed, and bright light spilled from his eyes, illuminating a small patch of the Wild Woods in front of them.

"And I wish Nanny Mae were here," Dorothy told Toad. "But if wishes were free we wouldn't have to bother with the baseball tournament. Now suck it up and help us find Alex. We have to assume Mrs. P. went after him, since she didn't stay with Nanny Mae, so we're looking for her too. Alex! Alex? Mrs. P.? Are you there?"

Toad jumped at a snapping twig in the darkness. "I don't know why you brought me along in the first place."

"Maybe because it's your fault he's gone?"

"What was that, what was that!?" Toad yipped. He grabbed Tik-Tok's head and swiveled it toward a noise, but there was nothing there. "Oh! If only Badger were here."

"Will you shut up about Badger?"

There was no path in the Wild Woods, so Dorothy, Toad, and Tik-Tok picked their way among the tall pine trees in roughly a straight line. Just in case they got turned around, Dorothy scattered sunflower seeds from the dugout bucket as they went. Unlike the unfortunate Hansel and Gretel (who now owned a bakery in the Emerald City's Little Germany), Dorothy, Tik-Tok, and Toad didn't have to worry about birds or other animals eating their seeds; there didn't seem to be anything else alive in the forest at all.

Leaves rustled nearby, and they froze. Perhaps there was something here with them after all.

"Who's there?" Dorothy called.

"He doesn't love me," somebody whispered.

"What? Who's there? Show yourself!"

"My parents will never get back together," a smaller voice said.

Tik-Tok's headlights swung to where the words were coming from, but all they caught was the blur of a shadow disappearing behind a tree.

"I'm never going to be famous. I'm never going to do anything."

"Nobody notices me."

"I'm not me when I take the medicine."

"I'm just a clown. They only like me because I make them laugh."

"It's Larks," Toad said. "They're Larks whose believers know better but refuse to give up their dreams, and it's driving them mad."

Each time Tik-Tok turned his head, they saw a different shadowy figure clawing at itself just before it slipped behind a tree away from the light.

"All right," Dorothy said. "I wish Badger were here too."

The three Cyclones drew closer together and crept forward, back to back to back.

"I'm so stupid," a Lark whispered.

"I'm going to get caught."

"I'm not good enough. I can't do it."

"I'm not real. I'll never be real."

"Alex?" Dorothy called. "That's him. It has to be him." She ran off into the darkness toward the voice. Tik-Tok's light bounced ahead of her as he tried to keep up. There—there was someone trying to get away. Dorothy put a hand out to the shadow and spun him around.

"Pinocchio? What are you doing here?"

The marionette stared at his feet. "I'm just a puppet. That's all I'll ever be. I'll never be a real boy."

"I'm not real," someone echoed nearby.

"Wait, that's our boy!" Toad cried. They let Pinocchio go and ran to where they'd heard the voice. Tik-Tok's light revealed Alex on the ground, curled up in a nest of pine needles. Mrs. P. was standing watch over him and hissed when they drew near, then purred and rubbed their legs when she saw who it was. Dorothy bent to scratch her head.

"Thanks for looking after him, P."

"I'm just a Lark," Alex whispered. "I'm nobody."

"Alex—Alex, it's Dorothy. We've come to take you back."

"Go away," Alex told them. "I don't want to go back."

"Let's get him up," Dorothy told Toad, and together they pulled Alex to his feet.

"Leave me alone!" Alex cried. "I don't want your help, and I don't want to play anymore! Just let me die in peace!" He pushed Dorothy away with both hands, knocking her back into one of the trees.

"Alex, remember yourself!" Toad cried, and for

a brief moment, Alex did remember himself. He remembered his mother and father, and his little sister. He remembered the hot pavement at the pool in summer, backyard baseball games that went so late they couldn't see the ball anymore, the taste of homemade ice cream and the smell of leather oil and the sound of a bat *thwack*ing a ball. But they weren't his memories. They were somebody else's. His entire life was a lie. He was a lie.

Alex staggered back into the forest. "Please," he whispered. "Just leave me alone."

"You really should listen to him," a gravelly voice said behind them. Tik-Tok's head swiveled around, and his light caught Pinocchio, who stood flanked by two huge trees.

No. Not trees. *Legs.* Great furry brown legs. Tik-Tok's light swept up and up and up, until it shone on the jagged, grinning face of the Big Bad Wolf.

"Don't you know it's dangerous to walk alone in the woods at night?" the wolf said, and he snapped Pinocchio up in his enormous jaws and swallowed him whole.

"*Run!*" Dorothy screamed, and there was chaos. Toad took off in one direction, Dorothy another, Mrs. P. yet another. The Big Bad Wolf swiped an enormous paw at Tik-Tok, who was too slow to run in any direction, and with a *crunk* the Wolf knocked the machine man's head off and sent it spinning into the darkness. The head rolled to a stop near the tree where Alex was hiding, and he watched the light from Tik-Tok's eyes flicker out, leaving the woods in total darkness.

"Oh, Tik-Tok," Alex whispered. His fear had drowned out his self-pity, if only for the moment.

"Yes, Mas-ter Al-ex?"

"Tik-Tok, you're alive!" But of course he was alive. Storybooks and Larks could be hurt, broken, taken apart, *swallowed* even, but they couldn't die.

"I hear you, Alex Metcalf," the wolf said somewhere nearby, and Alex held his breath. "I can smell you too. I can smell all of you. It's hard to run away in the darkness, isn't it?"

Escape was impossible, and they all knew it. Only Mrs. P. could see in the dark, and all she could do was run for Nanny Mae—who was probably still out of commission, or else she would have been there. The only way out of this was to fight. But how did you beat the Big Bad Wolf?

"Tik-Tok," Alex whispered, "you have an oven in your body, don't you? Do you think it's broken?"

"It is—op-er-a—tion-al," the machine man

told him. "My head—can con-trol—my bo-dy—
e-ven—when sep-a-ra-ted."

"Turn it on," Alex told him.

He groped around on the forest floor until he
found a stick. "I thought you said you wouldn't eat
anyone if they let you play baseball!" Alex shouted
to the wolf. He moved from where he'd been
standing as quickly as he could, swinging the stick
in front of him like a blind person's cane, trying to
hit the trees before they hit him.

"Well, a wolf has to eat," the Big Bad Wolf said.
His voice came from near where Alex had been.
"So I pop into the Wild Woods every now and
then for a snack. No one's going to miss a few
miserable souls who don't want to be here anyway. Isn't that why you came here, Alex Metcalf?
Don't you just want everyone to leave you alone?
To hide away in a den of your own despair? Why
don't you just tell me where you are, Alex Metcalf? Then I'll eat you up, and no one will ever
bother you again."

The wolf was close. Alex could hear his big
paws crunching in the pine needles on the forest
floor. Alex kept moving, sliding his feet forward,
foot by foot, searching for Tik-Tok's body. It had
to be around here somewhere.

"If I do, will you let my friends go?" Alex asked.

"Alex, no!" Dorothy cried from somewhere nearby in the darkness.

"Of course," the Big Bad Wolf said. "You have my word."

"Which counts for exactly naught," Toad called, also close by. "Don't listen to him, Alex!"

"Shall I huff and puff, then?" the wolf asked. From the sound of his voice he was only a few yards away, and Alex froze. "I huffed and puffed on top of the beanstalk to blow your nanny away, and when that didn't work I threw a tractor at her," the wolf said. "I was going to come after you then, eat you up, but I had to see where you were running off to. I never dreamed you would head for my neck of the woods."

Sniff sniff sniff—Alex could hear the wolf snuffling nearby. He had to keep moving. Something brushed his leg and he almost yelped before he realized it was Mrs. P., leading him toward something warm. Tik-Tok's body! He silently thanked Mrs. P. and felt around until he found the door to the oven in Tik-Tok's chest. He opened it and tried to get the stick to catch fire.

Come on, he thought. *Come on, come on, come on—*

"It's only a matter of time until I find you and eat you, Alex Metcalf. But that won't kill you, will it? Not as long as someone is still dreaming about you. I won't truly have gotten rid of you, and that bothers me, because I want to erase you from existence, Alex Metcalf. But then I had a thought. A very interesting thought. You're not a Storybook. You're a Lark. I *can* get rid of you, once and for all. All I have to do is eat your *dreamer* too."

Alex froze. So that was it. That was why the Big Bad Wolf had joined the Reapers. He was going to use his wish to become real and eat the real Alex too.

The stick in Tik-Tok's oven burst into flame and Alex was lit up for everyone to see. So was the wolf. His big face was right above Alex, his dripping fangs glinting in the light.

"Gotcha," he snarled.

"Got you!" Alex said.

Alex stabbed his torch into the dry bed of needles on the forest floor, and the wolf's eyes went wide. The wolf huffed, and he puffed, and he tried to blow out the fire—but his blast only fed the blaze. *Whoosh!* The dry woods around them exploded in flames, and Alex was blown back. But the wolf was too big to be knocked away. His fur caught fire and he howled, a monstrous sound like death itself dying.

It was the last thing Alex heard before a giant flaming paw swatted him deep into the dark Wild Woods.

THE PRINCESSES
AND THE PEA

20

H e's awake," said Scraps.

"Alex, it's good to have you back!" Jack said.

Alex blinked his eyes and stirred. He was lying on a bed of jerseys in a dugout. Puffy white clouds floated across the top of the outfield bleachers, and the flags whipped in the wind. He was inside the Fee-Fi-Fo-Forum, the stadium at the top of the bean-stalk. But when had he been brought here? Alex figured he must have been out all night.

He tried to sit up, but his head swam like he'd been hit by a pitch.

"Just rest," Dorothy told him. "You took a pretty nasty shot from the wolf."

"I told you, old boy, it's always better to just die and get it over with. Then it's not so painful."

"Toad, not now," Dorothy told him.

Alex closed his eyes. He had wished he was dead. Not when he was fighting the Big Bad Wolf, but before that. When he had gone to the Wild Woods and pulled his sorrow over him like a blanket. The knowledge that he wasn't real—that he never had been and never would be—that knowledge hurt, and he wanted the pain to end. But the woods were worse.

"Do I need to get some strips of fabric to tie him up?" Scraps asked quietly.

"No," Alex told them. "I'm not going back there. Really. I promise." He looked at Toad. "I mean it this time. I'm sorry."

"Quite all right, old bean," Toad told him. "We all get the urge to run off sometimes."

"Can we have a minute?" Dorothy asked, and the others left her alone with Alex. She sat down on the bench beside him. "You saved us back there. In the forest. We came to save you, and you ended up saving us."

"I was just scared. More scared of the wolf than I was of dying."

"Well, still. Thanks."

"So, how long until the wolf comes after me again?"

"Depends," Dorothy told him. "If he died in the fire, he would have popped back healthy and ready to go. If you just charred him, it could take him a while to heal."

"Oh! How is Nanny Mae? Is she all right?"

"Recovering nicely. She already bandaged herself up. Royal Army Nursing Corps and all that, you know."

Alex scratched at his arm. "Dorothy, I'm dying. He's giving up. The real Alex. He doesn't care anymore."

"I know," Dorothy told him.

Alex sat up, even though it hurt. "I'm so stupid. The Lark who thought he was real. I'll bet everybody got a pretty good laugh out of that one."

"Nobody was laughing at you, Alex."

He hung his head.

"Look," Dorothy told him, "I understand if you want to give up. You can sit here on the bench the rest of the time, and I'll move people around."

"You're already shorthanded, remember? Nanny Mae's hurt, and Tik-Tok's broken." The memory of that horrible scene in the dark woods came back to him, and he shuddered.

"Tik-Tok's already fixed. He's good as new. And Nanny Mae, as team nurse, has cleared herself to play. Although I'm not so sure we should be trusting the judgment of somebody who got hit in the head."

The Nanny sat knitting farther down the bench. Mrs. P. lay in her lap, catnapping, but Alex knew they were both still keeping an eye on him. He nodded his thanks.

"Look," Dorothy said, "the point is, I won't make you play."

"Heh. 'Make me play.'"

"You don't think I could? You're talking to the girl who took down the Wicked Witch of the West."

Alex gave her half a smile, which was as much as he could muster. "Scraps told me she's not so wicked after all."

"Well, she was then." Dorothy looked sidelong at him. "'Course, you could always help us win, and use your wish to not be forgotten, like the rest of us."

"Nobody else is going to use their wishes to be remembered, Dorothy. You've heard them."

"Then I'll wish it for them. I'll wish for all of us to be remembered. Even you."

Alex shook his head. "I thought about it, but it won't work. The real me is dying. When he dies, so do I." And if whatever was making him sick didn't get him, the Big Bad Wolf eventually would.

"Well, it's your call," Dorothy said. "I'm not going to push you anymore. Just don't go running off on us, all right?" She smiled. "We finally got used to having you around."

Dorothy left Alex alone at the end of the bench and gathered the team together for a pep talk. This was their last game before the finals. If they won, they would play the winner of the Reapers/Lost Boys game—but first they had to get through the Royals.

Although the team they faced actually included Cinderella, to call them a "Cinderella Team" would be a lie. Unlike the Cinderella of her story, this team was heavily favored to win, and had proven Ever After's oddsmakers right in every one of their previous games. The Royals treated victory as though it was their due, but their success had more to do with the amazing gifts their authors had given them than any hard work or determination.

"Bunch of stuck-up princesses," Br'er Rabbit said. "They was born on third and act like they hit a triple."

"Alex, you with us?" Dorothy asked as the Cyclones took the field.

"Yeah," he told her.

But though Alex was with them in body, he wasn't with them in spirit. His pitches weren't as sharp as they'd been against Pinocchio's Puppets, and when the Royals jumped out to an early lead Dorothy quietly swapped places with him on the mound. Back at first base, Alex was all right with anything hit or thrown right at him, but in the second inning he missed a low toss from Jack he might have saved before. It skipped into the stands and the runner was awarded an extra base. Even worse, Dorothy didn't get mad. She went easy on him just like she had with Button Bright.

Alex wasn't much better at the plate either. He did his best to stand in and take good swings, but he was late every time. His heart just wasn't in it. His Itch was getting worse too. He missed a clean throw from Toad in the fourth because he was busy scratching, and after that Dorothy called time-out and brought Scraps and Nanny Mae in from the outfield.

"Scraps, take Alex's place at first. Nanny Mae, I know you're always right, but would you play left today?"

"I think this one time I can be wrong," the Nanny said.

"All right," Dorothy said. "Alex, take right field."

Alex knew what that meant. Right field was where you put the players who couldn't be trusted anywhere else. It was the one place he could do the least amount of damage. He had gone from all-star to scrub. But that was where he belonged.

With Alex slumping and Scraps and Nanny Mae playing out of position, the Royals might have romped, but the score was kept close thanks to a trio of bad umpires—three little white mice with sunglasses and canes who made absolutely terrible calls. The Cyclones could never pull even, though, let alone ahead. It might have helped if Dorothy could touch home plate, but with Alex hitting behind her, there were few enough chances for her to score as it was.

"I say, old man, watch this," Toad whispered to Alex as they sat on the bench in the bottom of the seventh inning. Br'er Rabbit had lain down for a quick snooze between innings, and Toad crawled under the bench to stick a lit match between the rabbit's toes. The match curled its way up to Br'er Rabbit's foot, and when the flames touched him he yowled and shot into the air like a cartoon. Toad, Jack, Scraps, Pinkerton, even Dorothy busted out laughing, but Alex just went back to staring at the floor of the dugout and scratching at his Itch.

The Royals scored again in their half of the ninth inning, and the Cyclones came to bat trailing by four runs with only three outs to go. The Storybooks and Larks in the stands began to file out of the stadium, eager to catch the fairy home.

But everyone who left early missed an amazing sequence of events. Nanny Mae looped a liner to left to start the inning, and Scraps dragged a ball through the infield to put Cyclones on first and second. Jack Pumpkinhead tapped a sacrifice bunt back to the pitcher that moved the runners to second and third, and then the home plate umpire did his part, calling what should have been a third strike as ball four and putting Tik-Tok on to load the bases.

"What are you, blind!?" screamed Briar Rose from the pitcher's mound.

"Yes, actually," said the little mouse.

The princesses threw a royal fit, but the decision stood, and Pinkerton came to the plate with the bases loaded and only one out. The flying monkey smacked a double to right, scoring Scraps and the Nanny, and Toad stood in with two on, one out, and the Cyclones now down by two.

"Come on, Toad!" Dorothy called from the dugout.

"I shall hit like I have never hit before!" Toad

said, giving his bat a hefty practice swing.

"You never *have* hit before," said Br'er Rabbit.

But Toad surprised everyone in the stadium, the Cyclones included, when he singled sharply to center, scoring Tik-Tok and the fleet-winged Pinkerton to tie up the game. The crowd roared, and those who were not too far gone from their seats came back to cheer for the underdog.

Dorothy was up next. With one good swing of the bat she could put the Cyclones ahead without ever having to touch home plate herself.

Briar Rose still had barbs to throw, but Dorothy fought off a third strike with foul ball after foul ball. All the Storybooks and Larks in the stadium, save Alex, were on the edge of their seats.

The pitcher finally came after Dorothy with a pitch she could hit, and Dorothy sent it rocketing toward the outfield wall. The crowd rose to its feet and gasped—then sighed as one when Rapunzel climbed the center field wall and snared it for out two.

Toad was already halfway to third and had to scramble back to first. The throw bounced in and looked to have him beat, but the blind umpire at first called him safe, unleashing another tantrum from the princesses. They relented, though, when they saw which Cyclone was up next: Alex, who had struck out every single time at bat. Even a blind umpire couldn't walk Alex.

Dorothy stopped him on the way to the plate.

"Alex, we actually have a chance here. But we need you. I know you don't care about yourself anymore, but there are other people to think about. A Big Bad Wolf to beat. I'm just saying. *Please.*"

"I'll try," Alex told her. And he meant it, even if he didn't feel it. He didn't want to go back to the Wild Woods again, but he didn't want to be here, either. More than anything, he wanted to just curl up someplace and be alone. How was he supposed to care about balls and strikes when he was dying?

The first pitch hummed past Alex for strike one before he could even get his bat moving. In the Cyclones' dugout, Dorothy buried her head in her hands.

Alex tried to shake off his doldrums. Tik-Tok, Scraps, Jack Pumpkinhead, Br'er Rabbit, Nanny Mae, even Dorothy, they were all dying too, in a way, and they needed his help. But would winning the tournament really help? Was the Wizard powerful enough to actually work his magic on the real world, even though he was make-believe like the rest of them? Dorothy certainly thought so.

Alex had too, back when he thought he was real and wanted to go home. But what good was a wish from the Wizard now? Even if the Wizard could force the real Alex to believe in him, the real Alex was dying, and the dream Alex was dying with him.

Unless—

Briar Rose's second pitch zoomed past him for strike two.

Alex suddenly stood straighter. Had he been a cartoon character, the other players might have seen a lightbulb click on over his head. He'd been so stupid! All this time he'd been moping about himself, but Dorothy was right. *There were other people to think about.* Whether a wish from the Wizard could truly help or not, he didn't know— but it was worth trying for.

It was worth playing for.

The third pitch came whizzing in, and the old Alex was back. His bat flashed—*crack!*—and the ball leaped into the air. The Royals gasped, the crowd rose to its feet, and in the Cyclones' dugout Dorothy left the bench and came to the dugout rail to watch, tears welling in her eyes, as the baseball disappeared over the wall in left center and into the clouds for a game-winning home run.

THROUGH THE LOOKING GLASS
(AND WHAT ALEX FOUND THERE)

21

The final game of the Ever After Baseball Tournament was in the Emerald City, home of the wonderful Wizard of Oz—and the Cyclones. They were in the finals for the first time in the tournament's almost 150-year history, and their fans treated them to a ticker-tape parade down Verdigris Avenue as though they had already won. Perhaps they knew they'd better celebrate now while they could, Alex thought. The Cyclones had made it to the finals, but Ever After's odds-makers weren't giving them much of a chance to win. Their opponents, to the surprise of very few, would be the Grimm Reapers, who had won their place in the finals when the Lost Boys had been busted for performance enhancing pixie dust and

"No offense," Dorothy told the hedgehog, "but she's no Toad."

"No," Alex said, borrowing Mrs. Tiggy-Winkle's bonnet and putting it on Toad's head. "What if we play *Mrs. Tiggy-Winkle* there instead."

"You mean dress me up as a washerwoman?" Toad cried. "But—but it'll ruin my chances for election! I was going to parlay my dazzling on-field leadership skills and our ensuing victory into an election day win!"

The crowd cheered as Pinkerton doubled to right center.

"Toad, you're up next. It's now or never."

Toad's lip quivered. "Anything for the team," he said sadly. "That's my motto."

"But Alex," Dorothy asked while Toad made his quick change, "if 'Mrs. Tiggy-Winkle' is at short, we can't very well run the *real* Mrs. Tiggy-Winkle out there later in the game. What if—?"

"I'm not going anywhere," Alex assured her. "Not yet. I feel good. Better than I have in days. Seriously."

The problem of Toad was solved for the moment, but the Reapers had even more tricks up their black sleeves. In the second inning Br'er Rabbit went out to his position at third only to forced to forfeit their game. Now just two teams remained, with the final and deciding game to be played the following day.

In the meantime, most of the Cyclones had plans.

"Tonight, fellows, we party like there's no tomorrow!" Toad announced, and his teammates on the bus cheered.

Alex scratched again at his arms and worried that, for him at least, there really might not be a tomorrow.

Dorothy came down the aisle to his seat. "Alex, you coming? I know this great Winkie restaurant on Viridian Street."

"Sure," he said. He put his hand to the seat in front of him to pull himself up, but somehow he didn't grab it. Alex frowned. Had he reached for it and missed it?

He tried again and his hand went right through the seat.

"Dorothy, I—something's wrong. I can't—"

"Alex! Alex, no! Not yet!" Dorothy cried.

Alex looked down and saw straight through himself to the seat cushion.

He was fading away.

"Dorothy, I—I can't feel anything. I mean, I

can't even feel my heart beating, or my tongue, or my baseball jersey—"

"Alex, hang on!"

"To what?" he cried. His arms flailed as he tried to grab the seat, his glove, anything.

Dorothy reached out to him and yelled something, but it was like someone had pressed the mute button on her. No, on the whole world.

"Dorothy! Dorothy, I can't hear you! I can't hear anything!" he tried to say, but he couldn't even hear himself.

The world began to blur and turn dark. Alex put his hand to where Dorothy's was, and his fingers passed through hers like a ghost.

This was it. He was dying.

". . . I feel something!" Dorothy was saying. He could hear her again! And see her! Then he felt her too—a tingle, then a touch, and then his hand was in Dorothy's, and she was holding on like she was hauling him back up from a cliff, and Alex could feel his heart *thump-thump-thump*ing in his chest and taste the hot tears that ran down his face.

Dorothy sat down in the seat beside him, still squeezing his hand tight, and Alex was happy to leave it there for a while, happy to be holding on to anything real.

"There was nothing," Alex said, shivering. "It wasn't dark. It wasn't cold. It just . . . wasn't. Dorothy, I don't want to die. I know I ran off to the woods. I didn't want to deal with it, so I ran away and hid. I'm back now. I'm not going to run away from it. But that doesn't mean—"

"I know," she told him. "I know."

Alex slumped in his seat and scratched at his knee. "It's the real me. I've seen him. In my dreams. He's going to die soon, and he's giving up. Which means I'm going to die even sooner than he does."

Dorothy nodded. There wasn't anything she could say. He was right.

"I used to dream about him a lot, but not so much anymore. Maybe it's because he's forgetting me. How does it work, being a Lark?"

"I don't know," Dorothy told him.

"I wonder what he's doing right now. If he's with his friends and his family, or if he's hiding away, waiting to die. I wish I could see him."

"You really want to?"

"Sure. Wouldn't you?"

Dorothy seemed to come to a decision and nodded. "I know somebody who can show him to you. I'm not really supposed to, but . . . hang on." She took his hand again and clicked her heels and—nothing happened.

"Oh," she said. "I keep forgetting. No more magic shoes. We'll have to find another way to get there."

She led Alex outside and found Pinkerton, and soon he had them both in his arms and was flying them high over the rooftops of the Emerald City. Alex hoped he didn't start to fade away again before they got wherever they were going, or it was going to be a long fall—longer than the fall he'd taken from the rooftop. Behind them, in her motorcycle-turned-gyrocopter, flew the ever-watchful Nanny Mae and Mrs. P., complete with goggles and scarves.

Pinkerton swooped toward a tall green tower and glided in through an open balcony door to land in a wide, round room with no decoration but for a large gilded mirror hanging on the wall. The flying monkey set them down gently, and Nanny Mae landed behind them.

"Hello, Dorothy," the mirror said, making Alex jump. "Come to check your sales rank again?"

Dorothy blushed. "The Wizard keeps the Magic Mirror up here to keep an eye on 'persons of interest,' but I've been popping in to see if people remember me."

"You mean, it can see into the real world?"

"I'm hanging right here, you know," the mirror told him. "You don't have to talk about me like I'm not in the room. I'm always in the room."

"Sorry," said Alex.

"I've come to ask for something different today, Mirror," Dorothy told him. "Alex is a Lark, and he wants to see the boy who's dreaming him."

"Really?" the mirror asked.

Alex felt a twinge of excitement and fear. Until then, his only hint of the real him had been in vague, jumbled dreams. He wanted to see the real him, but he was almost scared to. In a way, it would prove once and for all that Ever After was real, not some weird, twisted nightmare.

"Yes," Alex said. "Please."

"Well, it's a first, that's for sure," the mirror told them. "All right. You know how this works."

"You have to ask him in rhyme, like in the story-books," Dorothy told Alex. "You know, 'Mirror, mirror, on the wall . . .' That sort of thing."

"Um. Okay. Mirror, mirror in front of me . . . show me who is dreaming me."

"You can't rhyme a word with itself," the mirror said.

"Come on, Mirror," said Dorothy.

"He used the word 'me' three times!"

"Just show him already."

The mirror sighed. "Poetry is a lost art. All right. Hold for signal . . ."

The mirror's glass face went staticky, then became clear like a television screen, showing the world from high in the clouds. Not Ever After, but the *real* world, a green and brown and blue map without words written on it. They swooped down, down, down toward the ground, and the world resolved itself into interstates and buildings and baseball fields and neighborhoods.

"I think I can see my house from here," Alex said, getting hopeful. Then they were dropping toward it, and through the roof, and into his bedroom. There were his posters of his favorite baseball players, his desk, his video games, his boxes of baseball cards. And there was his mother, sitting in bed with—

—with him. But not him, he realized. This wasn't *his* mother, and *his* room, and *his* things. This was the *other* Alex's world. The dreamer's world.

The real Alex lay with his head in his mother's lap, wrapped up in the blanket from his bed. She was reading to him from a picture book, something his little sister might have asked for, but Alex saw it was one of his favorites. Hearing her read it aloud to him made him feel like he was little again, without a care in the world, sitting in his mother's lap for a bedtime story, and he understood why the real Alex didn't complain.

". . . Max said 'BE STILL!'" she read. "And he tamed them with the magic trick of staring into all their yellow eyes without blinking once . . ."

The mirror, the tower, Dorothy, Pinkerton, the Emerald City, the tournament, The Itch—everything fell away as Alex watched his mother read him the rest of the story. When she was finished, she closed the book and set it aside and put her hand on the real Alex's bald head. Alex reached out, trying to touch his mother, but his fingers found only the flat surface of the mirror.

"Don't die," Alex whispered to his dreamer. "Just one more day. That's all I need."

The image faded, and Alex was looking at himself in the mirror again. He pulled his hand away from the glass. "Sorry."

"Think nothing of it," the mirror said.

Dorothy put a hand on Alex's shoulder. "It's going to be okay, Alex. We'll win tomorrow, and then you can use your wish to not disappear."

Alex nodded, but that wasn't what he planned to wish for at all.

THE EMERALD STADIUM OF OZ

22

The entry for "The Emerald City" in *Travels into Several Remote Regions of Ever After, in Four Parts,* by Lemuel Gulliver, devotes an entire page to Emerald Stadium, the crown jewel in a city built out of crown jewels. The grandstands and dugouts were carved out of shimmering emerald crystals that rose so high into the sky that the place felt more like a fairy castle than a baseball stadium. Green pennants hung from every roof, and a great green clock in center field ticked away the time. The infield was outlined with foul lines made of real diamonds, and the green grass of the field was so emerald it was hard to tell where the outfield ended and the wall began.

A sell-out crowd cheered as the emerald Jumbo-

Tron in right center came to life with bursts of flame around it. An enormous bald head, bigger than any giant's, took in the crowd with its big, round eyes.

"I am Oz, the Great and Terrible!" he thundered. "Welcome, one and all, to the final game of the annual Ever After Baseball Tournament! Two teams have survived this fantastic test of skill and determination—the Grimm Reapers, and our very own Oz Cyclones!"

The audience roared, and for the first time, Alex realized just what an accomplishment that was. He and Dorothy shared a nod. They had come this far together. Now they would finish it.

"As you know," the Wizard went on, "the winning team will be granted wishes by the Great and Terrible Oz. One wish for each player. Whatever they want. Their hearts' desires."

Alex turned to look at his friends on the bench. What would each of them wish for, if they won? Would they use their wishes not to be forgotten, or for something else? Scraps, Toad, Tik-Tok, Br'er Rabbit, Jack, the little hedgehog in an apron and a white dress who was knitting at the end of the bench . . .

Wait, who?

"Dorothy, who's that?"

"Oh. Um, that's Mrs. Tiggy-Winkle. She's an old friend."

"But what's she doing here?"

Dorothy wouldn't look at him. "I, um, I added her to the roster before the game. Just in case, you know, we need a pinch hitter late in the game."

Alex understood. "You mean, in case I disappear."

Dorothy looked heartbroken. "Please don't be upset, Alex. I'm sure you're not going to disappear. It's just, after what happened on the bus yesterday—"

"It's all right. If I don't make it, it's important that the rest of you do," he told her.

Dorothy still looked sick about it, but she nodded her thanks.

"And now, without any further humbug," the Wizard announced, "let the game begin!"

Emerald cannons shot greet confetti into the stands, the National Orchestra of Oz played a warbling anthem, and mighty Casey, a handlebar-mustachioed ballplayer in an old-timey uniform, threw out the ceremonial first pitch.

"What is it with Ever After and baseball?" Alex asked Scraps. "Why is everybody here so crazy for it?"

"Are you kidding?" she asked. "'Wait 'til next year' has to be the biggest dream of all time."

Dorothy and Alex took the lineup cards to the umpires, who were immediately familiar: They were the three magicians who had captured the Big Bad Wolf the day Alex had arrived in Ever After. He guessed they were there not only to umpire, but to keep watch over the Reapers' newest member, who came to home plate with Long John Silver to bring their lineup card.

"Hello, everyone," said Charles Wallace. "Merlin, the Fairy Godmother, and I will be your umpires today."

Merlin and the Fairy Godmother never took their eyes off the Big Bad Wolf, who now wore the black and red uniform of the Reapers. His hair didn't look charred, which meant he had probably died in the fire and come back. Alex couldn't help but smile at the thought, even though it had probably just made the wolf madder.

"We just have a few items to go over, and we'll get started," Charles Wallace said. "We flipped a coin, and the Cyclones will bat first. Reapers, that means you're the home team, and will bat last. Also, per tournament rules, there is to be no magic used by any of the players. Natural abilities are of course allowed, but the three of us are attuned to magic and wizardry of every kind, and we'll be keeping careful watch. Understood? And finally, the players in today's game are here at the discretion of the Wizard of Oz." He looked pointedly at the Big Bad Wolf. "Anyone who threatens or attacks anyone else will be removed. By force, if necessary."

The wolf put up a solemn paw. "A promise is a promise."

"He's lying!" Dorothy told them. "We saw him eat Pinocchio only two days ago! In the Forest of Fighting Trees!"

"Have thee any proof?" Merlin asked.

"Well, for one thing, Pinocchio's not around anymore," Alex said.

"Pinocchio has been known to disappear into the Wild Woods for days and weeks at a time," the Big Bad Wolf argued. "Who's to say he's not there right now?"

The Fairy Godmother's wings fluttered anxiously. "I'm afraid we can only concern ourselves with the here and now, dears."

"And now it is time for the game to begin," Charles Wallace said. "May the best team win."

"Aye. We intend to," said Long John.

"Care to make a wager on that?" Dorothy asked.

The wolf smiled. "Don't you think you've learned your lesson, little girl?" Her ruby and silver cleats glittered on his feet.

"What's wrong, Wolf? Chicken?"

Beside the wolf, Long John Silver growled. "Where I come from, lassie, to question a man's courage is to ask fer pistols at thirty paces."

"Yeah?" Alex said. "Well, where I come from, you're a fast-food chain."

"You lose, I get my cleats back," Dorothy told the wolf.

"And what do you have that I could possibly want?" the wolf asked.

Dorothy didn't have an answer to that question.

"Me," Alex said. "If we lose, I'll let you eat me. Without a fight."

"Alex, no!"

"Deal," the wolf said quickly, and with a worried frown and flick of her wand, the Fairy Godmother magically bound them to their word.

"Now, as I believe they say in athletic contests of this kind," Charles Wallace said, "'play ball.'"

The words were magically broadcast throughout the stadium, and a shout went up from the eager fans. On the way back to the dugout, Alex was tingling—and for the first time in days, it had nothing to do with The Itch.

"You shouldn't have done that," Dorothy told him.

"Doesn't matter," he said. "We're going to win, right?" He smiled. "You gotta believe."

"All right," Dorothy said when they got to the dugout. "Pinkerton, you're up first. Toad, grab a bat and—where's Toad?"

"That's what I'd like to know," said a policeman coming out of the dugout tunnel. He wore a blue uniform and sunglasses, and the patch on his sleeve said "Sheriff of Nottingham." He clicked a ballpoint pen and held it over his notebook. "He's not in the clubhouse, and he's not in the dugout. Tell me, when was the last time you saw the suspect?"

"The suspect?" Alex asked. "What's the charge?"

"Forty-seven counts of grand theft auto, and one hundred and sixteen counts of reckless endangerment. We got a tip from the other team that he'd be here today."

"Of course you did," Dorothy muttered.

Alex did a double take when he saw Scraps had four legs sticking out of her skirt—two of which had webbed feet. Alex gave Dorothy a nudge to let her know where Toad was hiding, and she edged the other direction so the sheriff kept his back to Scraps.

"I—we saw him this morning, but then he took off," Dorothy lied.

"Yes, he bought a motorcar and hit the open road," Alex added. "Told us he wasn't coming back. Off to see the world and all that."

The sheriff flipped his notebook closed and gave Alex his card. "All right. I'll check with the local wrecker services and hospitals. But I'm leaving some officers here in the stadium to keep a look-out. You'll let me know if you see him?"

"Er, yes. Of course."

"Toad," Dorothy whispered when the sheriff was gone. "Toad, what are we going to do? The game has started."

"O hapless Toad!" he moaned. "O ill-fated animal! Someone phone my solicitor. The jig is up. It'll be the ball and chain for me forever. I'm caught, dead to rights!"

"He will be if he takes the field," said Scraps.

"What else can we do?" Jack asked.

"We can play Mrs. Tiggy-Winkle instead," Alex told them.

A STORYBOOK FINISH

24

Alex was gone. Dorothy, Toad, and the rest of the Cyclone infielders stood huddled around where he had been at first base. There was nothing but footprints in the dirt to prove Alex had ever been there at all.

"Please," Dorothy begged the Fairy Godmother. "Help him. Bring him back."

"Oh, I'm sorry, dear. I can turn pumpkins into coaches and mice into footmen, but I can't make a Lark into something he's not. No magic can do that. I'm sorry. I truly am. This is why most teams don't use Larks, you know."

Dorothy didn't care what most teams did or didn't do. She didn't care what anybody else in the stadium, or Emerald City, or all of Ever After

find another, identical Br'er Rabbit already there. The doppelganger turned out to be a tar version of Br'er Rabbit, who got himself stuck when he picked a fight with it. In the third, a huff and puff from the Big Bad Wolf sent Pinkerton flying off course in the outfield, and in the fifth inning the horned King of Annwn "accidentally" smashed Jack's pumpkin head by sliding hard into second antlers first. Dorothy and Scraps had to chase Jack's body around until they could drag it back to the dugout, and it took an inning and a half to find a replacement pumpkin.

But Alex was the Cyclones' biggest problem. He kept telling everyone he was fine, but he was fading in and out more and more, and missing throws that sailed right through his open glove. Between his errors and the Reapers' tricks, the Cyclones were falling apart. By the end of the seventh inning, the Reapers led 7–2.

"We're going to lose," Dorothy said, sitting next to Alex on the bench. She punched a knife into the pumpkin she found to replace Jack's head and angrily sliced away at the line for his jagged mouth. "After everything we've done, after coming all this way, we're finished."

"It's just their pranks," Alex told her. "If this was a fair game, we could beat the pants off of them."

"So how do we level the playing field?" Jack asked, startling Alex. Jack's head had come back to life as soon as Dorothy finished cutting out his mouth, and Alex wondered again how everyone in Ever After could take all this weirdness in stride. But that was it, wasn't it? That was how the Reapers were beating them. They knew everything about his teammates—their strengths, their weaknesses, their obsessions. They could read the Cyclones like, well, like an open book.

"I know how we do it," Alex told them. "We have to beat them at their own game."

"How?" Dorothy asked.

"First," Alex said, "I need you to tell me some stories."

TRICK PLAYS

23

We all set then?" Alex asked the Cyclones. "We've only got two innings to pull this off." His teammates grinned at him and nodded. At the plate, Pinkerton grounded sharply to second, but Baba Yaga glided over on her mortar, scooped up the ball, and threw to first in plenty of time for the out.

"Okay. That witch is number one on the hit list," Alex told them.

Toad strode to the plate in his disguise as a washerwoman.

"Oh dear me," he said in a high-pitched voice. "How can I ever hope to replace that brave, wonderful, magnificent Toad?"

"Just shut up and hit, *Mrs. Tiggy-Winkle*," Dorothy called from the dugout.

Toad dinked the Wicked Stepsister's third pitch over the genie at short and jogged down to first base.

"Go up fer those, ye fool!" Long John yelled from first.

"As you command, O my master," the shortstop said, bowing.

Dorothy batted next, and worked a walk. When she was on first and Toad was on second, they nodded to each other and turned to the Baba Yaga, who floated between first and second.

"I say, Baba Yaga," Toad said in his washerwoman voice, "would you like me to wash those old rags you're wearing?"

The hag howled, losing a year off her life with Toad's question.

"Baba Yaga, what's seven times seven?" Dorothy asked.

The witch screamed, losing another year.

"Baba Yaga," Toad asked, "does this apron make me look fat?"

"Baba Yaga, why isn't there mouse-flavored cat food?"

"Do cats eat bats, Baba Yaga?"

"Or do bats eat cats?"

"Aaaaaaaaaaaaaaaaaaaa!" the decrepit old woman cried, and she flashed her claw-like fingers at both of them. With a *pop!* and a *pop!* Toad and Dorothy turned into chickens.

Alex charged onto the field, followed by the rest of the Cyclones. The Reapers came rushing from their dugout too. Before they could meet, the Fairy Godmother umpiring at first waved her wand with a shower of glitter and both teams froze mid-charge.

"Oh dear, oh dear, this will never do," she tutted.

"Unlawful use of magic," Charles Wallace agreed.

"Baba Yaga, thou art banished from this tournament!" Merlin cried. He swirled his wand, muttered an incantation, and the Baba Yaga disappeared with a *vumm*. The Fairy Godmother waved her wand, and the Cyclones and the Reapers became unstuck.

"Where did my second baseman go!?" the wolf roared.

"Forget her. What about Dorothy and Toa— Mrs. Tiggy-Winkle?" Alex asked.

"Not to worry," Charles Wallace told them. "Your teammates are still in there somewhere." He closed his eyes, searching with his mind. "Let's see. Yes. There's Dorothy," he said, and before their eyes one of the chickens transformed back into the Cyclones' leader. "And inside this one— oh. I think perhaps there is someone else in there, but Mrs. Tiggy-Winkle is as good a name as any," he said, and the second chicken transformed into Toad, who quickly pulled his washerwoman dress up around him.

"As for the Baba Yaga, rules are rules," the Fairy Godmother told the Wolf. "The Reapers will have to play shorthanded. Play on!"

The wolf growled, but there was nothing more he could do. Alex gave the base runners the thumbs-up—one Reaper down, eight to go.

In the bottom half of the inning, with the score 7–4, Br'er Rabbit slipped away from third to sneak up to the dragon, who lay curled with one eye closed and the other watching Long John's brass lamp.

"Don't even think about trying to steal my lamp," the dragon purred.

"Steal your lamp? I wouldn't think of it. I *was*

thinking it was awful plain-looking, though. A lot plainer looking than this one."

Br'er Rabbit pulled a solid gold lamp, polished to a shine, from his back pocket. Nanny Mae had produced it from her magic trench coat just for the occasion.

The dragon's eyes got wide and he stirred. "I don't suppose you would like to trade, would you?" he asked.

"Trade? Why, this golden lamp is priceless! Only thing I wish it did was work as a lamp. This one here's solid gold, through and through."

"This one works as a lamp," the dragon said. "Good one too."

"Well, that's something," Br'er Rabbit told him. "You got a deal."

The dragon collected the old brass lamp with his tail, and quickly swapped it out for the one Br'er Rabbit had. When the trade was made, the dragon snorted, little puffs of flame and smoke coming out of his nose as he laughed. "Fool! That old lamp is worthless."

"Says you," Br'er Rabbit said, and he began to rub it. Long John Silver, who had bunted out to first, saw Br'er Rabbit with the lamp and charged across the diamond.

"Arr! Ye great stupid beast! Get that treasure back!"

"I like this one better," the dragon said. "It's prettier."

Long John drew his flintlock pistol on Br'er Rabbit, but a blue mist was already escaping from the spout of the lamp and forming into the shape of a man.

"Say what thou wilt of me," the genie said. "Here am I, the slave of whoso hath in his hand the lamp."

"I ain't much on havin' slaves," Br'er Rabbit told him. "I give you your freedom, genie, to do with as you see fit."

The genie's eyes flared red, and it turned on Long John Silver.

"Oh bloody 'ell," the pirate said, backing away.

"Genie, shine my boot. Genie, get me a soda. Genie, wash my eye patch," the genie said. "I have been your slave for many moons, Silver. Now you will be mine."

Long John Silver fired his pistol into the blue cloud that enveloped him, but it didn't help. A few salty curses later he was gone, trapped inside the lamp. The genie turned on Br'er Rabbit and he flinched, but the genie's eyes were softer now, and he bowed low.

"A thousand blessings upon you, most compassionate and wise little rabbit. I thank you, and take my leave." The blue mist swirled, picked up its lamp, and was gone.

"This isn't fair!" the wolf cried. "I just lost my shortstop and my first baseman!"

"Play on, play on," the Fairy Godmother called with a smile.

The Cyclones came to bat in the ninth inning with the score 8–4, but with more than half of the Reapers' infield gone, they were quickly able to load the bases.

But it was up to Jack Pumpkinhead to drive them in.

"Oh, Alex!" Jack moaned. "Your plan is working, only I'm still awful at baseball. I'm the weak link. The rotten apple. The wrench in the works. The—"

"All right, all right. Don't beat yourself up, Jack."

"I wish I had a head for baseball like you! For a minute there when Dorothy was carving me a new head her knife made me sharp, but now I've got a head full of nothing again."

"Hang on, Jack. I've got an idea." Alex picked up a baseball, but it started to slip through his fingers. He was fading again! He instinctively tried to catch the falling ball, and he did, his hands rematerializing. The fading was getting worse, though. He didn't know how much time he had left. Focusing all his thoughts and energy on staying solid, Alex lifted the lid on Jack's head and dropped the ball inside.

Jack sat up straight. "'Earned run average is calculated by dividing the number of earned runs allowed by the number of innings pitched and multiplying by nine,'" Jack recited. "Alex! You've done it! I know everything there is to know about baseball!" Jack wobbled his head, and the baseball *thunk-thunk*ed against the sides.

"All right, Professor. Go get 'em!"

"Easy out, easy out," the raccoon-like Tanuki called from the outfield. Everyone in the stadium must have thought the same thing, including the Wicked Stepsister, who threw a lollipop of a pitch right over the plate. Jack hitched his bat, planted his foot, and turned on the ball like an all-star, belting it to deep left field. Back, back, back it went, and before the sleepy dragon playing all of left and center could even think to take flight, the ball was gone for a grand slam.

"Yeah! Yeah! Yeah! Jaaaaaaaack!" Alex screamed.

Emerald fireworks boomed in the sky overhead. The Cyclones streamed out onto the field to welcome Jack at home plate and lift him on their shoulders to parade him back to the dugout. The score was tied. It was a whole new ball game with less than an inning left to play.

Two batters later, Dorothy hobbled to the plate in obvious pain.

"Are you all right?" Charles Wallace asked.

"It's these glass cleats," Dorothy told him. She was wearing a spectacularly uncomfortable pair pulled, again, from Nanny Mae's bottomless pockets. "Whoever can wear them hits and pitches like a Hall of Famer, but they don't—they don't seem to fit."

"Of course they don't fit you!" cried the Wicked Stepsister. She called time-out and hurried in from the pitcher's mound. "Here. Let me try them on."

"Leave it alone!" the wolf cried from first, where he'd moved when Long John Silver had been swept away by the genie. "They're tricking you!"

The Wicked Stepsister ignored him, and wedged her feet into the tiny glass cleats. They clearly didn't fit, but she wouldn't admit it.

"You see? How could a—how could a loser like

you ever—wear the shoes of a Hall of Famer? If I'd had these a month ago, I could have—*ow!*—I could have played for the Royals!"

"You're right," Dorothy told her. "They fit like they were made for you. I guess you're the one who gets to hit happily ever after."

The Wicked Stepsister put her nose in the air and limped back to the mound. She fell twice along the way.

"Take those off!" Rumpelstiltskin called from third. "You'll never be able to pitch in them!"

The Wicked Stepsister went into her windup and grunted as she threw. Her first pitch went well over the reach of the towering King of Annwn at catcher, and after four shaky pitches Dorothy had an easy walk.

"Think she'll ever figure out those shoes make her worse?" Alex asked the other Cyclones as he grabbed his bat.

"Not the way she's written, old man," Toad said.

The Reapers were beginning to look like a backyard baseball team. The wolf sent the Wicked Stepsister to first and took over for her on the mound, but the only other infielder was Rumpel-stiltskin, who had moved from third to somewhere near short. In the outfield, only Tanuki and the

dragon remained. The wolf was a tricky south-
paw, but the Cyclones were still able to score once
more with the Reapers so spread out behind him,
putting them in the lead by a single run with only
three outs separating them from being crowned
tournament champs.

"We're winning!" Dorothy told Alex as they
changed sides. "We're actually winning!"

"Was there ever a doubt?" he joked, and Dorothy laughed.

The first Reaper to bat was Rumpelstiltskin,
who had a knack for turning bad pitches into gold.
He drove a two and one pitch into short right field
and stopped at first, and the Reapers had something going with the Wicked Stepsister up next.

Dorothy got the ball back and worked it over
in her hands, pacing around the mound. Sure, letting a runner on base with no outs wasn't the best
way to start the bottom of the ninth in a one-run
game, Alex thought, but if she lost her cool now
it was all over for sure. He called time-out and
jogged to the mound with Toad to check on her.

"Dorothy, what's—" He was going to ask her
what was wrong, but when she looked up she was
grinning.

"Heya, Golden Boy," she said, putting her arm

around him and giving him an enthusiastic hug.

Alex and Toad looked at each other, stunned. Dorothy was smiling? Giving out hugs?

While Dorothy still had her arm around him, Alex felt something hard press into his armpit from behind. *The ball.* Dorothy was passing him the ball for a hidden ball trick!

"How ya been, Golden Boy?" she said, shaking him with another hug as she worked the ball farther under his sleeve. "You good?"

"Yeah," Alex told her with a smile. "I'm good."

"You've both gone mad," Toad said, not understanding at all. "Have you been bewitched, old girl? Is this some kind of spell?"

"No, it's all good, Tiggy-Winkle. Time in!"

Toad shook his head and went back to shortstop, and Alex jogged back to his position. Rumpelstiltskin took a lead-off first, and when he was a few steps away Alex dropped the ball from his armpit into his glove and tagged the dwarf on the shoulder.

"Out!" cried the Fairy Godmother, and the crowd laughed and applauded as the JumboTron replayed what had happened.

"What?" Rumpelstiltskin cried. "No! Not fair! Not fair not fair not *fair!*" On the last *not fair!* he stomped so hard he buried his right leg up to his knee. The ground shifted and rumbled, and the laughter in the stands became a gasp as the stadium shook. A crack opened up in the ground near first base, and Rumpelstiltskin tumbled into its black depths, crying *"Not faaaaaaaaaair!"* as he disappeared.

Dorothy and Jack joined Alex at the edge of the hole and peered down into the nothingness.

"Wow. Um, you guys didn't tell me that part of his story," Alex said.

"It's an old variant," Dorothy said. "I'd forgotten it."

"Hmm," the Fairy Godmother said, flitting about over the chasm. "Can't have unsafe playing conditions, now, can we?" She waved her hand over the crack in the infield and sewed the two sides back together like stitching closed a seam. "Play on!" she said happily.

"Nice one, *Kansas*," Alex told Dorothy. He went to put the ball in her glove, but it dropped through his hand and *thunk*ed on the ground. He was fading away again!

"No—not yet," he said. "Not yet!"

Alex grabbed for Dorothy's hand, but he felt nothing, not even a tingle. The world grew fuzzy and black. Dorothy was yelling something, panic written all over her face, but he couldn't hear her. He couldn't hear anything. It was quiet again, so silent he couldn't even hear his own breath, and the last thing he saw before the world went away was Jack and Toad and the rest of the Cyclones running toward him, reaching out for something that wasn't there.

did. She dropped to her knees and cried—big fat tears that plopped into the dust like meteors leaving craters on the moon.

"We'll wait then," she said. "We'll wait until he comes back."

At the top of the Reapers' dugout steps, the Big Bad Wolf cleared his throat.

"I'm afraid we must play on, dear," the Fairy Godmother told her.

Toad put a hand on Dorothy's shoulder. "They shall sing songs of him," he told her, but it only made her cry again.

"We'll wait," she said again. "He'll come back. Button Bright came back once or twice before he—"

"Button Bright's in a book, old girl. There was always a chance someone new would come along and discover him. But Alex—"

Toad didn't have to say any more.

"I would just like to remind everyone that my team has lost many of its players, without causing an interruption," the wolf said. "We have a game to finish. Unless the Cyclones wish to forfeit?"

Dorothy dragged the backs of her wrists across her eyes, smudging them with dirt and tears. "No," she said. "We're not quitting. Not now.

Toa—Tiggy-Winkle, shift over toward second. Jack—" she began, but she couldn't finish.

"I know what to do," Jack said. He tapped his head. "Alex taught me everything."

"I suppose with my charge gone, my mission is at an end," Nanny Mae said, her metal hat in her hand. "I'll stay on, though, until I get new marching orders. For the team."

Toad and Jack helped Dorothy to her feet, and she climbed back up on the mound and tried to see Tik-Tok through her watery eyes. They only needed two more outs. She took a deep breath. *I can do this,* she thought. *First, we win. Then I can crawl in a hole and never come out.*

"You know, my only regret is that your Lark wasn't around long enough for me to eat him," the wolf called from the Reapers' dugout.

Dorothy's tears turned to ice. Her leg kicked, her arm whipped, and she threw—not pitched— as hard and as fast as she could. There was nothing tricky about it, and the Wicked Stepsister, even with her hobbled feet, blooped a single to left and stumbled her way to first. The Reapers had a new base runner.

"They work! They work! The glass slippers work!" the Wicked Stepsister said. In her celebration she turned an ankle in the ill-fitting shoes and fell down on the bag.

The Big Bad Wolf growled. "Take off your shoes and run, or I'll eat you up!" he yelled, and the Wicked Stepsister quickly did as ordered. But she didn't have to do any running during the next at bat after all: The Japanese trickster Tanuki drew a walk, and the Reapers had runners on first and second with only one out.

"Dorothy, you need to keep your center of gravity over your waist and snap your wrist as you throw," Jack told her. "You're—"

"I know what I'm doing!" Dorothy shot back, and Jack let her be.

The King of Annwn glided to the plate, his great skull mask and bone antlers looming tall over Tik-Tok and the umpire. He tapped the dirt from his cleats with his bat and got ready to hit.

"You can't win, Dorothy," the Big Bad Wolf told her. "You needed a Lark to beat me, and now you don't even have that. I wonder: Will your magic shoes work in the real world? It'll be fun to find out."

"Raaaaah!" Dorothy grunted, and threw as hard as she could. The Welsh King of the Dead killed the pitch, driving it down the third base line. Br'er Rabbit dove, snared the ball on the bounce, and hopped back up. He was too late to get the Wicked Stepsister at third so he threw on to second, where Tanuki slid in at the same time as the ball.

"Out!" cried Merlin.

Toad leapfrogged the raccoon-dog and threw on to Jack for the double play, but his dress got caught up in Tanuki's paws and the throw went wide. Jack stretched his long body out as far as he could and saved the ball from skipping into the stands, but he was pulled off the bag toward home. The King of Annwn was coming fast, only heartbeats away, and Jack swung around to tag him.

"Gah!" he said, backing away. The horns on the skull mask the king wore had already speared Jack's pumpkin head once that day, and Jack clearly didn't want it to happen again.

"Use the name! Use the name!" Toad cried.

Jack closed his eyes and said "Arawn!" just as they were about to collide, and a bolt of lightning split the air—*kra*KOOM! The Welsh King of the Dead burst into flames, and he and the Cyclones' second baseman were swallowed in a ball of fire.

"Jack!" Dorothy cried, but when the flames

and the smoke curled away into the sky, Jack was still there. A bit singed, but still there.

"Whoa," he said. "I didn't know *that* would happen."

"The runner is out, I suppose," the Fairy Godmother said.

The Big Bad Wolf erupted from the Reapers' dugout. "Illegal use of magic! Illegal use of magic! Throw him out!"

"It's not using magic to say someone's name," Charles Wallace ruled, "even if, I suppose, saying his name makes him burst into flame."

The wolf howled in anger and started to grow. His Reapers jersey spilt open at the seams and fell to the ground as he grew larger and larger, dwarfing everyone else on the field. He huffed, and he puffed, and storm clouds gathered overhead. Fans screamed and ran for the exits, and the Cyclones braced themselves against the storm.

"Wolf!" Merlin cried, his robes whipping in the wind. "Thou hast been warned. If thou attackest anyone on this field, the game shall be forfeit and thou shalt be banished to the Black Forest!"

Tanuki scurried off into the stands to hide among the fans, and the great dragon flapped his wings and took to the air, abandoning his team.

The only other Reaper left, the Wicked Stepsister, tried to slip away from third base, but the wolf snarled and snapped at her.

"Stay where you are!" he thundered, making his teammate cower. "We're going to finish this. When I hit a home run—and I *will* hit a home run, Dorothy—she will score, and I will score, and you will lose. You will lose everything."

"I've already lost everything," Dorothy said, the wind carrying her words away.

The Big Bad Wolf was as tall as the upper deck now, and he ripped a post from the protective netting behind home plate to use as a bat. Dorothy looked to see if all her teammates were behind her, but none of them had run away. They were the Cyclones. They were a team, even to the last.

In the twisting tornado, Dorothy found a kind of peace. She was Dorothy Gale, after all. She knew a thing or two about riding out a cyclone. The wolf was giant-sized now, and it didn't matter if she pitched or threw. She aimed high and lobbed the ball through the swirling winds to pass through the wolf's strike zone, and Tik-Tok ran it down on the other side of the plate.

"Strike one!" Charles Wallace called out over the windstorm.

"You think you can win, Dorothy," the wolf told her, "but you can't."

Dorothy lobbed the ball again, and again the wolf didn't swing.

"Strike two!"

"You think this is a game, but it isn't. You cannot beat me," the Big Bad Wolf told her. "No one can."

He was playing with her again. Letting her think she was doing well. But the wolf was always there in the end, waiting to get you. He was always going to win. Dorothy saw that now.

Still, there was nothing to do but play the game.

As the winds that had first carried her to Oz swirled around her, Dorothy reached back and threw.

The ball twisted and turned in the gale. The wolf hitched his bat.

"Alex!" Jack Pumpkinhead cried, and there Alex was, standing at first. He blinked, staring down at his glove as his mop of hair whipped around his head, as though he didn't know where he had gone, or how long he had been there. But Alex was back!

The wolf's eyes flashed to Alex, distracted, then back to the ball, and as the pitch came bending in he hurried his swing and hit underneath it, sending it high, high, high into the churning storm above the infield. He and the Cyclones watched it until they could no longer see it, and only then did the Big Bad Wolf realize he should run.

"Who's got it? Who's got it?" Jack cried, the only one of them to keep his head. Dorothy, Br'er Rabbit, Toad, Jack, Tik-Tok: None of them could see it. Worse, the winds were so strong now they could barely stay on their feet. Tik-Tok was the heaviest of them, and the infielders grabbed hold of him so they wouldn't be swept away. In the outfield, Pinkerton snatched up Scraps to fly her to safety, and Nanny Mae deployed another parachute and flew up into the sky.

Alex was the last of the outfielders to grab on to the chain of Cyclones, grabbing Dorothy's hand just before they were all lifted by the wind like a kite with steadfast Tik-Tok as their anchor.

The Wicked Stepsister scored and ran away. Unless someone caught the ball, hers was the tying run. The winning run, the Big Bad Wolf, fought against his own storm and rounded first with huge, thundering strides.

"What's the score?" Alex yelled to Dorothy over the roar of the wind.

"Ten to nine!"

"How many outs?"

"Two!"

The Big Bad Wolf rounded second and leaned into the wind, headed for third.

"We have to get that ball!" Alex yelled.

Dorothy shook her head. *"We can't! Alex, we can't beat him! It's over!"*

"No it's not! Not until I'm gone!" He looked up into the eddy of storm clouds above them. *"Dorothy, you have to let me go!"*

"What? No!" she yelled, holding his hand even tighter. *"We just got you back!"*

"What's the worst that could happen?" Alex asked her.

"You could be thrown ten miles from here! You could die!"

Alex smiled at her. Dying was nothing to him, and they both knew it. He was a Lark.

"You could disappear for good, and I'd never see you again," Dorothy said, finally admitting why she wouldn't let go.

"So what do we do, just crawl off to the Wild Woods and quit? Or do we play the game?"

The Big Bad Wolf made the turn at third and headed for home.

"Dorothy," Alex told her, *"you have to let me go."*

Dorothy closed her eyes, the wind whipping tears from her face. Very slowly she opened her hand, and Alex slipped from her fingers and away up into the storm.

THE BOY WHO COULD FLY

25

Alex fell up.

The tornado lifted him high into the sky, and he watched Dorothy and the rest of the Cyclones tethered to Tik-Tok grow tiny as the Emerald City stadium spun down and away from him. This was falling like he had always thought falling would be, in slow motion, with everything floating slowly by.

In the swirling storm, pieces of the world went sailing by: a "VOTE TOAD" card, the Cyclones' pink bus, a piece of string, a theme park bench with the words "Carpe Diem" written on it, a paintbrush, a dripping tangle of socks tied together, Nanny Mae, a dented golf cart, a tree branch, a baseball.

Alex reached out and grabbed the baseball.

"Out!" called the Fairy Godmother, who floated by.

"Good show, young man," the Nanny said, clapping. "Absolutely whiz-bang."

The wind died down, and Alex began to fall the right way this time—that is to say, he fell down, and not up. But this time he wasn't scared. There was only one way to die in Ever After, and this wasn't it.

The wolf stood on home plate, howling in triumph, as Alex floated into the arms of his team-mates. They crowded around him to welcome him back, and soon they had him raised on their shoulders, where he held the ball up for everyone to see.

"Impossible!" the wolf roared, his big teeth glinting in the sunlight that broke through the clouds.

"Oh no," the Fairy Godmother told them. "It's the same ball, all right. I saw him catch it on the fly."

"So to speak," said Toad.

"Neither run counts," Charles Wallace announced. "The Cyclones win."

The wolf's eyes went wide as he understood. He clicked his heels together, trying to escape, but he didn't disappear. The ruby and silver cleats were gone.

"Looking for these?" Dorothy asked. The shoes were back on her feet where they belonged. They had returned, magically, the moment the bet had been won.

The Big Bad Wolf snarled and lunged for them, but the three wizards combined their talents again, and the wolf was caught up in another purple cloud.

"I sense there are quite a few people in there," Charles Wallace said. "Should we get them out now?"

"There can be no better time than the present," said Merlin. The wizard waved his wand, and to Alex's surprise a long gash opened up in the Big Bad Wolf's stomach. Even more surprising, people began to climb out. Lancelot and Galahad, nine little pigs, Lester the bus driver, a giant spider, a Cheshire Cat like the one Dorothy had lost her cleats to, and more. Dozens more. Storybooks of all shapes and sizes that Alex didn't recognize climbed out of the monster's belly like clowns from a circus clown car. Pinocchio was there too, from the Wild Woods, and Larks, lots of them—more than a few with The Itch.

Alex caught himself scratching at his own Itch while the Cyclones welcomed the lost Storybooks and Larks back to Ever After. Dorothy noticed it too.

"I hate to cut this celebration short," she told everyone. "But we've got wishes that can't wait."

The Cyclones gathered around her, arm in arm, and with a click of Dorothy's heels they were gone.

HAPPY EVER AFTER

26

The Cyclones' victory, combined with the return of the Big Bad Wolf to the Wild Woods, was cause for a wild rumpus. Throughout the Emerald City, feasts were served, toasts were made, and songs were sung—most of them by and about Toad. But while there would be parades and speeches and parties to come, the Cyclones wanted only one thing: their hearts' desires.

The Cyclones had made sure Alex went in first, before he disappeared again. After a lengthy apology from the Wizard for sending the Nannies after him and ever thinking about giving him to the wolf, Alex's wish was granted and he rejoined his teammates in a great banquet hall filled with food and drink in their honor. One by one they went in and came back out, each granted his or her greatest wish.

The doors to the Wizard's great Throne Room opened, and Br'er Rabbit came out to where the others celebrated.

"How'd it go, Ears?" Alex asked. "What'd you wish for?"

"What I said I was gonna wish for. More wishes! And I got 'em too, suckers! The Wizard said I could come back tomorrow and have another wish!"

"Just one more wish? What will you wish for then?"

"Another wish, of course."

Alex wanted to point out that if he kept wishing for one more wish he would never actually get to use a wish on anything else, but Br'er Rabbit seemed happy enough, which was all that really mattered.

"All right, Pinkerton. You're up," Dorothy told the flying monkey, and he hopped through the doors to the Throne Room.

"Huzzah!" cried Toad. He had been glued to a flat-screen television the whole time, and the rest of the Cyclones went over to join him. "I've done it! I've been elected prime minister!"

"That isn't a surprise, is it?" Alex asked. "Isn't that what you wished for?"

Toad blushed. "Well, I had *thought* to wish for that, especially after playing disguised as Tiggy-Winkle starched, as it were, my chances for worldwide acclaim. But when I was standing there in front of the Great and Terrible Oz and he said, 'Toad of Toad Hall, what is your heart's desire?' Well . . . if I was being *totally* honest with myself, and I admitted my *true* heart's desire . . ."

"You wished for a car, didn't you?" Dorothy asked.

"Not just any car. A one-of-a-kind original! Timber-spoked wheels, red and white cedar boat for a back carriage, dashboard straight from a British Sopwith Camel biplane, brass fittings, copper piping, and . . ." Toad hopped with excitement. "Press a button and wings pop out and it flies! Absolutely smashing!"

"Then how did you win the election?" Alex asked.

"Word of my selfless deed dressing up as Tiggy-Winkle somehow spread through the Internet."

"Maybe because you blogged about it?" Scraps said.

"However it was leaked, I've gone viral," Toad told them. "Storybooks and Larks voted for me in droves! It's a come-from-behind, landslide victory! A mandate from the masses!" Toad put his webbed hands around Alex and Dorothy. "Who would have thought being humble could be so rewarding? Amazingly humble: That's my new motto! In fact, I think I shall write a song about it."

Toad's teammates were in such good spirits they began to compose Toad's song for him, and Alex and Dorothy drifted away to one of the big green glass windows at the far end of the hall.

"When you came out of the Throne Room, everybody was celebrating," Dorothy said. "You never told us what you wished for."

"Neither did you. Did you wish to save everybody?"

"Look at them," Dorothy said. "They all should have wished they wouldn't be forgotten, but is that what they did? No. Toad wished for a flying car. Jack wished for a bucket of baseballs, so he can stuff his head full of them and be a baseball super genius. Br'er Rabbit wished for more wishes. Tik-Tok wished for a new mainspring. Scraps won't tell me what she wished for, but I don't think she wished for not being forgotten. They all had the chance to live forever, and they didn't take it." She sighed. "So no. I didn't do it. I didn't use my wish on any of them. I guess I figured, if they didn't choose that for themselves when they could, what right did I have to choose it for them?"

"So what about you?" Alex asked. "Did you wish you would live forever?"

"I meant to. That's what I was playing for. But I started to think that maybe everybody else was right."

"'*Maybe everybody else was right*'?" Alex put a hand to Dorothy's forehead. "Are you feeling all okay? Was Toad right? Are you under a spell?"

She batted his hand away, but grinned. "Shut up. No. Maybe it's possible. Maybe Storybooks can live forever. Maybe we can't. I don't know. But I was so worried about it I forgot to be happy. I used to be happy, and I liked it. So I—I wished I was happy again."

Across the room, the Cyclones sang a song making fun of Toad, and Toad sang along, louder than any of them. Dorothy laughed.

"I still wish Scraps would tell me what she wished for," she said.

"Oh, I think she got her wish," Alex said. Across the room, Scraps waved happily at them both.

Pinkerton came out of the Throne Room, looking smug.

"Pinky!" Alex called. "What'd you wish for?"

The flying monkey cleared his throat. *"Don't call me Pinky."*

"Pinkerton!" Dorothy cried. "You wished for speech!"

"Wait, you mean he couldn't talk before?" Alex said. "I thought he was just cranky."

Dorothy laughed again. "No. And I think maybe he used up his wish just to tell you to stop calling him Pinky!"

Pinkerton had all manner of other things to say to the Cyclones though, and he happily chattered away with his newly granted power of speech.

Dorothy nudged Alex. "Okay. Pinkerton's talking. Now you. Spill it. Did you wish for somebody else to believe in you?"

"No. I wished for the real me not to be sick anymore."

Dorothy pulled away from him. "What? Wait. Alex, you know what you've done, right? If your dreamer gets better—"

"I know. He won't need me anymore, and he'll forget about me."

"And when he forgets about you, you'll disappear. You just—you just wished for your own death!"

"Maybe. But how is that any worse than him dying and taking us both with him? At least this way, one of us gets to live."

Dorothy leaned back against the windowsill and shook her head. "I never thought you were the sacrifice bunt kind of guy. Always figured you to swing away."

Alex shrugged. "Anything for the team: That's my motto."

"Do you think it will work?" Dorothy asked. "Do you think a dream can really affect a dreamer?"

Alex shrugged. "I don't know. But I'm not Itching anymore. Not yet, at least. I like to think that's because he's getting better. That maybe I saved him, and he's out there playing baseball again. You gotta believe, right?"

Dorothy smiled. "Right."

"So. The tournament's over, and we all got what we wished for. What now?" Alex asked.

"Now we start practicing for the next tournament."

"The next tournament? We just won this one!"

"Yeah," Dorothy told him, "but just wait until next year . . ."

THE END

Acknowledgments

Thanks to Steve North for the house call, to Laurel Snyder for helping me see what this book was really about, to Liz Waniewski for going to bat for me (again), to Heather Alexander for coming off the bench to pinch hit, to Regina Castillo for playing catcher, to Bob for waving the foam fingers and cheering me on, to the American School in Japan for bringing me and *Fantasy Baseball* to Tokyo for the road trip of a lifetime, and of course, as always, to Wendi and Jo for putting up with my usual nonsense along the way.

Very special thanks to Brian Jacques and the Redwall Companies for their permission to use the wonderful world of Redwall and its terrific characters from Brian's work, to the estate of Madeleine L'Engle for allowing Charles Wallace, Mrs. Which, and Mrs. Whatsit to work their magic in my story, to the estate of Ruth Spencer-Davies for letting me borrow the inimitable Nanny Mae and her feline companion Mrs. P., and to Ingrid Law, who had the savvy to let me use her pink bus and equally colorful Lester Swan. Thanks too to all the other children's book authors past and present whose fantastic characters live on happily in Ever After.

ORANGE-SPICED PECAN BRITTLE

- ½ cup (125 mL) granulated sugar
- ½ cup (125 mL) packed brown sugar
- ¼ cup (50 mL) dark corn syrup
- 2 tablespoons (25 mL) water
- ¼ teaspoon (1 mL) salt
- ¼ teaspoon (1 mL) ground cinnamon
- ¼ teaspoon (1 mL) ground nutmeg

- 1 cup (250 mL) chopped pecans
- 1 tablespoon (15 mL) butter or margarine
- 1 teaspoon (5 mL) baking soda
- ½ teaspoon (2 mL) orange extract or homemade Orange Extract, page 278

¾ lb. (375 g) or
2 cups (500 mL) crushed

1 Line large baking sheet with foil. In large bowl, combine granulated sugar, brown sugar, corn syrup, water, salt, cinnamon and nutmeg. Microwave at High 5 minutes. Stir in pecans. Insert microwave candy thermometer. Microwave at High 1½ to 4½ minutes, or until temperature is 300°F/150°C (hard crack stage*), stirring after each minute.

2 Stir in butter, baking soda and orange extract until light and foamy. With rubber spatula, quickly spread to thin layer on prepared baking sheet. Cool. Break apart. Serve as a snack, or crush for use as a dessert topping. Store in airtight container no longer than 2 months.

Hard Crack Stage: *Syrup separates into hard, brittle threads when dropped into cold water.*

AMARETTO GLAZED ALMONDS

- 3 tablespoons (50 mL) Amaretto
- ½ cup (125 mL) blanched whole almonds

½ cup (125 mL)

Place Amaretto in 9" (23 cm) pie plate. Stir in almonds, tossing to coat. Microwave at High 4 to 5 minutes, or until glazed and light golden brown, stirring after each minute. Almonds will continue to toast after they are removed from oven. Spread on sheet of foil to cool. Store in airtight container. Serve as a snack or dessert garnish.

271

FRUIT-FLAVORED POPCORN BARS

- 1 bag (10 oz./300 g) large marshmallows
- ¼ cup (50 mL) butter or margarine, cut up
- 3 tablespoons (50 mL) fruit-flavored gelatin powder (any flavor)
- 8 cups (2 L) popped popcorn
- ½ cup (125 mL) dry-roasted peanuts (optional)

16 popcorn bars

1 Grease 9" (2.5 L) square baking dish. Set aside. In large mixing bowl, place marshmallows and butter. Microwave at High 2 to 3 minutes, or until marshmallows puff and mixture can be stirred smooth, stirring 2 or 3 times.

2 Add gelatin. Mix well. Add popcorn and peanuts. Stir to coat. With buttered fingers, press popcorn mixture into prepared baking dish. Let mixture cool, and cut into 16 bars.

Fruit-flavored Popcorn Sculptures:
Follow recipe above, except shape popcorn mixture into any desired shape on greased baking sheet.

RED HOT POPCORN BALLS

- 6 tablespoons (75 mL) butter or margarine
- ½ cup (125 mL) red cinnamon candies
- 10 large marshmallows

- ⅓ cup (75 mL) packed brown sugar
- 2 tablespoons (25 mL) light corn syrup
- 8 cups (2 L) popped popcorn

6 popcorn balls

1 In large mixing bowl, combine butter and cinnamon candies. Microwave at High 3½ to 4 minutes, or until candies are melted and can be stirred smooth. Add marshmallows, brown sugar and corn syrup. Microwave at High 1 to 1½ minutes, or until marshmallows puff and mixture can be stirred smooth, stirring 2 or 3 times. Add popcorn. Stir to coat.

2 With buttered fingers, shape popcorn mixture into 6 balls. Let popcorn balls cool. Wrap with plastic wrap, and tie with ribbon, if desired.

Popcorn Sculptures: Follow either popcorn recipe, except shape prepared popcorn mixture into any desired shape on greased baking sheet. Decorate with prepared frosting, jelly beans or decorator sprinkles.

CARAMEL CORN

- 3 tablespoons (50 mL) butter or margarine
- ¾ cup (175 mL) packed brown sugar
- ⅓ cup (75 mL) shelled raw peanuts
- 3 tablespoons (50 mL) dark corn syrup
- ½ teaspoon (2 mL) vanilla
- ¼ teaspoon (1 mL) baking soda
- Pinch salt
- 5 cups (1.25 L) popped popcorn

5 cups (1.25 L)

Soft Crack Stage: *Syrup separates into hard but not brittle threads when dropped into cold water.*

1 Place butter in 8-cup (2 L) measure or large bowl. Microwave at High 30 to 45 seconds, or until melted.

2 Stir in brown sugar, peanuts and corn syrup. Insert microwave candy thermometer.

3 Microwave at High 3 to 4 minutes, or until mixture reaches 280°F/ 135°C (soft crack stage*).

4 Mix in vanilla, baking soda and salt. Place prepared popcorn in large bowl.

5 Pour hot mixture quickly over popcorn, stirring to coat. Microwave popcorn at High 2 minutes, stirring after half the time.

6 Stir again. Cool about 30 minutes, stirring occasionally to break apart.

LOLLIPOPS

- 1 cup (250 mL) sugar
- ½ cup (125 mL) light corn syrup
- ¼ cup (50 mL) water
- ¼ teaspoon (1 mL) orange, lemon (page 278) or peppermint extract
- Food coloring (orange, yellow or red)
- 12 wooden popsicle sticks or lollipop sticks

12 lollipops

Hard Crack Stage: *Syrup separates into hard, brittle threads when dropped into cold water.*

1 Mix sugar, corn syrup and water in 8-cup (2 L) measure. Use wet pastry brush to wash sugar crystals from sides of measure. Insert microwave candy thermometer.

2 Microwave at High 9 to 12½ minutes, or until mixture reaches 310°F/155°C (hard crack stage*), stirring every 2 minutes. Stir in desired extract and food coloring.

3 Pour over sticks arranged on buttered foil, or pour into lollipop molds, below. Let stand about 1 hour, or until hard. Wrap in plastic wrap. Store in a cool, dry place.

HOW TO MAKE LOLLIPOP MOLDS

1 Cut 1" (2.5 cm) off top of twelve 9-oz./275 mL wax-coated paper drinking cups.

2 Grease inside of top portion of cup. Punch small hole in side of mold; insert stick.

3 Place molds on buttered foil. Fill as directed, above.

GRANOLA

- 3 cups (750 mL) old-fashioned rolled oats
- ½ cup (125 mL) shredded coconut
- ⅓ cup (75 mL) sliced almonds, chopped
- ⅔ cup (150 mL) honey
- ¼ cup (50 mL) packed dark brown sugar
- ¼ cup (50 mL) vegetable oil

- 1 teaspoon (5 mL) ground cinnamon
- 1 teaspoon (5 mL) vanilla
- 1 teaspoon (5 mL) molasses
- ½ cup (125 mL) raisins
- ⅓ cup (75 mL) chopped dried apples

6 cups (1.5 L)

← GRANOLA BARS

- 6 cups (1.5 L) Granola (opposite)
- ½ cup (125 mL) butter or margarine
- ½ cup (125 mL) packed dark brown sugar

- Pinch salt
- 2 eggs, slightly beaten
- ¼ teaspoon (1 mL) almond extract

12 bars

1 Prepare granola as directed, except omit raisins. Set aside. Place butter in 2-cup (500 mL) measure or medium bowl. Microwave at High 45 seconds to 1½ minutes, or until melted. In medium bowl, combine brown sugar, salt, eggs and almond extract. Beat in butter until combined. Stir in granola until coated. Press into greased 12" x 8" (3 L) baking dish.

2 Microwave at High 6 to 9 minutes, or until firm to the touch, rotating dish ½ turn and pressing mixture with spatula every 2 minutes. Cut into twelve 4" x 2" (10 x 5 cm) bars. Cool completely before removing from dish. Store in refrigerator no longer than 1 week.

HOW TO MICROWAVE GRANOLA

1 Mix rolled oats, shredded coconut and chopped almonds in large bowl. Set aside.

2 Combine remaining ingredients, except raisins and apples, in 8-cup (2 L) measure. Microwave at High 2 to 3 minutes, or until boiling, stirring after each minute.

3 Pour the honey mixture over the oats, tossing to coat. Microwave at High 4½ to 7 minutes, or until the mixture begins to stiffen and appear dry, stirring every 2 minutes. For crisper cereal, microwave 30 to 60 seconds longer, or until the coconut begins to brown lightly.

4 Stir in raisins and apples. Allow mixture to cool about 1 to 1½ hours, stirring to break apart 1 or 2 times during cooling.

← CANDIED PINEAPPLE

- 1 cup (250 mL) sugar
- 1 can (20 oz./ 570 mL) pineapple slices, packed in own juice, drained and ⅓ cup (75 mL) juice reserved
- 2 tablespoons (25 mL) light corn syrup
- Sugar

10 slices

1 In 3-qt. (3 L) casserole, combine 1 cup (250 mL) sugar, ⅓ cup (75 mL) reserved pineapple juice and the corn syrup. Arrange five pineapple slices in single layer over sugar mixture. Microwave at High 8 to 12 minutes, or until sugar dissolves and slices are glossy and transparent on edges, turning over and rearranging every 4 minutes. Remove slices to wire rack to cool. They will become more transparent as they stand.

2 Add remaining slices to hot syrup. Microwave as directed above. Cool. When slices have cooled completely, coat with sugar. Cover with wax paper and let stand on wire rack at least 24 hours to dry. Re-coat with sugar. Slices will be slightly sticky. Store in airtight container with wax paper between layers no longer than 2 weeks.

← LEMON OR ORANGE EXTRACT

- 1 lemon or orange
- ½ cup (125 mL) vodka

½ cup (125 mL)

Remove peel from lemon with vegetable peeler or zester. Do not include white membrane. Place peel in 4-oz. (125 mL) bottle. Add vodka. Microwave at High 30 to 45 seconds, or until bottle is warm to the touch. Cap bottle. Let stand at room temperature about 2 weeks before using.

STEWED FRUIT

- 1 cup (250 mL) dried fruit (prunes, apricots, apples or mixed dried fruit)
- ½ cup (125 mL) water

1 cup (250 mL)

Place dried fruit in 1½-qt. (1.5 L) casserole; sprinkle with water. Cover. Microwave at High 2 to 4 minutes, or until water boils, stirring after each minute. Let stand, covered, 5 minutes. Stir before serving. Sprinkle with cinnamon, if desired.

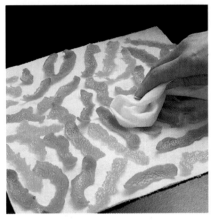

CANDIED PEEL

- 3 large oranges
- 1 lemon
- 6⅓ (1.575 L) cups water, divided
- ⅔ cup (150 mL) granulated sugar
- ¼ cup (50 mL) powdered sugar

1 cup (250 mL)

1 Remove peel from oranges and lemon with vegetable peeler or zester. Do not include the white membrane of fruit.

2 Combine 2 cups (500 mL) water and the strips of peel in 4-cup (1 L) measure or medium bowl. Microwave at High 4 to 6 minutes, or until the water boils. Drain.

3 Repeat process 2 more times, boiling all the peel in 2 cups (500 mL) of water each time. Rinse peel. Drain on paper towels; pat dry.

4 Combine ⅓ cup (75 mL) water and the granulated sugar in 3-qt. (3 L) casserole. Stir in peel. Microwave at High 6 to 8 minutes, or until sugar dissolves and peel is glossy and transparent, stirring every 2 minutes.

5 Remove peel with slotted spoon to rack. Cool. Sift powdered sugar over peel. Let cool completely. Store in airtight container no longer than 1 month.

6 Serve as a dipper for chocolate fondue, or add one strip of peel to cup of coffee or hot chocolate to flavor the drink.

Gifts from
the Kitchen

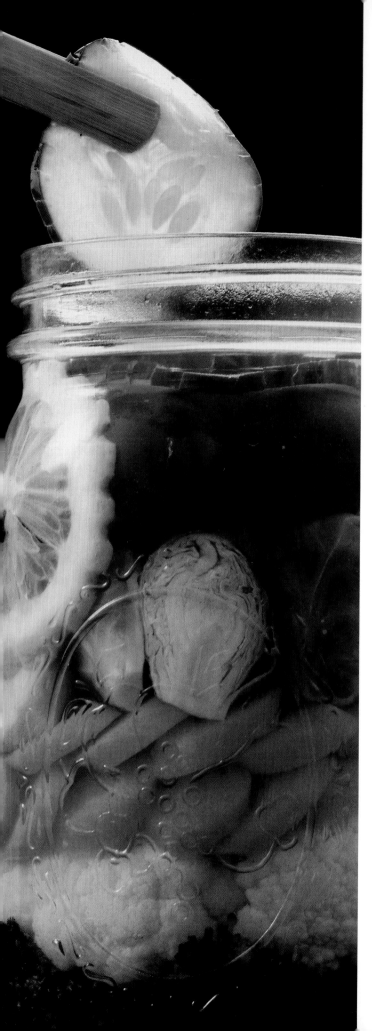

PICKLES & RELISHES

Putting up pickles and relishes once meant hours of effort at harvest time. With most ingredients available year-round, modern cooks can microwave small batches of these items as they are needed. Microwaving is cooler, cleaner, and faster than conventional methods, and small batches can provide more variety. These home-made specialties have true, natural flavor. They make welcome gifts when presented in an attractive bottle.

Experiment with a variety of pickles, your own home-made salsa, or trend-setting specialty mustards, which add spice to meals and cost less than those purchased from gourmet food shops.

The recipes on pages 282-290 are packed into sterilized jars after microwaving. They are not pressure- or water bath-canned, so they do require refrigeration.

ANTIPASTO JAR

Pickling Liquid:
- 1 cup (250 mL) water
- ½ cup (125 mL) Onion-Garlic Vinegar (page 291), or cider vinegar
- 1 tablespoon (15 mL) salt
- 1 tablespoon (15 mL) vegetable oil

Three cups (750 mL) fresh vegetables: Use a combination of the following to equal 3 cups (750 mL):
- Broccoli flowerets and stalks, sliced ¼" (5 mm) thick
- Brussels sprouts (¼ lb./125 g), cut in half lengthwise
- Sliced carrots, ¼" (5 mm) thick
- Cauliflowerets
- ½ cup (125 mL) water

One cup (250 mL) fresh vegetables: Use a combination of the following to equal 1 cup (250 mL):
- Fresh whole mushrooms, 1" (2.5 cm) diameter
- Green or ripe olives
- Green pepper, cut into 1" (2.5 cm) pieces
- Sliced cucumber

Garnish: Add one or more of the following:
- 1 lemon slice
- 1 bay leaf
- 1 sprig fresh dill, basil or oregano

1 quart (1 L)

PICKLED CARROTS

- 12 oz. (375 g) fresh tiny whole carrots
- ¼ cup (50 mL) water

Pickling Liquid:

- ½ cup (125 mL) cider vinegar
- ⅓ cup (75 mL) sugar
- ½ to 1 teaspoon (2 to 5 mL) salt
- Pinch celery seed
- Pinch mustard seed
- Pinch dried crushed red pepper
- 4 whole cloves
- 4 whole peppercorns
- 2 small cloves garlic, peeled
- 1 bay leaf
- 1 stick cinnamon

1 pint (500 mL)

1 Wash and scrub or peel carrots; trim ends. Place in 1½-qt. (1.5 L) casserole. Add water; cover. Microwave at High 3 to 4 minutes, or until tender-crisp, stirring after half the time. Place under cold running water until cool. Drain. Pack into sterilized 1-pint (500 mL) jar or two ½-pint (250 mL) jars. Set aside.

2 In 2-cup (500 mL) measure, combine pickling liquid ingredients. Microwave at High 1 to 2 minutes, or until boiling, stirring after half the time to dissolve the sugar and salt. Pour over carrots in the jar. Cover. Refrigerate 1 week before serving. Store in refrigerator no longer than 1 month.

1 Mix pickling liquid in 4-cup (1 L) measure. Microwave at High 3½ to 5½ minutes, or until boiling, stirring after half the time.

2 Combine desired 3 cups (750 mL) vegetables in 2-qt. (2 L) casserole. Add ½ cup (125 mL) water. Cover.

3 Microwave at High 2 to 4 minutes, or until color of vegetables intensifies, stirring once.

4 Place immediately under cold running water until cool. Drain. Add remaining 1 cup (250 mL) vegetables.

5 Pack vegetables into sterilized 1-qt. (1 L) jar, layering if desired. Include choice of garnish.

6 Pour pickling liquid over the vegetables. Cover. Refrigerate 2 to 3 days before serving. Store in refrigerator no longer than 1 month.

283

WATERMELON PICKLES

- 1 lb. (500 g) watermelon rind
- ½ cup (125 mL) sugar
- ½ cup (125 mL) cider vinegar
- 1 tablespoon (15 mL) chopped cyrstallized ginger
- 2 teaspoons (10 mL) grated fresh orange peel or 1 teaspoon (5 mL) dried orange peel
- 4 whole cloves
- 1 stick cinnamon

1 pint (500 mL)

1 Trim dark green outer skin from rind. Cut trimmed rind into 1" (2.5 cm) chunks. (Yields 3 cups/750 mL.) Place chunks in 1½-qt. (1.5 L) casserole. Add sugar, tossing to coat. Cover and let stand overnight.

2 Stir in vinegar, ginger, orange peel and cloves. Add cinnamon. Microwave, uncovered, at High 10 to 13 minutes, or until chunks are transparent, stirring every 3 minutes. Remove cinnamon stick. Spoon into hot sterilized 1-pint (500 mL) jar; cover. Refrigerate 1 week before serving. Store in refrigerator no longer than 1 month.

CABBAGE RELISH

- 2½ cups (625 mL) shredded green or red cabbage
- ¾ cup (175 mL) chopped red onion
- ½ cup (125 mL) chopped green pepper
- 1 cup (250 mL) white vinegar
- ⅔ cup (150 mL) sugar
- 2 teaspoons (10 mL) salt
- ½ teaspoon (2 mL) celery seed
- ½ teaspoon (2 mL) mustard seed
- ¼ teaspoon (1 mL) ground turmeric

2 pints (1 L)

1 In medium bowl combine cabbage, red onion and green pepper. Divide mixture equally between two sterilized 1-pint (500 mL) jars. Set aside.

2 In 4-cup (1 L) measure, combine vinegar, sugar, salt, celery seed, mustard seed and turmeric. Microwave at High 2 to 4 minutes, or until boiling, stirring after half the time to dissolve sugar and salt. Divide between two jars; cover. Refrigerate 1 week before serving. Store in refrigerator no longer than 1 month.

APPLE-PEAR CHUTNEY

- 2 medium apples, cored and chopped
- 2 medium pears, peeled, cored and chopped
- 1½ cups (375 mL) packed dark brown sugar
- 1 cup (250 mL) cider vinegar
- ¾ cup (175 mL) chopped onion
- ⅔ cup (150 mL) chopped green pepper
- ½ cup (125 mL) chopped dates
- 1 tablespoon (15 mL) chopped crystallized ginger
- 1 teaspoon (5 mL) salt
- 1 teaspoon (5 mL) dry mustard
- 4 whole cloves
- 4 whole allspice
- 2 bay leaves
- 1 stick cinnamon

2 pints (1 L)

1 Combine apples, pears, brown sugar, vinegar, onion and green pepper. Process in food processor, turning motor on and off 4 to 6 times, or place in blender and process 10 to 15 seconds, or until chopped but not puréed. (Process in two batches, if necessary.) Place the mixture in 2-qt. (2 L) casserole. Stir in remaining ingredients.

2 Microwave at High 18 to 25 minutes, or until very thick, stirring 3 or 4 times. Cool to room temperature. Discard bay leaves and cinnamon stick.

3 Divide equally between two sterilized 1-pint (500 mL) jars; cover. Refrigerate 1 week before serving. Store in refrigerator no longer than 1 month.

NOTE: *Use as a condiment for meat or curry dishes.*

TRANSFORM LEFTOVERS

Save watermelon rind for Watermelon Pickles, opposite. Use leftover cabbage in Cabbage Relish, opposite. When you fix a selection of raw vegetables for a relish or appetizer tray, set some aside to make an Antipasto Jar (page 282) the next day.

CORN RELISH

- 3 cups (750 mL) frozen whole kernel corn
- ½ cup (125 mL) chopped green pepper
- ¼ cup (50 mL) chopped onion
- 2 tablespoons (25 mL) chopped pimiento, drained
- 1 cup (250 mL) white vinegar
- ⅔ cup (150 mL) sugar
- 1 teaspoon (5 mL) salt
- 1 teaspoon (5 mL) celery seed
- ½ teaspoon (2 mL) mustard seed
- ½ to ¾ teaspoon (2 to 4 mL) red pepper sauce

2 pints (1 L)

1 In medium bowl, combine corn, green pepper, onion and pimiento. Microwave at High 1½ to 2½ minutes, or until corn is defrosted but cool to the touch, stirring after half the time. Divide equally between two sterilized 1-pint (500 mL) jars. Set aside.

2 In 4-cup (1 L) measure, combine remaining ingredients. Microwave at High 2 to 4 minutes, or until boiling, stirring after half the time to dissolve sugar and salt. Divide mixture between the two jars; cover. Refrigerate 1 week before serving. Store in refrigerator no longer than 1 month.

MIXED PICKLE RELISH

- 1 cup (250 mL) peeled, seeded and chopped cucumber
- 1 cup (250 mL) chopped onion
- 1 cup (250 mL) chopped red pepper
- 1 cup (250 mL) chopped green pepper
- 1 tablespoon (15 mL) pickling salt
- ⅔ cup (150 mL) sugar

- ½ cup (125 mL) white wine vinegar
- 2 teaspoons (10 mL) dry mustard
- ½ teaspoon (2 mL) grated fresh gingerroot
- ¼ teaspoon (1 mL) ground turmeric
- Pinch ground allspice
- Pinch cayenne
- 1 clove garlic, minced

1-pint (500 mL) jar

1 In colander, place cucumber, onion, red and green peppers. Sprinkle with salt. Toss lightly to mix. Let colander stand over bowl 1½ hours, stirring occasionally.

2 Place salted vegetables in 1½-quart (1.5 L) casserole. Add the remaining ingredients. Mix well. Microwave at High 20 to 30 minutes, or until mixture thickens slightly, stirring twice. Spoon mixture into sterilized 1-pint (500 mL) jar. Cover and refrigerate overnight before serving. Store relish in refrigerator no longer than 1 month.

CHRISTMAS OVERNIGHT PICKLES

- 1 large cucumber (¾ lb./375 g), peeled and cut crosswise into 3 pieces
- 4 whole allspice
- 4 whole cloves
- ½ cup (125 mL) water

- ½ cup (125 mL) cider vinegar
- ½ cup (125 mL) sugar
- ¼ teaspoon (1 mL) salt
- ¼ teaspoon (1 mL) ground nutmeg

- ½ teaspoon (2 mL) red food coloring
- ½ teaspoon (2 mL) green food coloring

4 to 6 servings

1 Scoop out and discard seeds from cucumber; slice hollow pieces into ¼" (5 mm) rings. Divide cucumber rings evenly between two plastic food-storage bags. Add 2 allspice and 2 cloves to each bag. Set aside.

2 Combine remaining ingredients, except food colorings, in 2-cup (500 mL) measure. Microwave at High 2 to 5 minutes, or until mixture boils, stirring once to dissolve sugar and salt. Divide mixture into two portions. Stir red coloring into one portion. Stir green coloring into remaining portion. Cool slightly.

3 Pour red vinegar mixture over cucumbers in one food-storage bag. Pour green vinegar mixture into remaining bag. Tie securely and refrigerate bags overnight. Drain pickles before serving. Store in refrigerator no longer than 3 days.

YELLOW SUMMER SQUASH PICKLES

- 3 cups (750 mL) thinly sliced yellow summer squash
- ½ cup (125 mL) coarsely chopped red pepper
- 1 small onion, thinly sliced and separated into rings
- 8 whole peppercorns
- 1 large clove garlic, cut into quarters (optional)
- 1 cup (250 mL) white wine vinegar
- ⅔ cup (150 mL) sugar
- 2 teaspoons (10 mL) pickling salt
- ¼ teaspoon (1 mL) celery seed
- ¼ teaspoon (1 mL) mustard seed

Two 1-pint (500 mL) jars

1 In medium mixing bowl, mix squash, red pepper and onion. Divide mixture and pack evenly into two sterilized 1-pint (500 mL) jars. Place 4 peppercorns and 2 garlic quarters in each jar. Set aside.

2 Combine remaining ingredients in 2-cup (500 mL) measure. Microwave at High 2 to 5 minutes, or until mixture boils, stirring once to dissolve sugar and salt. Pour mixture evenly into jars. Cover and refrigerate at least 5 days before serving. Store in refrigerator no longer than 1 month.

PICKLED EGGS

- Juice from 1 can (16 oz./454 g) sliced beets
- Water
- ⅔ cup (150 mL) cider vinegar
- 3 tablespoons (50 mL) packed brown sugar
- ¾ teaspoon (4 mL) salt
- 6 whole cloves
- 6 whole allspice
- 6 whole peppercorns
- 1 medium onion, thinly sliced
- 6 hard-cooked eggs, peeled

6 servings

Add enough water to beet juice to measure 1 cup (250 mL). (Reserve beets for future use, if desired.) In medium mixing bowl, combine beet juice mixture, vinegar, sugar, salt, cloves, allspice and peppercorns. Add onion. Cover with plastic wrap. Microwave at High 6 to 8 minutes, or until onion is tender-crisp, stirring once. Add eggs. Cover and refrigerate 1 to 2 days, turning occasionally to ensure even-colored eggs. Drain and slice eggs. Serve on platter or in salads.

PICKLED GREEN BEANS

- 1 pkg. (10 oz./300 g) frozen cut, or French-cut, green beans
- 1 small onion, cut in half lengthwise and thinly sliced
- ½ cup (125 mL) sliced black olives
- 1 cup (250 mL) white vinegar
- ⅔ cup (150 mL) sugar
- 2 teaspoons (10 mL) pickling salt
- ¼ teaspoon (1 mL) dried tarragon leaves or dried dill weed or stem

Three ½-pint (250 mL) jars

1 In medium mixing bowl, microwave beans at High 4 to 6 minutes, or until defrosted, breaking apart once. Drain thoroughly. Add onion and black olives. Mix well. Divide mixture and pack evenly into three sterilized ½-pint (250 mL) jars. Set aside.

2 Combine remaining ingredients in 2-cup (500 mL) measure. Microwave at High 2 to 5 minutes, or until mixture boils, stirring once to dissolve sugar and salt. Pour mixture evenly into jars. Cover and refrigerate at least 5 days before serving. Store in refrigerator no longer than 1 month.

PICKLED GARDEN RELISH

- 3 cups (750 mL) fresh cauliflowerets, 1" (2.5 cm) pieces
- 2 medium carrots, cut into 2" x ¼" (5 cm x 5 mm) strips
- ¼ cup (50 mL) water
- 1 medium red pepper, cut into 2" x ¼" (5 cm x 5 mm) strips
- 2 stalks celery, sliced ½" (1 cm) thick
- ⅔ cup (150 mL) whole green or black olives
- ¾ cup (175 mL) white wine vinegar
- ½ cup (125 mL) olive oil
- 2 tablespoons (25 mL) sugar
- 1 teaspoon (5 mL) salt
- ½ teaspoon (2 mL) dried oregano leaves
- ¼ teaspoon (1 mL) pepper

About 6 cups (1.5 L)

1 In 1½-quart (1.5 L) casserole, combine cauliflower, carrots and water. Cover. Microwave at High 3 to 5 minutes, or until vegetables are hot, but still crisp, stirring once. Stir in red pepper, celery and olives. Set aside.

2 In 2-cup (500 mL) measure, blend vinegar, olive oil, sugar, salt, oregano and pepper. Pour vinegar and oil mixture over vegetables. Mix well. Re-cover. Chill at least 8 hours or overnight. Drain before serving.

FLAVORED VINEGARS

To speed the release of flavors into vinegar, microwave until warm to the touch, not hot. Use any well-washed bottle from catsup or other condiments. Avoid flawed or chipped bottles.

ONION-GARLIC → VINEGAR

- 2 cloves garlic, peeled
- 2 pearl onions, peeled
- Wooden skewer, 6" (15 cm) long
- 1 or 2 cups (250 or 500 mL) white or cider vinegar

1 or 2 cups (250 or 500 mL)

Alternate garlic cloves and pearl onions on a skewer. Drop into bottle. Add vinegar. Microwave, uncovered, at High 30 seconds to 1½ minutes, or until bottle is just warm to the touch; check every 30 seconds. Cap and let stand in a cool, dark place 2 weeks before using. After opening, store in refrigerator no longer than 2 months.

HERB VINEGAR

- 1 sprig fresh mint, fresh tarragon, or fresh oregano
- 1 or 2 cups (250 or 500 mL) white or cider vinegar

1 or 2 cups (250 or 500 mL)

Place one or more sprig desired herb in bottle. Add vinegar. Microwave, uncovered, at High 30 seconds to 1½ minutes, or until bottle is just warm to the touch; check every 30 seconds. Cap and let stand in a cool, dark place 2 weeks before using. After opening, store in refrigerator no longer than 2 months.

JELLIES & SYRUPS

← WINE JELLY

- 2¾ cups (675 mL) rosé wine, white wine or pink champagne
- 1 box (1¾ oz./57 g) powdered fruit pectin
- 1 stick cinnamon
- 3 whole cloves
- 3½ cups (875 mL) sugar

2½ pints (625 mL)

1 In 3-qt (3 L) casserole or 8-cup (2 L) measure, combine wine, pectin, cinnamon stick and cloves. Microwave at High 5 to 10 minutes, or until boiling, stirring every 3 minutes. Boil 1 minute. Gradually stir in sugar until blended.

2 Microwave at High 3 to 6½ minutes, or until mixture returns to a boil, stirring carefully every 2 minutes to prevent boilover. Boil 1 minute. Skim any foam from top. Pour into hot sterilized ½-pint (250 mL) jars, or glasses. Cover with hot sterilized lids and screw bands. Invert jar and quickly return to upright position. Or, if desired, seal jars with paraffin wax. Store in a cool, dark place no longer than 6 months.

← FRUIT JELLY

- 1 can (6 oz./170 mL)* frozen apple, grape, pineapple or tangerine juice concentrate
- 2 cups (500 mL) water
- 1 box (1¾ oz./57 g) powdered fruit pectin
- 3½ cups (875 mL) sugar

2½ pints (625 mL)

1 In 3-qt. (3 L) casserole or 8-cup (2 L) measure, combine juice concentrate and water. Stir in pectin until dissolved. Microwave at High 7 to 14 minutes, or until boiling, stirring every 3 minutes. Boil 1 minute. Gradually stir in sugar until blended.

2 Microwave at High 5 to 7 minutes, or until mixture returns to a boil, stirring carefully every 2 minutes to prevent boilover. Boil 1 minute. Skim any foam from top. Pour into hot sterilized ½-pint (250 mL) jars. Cover with hot sterilized lids and screw bands. Invert jar and quickly return to upright position. Or, if desired, seal jars with paraffin wax. Store in a cool, dark place no longer than 6 months.

VARIATIONS:

Zesty Grape Jelly: *Stir 1 teaspoon (5 mL) fresh lemon juice into Grape Jelly after skimming foam.*

Mint Apple Jelly: *Stir 5 to 7 drops green food coloring and 1 teaspoon (5 mL) mint extract into Apple Jelly after skimming foam.*

If 6-oz. (170 mL) can not available, use half of 12-oz. (341 mL) can.

LAYERED JELLIES ↑

Jellies can be layered in wine glasses, coffee mugs or creamers as well as pint jars and jelly glasses. Sterilize the containers before use.

Choose jellies that have attractive color contrast and good flavor combination, such as Apple, Mint Apple and Grape, above.

Try Pineapple and Tangerine with a middle layer of Rosé or White Wine Jelly. For variety, suspend a piece of Candied Pineapple (page 278) or a maraschino cherry in the layer of Wine Jelly. Three batches of jelly yield 7½ pints (1.875 L).

1 Fill each jelly glass or other container one-third full. The first layer must begin to set before the next layer is added.

2 Prepare second layer. When first layer is sufficiently set, carefully spoon second layer into jar. Allow to set slightly.

3 Add final layer, carefully spooning over second layer. Top with paraffin wax.

BLUEBERRY-KIWI
REFRIGERATOR JAM ↑

- 2 cups (500 mL) peeled, cored and sliced kiwi fruit
- 2 cups (500 mL) frozen blueberries
- 2 cups (500 mL) sugar
- 1 pkg. (3 oz./85 g) lemon gelatin

Three ½-pint (250 mL) jars

In medium mixing bowl, combine kiwi fruit, blueberries and sugar. Mix well. Microwave at High 15 to 25 minutes, or until fruit is very soft, stirring 3 or 4 times. Add gelatin, stirring until dissolved. Divide mixture evenly among three sterilized ½-pint (250 mL) jars. Cover and chill until set, about 2 hours. Store jam in refrigerator no longer than 1 month.

Blueberry-Kiwi Light Jam: Follow recipe above, except substitute 1 pkg. (0.3 oz./11 g) low-calorie lemon gelatin for the 3-oz. (85 g) pkg.

CHERRY-ALMOND
REFRIGERATOR JAM

- 4 cups (1 L) frozen pitted dark sweet cherries
- 2 cups (500 mL) sugar
- 1 pkg. (3 oz./85 g) cherry gelatin
- ¼ teaspoon (1 mL) almond extract

Three ½-pint (250 mL) jars

In medium mixing bowl, combine cherries and sugar. Mix well. Microwave at High 15 to 25 minutes, or until cherries are very soft, stirring 3 or 4 times. Add gelatin, stirring until dissolved. Stir in almond extract. Divide mixture evenly among three sterilized ½-pint (250 mL) jars. Cover. Chill until set, about 2 hours. Store jam in refrigerator no longer than 1 month.

Cherry-Almond Light Jam: Follow recipe above, except substitute 1 pkg. (0.3 oz./11 g) low-calorie cherry gelatin for the 3-oz. (85 g) pkg.

STRAWBERRY-RHUBARB REFRIGERATOR JAM

- 4 cups (1 L) frozen cut-up rhubarb
- 2 cups (500 mL) sugar
- 1 pkg. (3 oz./85 g) strawberry gelatin
- 2 teaspoons (10 mL) lemon juice

  Three ½-pint (250 mL) jars

In medium mixing bowl, combine rhubarb and sugar. Mix well. Microwave at High 15 to 25 minutes, or until rhubarb is very soft, stirring 3 or 4 times. Add gelatin, stirring until dissolved. Mix in lemon juice. Divide mixture evenly among three sterilized ½-pint (250 mL) jars. Cover. Chill until set, about 2 hours. Store jam in refrigerator no longer than 1 month.

Strawberry-Rhubarb Light Jam: Follow recipe above, except substitute 1 pkg. (0.3 oz./11 g) low-calorie strawberry gelatin for the 3-oz. (85 g) pkg.

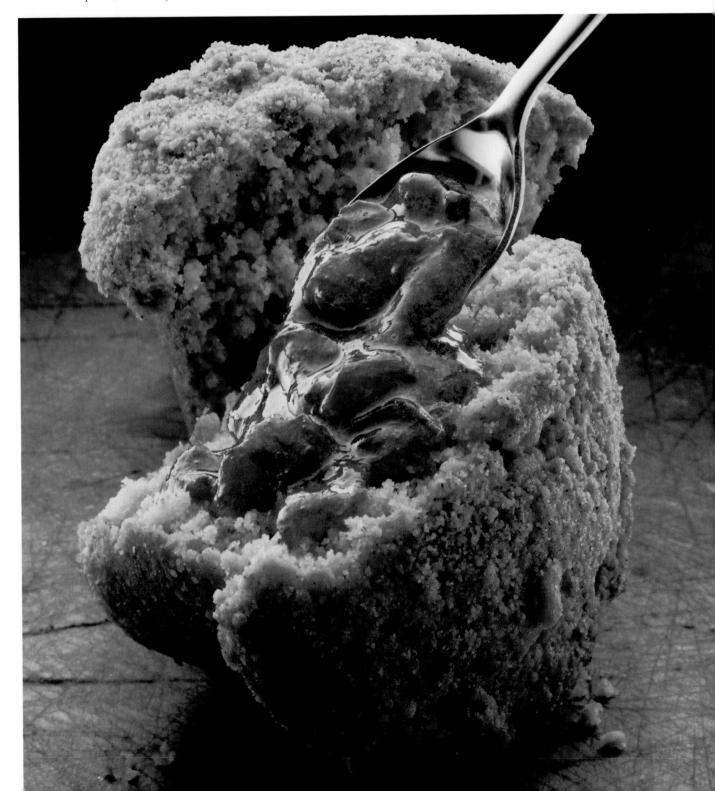

APPLE
← BUTTER

- 3 lbs. (1.5 kg) cooking apples, peeled, cored and cut into quarters
- ¼ cup (50 mL) apple cider
- 1½ cups (375 mL) granulated sugar
- ½ cup (125 mL) packed brown sugar
- 2 tablespoons (25 mL) cider vinegar
- 1½ teaspoons (7 mL) ground cinnamon
- ¼ teaspoon (1 mL) ground allspice
- Pinch ground nutmeg

Three ½-pint (250 mL) jars

1 Place apples in 3-quart (3 L) casserole. Add apple cider. Cover. Microwave at High 18 to 23 minutes, or until apples are very soft, stirring once or twice. Place mixture in food processor or blender, and process until smooth.

2 Return apple mixture to 3-quart (3 L) casserole. Stir in remaining ingredients. Microwave, uncovered, at High 30 to 45 minutes, or until mixture is very thick, stirring 3 or 4 times. Spoon mixture evenly into three sterilized ½-pint (250 mL) jars. Cover and refrigerate overnight before serving. Store Apple Butter in refrigerator no longer than 1 month.

PEAR HONEY

- 2 lbs. (1 kg) pears (4 medium), peeled and cored
- 2¼ cups (550 mL) sugar
- 1 can (8 oz./227 mL) crushed pineapple
- 1 tablespoon (15 mL) lemon juice
- ½ teaspoon (2 mL) grated lemon peel

Three ½-pint (250 mL) jars

Cut each pear into 6 pieces. Place in food processor or blender. Process until finely chopped. Place chopped pears in 3-quart (3 L) casserole. Stir in remaining ingredients. Mix well. Microwave at High 30 to 40 minutes, or until pears are translucent and very tender, stirring 2 or 3 times. Divide mixture evenly among three sterilized ½-pint (250 mL) jars. Cover and refrigerate overnight before serving. Store in refrigerator no longer than 1 month.

BRANDIED FRUIT

- ¾ cup (175 mL) water
- ½ cup (125 mL) packed brown sugar
- ⅓ cup (75 mL) granulated sugar
- ½ teaspoon (2 mL) ground cinnamon
- Pinch ground allspice
- Pinch ground nutmeg

- ½ to ¾ cup (125 to 175 mL) brandy
- 1 cup (250 mL) dried apricots
- 1 cup (250 mL) dried apples
- 1 cup (250 mL) pitted prunes
- ½ cup (125 mL) raisins
- ¾ cup (175 mL) drained maraschino cherries (optional)

1 quart (1 L) fruit

1 In medium mixing bowl, combine water, sugars, cinnamon, allspice and nutmeg. Mix well. Microwave at High 4 to 6 minutes, or until mixture boils and sugar dissolves, stirring once.

2 Stir in remaining ingredients. Microwave at High 9 to 14 minutes, or until apricots and apples are tender, stirring once or twice. Cover and refrigerate at least 3 days before serving. Store in refrigerator no longer than 3 weeks. Serve fruit over plain cake or ice cream, if desired.

FRUIT SYRUPS

- 1 bag (16 oz./500 g) frozen raspberries, blackberries or blueberries
- 1 cup (250 mL) sugar
- ¾ cup (175 mL) light corn syrup

1 pint (500 mL)

1 Place frozen fruit in medium bowl or 4-cup (1 L) measure. Cover with plastic wrap. Microwave at High 6½ to 10 minutes, or until boiling, stirring every 3 minutes.

2 Line strainer with cheesecloth; place in 8-cup (2 L) measure or 3-qt. (3 L) casserole. Pour hot fruit into lined strainer.

3 Mash fruit with back of spoon to press the juice through strainer. (Yields about ½ to ¾ cup/125 to 175 mL juice.) Discard pulp.

4 Add sugar and corn syrup to the strained juice. Microwave at High 3 to 6 minutes, or until boiling, stirring every 2 minutes.

5 Boil 1 minute. Skim any foam from top. Pour the syrup into hot sterilized 1-pint (500 mL) jar or catsup bottle; cap.

6 Refrigerate or store in a cool, dark place no longer than 6 months. Serve over pancakes, waffles or desserts.

FRESH STRAWBERRY SYRUP ↑

- 1 pint (500 mL) fresh strawberries, hulled
- 1 cup (250 mL) sugar
- ¾ cup (175 mL) light corn syrup

1 pint (500 mL)

1 Cut strawberries in half. Place in large bowl. Mash with fork. Cover. Microwave at High 4 to 5 minutes, or until boiling, stirring every 2 minutes. Line strainer with cheesecloth; place in 3-qt. (3 L) casserole or 8-cup (2 L) measure. Pour hot fruit into lined strainer. Mash fruit with back of spoon to press the juice through strainer. (Yields ½ to ¾ cup/ 125 to 175 mL juice.) Discard pulp.

2 Add sugar and corn syrup to strained juice. Microwave at High 3 to 6 minutes, or until boiling, stirring every 2 minutes. Boil 1 minute. Skim any foam from top. Pour syrup into hot sterilized 1-pint (500 mL) jar or catsup bottle; cap. Refrigerate or store in a cool, dark place no longer than 6 months. Serve over pancakes, waffles or desserts.

Heat Syrup for Serving: *Remove cap from bottle or jar. Microwave at High 30 to 60 seconds, or until bottle is warm to the touch.*

FRESH PLUM SYRUP →

- 1 lb. (500 g) very ripe purple plums
- 1 cup (250 mL) sugar
- ¾ cup (175 mL) light corn syrup

1 pint (500 mL)

1 Cut plums in half; remove pits. Cut halves into small pieces. Place in large bowl; cover. Microwave at High 5 to 8 minutes, or until plums cook down and mash easily, stirring every 2 minutes.

2 Line strainer with cheesecloth; place in 3-qt. (3 L) casserole or 8-cup (2 L) measure. Pour hot fruit into lined strainer. Mash fruit with the back of spoon to press juice through strainer. (Yields ½ to ¾ cup/125 to 175 mL juice.) Discard pulp.

3 Add sugar and corn syrup to strained juice. Microwave at High 3 to 6 minutes, or until boiling, stirring every 2 minutes. Boil 1 minute. Skim any foam from top.

4 Pour syrup into hot sterilized 1-pint (500 mL) jar or catsup bottle; cap. Refrigerate or store in a cool, dark place no longer than 6 months. Serve over pancakes, waffles or desserts.

SOFTENING CREAM CHEESE

In small mixing bowl, microwave cream cheese as directed in chart (below), or until softened. DO NOT microwave cream cheese in the foil wrapper. For use in dips and spreads, blend softened cream cheese with favorite flavors, as directed in chart (opposite).

Amount	Power Setting	Microwave Time
1 pkg. (3 oz./85 g)	High	15 to 30 seconds
1 pkg. (8 oz./250 g)	50% (Medium)	1½ to 3 minutes

TIP: Cream cheese softens quickly in the microwave and spreads easily. Softened cheese is easier to blend in your favorite appetizer, main dish or dessert recipe.

HOW TO MAKE FLAVORED CREAM CHEESES

1 Microwave 8 oz. (250 g) cream cheese in small mixing bowl as directed in chart (above), stirring once or twice.

2 Blend in additional ingredients for desired flavor (opposite).

3 Serve flavored cream cheeses as directed (opposite); store cream cheese as recommended.

Flavor & yield	To 8 oz. (250 g) cream cheese blend in:	Serving suggestions	Store up to:
Cheddar & Chive Cream Cheese about 1¼ cups (300 mL)	½ cup (125 mL) finely shredded Cheddar cheese, 1 tablespoon (15 mL) sliced green onion, 1 teaspoon (5 mL) freeze-dried chives, pinch garlic powder	Dip for vegetables; topping for hot cooked vegetables; spread for crackers, bread	2 weeks
Cocoa Cream Cheese Frosting about 1¼ cups (300 mL)	½ cup (125 mL) powered sugar, 2 tablespoons (25 mL) cocoa, ½ teaspoon (2 mL) vanilla	Frosting for graham crackers, brownies, bars, cakes	2 weeks
Italian Herb Cream Cheese about 1 cup (250 mL)	2 tablespoons (25 mL) fresh snipped parsley, ½ teaspoon (2 mL) Italian seasoning	Spread for sandwiches or crackers; topping for hot cooked vegetables	2 weeks
Lemon-Basil Cream Cheese about 1¼ cups (300 mL)	2 teaspoons (10 mL) lemon juice, ½ teaspoon (2 mL) dried basil leaves (crushed), ¼ teaspoon (1 mL) garlic powder	Dip for vegetables; spread for bagels, French bread, cheese croissants	2 weeks
Mustard Relish Cream Cheese about 1¼ cups (300 mL)	2 tablespoons (25 mL) sweet relish, 1 tablespoon (15 mL) chopped onion, 2 teaspoons (10 mL) Dijon mustard	Spread for bagels, sandwiches, crackers	2 weeks
Orange Spice Cream Cheese about 1 cup (250 mL)	2 tablespoons (25 mL) sugar, 2 tablespoons (25 mL) orange juice, 1 teaspoon (5 mL) grated orange peel, pinch ground allspice	Spread for fruit muffins, bagels, croissants, quick breads	2 weeks
Red Wine Onion Cream Cheese about 1¼ cups (300 mL)	2 tablespoons (25 mL) chopped onion, 2 tablespoons (25 mL) red wine, pinch salt, pinch pepper	Dip for vegetables and crackers	2 weeks
Strawberry Cream Cheese about 1⅓ cups (325 mL)	½ cup (125 mL) fresh sliced strawberries, 2 tablespoons (25 mL) sugar, 1 teaspoon (5 mL) vanilla	Dip for fruit; spread for pound cakes, quick breads	3 days

CANDY COATING ORNAMENTS

- ¼ lb. (125 g) chocolate or white candy coating
- 1 heat-sealable pouch, 1-qt. (1 L) size
- Coloring book (optional)

About 10 ornaments

Choose the Right Pouch: *Be sure to use a heat-sealable, boilable pouch when melting candy coating. Do not use ordinary food-storage or freezer bags; they are not designed to withstand the high temperature.*

1 Break candy coating into pieces. Place in heat-sealable pouch. Do not seal pouch.

2 Microwave at 50% (Medium) 3 to 4 minutes, or until soft to the touch. (Candy should be warm, not hot.)

3 Sqeeze softened candy coating into one corner of pouch. Snip corner with scissors to form writing tip.

4 Draw designs with candy coating onto wax paper, or trace designs onto wax paper over coloring book for pattern ideas.

5 Let stand until firm. Peel design off wax paper. Place thread through ornaments for hanging.

6 Decorate ornaments while still soft. Use red hot candies, chocolate chips or miniature marshmallows, if desired.

DOG BISCUITS

- 1 cup (250 mL) whole wheat flour
- ½ cup (125 mL) all-purpose flour
- ¾ cup (175 mL) non-fat dry or skim milk powder
- ½ cup (125 mL) quick-cooking rolled oats
- ¼ cup (50 mL) yellow cornmeal
- 1 teaspoon (5 mL) sugar

- ⅓ cup (75 mL) shortening
- 1 egg, slightly beaten
- 1 tablespoon (15 mL) instant chicken or beef bouillon granules
- ½ cup (125 mL) hot water

  1½ dozen cutouts or 5½ dozen nuggets

VARIATION:

Cheese Dog Biscuits: *Omit bouillon granules. Add ¼ cup (50 mL) grated cheese to dry ingredients. Continue as directed below.*

1 Combine flours, milk powder, rolled oats, cornmeal and sugar in medium bowl. Cut in shortening until mixture resembles coarse crumbs.

2 Stir in egg. Stir instant bouillon granules into hot water until dissolved. Slowly pour into the flour mixture, stirring with a fork to moisten.

3 Form dough into ball and knead on floured board 5 minutes, or until smooth and elastic. Divide dough in half and roll out each ½" (1 cm) thick.

4 Make cutouts with cookie cutter. Or, make nuggets by rolling dough into 1" (2.5 cm) diameter log; cut off ½" (1 cm) pieces.

5 Arrange 6 cutout shapes or 24 nuggets on 10" (25 cm) plate. Microwave at 50% (Medium) 5 to 10 minutes, or until firm and dry to the touch.

6 Rotate plate every 2 minutes and turn shapes over after half the time. Cool on wire rack. Shapes will crisp as they cool.

DOUGH ART

The microwave oven dries baker's clay in minutes rather than the hour or two needed conventionally. Use this inedible dough to make baskets, picture frames, ornaments, candle holders, necklace pendants or to sculpt small figures.

The dough can be applied to microwave oven-safe objects, such as clay pots or glass jars. To test dish safety, place in oven. Place ½ to 1 cup (125 to 250 mL) water in glass measure. Set on or next to dish. Microwave at High 1 to 2 minutes. If dish remains cool, it is microwave-safe. Before shaping dough over glass bottles, jars or bowls, check the glass carefully for flaws. Do not use imperfect glass, as heat and steam from the dough could cause it to break.

Always elevate objects on a microwave roasting rack. The dough adheres to glass and clay, so no glue is needed. If you plan to remove the shaped object from the glass after microwaving, first spray the glass with a nonstick vegetable spray. Allow items shaped over glass to cool in the oven; rapid temperature changes can cause the glass to break.

Useful tools for dough art are a rolling pin; a ruler; cookie cutters, pastry cutter, drinking glass with floured rim, or a small knife for cutting out objects; a drinking straw for making holes to hang ornaments; flat wooden sticks for sculpting or engraving designs; wooden picks for interior support of arms, legs or neck of sculptured figures; garlic press to produce textures like hair or fur; and a paint-brush to moisten pieces for joining. After thorough drying, paint your work with acrylic or enamel colors or finish with a sealer to prevent brittleness.

HOW TO MAKE DOUGH ART*

- 3 cups (750 mL) all-purpose flour
- ¾ cup (175 mL) salt
- ¾ teaspoon (4 mL) powdered alum

- Food coloring (optional)
- 1¼ cups (300 mL) water

1 In large bowl, combine flour, salt and alum. If colored dough is desired, add food coloring to water. Mix water into flour. Shape dough into ball. Knead dough on lightly floured surface about 5 minutes, or until dough is smooth. Store in plastic bag.

2 If dough becomes too stiff, sprinkle lightly with water while kneading. If dough is too moist, knead in additional flour to achieve desired consistency. Most dough shapes are microwaved on microwave roasting rack or microwave baking sheet sprayed with nonstick vegetable cooking spray. Microwave at 30% (Medium-Low) at 2-minute intervals.

3 Microwave dough drying is *not* a complete drying process. Small areas of most objects may remain moist but firm to the touch. Allow all microwave-dried pieces to air-dry for at least 24 hours before finishing. All dried objects require finishing to prevent brittleness or breakage. Paint both sides of exposed areas with acrylic sealer, shellac, varnish or lacquer.

***NOTE:** This dough is for decoration only.*

HOW TO MAKE DOUGH BASKETS

1 Prepare dough as directed (page 305). Select glass bowl the size and shape desired for basket. Dough is shaped over outside of bowl. Spray outside of the bowl with nonstick vegetable cooking spray. Place bowl upside down.

2 Roll dough on lightly floured surface to ¼" (5 mm) thickness. Using pastry wheel or knife, cut ½" (1 cm) wide strips long enough to go across side, bottom and other side of bowl with 1" (2.5 cm) overhang on each side.

3 Weave bottom by starting in center and laying parallel strips across bottom. Pull back every other strip to center and place another strip at right angles. Lift alternate strips and place another strip at right angles. Continue with additional strips until bottom is woven.

4 Cut ½" (1 cm) wide strips long enough to go around bowl. Weave in and out of strips on bowl until sides are completed. Join ends of strips by moistening with small amount of water. (A paintbrush works well.) Trim strips even with top of bowl.

5 Form rope long enough to go around top of basket by rolling two equal pieces of dough between hands. Lay pieces side by side and twist one over the other, starting at center. Moisten top basket edge with water and press rope onto woven pieces. Moisten ends to join.

6 Microwave one basket at a time at 30% (Medium-Low) 4 minutes, rotating 2 or 3 times. Check; rotate if basket is not dry. Continue to microwave at 2-minute intervals, checking and rotating after each minute. Cool in oven. Remove from bowl and finish as directed (page 305).

HOW TO MAKE DOUGH CUTOUTS

1 Prepare dough as directed (page 305). Spray microwave baking sheet with nonstick vegetable cooking spray.

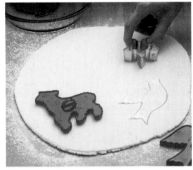

2 Roll dough on lightly floured surface to ¼" (5 mm) thickness. Dip edges of cutters in vegetable oil. Cut desired shapes.

3 Arrange four pieces at a time on prepared baking sheet. Cutouts can be appliquéd with small designs, if desired.

4 Shape designs for appliqué out of very small pieces of dough. Moisten area on cutout to be decorated. Place appliqué on wet area as directed (page 309).

5 Punch small hole at top of cutout with wooden pick or drinking straw if object is to be hung. Microwave pieces at 30% (Medium-Low) 2 minutes.

6 Check; rotate if pieces are not dry. Continue microwaving at 2-minute intervals, checking and rotating after each minute. Cool and finish as directed (page 305).

HOW TO MAKE PICTURE FRAMES

1 Prepare dough as directed (page 305). Spray microwave baking sheet with nonstick vegetable cooking spray. Roll dough on lightly floured surface to ¼" (5 mm) thickness.

2 Use pastry wheel or knife to cut ½" to 1" (1 to 2.5 cm) wide strips long enough to form 3" x 5" (8 x 13 cm) or 5" x 7" (13 x 18 cm) rectangles. Cut circles with a jar, using a smaller jar to cut out center.

3 Assemble the frame on prepared baking sheet. Wet cut edges with water and press together gently. Appliqué with cutout designs, if desired.

4 Microwave at 30% (Medium-Low) 2 minutes. Check; rotate if pieces are not dry. Microwave at 2-minute intervals, checking and rotating after each minute.

5 Cool and finish as directed (page 305). Cut cardboard to fit back and cover with fabric. Glue cardboard onto three edges of frame back.

6 Leave one edge of frame open to insert picture. Attach picture hanger, paper clip or easel backing.

HOW TO MAKE APPLIQUÉS FOR CLAY POTS

1 Prepare dough as directed (page 305). Cut or shape desired designs. Wet one side of cutout designs and area on pot where designs are to be applied.

2 Press designs onto dampened surface. Place pot directly on microwave oven floor. Microwave at 30% (Medium-Low) 2 minutes; check. Rotate if piece is not dry.

3 Microwave at 1-minute intervals, checking and rotating after each minute. Cool in microwave oven. Finish as directed (page 305).

HOW TO MAKE DECORATED JARS

1 Prepare dough as directed (page 305). Roll dough on lightly floured surface to ¼" (5 mm) thickness. Press dough over jar until it adheres.

2 Appliqué as desired. Place in microwave oven upside down on roasting rack. Microwave at 30% (Medium-Low) 2 minutes; check. Rotate if the piece is not dry.

3 Microwave at 1-minute intervals, checking and rotating after each minute. Cool in microwave oven. Finish as directed (page 305).

PATTERNS

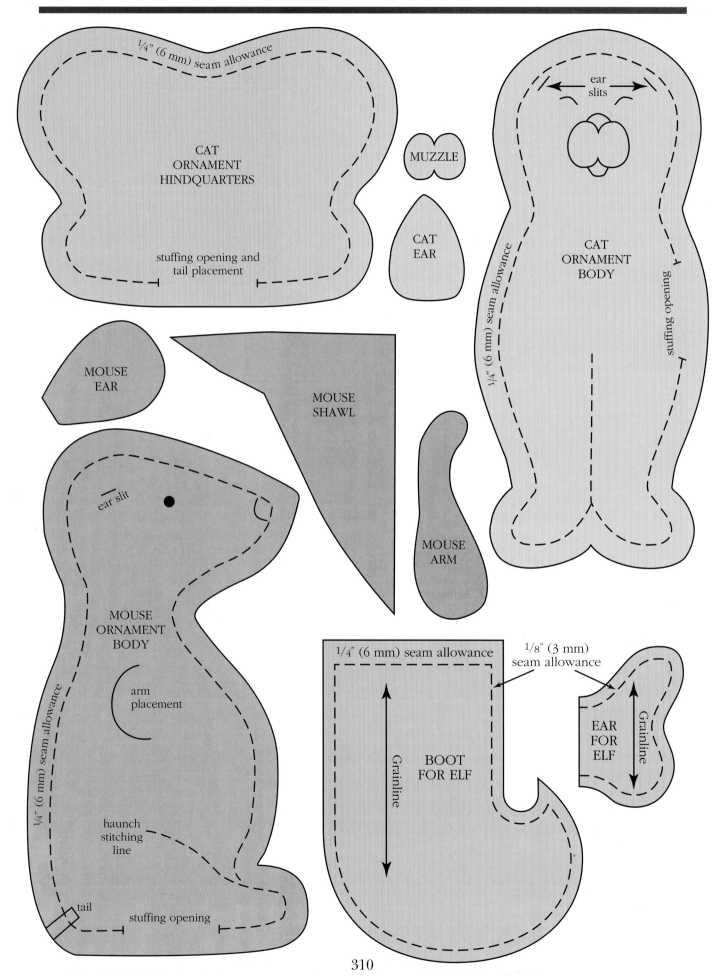

310

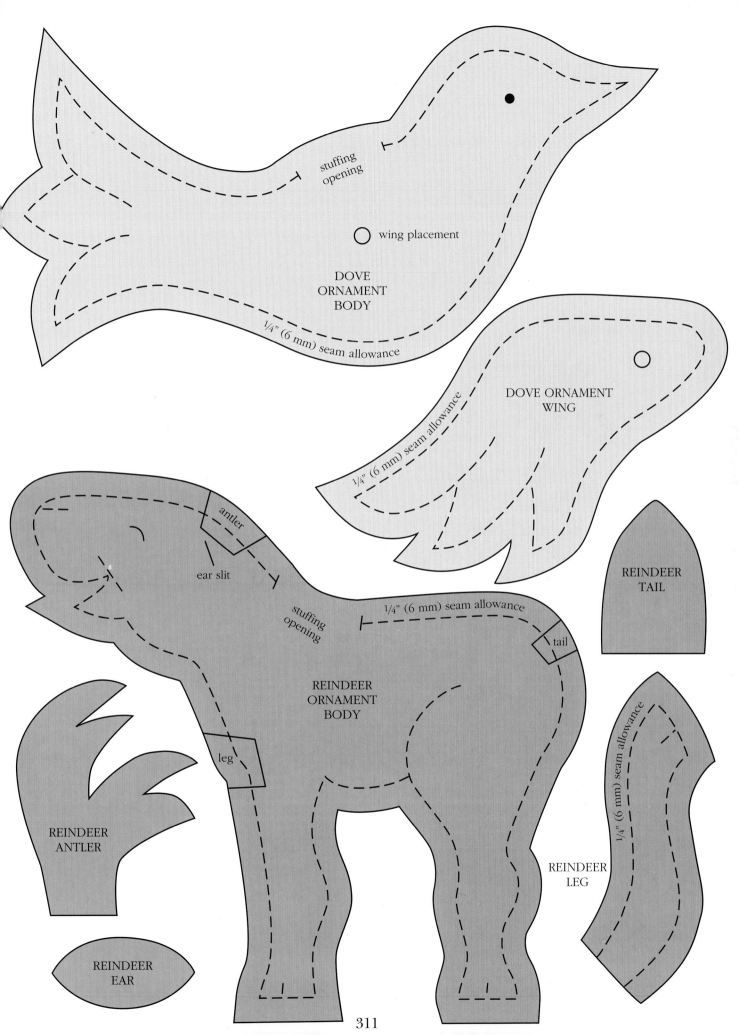

stuffing
opening

wing placement

DOVE
ORNAMENT
BODY

¼" (6 mm) seam allowance

DOVE ORNAMENT
WING

¼" (6 mm) seam allowance

¼" (6 mm) seam allowance

REINDEER
TAIL

antler

ear slit

stuffing
opening

¼" (6 mm) seam allowance

tail

REINDEER
ORNAMENT
BODY

leg

REINDEER
ANTLER

¼" (6 mm) seam allowance

REINDEER
LEG

REINDEER
EAR

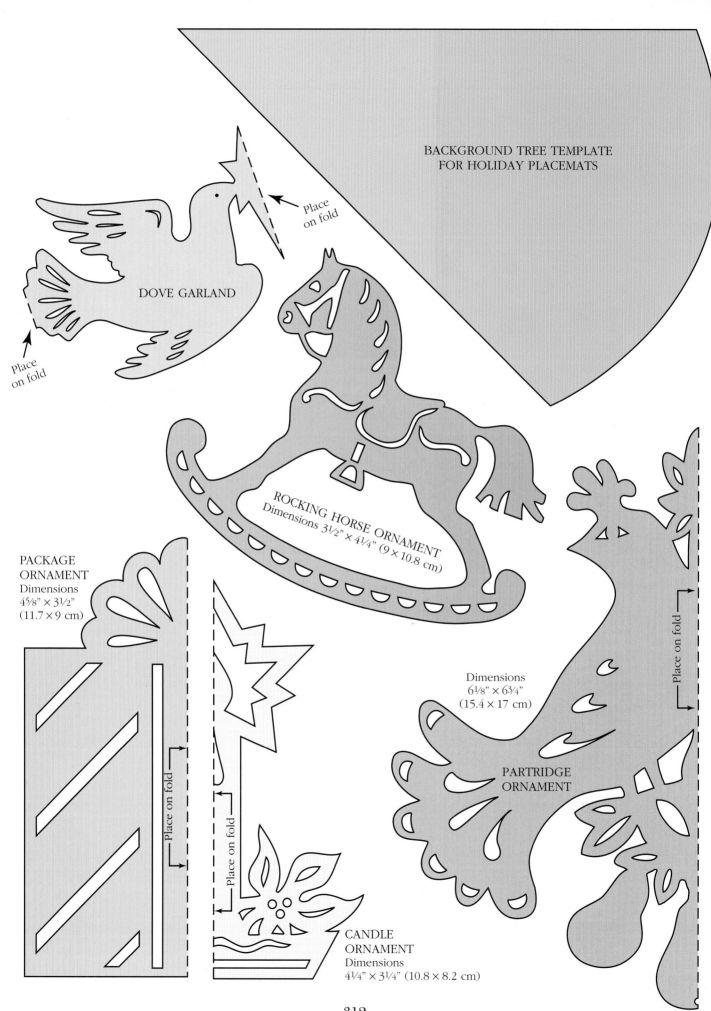

BACKGROUND TREE TEMPLATE
FOR HOLIDAY PLACEMATS

Place
on fold

DOVE GARLAND

Place
on fold

ROCKING HORSE ORNAMENT
Dimensions 3½" × 4¼" (9 × 10.8 cm)

PACKAGE
ORNAMENT
Dimensions
4⅝" × 3½"
(11.7 × 9 cm)

Place on fold

Place on fold

Dimensions
6⅛" × 6¾"
(15.4 × 17 cm)

Place on fold

PARTRIDGE
ORNAMENT

CANDLE
ORNAMENT
Dimensions
4¼" × 3¼" (10.8 × 8.2 cm)

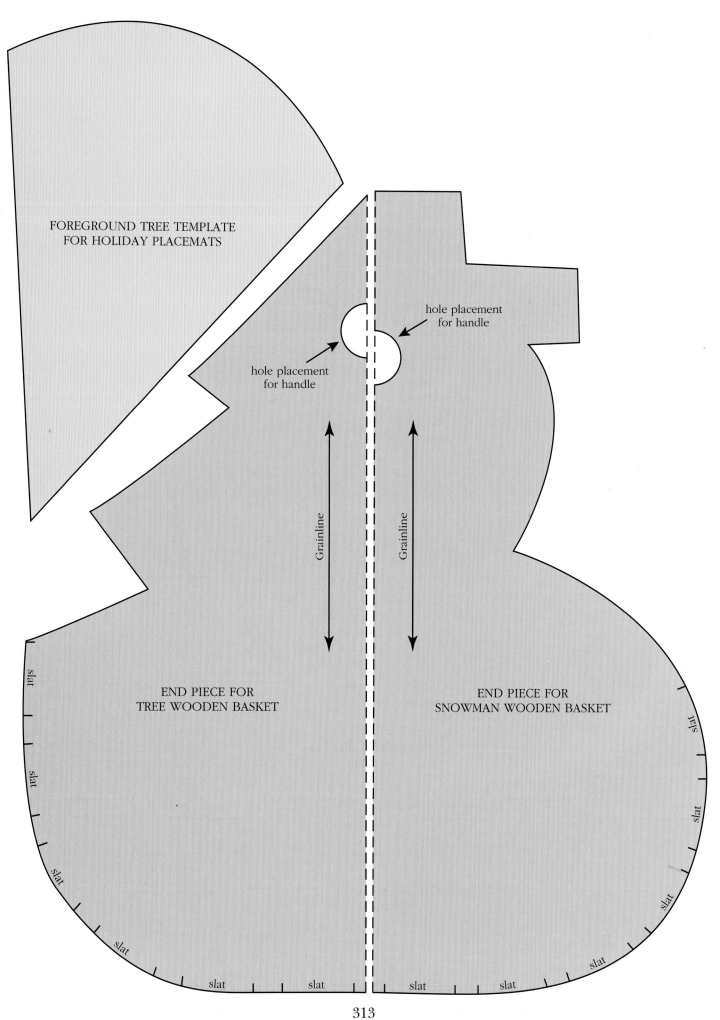

FOREGROUND TREE TEMPLATE
FOR HOLIDAY PLACEMATS

hole placement
for handle

hole placement
for handle

Grainline

Grainline

END PIECE FOR
TREE WOODEN BASKET

END PIECE FOR
SNOWMAN WOODEN BASKET

slat

slat

slat

slat

slat

slat

slat

slat

slat

slat

slat

slat

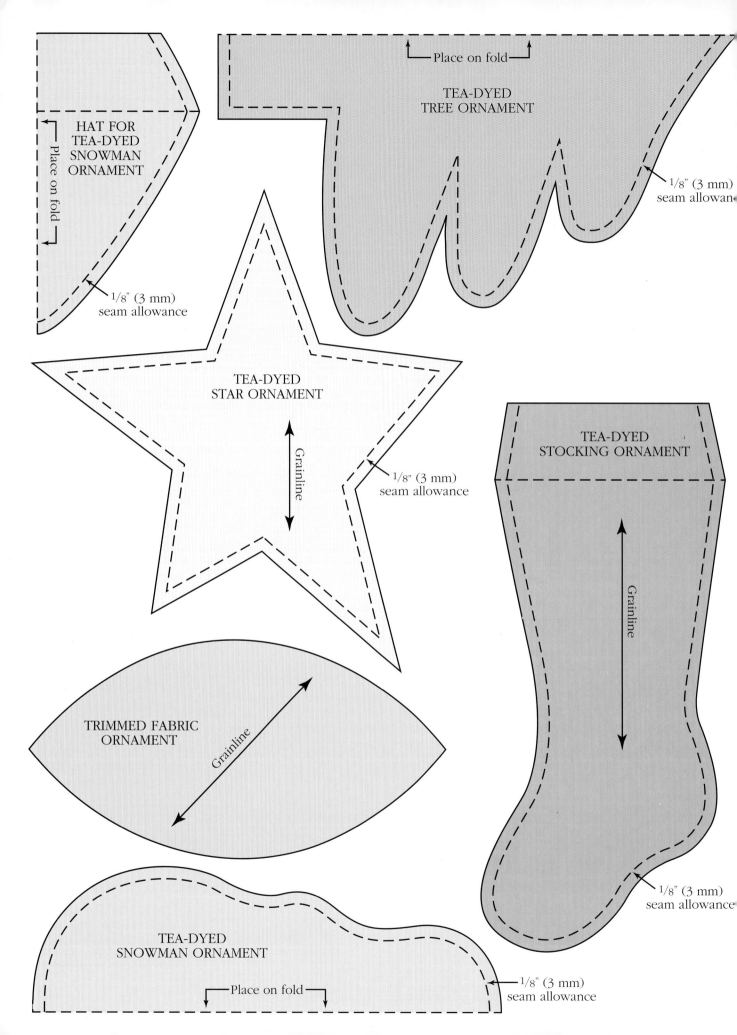

HAT FOR
TEA-DYED
SNOWMAN
ORNAMENT

Place on fold

1/8" (3 mm)
seam allowance

Place on fold

TEA-DYED
TREE ORNAMENT

1/8" (3 mm)
seam allowance

TEA-DYED
STAR ORNAMENT

Grainline

1/8" (3 mm)
seam allowance

TEA-DYED
STOCKING ORNAMENT

Grainline

TRIMMED FABRIC
ORNAMENT

Grainline

1/8" (3 mm)
seam allowance

TEA-DYED
SNOWMAN ORNAMENT

Place on fold

1/8" (3 mm)
seam allowance

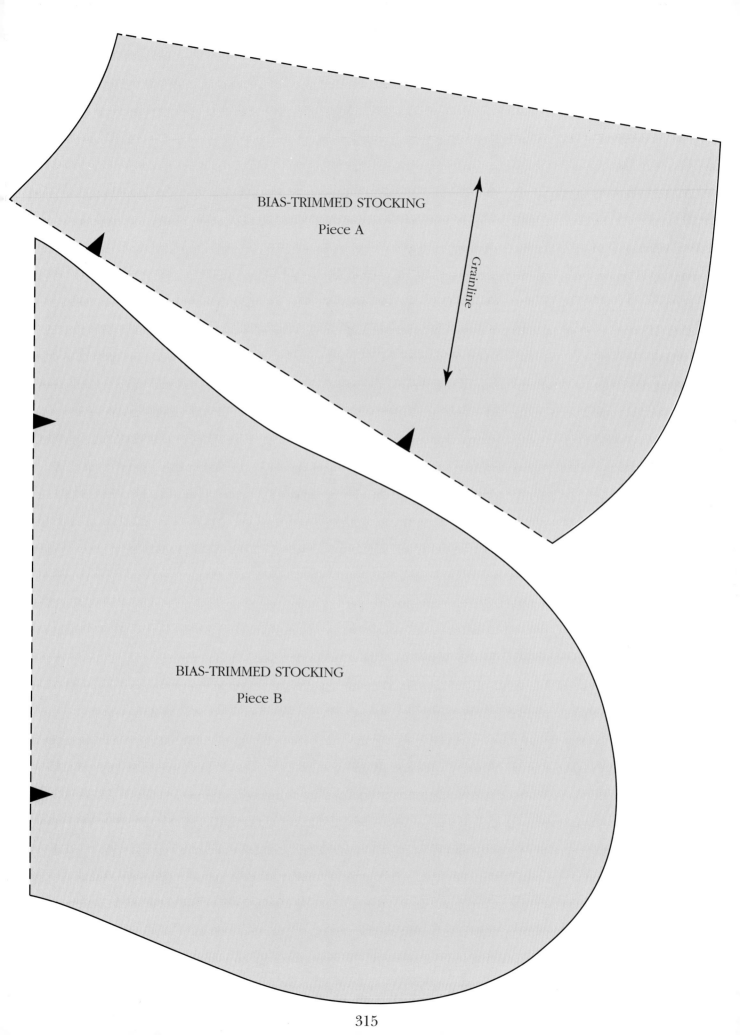

BIAS-TRIMMED STOCKING

Piece A

Grainline

BIAS-TRIMMED STOCKING

Piece B

INDEX

Creative Publishing international, Inc. offers a variety of how-to books. For information write:
  Creative Publishing international, Inc.
  Subscriber Books
  5900 Green Oak Drive
  Minnetonka, MN 55343